D0222293

BILATERAL ECOPOLITICS

Global Environmental Governance

Series Editor: John Kirton
Munk Centre for International Studies, Trinity College, Canada

Global Environmental Governance addresses the new generation of twenty-first century environmental problems and the challenges they pose for management and governance at the local, national, and global levels. Centred on the relationships among environmental change, economic forces, and political governance, the series explores the role of international institutions and instruments, national and sub-federal governments, private sector firms, scientists, and civil society, and provides a comprehensive body of progressive analyses on one of the world's most contentious international issues.

Titles in the series

Governing Global Desertification
Linking Environmental Degradation, Poverty and Participation
Edited by
Pierre Marc Johnson, Karel Mayrand and Marc Paquin
ISBN 0 7546 4359 X

Sustainability, Civil Society and International Governance
Local, North American and Global Contributions
Edited by
John J. Kirton and Peter I. Hajnal
ISBN 0 7546 3884 7

A World Environment Organization
Solution or Threat for Effective International Environmental Governance?
Edited by
Frank Biermann and Steffen Bauer
ISBN 0 7546 3765 4

Hard Choices, Soft Law
Voluntary Standards in Global Trade, Environment and Social Governance
Edited by
John J. Kirton and Michael J. Trebilcock
ISBN 0 7546 0966 9

Bilateral Ecopolitics

Continuity and Change in Canadian-American Environmental Relations

Edited by

PHILIPPE LE PRESTRE
Université Laval, Canada

PETER STOETT
Concordia University, Canada

ASHGATE

Published by
Ashgate Publishing Limited
Gower House
Croft Road
Aldershot
Hampshire GU11 3HR
England

Ashgate Publishing Company
Suite 420
101 Cherry Street
Burlington, VT 05401-4405
USA

Ashgate website: http://www.ashgate.com

British Library Cataloguing in Publication Data
Bilateral ecopolitics : continuity and change in
Canadian-American environmental relations. - (Global
environmental governance)
1. Environmental policy - Canada 2. Environmental policy -
United States 3. Canada - Relations - United States 4. United
States - Relations - Canada
I. Le Prestre, Philippe G. II. Stoett, Peter J. (Peter John),
1965-
363.7'00971

Library of Congress Cataloging-in-Publication Data
Bilateral ecopolitics : continuity and change in Canadian-American environmental relations / edited by Philippe Le Prestre and Peter Stoett.
p. cm. -- (Global environmental governance)
Includes bibliographical references and index.
ISBN 0-7546-4177-5
1. Canada--Foreign economic relations--United States. 2. United States--Foreign economic relations--Canada. 3. Environmental policy--Canada. 4. Environmental policy--United States. I. Le Prestre, Philippe G. II. Stoett, Peter J. (Peter John), 1965- III. Series: Global environmental governance series.

HF1480.15.U5B55 2006
333.70973--dc22

2006012571

ISBN 10: 0 7546 4177 5
ISBN 13: 978-0-7546-4177-3

Printed and bound in Great Britain by MPG Books Ltd, Bodmin, Cornwall.

Contents

List of Tables

List of Acronyms

ACIA	Arctic Climate Impact Assessment
AEPS	Arctic Environmental Protection Strategy
AES	Arctic Environmental Strategy (Canada)
AMAP	Arctic Monitoring and Assessment Program
AMEC	Arctic Military Environmental Cooperation
AQA	Canada-United States Air Quality Agreement
AQC	Canada-United States Air Quality Committee
ASAP	Anti-Smog Action Plan (Ontario)
AWPPA	Arctic Waters Pollution Prevention Act (Canada)
BCR	Bird Conservation Regions
BRCG	Bilateral Research Consultation Group on the Long-Range Transport of Air Pollutants
CAA	Clean Air Act (U.S.)
CAFF	Conservation of Arctic Flora and Fauna
CAIR	Clean Air Interstate Rule
CARC	Canadian Arctic Resources Committee
CBD	Convention on Biological Diversity
CCME	Canadian Council of Ministers of the Environment
CEC	Commission for Environmental Cooperation
CEPA	Canadian Environmental Protection Act
CIIA	Canadian Institute for International Affairs
CITES	Convention on International Trade in Endangered Species of Wild Flora and Fauna
COSEWIC	Committee on the Status of Endangered Wildlife in Canada
CSRM	Committee on Standards Related Measures
CWS	Canada-Wide Standards
CWS	Canadian Wildlife Service
DEW	Distant Early Warning
DFO	Department of Fisheries and Oceans (Canada)
DIAND	Department of Indian Affairs and Northern Development (Canada)
DND	Department of National Defence (Canada)
DOE	Department of Energy (U.S.)
EBA	Endemic Bird Areas
ECOS	Environmental Council of the States
ECTSIG	Eastern Canada Transboundary Smog Issue Group

EPA	Environmental Protection Agency (US)
EPPR	Emergency Prevention, Preparedness and Response
ERP	Environmental Regulatory Protection
FTA	Free Trade Agreement
FWS	Fish and Wildlife Service (U.S.)
GEF	Global Environment Facility
GLWQA	Great Lakes Water Quality Agreement
GMOs	Genetically Modified Organisms
IAQAB	International Air Quality Advisory Board (IJC)
IBA	Important Bird Areas
ICC	Inuit Circumpolar Conference
ICJ	International Court of Justice
ICLEI	International Council for Local Environmental Initiatives
ICSID	International Center for the Settlement of Investment Disputes (World Bank)
IJC	International Joint Commission
IMO	International Maritime Organization
JPAC	Joint Public Advisory Committee (NAEEC)
LRTAP	Convention on Long Range Transboundary Air Pollution
NAAEC	North American Agreement on Environmental Cooperation
NAAQS	National Ambient Air Quality Standards
NABCI	North American Bird Conservation Initiative
NAEWG	North American Energy Working Group
NAFTA	North American Free Trade Agreement
NARSTO	North American Research Strategy on Tropospheric Ozone
NAWMP	North American Waterfowl Management Plan
NEG/ECP	New England Governors/Eastern Canadian Premiers
NEPA	National Environmental Policy Act (U.S)
NESCAUM	Northeast States for Coordinated Air Management
NSPS	New Source Performance Standards
NGOs	Non-Governmental Organizations
NOAA	National Oceanic and Atmospheric Administration (U.S.)
OTAG	Ozone Transport Assessment Group
OTC	Ozone Transport Commission
PAME	Protection of the Arctic Marine Environment
PCBs	Polychlorinated Biphenyls
PEMA	Pollution Emission Management Area
PM	Particulate matters
POPs	Persistent Organic Pollutants
PSD	Prevention of Significant Deterioration
RAP	Great Lakes Remedial Action Plan
RGGI	Regional Greenhouse Gas Initiative
RPS	Renewable Portfolio Standard
SIP	State Implementation Plan

SMOC	Sound Management of Chemicals (CEC)
TAPIR	Transboundary Air Pollution Transport Regions
TFSD	Task Force on Sustainable Development (Arctic)
UNCITRAL	United Nations Commission on International Trade Law
UNCLOS	United Nations Conference on the Law of the Sea
UNDP	United Nations Development Programme
UNEP	United Nations Environment Programme
USSR	Union of Soviet Socialist Republics
VOCs	Volatile Organic Compounds
WTO	World Trade Organization

List of Contributors

Samuel Barkin is Associate Professor of Political Science at the School of Natural Resources and the Environment at the University of Florida. His most recent book is *International Organization: Theories and Institutions* (Palgrave, 2006). He is also co-editor, with George Shambaugh, of *Anarchy and the Environment: The International Relations of Common Pool Resources* (SUNY Press, 1999).

Robert Boardman is McCulloch Professor of Political Science at Dalhousie University. His publications include *The International Politics of Bird Conservation: Biodiversity, Regionalism and Global Governance* (2006), *The Political Economy of Nature: Environmental Debates and the Social Sciences* (2001), and *Canadian Environmental Policy: Context and Cases*, 2nd edition, edited with Debora VanNijnatten (2002).

Mary Durfee is Assistant Provost for Academic Improvement at Michigan Technological University and a member of the Social Sciences Department. She is co-author of *Thinking Theory Thoroughly*, a member of the USEPA Science Advisory Board's new Homeland Security Advisory Committee, and active in the Michigan Tech's Sustainable Futures Institute. She served for five years on the Binational Forum for Lake Superior.

Rob Huebert is an Associate Professor with the Department of Political Science and is the associate director of the Centre for Military and Strategic Studies at the University of Calgary. His main area of research is on the topics of Arctic security, maritime security, and Canadian security policy. He is the co-editor of books on the use of commercial satellite imagery for Canadian security needs and renewable resource and ocean development in the Canadian north. He is now working on books on Canadian Arctic sovereignty and security.

John Kirton is a professor of Political Science at the University of Toronto and was principal investigator for the "Strengthening Canada's Environmental Community through International Regime Reform" project (EnviReform). Recent publications include, with V. Maclaren, *Linking Trade, Environment and Social Cohesion: NAFTA Experiences, Global Challenge*, (Aldershot: Ashgate, 2002).

Philippe Le Prestre is Professor of Political Science and Director of the Hydro-Quebec Institute on Environment, Development, and Society at Laval University

(Quebec, Canada). His most recent book is *Protection de l'environnement et relations internationales* (Paris: Armand Colin, 2005); he recently edited *Governing Global Biodiversity* (Aldershot: Ashgate, 2002).

Don Munton is a Professor of International Studies at the University of Northern British Columbia. His recent research has focused on environmental policy, internationalism, Canadian foreign policy, and the Cuban missile crisis. He is editor of *Hazardous Waste Siting and Democratic Choice* and of *Measuring International Behaviour*, co-editor (with John Kirton) of *Canadian Foreign Policy: Selected Cases*, and co-editor (with Hans Rattinger) of *Debating National Security*.

Robert Paehlke teaches Environmental and Resource Studies at Trent University. He is a founding editor of *Alternatives: Canadian Environmental Ideas & Action* and most recently the author of *Democracy's Dilemma: Environment, Social Equity and the Global Economy* (MIT, 2004) and co-editor of the new edition of *Managing Leviathan: Environmental Politics and the Administrative State* (Broadview, 2005).

Ian H. Rowlands is Associate Professor in Environment and Resource Studies at the University of Waterloo, Canada, and Director of the Environment and Business Program in the University of Waterloo's Faculty of Environmental Studies. His research focuses upon energy policy, corporate environmentalism, and international environmental relations. Recent work by Professor Rowlands has appeared in *Energy Policy*, *Renewable Energy* and *Renewable & Sustainable Energy Reviews*.

John Nick Sanders has a Master's degree in Public Policy and Political Administration and a Graduate Degree in Environmental Impact Assessment from Concordia University in Montreal. He is a founding partner of Sustainable Futures International, and currently works as a Policy Analyst with Canadian Wildlife Services of Environment Canada.

Alan M. Schwartz, Ph.D (University of Pennsylvania) is a Professor in the Department of Environmental Studies at St. Lawrence University. His research focuses on issues of conflict in the Canada-U.S. environmental relationship and mechanisms for their resolution.

Henrik Selin is an Assistant Professor in the Department of International Relations at Boston University. His research focuses on global and regional politics and policy-making on environment and sustainable development. His chapter for this volume, co-authored with Stacy D. VanDeveer, presents results from an ongoing research project on North American climate change policy-making and action at national, regional and local levels.

Mirit Shamir, a lawyer, has represented the Israeli Attorney General in environmental cases such as ground water pollution and air pollution. She is currently completing an MS in Environmental Policy at Michigan Technological University. Her thesis is on the international legal status of the precautionary principle.

Peter Stoett is Associate Professor and Chair of the Department of Political Science, Concordia University, Montreal. His work focuses on human rights and environmental issues; he is currently working on a book on global biosecurity concerns. Recent books include *Human and Global Security: An Exploration of Terms* (University of Toronto Press, 2000); he recently co-edited *International Ecopolitical Theory: Critical Approaches* (UBC Press, 2006).

Stacy D. VanDeveer is the 2003-2006 Ronald H. O'Neal Associate Professor of Political Science at the University of New Hampshire. His research interests include international environmental policy-making and its domestic impacts, the connections between environmental and security issues, and the role of expertise in policy-making. He recently co-edited *EU Enlargement and the Environment: Institutional Change and Environmental Policy in Central and Eastern Europe* (Routledge, 2005).

Debora VanNijnatten is Associate Professor in the Department of Political Science at Wilfrid Laurier University. Her research focuses on various aspects of Canadian-American environmental politics, including transboundary decision processes, air quality policy, climate change policy and state-province policy innovations. She is co-editor of *Canadian Environmental Policy: Context and Cases* (Oxford, 2002).

Preface

Many books are, to use an old phrase, a long time coming. This is no exception. In November of 2002, we decided to express our mutual dismay at the lack of academic literature dealing with the theme of Canadian-American Environmental Relations, despite its obvious centrality to the relationship. We wanted to explore the evolving interaction between these two colossal states, with the goal of detecting current trends and adding to a very necessary cross-border discussion. Though it has taken some time to collect and assemble these chapters, we are confident that the result is a solid contribution to the literature and ongoing debate. With Ashgate's welcome encouragement, we pushed ahead, and the final product is in your hands.

Special thanks go to John Nick Sanders, who co-wrote one of the articles in the book but, as a hired hand, played a much larger role in the final editing and design of the text. Cristina Romanelli, Althea Arivis, and Elaine Carsley helped with the production as well. We also thank family and friends for sustenance, and dedicate this book to Canadian and American youth, who will have to confront the ecological legacy currently being shaped by the dynamics of Canadian-American ecopolitical relations. As this book demonstrates, Canadians and Americans face many common problems, and there will always be friction at some level of interaction. But that is also where the opportunity lies.

Philippe Le Prestre, Peter Stoett,
Montreal, 2006.

Chapter 1

From Neglect to Concern: The Study of Canadian-American Ecopolitics

Peter Stoett and Philippe Le Prestre

Introduction: Continental Ecopolitics

Former Canadian Prime Minister Paul Martin had a wide range of topics to discuss during his first official visit to Washington in April 2004. While the agenda was, as usual, dominated by security concerns such as the ongoing crises related to the invasion of Iraq, and economic issues such as Canadian beef and lumber exports, several environmental issues were also raised, inspired largely by provincial concerns. They included air pollution from Midwestern factories affecting Ontario, waste dumps on the Quebec-Vermont border, and the state of Devil's Lake in Manitoba, where a proposed diversion scheme was raising renewed concerns over the possible unwelcome appearance of invasive species.

The list of transboundary disputes could be much longer: planned power plants in Washington state threaten the Fraser Valley, a project by the U.S. Army corps of engineers intends to widen the St. Lawrence Seaway, biosafety concerns persist in Canadian agricultural industries, disputes over salmon rights between Washington State and British Columbia drag on, and the Bush Administration's long-term intention to allow exploratory oil drilling in the Arctic National Wildlife Refuge remains a hot issue. Disputes are also evident at the global level; controversies over the protection of Arctic waters are fuelled by fears that climate change will increase their vulnerability to both commercial and military shipping. Meanwhile the pre-Harper Canadian government clashed directly with the Bush Administration over the merits (if not the realities) of implementing the Kyoto Protocol on global warming. In what might have been an all-time low in public diplomacy, Martin chastised the United States for acting without a "global conscience" during the Conference of the Parties to the UNFCCC[1] in Montreal in December of 2005.

1 United Nations Framework Convention on Climate Change. The fact that Martin's statement occurred on the eve of a Canadian national election – one Martin would go on to lose – further irked the Americans. Meanwhile, ex-President Bill Clinton appeared at the conference as well, and added his own criticisms of the Bush Administration's inaction on climate change.

The central theme of this volume is the need to study the new dimensions and interdependent nature of this evolving relationship and, in so doing, recognize that, for Canadians and Americans alike, ecopolitics is less and less national but rather must be considered continental in scope. Arguably, this was always the case: the border is but an artificial construction that cannot change the natural heritage and geophysical features of the land. Accordingly, the concept of shared stewardship has shaped the political relationship in several areas where values and interests converged, notably wildlife and water. But the Canadian-American environmental relationship has become considerably more ambivalent in recent decades, a mix of conflict and cooperation reflecting common long-range concerns, more immediate crises, the rise of environmental activism on both sides of the border, and the evolution of international regimes. The broader Canadian-American relationship, which has remained generally amicable even during episodes of open disagreement, permeates all aspects of ecopolitics in Canada, even relatively local issues such as waste dumping or energy production. At the same time, high-level environmental issues in turn affect the broader Canada-United States relationship in evolving ways, and Canadian citizens and policymakers must strive to understand the institutional context as well as the complexities of specific issue-areas.[2] Although historians have focused on specific issues, highlighting the continuity in the dynamics observed (Dorsey, 1998; Carroll, 1983), there have been few recent concerted efforts to analyse the Canadian-American relationship with environmental policy foremost in mind. This is unfortunate, because environmental issues, from salmon to caribou to acid rain to energy exports, have been thematic mainstays for several decades now. Indeed, we might argue that environmental questions have always permeated the relationship, and not just in the economic sense of resources, both raw and processed, flowing back and forth across the border, but in the broader sociological sense of mutual understanding between these colossal states.

Many Americans, when not in Toronto, Montreal, or Vancouver, view Canada as a vast storehouse of resources, mainly natural, awaiting eventual human utilization. This may be unfair to those who have a more sophisticated view; then again, many Canadians consider the United States an overzealous consumer of resources that will prove too eager to appropriate Canadian resources to feed a wasteful economy and life-style, and to be a poor steward of its own natural and built environment, not to speak of the global commons. Some Canadians still cling to the notion that Canada is a virtual green paradise in comparison with the pollution-belching United States, and that Canada's reputation is similarly admired around the world, while the U.S. evades its global ecological responsibilities. While it is obvious that a tremendous discrepancy in size produced a commensurate difference in pollution levels, it is

2 Although Mexico is obviously intrinsically involved in continental ecopolitics, this volume will mostly engage the Canadian-American relations dimension. However, references to the NAFTA and CEC are obviously inclusive of Mexican participation, and many of our chapters deal with Mexico at some length.

certainly not the case that Canadian environmental policies are considerably more forceful or effective than American ones.

Historically, largely because of its economic and security dimensions, the environment has been central to Canadian-American relations. Geography, both real and perceived, also plays a key role in the cultural definitions that inform our views. The two countries share a 9000 km-long border which cuts through a wide diversity of ecosystems, such as shared river basins and the Great Lakes, mountain ranges, Arctic wilderness, coastal zones, and old-growth forest. Prevailing winds means that air pollution from the Midwest finds its way to New England and the Canadian East. Native Americans and First Nations Canadians are often more prone to recognize this ecosystemic continuity than they are any borderline negotiated by Europeans (startling findings of PCBs and other toxic pollutants in the breast milk of Inuit mothers in the late 1980s offered evidence of this interdependence, and the asymmetrical vulnerability it reflects; see Dewailly, 1989). And the similarities between Canadian and American economic systems, with their intensive consumption of resources and disposal of waste, make the treatment of nature an even more obvious topic for sustained analysis.

This volume aims to present the reader with updated analyses of several of the institutional and issue-based ecopolitical dilemmas affecting both policymakers and citizens in both states. Ecopolitics may be defined as the space where environmental issues and politics become inseparable. This demands further explication. Environmental issues are contentious and cut deeply into the social fabric of human communities. For our purposes, when questions about land use, water allocation, wildlife management, air and water quality, and others become the source of conflict – even though other factors, such as social or racial inequality, economic instability, or even military conflict, might have put these questions in bold relief in the first place – then they become the stuff of ecopolitics. This also entails the study of the various actors involved in creating, sustaining, and opposing institutional structures and ideologies created to "manage" the natural environment and control the conflict that results from disparate approaches, designs, and activity. This is not to reveal prejudice toward conflict as the most worthy object of study, since more often than not the end result is sustained, if somewhat tenuous, cooperation. But without a conflict between at least two human beings over the best path to take, we would not be interested in public policy debates but in the study of utopia.

North America is many things, but it is most assuredly not utopia. In fact, a quick look at the overall picture paints a rather different picture. Air pollution, contaminated and depleted water resources, land degradation, toxic chemicals, degradation of coastal waters and depletion of fisheries due to agricultural runoff and overfishing, highly wasteful consumption, poor urban infrastructures, habitat fragmentation or destruction, and declining biodiversity: we have it all, even if trends do vary and significant inroads have been made in some areas, notably air quality (especially in the U.S.), reduction of phosphorous loadings into the Great Lakes and of mercury emissions in the atmosphere, and sustainable forestry (in Canada) (see UNEP 2002, 2005). Nor, on matters environmental is there anything approaching political harmony; rather, significant historical dissent has arisen over the environment and resources. The Pacific Fur Seals controversy in the early 1900s, which resulted in a historic treaty signed by Japan, Russia, the United States and Great Britain (the latter on behalf of Canada) in 1911, was already a transnational as well as an international issue. Later, and more famously, the Trail Smelter case of 1935 set a milestone in international environmental law (see Allum, 1995).[3] The acid rain debate polarized Ottawa and Washington for many years (see Munton, 1997 and this volume). Canada has been threatened with American sanctions because of the Inuit bowhead whale hunt. And divergence on the utility of contemporary multilateral approaches to global environmental governance is as common as convergence, especially since the arrival of the G.W. Bush Administration in the White House. Thus the need for the present text, which looks at these issues with both conflict and cooperation in mind.

Indeed, there are notable similarities between the two states. Put bluntly, both are huge. Canada is the second largest country in the world (next to Russia), and the United States third. Canada's population, at 32 million, pales beside the United States' 300 million (the third largest), but 32 million remains significant since it is largely concentrated within one hundred kilometres of the Canada-U.S. border. In the Canadian case, Canada's major urban centres are as populated, and polluted, and challenged, as most of the large American cities. Because of their size, the variety of ecosystems, geographic and socio-economic conditions in both states is tremendous, and managing these widespread polities under federal systems presents similar challenges to both governments. Size may be good thing, but it certainly creates its own set of problems, including the question of appropriate degrees of centralization in the name of environmental protection (see Weibust, 2000). One can easily argue, for example, that, as far as environmental issues are concerned, geography more than political institutions brings different polities together. Regional similarities along a transborder North-South axis create interests that trump political divisions, which have led to analytic and political attention to transborder cooperation (see, for example, Findlay and Coates, 2002).

Both states have relatively young public histories replete with stories of forging civilization out of the wilderness, heroic tales of conquering pioneers who applied European technology to a new world. Of course, these are but parcels of a past that includes what many would consider genocidal policies affecting indigenous peoples, the institutionalization of slavery of Africans, and the careless application of large-scale industrial infrastructure. Though one state has a revolution and bloody civil war to its character-building credit, the other underwent numerous rebellions and, more recently, near-partition. Both had formative experiences in two world wars. And

3 A zinc and lead ore smelter in Trail, British Columbia, had damaged cross-border farmland with its sulphur dioxide emissions. After protracted diplomatic failures, the Trail Smelter Tribunal was established, which ultimately (1941) found the Canadian government culpable; the latter paid compensation and thus was established the principle that "no state has the right to use or permit the use of its territory in such a manner as to cause injury by fumes in or to the territory of another..." See also Cassesse, 2001:376-377.

both must constantly struggle with similar questions: how can we make the most of the bountiful renewable resources here, and retain their value for later generations, not only in North America but also for the rest of the world? How can we use non-renewable resources more effectively and minimise the negative impacts of their exploitation, without destroying them? This is, obviously, a problem that cries out for cooperation. To take a dramatic but quite empirical example, there are over 4,500 known hazardous waste sites on both sides of the border in the Great Lakes Basin alone (Fletcher, 1998). Canada and the United States are co-joined, federalist twins in many ways, but environmental issues may be their closest link of all.

This tends to bother Canadians a good deal more than it does their southern neighbours. Canada lives upstairs to the world's mightiest economy, and the most prolific polluter in world history. China, India, Brazil, and even the relatively green-friendly European Union may overtake the United States in both or either of these distinctions in the future, but Canada and Mexico have lived out the height of the empire, and the smokestacks of the American Midwest and the chemical wastelands and polluted land that came with it. But Canadians too have caused their own share of ecological damage (largely the result of extractive industries, such as mining and fishing), and with repeated determination. Indeed, Americans have serious environmental issues with Canada to contend with as well, as many of the chapters in this volume attest. One cannot escape the notable discrepancy, however, between the size of the two economies, and the comparative aggregate consumption this affords. Yet, similar lifestyles, development and natural endowments make for very similar consumptive behaviour. Thus the propensity to approach the bilateral relationship as "David versus Goliath" is an obvious oversimplification and contributes little to our overall understanding. Cooperation has been at least as common as conflict in the ecopolitical issue-areas with which we are concerned. Environmentalists may argue that this amounts to a common approach to exploiting the land, but foreign policy specialists may be more interested in the implications for Canadian-American relations.

Despite intense and long-standing disputes, the continent has also been the theatre of much cooperation, and the birthplace of two major international institutional innovations: the International Joint Commission and the Commission for Environmental Cooperation, both of which are treated at length in this volume. Generally, cooperation first addressed commercial concerns or specific pollution problems, then expanded into a larger approach of environmental protection. Environment Canada estimates that there are about thirty such bilateral mechanisms (Environment Canada, 2000), which leaves out the agreements at the provincial and state levels, such as the New England Governors/Eastern Canadian Premiers Climate Change Action Plan of 2001 or the Council of Great Lakes Governors (which includes the Ontario and Quebec Premiers) Great Lakes Charter of 1985 or more recent ones on the derivation of Great Lakes waters. Indeed, the sub-state level of cooperation appears to be on the rise as bilateral efforts are clogged by other foreign policy concerns; transnational citizens movements (such as Great Lakes United) are also increasingly important in the study of bilateral environmental diplomacy, a point that surfaces throughout the chapters to follow.

This volume is an effort to bring several analyses of continental ecopolitics together in one place, so that we might learn more about the general path being taken. We have selected a wide variety of topics, reflecting the breadth of the related issue-areas; and we have asked our contributors to suggest ways in which environmental protection can be both increased and instilled as a permanent part of the relationship between Canada and the United States. That relationship is, itself, the core empirical platform for the study of bilateral ecopolitics, and we turn now to a brief discussion of the academic pursuit of understanding its contours.

The Development of a Sub-Discipline: Bilateral Ecopolitics

Little attention has been paid to the Canadian-American bilateral relationship, which is both a source of surprise and dismay. Given the global importance of North America and the central importance of the United States to Canadian policy, foreign and domestic (and conversely), it is rather surprising an entire cottage industry of academia has not formed around the questions raised by those brave few who have made it their scholarly purpose. Indeed, Canadian-American relations as a topic was exceptionally slow to develop as a field unto itself, and was even labelled a "non-subject" (see Clarkson, 1973). There are explanations for this, of course: the lack of heightened conflict between the two states made for boring study in a field, namely international relations, dominated by the study of war; Cold War concerns took precedence over everything else; and Canada was condemned by many to be little more than a glorified American satellite and therefore it was unnecessary, even superfluous, to study the foreign policies of a state with such limited foreign policy latitude.[4]

Yet, the formal study of the relationship did evolve. Early work was mostly diplomatic history, largely in the realist tradition (Eayrs, 1961; Holmes, 1971), and pondered Canada's reactions to American power dilemmas or, more engagingly, focussed on Canadian autonomy vis-à-vis the United States (most famously, Grant, 1965). It was not until the mid-1970s that Canadian-American relations were deemed to make a significant contribution to the broader field of International Relations (IR) theory, and even here it was largely within a rather narrow debate between the dependency and interdependency schools of thought (see Smythe, 1980). Works on the impact of integration (Axline, et al., 1974) and comparisons of dispute resolution (Fox, et al., 1974) gave clues as to the direction of the relationship, but seemed as though they were collected by incidence, serving primarily as empirical grist for fashionable theoretical mills. This was, after all, a remarkably observable "dyad"; and "some curiosity might be in order concerning the relationship between dyadic

4 This despite obvious differences that arose even during relatively smooth periods, such as Canada's opposition to aspects of the Viet Nam war (though Canada did contribute napalm production and aided the war effort in other ways) and policy toward Cuba. For a recent treatment of the 1963-1968 period, see Donaghy, 2002.

disparity and the definition of Canada's goals. It may be that anticipated American reaction heavily circumscribes Canada's foreign policy objectives in the dyad" (Smythe, 1980:135). This is rather self-evident today, when the Canadian debate over participation in the Bush administration's national missile defence plan centred largely not on the dubious merits of the plan but on the willingness to upset American policymakers.

The power differential between the two countries has been seen as fundamental to the relationship, with the structural power of the much larger pole in a dyad being strongly determinative (Redekop, 1976). Others, such as Clement (1977) have stressed the obvious economic/investment factor, American investment having largely moulded the capitalist elite of Canada. So analysis of the relationship has always been about relative power and influence, though some of it has focused on the evolution of a security community, defined succinctly by Kitchen as the development of "dependable expectations of peaceful change arising from a shared identity and meanings" (Kitchen, 2004:703; Adler and Barnett, 1998). Yet, questions have been raised with respect to the explanatory power of this asymmetry across time, issue-areas and political contexts, notably by the interdependence school (Keohane and Nye, 1977). Thus, a more nuanced understanding of the policy process across borders was at least partially inspired by the relationship as well, giving us constructs such as the distinction between transgovernmental and transnational relations. Transgovernmentalism involves *direct interaction between agencies and governmental subunits*, acting relatively autonomously from their central government; transnational relations are *interactions involving at least one nongovernmental actor* (Fox et al. 1974). We adopt this distinction throughout this text, as both are highly relevant to bilateral ecopolitics: they serve as indicators of integrational tendencies (Axline, 1974) as well as sources of potential conflict, but may in some cases describe the most effective routes toward environmental protection.

Even within this limited corpus of work, little bore directly on environmental policy. This is again somewhat surprising given the economic integration of the two countries, the simultaneous rise of environmental activism (Friends of the Earth was founded in 1969 in the U.S. and Greenpeace in 1971 in Canada) emergence of ecology on the national and political agenda with the United Nations Conference on the Human Environment (UNCHE) in Stockholm, 1972, coupled with the Club of Rome report that same year on the *Limits to Growth*. Environmental issues were quite alive, on the ground: the continued work of the International Joint Commission (IJC) (see Cohen, 1975) assumed an increasingly ecological rationale with the adoption of a watershed perspective and the development of the ecosystem approach in the 1970s and 1980s; the coastal fisheries were beginning to crackle with conflict, the Law of the Sea was under intense negotiation. Further, "low-level" politics involved specific and prolonged disputes over river diversion and dam construction, not atypical of other ecologically-linked dyads.[5]

Gradually, this activity would become not only newsworthy but deserving of scholarly analysis as well. Greene and Keating (1980:750), for example, would focus on the increasing influence of the domestic lobby on the west coast fishery dispute, concluding that "[t]here is little doubt that nongovernmental involvement is both desirable and in democratic societies at least to some degree inevitable. Such involvement does, however, increase the difficulty of concluding bilateral agreements". This theme transpires throughout the present volume as well. Others would focus on Arctic sovereignty questions (Dosman, 1976; Munton and Kirton, 1992), yet another theme with increasing salience today in the age of global warming.[6] The International Joint Commission, which plays a key role in the management of transboundary resources, received increased attention as an object of study as well (see Spencer, 1981). Carroll's 1983 book marks a turning point in the mainstream significance of the overall topic. From here on, though the term itself was not employed, bilateral ecopolitics were the subject of concerted, if still rather consigned, study. Nonetheless, it was not until 1997 that a special volume of *The American Review of Canadian Studies* was devoted to the topic (see Rabe, 1997).

Environmental relations only grew in importance with the signing of NAFTA and the parallel creation of the CEC, the body responsible for "overseeing" the environmental impact of the trade accord. Not only does the environmental impact of the trade regime remain controversial, it has resulted in a wealth of publications by the CEC itself. The more traditional zones of bilateral conflict, such as air quality issues (see VanNijnatten, this volume, and Allison, 1995) continue to draw attention, but they have been joined by concerns for transnational wildlife protection (see Sanders and Stoett, Boardman, and Barkin, this volume), potential bulk water exports (see Durfee, this volume), the clean-up of dismantled Distant Early Warning

5 For example, the ongoing dispute over the Garrison Diversion Project involves the 125-year old plan to divert the Missouri River water northward, introducing unwanted water and biota into watersheds draining into Manitoba (see Carroll, 1983, 175-76; Nossal, 1978). The IJC recommended the project be halted in the late 1960s. Another dispute broiled between the city of Seattle and the Province of British Columbia: Seattle wanted to raise a dam on the Skagit River for hydroelectricity, and BC objected since this would flood land on the Canadian side. The IJC mediated in 1982, and by 1984, BC agreed to supply Seattle with electricity and Seattle agreed not to raise the dam high enough to affect Canadian land. These are just two examples of how sub-state actors and relations are often dominant in continental politics.

6 See the chapter by Huebert in this volume, along with a recent piece by Griffiths who argues that claims that global warming will make the Northwest Passage passable on a yearly basis – and thus present a threat to Canadian sovereignty – are overblown: "Arctic ice is decidedly not what it used to be. But neither is the threat of commercial shipping to Canada's Arctic sovereignty" (2003: 257). Meanwhile this theme was revisited by a major report released by the Arctic Council (Arctic Climate Impact Assessment, 2004). For a recent analysis of the Canadian diplomatic role in the Arctic Council, see Stoett, 2000.

Systems in the north and proposed oil drilling in the Arctic National Wildlife Refuge (see Huebert, this volume), and differences of opinion on multilateral approaches to global environmental governance on such issues as UNEP reform, control of persistent organic pollutants, biodiversity, or climate change. The latter may reflect the most serious rift that has emerged since the election of G.W. Bush in 2000, as a relatively unilateralist United States refuses to participate in the Kyoto Protocol on global warming recently ratified by Ottawa and Russia. This volume aims to capture some well-informed views on these, and many other, complex contemporary ecopolitical dilemmas, and as such to add to the steadily growing body of literature that considers the ecopolitical dimension of the utmost importance for the future overall bilateral relationship.

The context in which environmental policy decision-making occurs has changed, resulting from widening environmental *problématiques*, increased demands from groups and citizens, continuing pressure on the continent's resources, and normative shifts. But the complexity of current issues is related also to an even broader contextual shift: the globalization of environmental issues exacerbated by trade liberalization, especially on the regional level but also the global, and the potential contradictions between the trade and environmental international agenda that this implies. While it is clear that Canadian and American bilateral environmental policy must consider the vagaries of both states, it is within the coterminous globalization framework that many decisions will be made as well. Thus, we stand at a unique, and highly challenging, time to analyse Canadian-American environmental relations, especially from a Canadian perspective. Can we learn from the evolution of historical conflicts in this regard? Or, are the immediate urgencies and political idiosyncrasies of the day still far more relevant? Indeed, has the environmental governance anticipated by transgovernmental relations specialists actually declined in recent years? Relatedly, how do these governments attempt to influence each other? For example, Hoberg (2002) writes of several routes, including working-level arrangements, direct diplomacy, the use of international institutions, leading by example ("putting our own house in order"), mobilizing U.S. domestic support, and fostering analytic capacity. All of these have been used, with varying degrees of success, in recent years. But influence-strategy is but one of the many issue-areas we need to discuss. Each chapter in this volume takes a unique focus on one aspect of the overall bilateral ecopolitical relationship and advances our efforts to understand it as a whole.

The Text

This volume features chapters written by both Canadian and American scholars interested in the evolution of bilateral ecopolitics. A growing body of literature is devoted to the contemporary significance of borders (see Nicol and Townsend-Gault, 2004). The Canadian-American border has shaped our abilities to both exploit and conserve nature, and we seek to understand the ways in which this has occurred over the last century. The present contributions demonstrate that, with a few notable exceptions, ecopolitics is largely occurring at the sub-state level. Policy networks, including civil society actors, play the major role, as has been suggested in studies of the development of agro-environmental policy in both states (Montpetit, 2003). States and provinces are taking more concrete steps toward greenhouse gas reductions than national governments (see Rabe, 2004). So it is immediately apparent that we must employ a level of analysis that goes beyond bilateral relations to encompass transgovernmental and transnational relations as well. Beyond this analytic openness, we have made no effort to impose ideological or even theoretical perspectives on the authors, who range quite widely in terms of their approaches and convictions.

We wish also to explore the factors that shape this multi-faceted relationship. One concerns the impact of power asymmetries, as discussed above. The question is not whether it has an impact, but when, on what aspects and under what conditions. In many cases, Ottawa is quite willing to duke it out with Washington; in others, less so. While we naturally expect the United States to exert tremendous influence, other domestic and external influences affect the shape of the relationship, starting with the international norm-complex of "liberal environmentalism", which embraces "economic expansion, free trade, and market forces and incentives as a means to address global environmental issues" (Bernstein and Cashore, 2002:213).

A key question to explore, then, is how the changing context of continental trade liberalization and ideological shifts in the U.S. has impacted the environmental relationship of the two countries. The United States imports more oil from Canada than from any other state. Some 86 percent of Canadian trade goes to the United States, while 25 percent of American trade goes to Canada; this remains the single largest trading relationship in the global economy (Kitchen, 2004:694). To what extent, and under what conditions, has it fostered environmental disputes or policy convergence? How have the two countries attempted to reconcile expectations and norms carried respectively by trade and environment regimes? In this context, is an institutionalized pattern of environmental governance emerging? We open the book with John Kirton's treatment of the NAFTA trade-environment regime to reflect the centrality of this contextual factor. Indeed, NAFTA is one of the few trade agreements that actually institutionalizes environmental policy concerns, though it is often criticized as weakly reinforced in this regard. Despite a mixed record, Kirton believes the interplay between Canada and NAFTA reveals that Canada has sustained a policy of embedded ecologism throughout several trade/environment disputes in the time since NAFTA's conception. Readers can decide for themselves whether NAFTA has enhanced environmental protection in North America; Kirton provides an impressively detailed analysis suggesting it does. He goes as far as to suggest that the environmental regime within NAFTA "has the potential to serve as a model and foundation for building a more equitable and socially sensitive trade-environment regime on a global scale, and for proceeding with deeper integration and regional community building within North America itself."

Debora VanNijnatten is similarly concerned with institution-building, and posits a multi-level approach to examine the establishment of a ground-level ozone regime between Canada and the United States. Her analysis takes us across a wide spectrum of actors and institutions, including the Environmental Protection Agency, various state and provincial governments, and an epistemic community of concerned professionals. Many Canadians might be surprised to learn that the main problem in implementing a more robust regime was the weak regulatory policy of the government of Ontario, not the United States. The difficulties of federal-provincial policy co-ordination are thus made evident early in the text, a theme to which many other authors return.

Our next chapter is written by Don Munton, who keeps the focus at the diplomatic bilateral level as he revisits a theme he introduced in the 1980s, that of environmental dependence, "a situation in which the environmental quality and/or valued resources of a country are endangered by transboundary pollution…" He applies this theme specifically to the case of acid rain and ground-level ozone negotiations between Canada and the United States, which culminated in and affected the Air Quality Agreement; and particulate matter, which he believes is "the emerging issue in Canada-United States air quality relations in the 21st century." Munton suggests we have moved away from the openly confrontational bargaining model demonstrated by the acid rain negotiations, and toward a much more quite diplomacy on ozone and particulate matter; away from politicization and toward bureaucratization. The reason for this shift, he asserts, is that the level of governmental support for air quality improvement has remained stagnant, or decreased, since the initial Air Quality Agreement negotiations.

Next, Henrik Selin and Stacy VanDeveer continue on the theme of air pollution, but take us back toward the sub-state level with their detailed analysis of the joint Climate Change Action Plan adopted by the New England Governors (NEG) and the Eastern Canadian Premiers (ECP) in August 2001. Their focus on regionalism transcends the Canada-United States relationship, emphasizing the ecological and political regional circumstances that have forced state and provincial leaders to pursue public commitments that in effect exceed the willingness of national and federal politicians. Selin and VanDeveer suggest there are three principal forces driving climate change policy development in Northeast North America: "(1) developments in international scientific and political debates about climate change; (2) changing political pressures and incentives for regional office holders; and (3) an advocacy coalition of active networking and leadership activities on the part of state/provincial level civil servants." The NEG-ECP Action Plan will not reverse the trend toward global warming, but it may signal a new direction in ecopolitics.

One area where we might see the resumption of much more publicly confrontational diplomacy is the Arctic. Here, Canada is the main territorial player, but Alaska remains not only a vital part of the circumpolar ecosystem, in some ways it is also its most controversial given the Bush administration's expressed desire to open up the Arctic National Wildlife Refuge to further oil exploration and possible drilling. Though this is perhaps the most high-profile issue related to bilateral Arctic affairs, Rob Huebert reminds us that there are many others, most of them centered on the long-term prospects for the North's people and ecosystem alike. This is an issue-area where multilateral cooperation is also necessary, adding another layer of analysis to the chapter. Huebert notes that in the case of Arctic relations, rhetorical commitments are relatively strong, while actual funding commitments relatively weak. In the post-Cold War era, the northern relationship will reflect changing conditions on the Arctic ground: the impact of global warming, and the demand for natural gas and pipeline construction.

Perhaps the most well-known shared resource, however, is the Great Lakes. Indeed, the co-management regime established by the Boundary Waters Treaty of 1909, described in detail by Al Schwartz in Chapter 7 of this volume, is used as a textbook example of regional cooperation, and we have devoted two chapters to issues related to the work of the International Joint Commission; another deals with invasive species in the region. As one of the greatest single sources of freshwater in the world, the lakes are legendary for their size and the amount of trade traffic that crosses them since the opening of the Saint Lawrence Seaway. Schwartz goes beyond the lakes, however: he is concerned not only with the Great Lakes Water Quality Agreements of the 1970s, but brings us also to a discussion of recent proposals by the IJC to create Transboundary Watershed Boards across the entire Canada/U.S. border. This represents a giant leap in the regulatory potential of this bilateral institution, though it raises many problems of coordination in the process. While subnational political units may encourage greater transborder cooperation, Schwartz suggests they can also be threatened by the ecosystemic approach to resource management. Indeed he concludes that watershed boards may not be politically feasible until a true convergence on interests among the myriad actors is found.

Mary Durfee and Mirit Shamir identify another threat to Great Lakes bilateral management: the multilateral trade environment. While Kirton is ultimately optimistic about the environmental consequences of the NAFTA regime, these authors point to both NAFTA and the WTO as potential challengers to the IJC in particular. One of the principal concerns here is that of bulk water exports; though there has been considerable resistance to this development, especially in Canada, Durfee and Shamir address the common fear that, once begun, such exports would be legally sanctioned and in fact become obligations under NAFTA. They are also concerned that the science-based ecosystemic approach will be overridden by trade law and its differing normative context. They suggest that strengthening the validity of the precautionary principle, which has become to some extent a cornerstone in international environmental law, may prevent the collapse of the ecological dimension of this bilateral arrangement.

If precaution is valuable, it is certainly in order when it comes to the preservation of biodiversity. This is a much more important crossborder issue than many people realise, and we have devoted three chapters to it. We begin with Peter Stoett and John Nick Sanders, who focus attention on transborder conservation efforts. They argue that there has been a general paradigm shift among conservationists, from a species and park-based approach to a much more ambitious focus on regional ecosystems, and this has of course meant that transborder cooperation is vital in contemporary efforts to both save endangered species and protect extant biodiversity from encroachments by invasive species. In both cases, cooperation on a state-provincial level has been the main approach taken, but non-state actors have played a more important role in encouraging governmental action and implementing concrete protection and prevention efforts. They present several case studies to illustrate this point: the protection of rangelands for the Yellowstone wolf; the Yellowstone to Yukon Conservation Initiative (Y2Y); the 2 Countries, 1 Forest (2C1Forest) initiative in the Northern Appalachian and Acadian Forest Ecoregion; and the zebra mussel infestation of the Great Lakes, where the irreversibility of the invasion only stresses the vital importance of future prevention efforts.

Another area where governance is characterized by what Robert Boardman refers to as "dense thickets of non-governmental organizations" is that of migratory bird conservation. In Chapter 10, Boardman offers a detailed examination of this governance structure, which is held together with bilateral and multilateral agreements such as the North American Waterfowl Management Plan, put in place in 1986 (and which Mexico joined in 1994). Here too we see a paradigm shift, from a system based largely on conserving game species to one more concerned with overall ecosystemic health as reflected in bird populations regardless of their game value. Hunting controls are only part of a complex story that involves Native Americans, coastal communities, habitat protection efforts, the Trilateral Committee for Wildlife and Ecosystem Conservation and Management, continental "flyway councils", and birdwatching enthusiasts. What emerges is a complex picture of governance structures, where the "emerging core tasks of conservation governance in North America lie not so much in the design of new continental architecture, but rather in the creative forging of more robust trans-level and inter-actor linkages." [7]

Perhaps few species have so high-profile an image attached to their plight as the Pacific salmon, which is under increasing threat because of both habitat destruction and overfishing. Indeed, the west coast salmon dispute has been one of the sharper areas of division between Canadian and American actors for many years now. And, again, we see that subnational units are not only the key players but the primary antagonists. Samuel Barkin argues in Chapter 11 that the "politics of salmon quota negotiations highlight the difficulties of negotiations between governments in a federal system, when the two national governments do not have full authority over the issue, and where the distribution of authority between national and sub-national governments is different in the two countries." Clearly, the bilateral Pacific Salmon commission has not been up to the task of reconciling differences. Barkin goes on to utilize international environmental relations theories on common and directional resource problems to discuss possible paths of cooperation.

7 Indeed, the emergence of multiple actors and multi-level governance raises issues that pertain to the relative influence of specific actors at different governance levels: the legitimacy of the decisions made; the effectiveness both of the process of reconciling conflicting norms, perspectives and interests, and of the policies adopted in solving the environmental problem. These dimensions are interdependent but not necessarily related positively; the resulting dynamics indeed deserve greater scrutiny.

Our next chapter discusses the growing need for "green energy" production on the North American power grid, and the political implications of such a development. After the power blackout in the summer of 2003, much more attention is being paid to the question of energy security; and as the chapter by Selin and VanDeveer suggests, more substate actors are looking for practical solutions than ever before. How can electricity generated from solar, wind, small hydro and biomass resources be encouraged on a continent with such a long history of fossil fuel electricity production? What impact could this have on continental relations? Ian Rowlands advocates a middle ground between the current approach, which is largely focused on local approaches to innovation, and a bilateral or continental one that will homogenize energy production even further. The chapter adds further evidence to our central claim that bilateral ecopolitics is both a high-level and, even, security issue, but is dominated by substate and transnational actors and, increasingly, institutions. Whether we can move ahead in the area of renewable energy sources will, of course, be a central issue in the years to come.

Naturally there are many issue-areas this text does not adequately cover, though most relevant issues are at least mentioned throughout the various chapters assembled here. Policy co-ordination between Canada and the United States can only take us so far, however, if there is no grander vision for the future of environmental policy in both states. While the United States remains the world's only "superpower", its troubled legitimacy in this role since the invasion of Iraq and repeated rejections of multilateral approaches to solving common problems has forced Canada and other states to respond to unilateralism with policy statements that indicate either unqualified support or, more often, distinct unease. There have been many excellent discussions of Canadian foreign policy, toward the U.S. and elsewhere, in the post 9/11 climate (see for example, Stairs, 2003; Pentland, 2003; Haglund, 2003; Cohen, 2003; Condon and Sinha, 2003), but how will this shape the policy landscape in upcoming years with regard to environmental protection? To this end, Robert Paehlke's closing chapter offers a perspective, largely from the Canadian point of view, of what directions policy might, can, and should take given the context of globalization. After contrasting competitiveness and sustainability concerns, he pushes forth his vision for a democratic sustainability, as well as more specific guidelines he feels should guide Canadian environmental diplomacy and policy, especially in the continental context. In so doing, Paehlke raises challenging assertions and provokes further thinking.

It will be apparent to the reader that we have assembled a diverse array of authors here, many of whom openly contradict each other regarding policy outcomes, priorities, and possibilities. This was our intention, and we hope it stimulates as much debate as interest amongst readers. But several themes strongly emerge as the chapters progress, including the necessity to go beyond simple state-state politics in order to understand these complex issue-areas; the tension between the search for consensus among an increasing diversity of legitimate actors and the quest for policy effectiveness; the need to anticipate future developments in terms of demand for innovation and change; the requirement to delve deep into the details of case studies to achieve a better understanding and respect for the precautionary principle; and the need to develop a longer-term perspective of the common directions we can and should follow.

Conclusion

In an eclectic work such as this, it might be haphazard to attempt to draw firm overall conclusions. What becomes clear is that the various authors assembled here all believe the Canadian-American relationship is a fluid and ongoing work in progress. Several animating themes drive this text, and our contributors have each had to struggle with them. These include the impact of, and on, the overall nature of the relationship between Canada and the United States as it pertains to ecopolitics. It also entails consideration of the impact, again, both of and on, the federal political structure of both states, the role of regionalism, and globalization. It is clear that a cursory dismissal of the topic as simply the byproduct of a power discrepancy is unwarranted. Looking through ecopolitical lenses at the Canadian-American relationship will produce a distinct, if not entirely unique, picture than one obtained from the more traditional way of looking at the relationship, one emphasizing economic and ecological integration, as well as centrifugal forces, complex interdependence, and decision-making autonomy that is more limited than both states are ready to recognize.

It is also clear that transgovernmental and transnational activity is as often as not the most important locale of political activity, especially in terms of co-operative ventures. However, as our concluding chapters remind us, both states are situated within the complexities of the global economy, and decision-making will reflect priorities sustained by political determination and long-term vision. Hopefully, environmental security will be a paramount factor in such a vision, and this volume will aid that development.

Chapter 2

Managing Canada's U.S. Relations Through NAFTA's Trade-Environment Regime

John Kirton

Introduction

In the long, intense continental relationship between Canada and the United States, both environmental and trade issues have recurrently been at the centre of controversy and conflict (Nye 1976). They have equally been at the centre of co-operative steps, including the construction of pioneering bilateral institutions such as the International Joint Commission (IJC) and those created or catalyzed by the Free Trade Agreement (FTA) of 1988 (Spencer, Kirton, and Nossal, 1981). Moreover, many of the controversies – notably the *Arctic Waters Pollution Prevention Act* of 1970 and the FTA itself in 1988 – and the co-operative initiatives and institutions that have arisen to govern them, have inherently involved tradeoffs and other linkages between trade and investment on the one hand and the environment and associated social values on the other (Munton and Kirton 1992).

Yet it was only in the 1990s, with the advent of the North American Free Trade Agreement (NAFTA), that trade and environment became formally fused in a single regional regime encompassing Canada and the United States (Kirton, 1998b; Kirton, 1997; Munton and Kirton, 1996; Magraw and Charnovitz, 1994; Lowry, 1992). It is truly paradoxical that the countries with the largest two-way trading relationship in the world and with vast borders that join their massive ecological capabilities and vulnerabilities should have waited until the arrival of Mexico and the trilateralism it brought to forge their direct international institutional trade-environment link. It is even more paradoxical that these two world-leading G8 trade and environmental powers and pioneers of broad multilateral trade and environment institutions in the 1990s, notably the World Trade Organization (WTO) and the Rio bodies, should have set aside such multilateral institutions as important instruments to address the trade-environment relationships within their continental home. For it has largely been the trilateral NAFTA regime, rather than available bilateral or multilateral alternatives, that have defined how trade and environment processes and values have been fused within the North American region.

After a decade in formal operation, and a further three years in serious negotiation and anticipation, the impact of this revolutionary NAFTA regime remains the subject of considerable controversy (Audley et al., 2003; Abbott, 2000; Groetzinger, 1997; CEC, 1999; Grossman, 2000; Jansen, 2001; Rugman and Kirton, 1998). Those examining the NAFTA trade-environment regime in general terms from realist perspectives have concluded that it offers very limited institutionalization and effectiveness relative to the European Union, and thus does little to constrain a predominant United States (Steinberg, 1997). More constructivist scholars claim that its rules and decision-making procedures have not been underpinned by genuine changes in underlying norms or principles, and that the regime has been largely ineffective as a result (Audley, 1997; Mayer, 1998). Liberal institutionalist scholars with a "legalization" bias, along with NAFTA's many critics, argue that NAFTA's new environmental institution, the Commission for Environmental Cooperation (CEC), has done little to fulfil what they see as its core purpose of ensuring the effective enforcement of national environmental regulations (Abbot et al., 2000; Mumme and Duncan, 1996; Public Citizen, 1995; Economic Policy Institute, 1997).

Other assessments are more favourable to the core liberal-institutionalist argument that international regimes have an autonomous impact in enhancing the co-operative behaviour, if not the underlying interests and identities, of their member governments. Here the most popular claim is that NAFTA's far reaching trade and investment liberalization rules has unleashed a more intense competition among the countries and companies of North America. This has allegedly led, first, to a "race" to the bottom in regulation and industrial relocation; second, to "regulatory" chill in the face of rising environmental problems, awareness and demands; third, to "restraint" on the ability of national and subfederal governments to regulate freely to supply the demanded environmental protection, and fourth to a strong trade community and U.S. benefiting at the expense of a weaker environmental community and Canadian and Mexican neighbours. In particular, attention has focused on the way NAFTA's Chapter 11 investment dispute settlement mechanism has rewarded U.S.-based multinational corporations (MNCs) at the expense of Canadian and Mexican environmental regulators. In contrast, the counterpart Article 14-15 citizen complaint process in NAFTA's environmental side agreement, the North American Agreement on Environmental Cooperation (NAAEC), instituted to ensure governments enforce their existing environmental laws and regulations, has offered little offsetting balance (Kibel, 2001; Mann and von Moltke, 1999).

In contrast, those more faithful to liberal institutionalist traditions should take seriously the fact that NAFTA was not only a pioneering trade and investment agreement, but an historic trade-environment agreement as well. It came with innovative and potentially powerful environmental principles, norms and rules in both the core NAFTA and its environmental side agreements, with 50 or more new trilateral institutions the agreements created or inspired, and with the unique creation of a regional organization – the CEC – that the trade and investment component of the overall NAFTA regime lacks. Some early analyses saw the CEC as an institution with considerable potential (Munton and Kirton, 1994; Johnson and Beaulieu, 1994;

Abbott, 1996; Johnson, 1999). Others saw the NAFTA regime's rules and institutions more broadly as engendering effective environmental cooperation among the parties in several instances, as well as constraining national and subfederal environmental regulations that serve as barriers to trade (Rugman, Kirton and Soloway, 1997, 1999; Rugman and Kirton, 1999, 1998; Kirton and Rugman, 1999; Kirton and Fernandez de Castro, 1997; Kirton 1998b, 1997; Weintraub, 1997). Such analyses raise the possibility that the NAFTA regime might over time alter the underlying interests and even identities of its governments, corporate communities, and civil society and citizens, in ways that enable a new trade-environment balance to emerge in North America, provide a model for the wider world and a nest for regional community building in North America.

What does the record of the first decade reveal? This chapter reports the results of a comprehensive exploration of how NAFTA and its institutions have altered the process and outcomes in the full universe of cases of broadly defined "environmental regulatory protection' involving at least two of the three NAFTA member countries from 1980 to mid 1998, and in critical selected areas in subsequent years.[4] It first specifies as an anchor for the analysis Canada's fixed national interests and distinctive national values in the trade-environment domain, as they are expressed in declared government policy and mass public opinion. Second, it identifies the cases of "environmental regulatory protection" (ERP), arising from new conditions of "complex institutional responsiveness (CIR)," the process through which these cases are handled, and the outcomes that result. Here it explores in particular how the balance of outcomes changes across issue areas, industry sectors, from the pre-NAFTA to post-NAFTA period, as the NAFTA institutions are involved, and as the CEC, rather than NAFTA's trade institutions, are employed. Third, it explores the overall record of the 36 cases initiated under Chapter 11 from 1994 to 2004. Fourth, it similarly analyzes the 49 cases initiated under Article 14-15 from 1994 to 2004. Fifth it considers the five cases initiated under the CEC's "roving spotlight" instrument of Article 13.

This analysis reveals that Canada has long had deeply embedded foreign policy priorities and distinctive national interests of "embedded ecologism"; environmental protection has come to assume first place in Canadian foreign policy priorities, and take primacy over the trade liberalization with which it is now integrally linked. These preferences coincide with the proliferation of ERP cases in North America from the 1980s to the NAFTA era of the 1990s. This proliferation shows that NAFTA-ensconced governments in the U.S., Canada and Mexico have had no diminished appetite or ability to regulate for environmental protection in ways that affect trade. In resolving such cases, the three North American governments have tended to find solutions that generate both higher and more convergent environmental regulations, and greater trade and investment liberalization as well. Despite the overwhelming economic power of the United States in the NAFTA region, and of the trade-investment community centered in it, the outcomes of such cases move toward equality among the member countries and between their trade and environment communities as the NAFTA era arrives, and as the NAFTA institutions in general, and the CEC in particular, assume consequential roles. The record of Chapter 11 and Article 14-15, where societal actors have direct access to international tribunals, contributes to and confirms such results. The impact of the Article 13 cases, reflecting the autonomous power of the CEC Secretariat, points in the same direction as well.

In short, relative to the previous regime and available alternatives, the NAFTA regime has worked well for Canada, and for its management of its relationship with the U.S. The NAFTA regime has provided an incentive and an instrument for governments in Canada, as well as the U.S. and Mexico, to regulate more aggressively and successfully in order to secure higher levels of environmental protection, through a more equal process of mutual adjustment, that yields outcomes that more equally benefit each of the region's three countries and both of its environment and trade communities. In particular, NAFTA has given Canada and its partners both a reason to recognize, and a regime to respond to, the new trade opportunities and ecological vulnerabilities that the trilateral community brings, and to do so in ways that benefit all. The opening of international institutions to allow direct access for corporations and citizens has strengthened the equalizing and community-building effects of the innovative NAFTA trade-environment regime. It thus has the potential to serve as a model and foundation for building a more equitable and socially sensitive trade-environment regime on a global scale, and for proceeding with deeper integration and regional community building within North America itself.

Embedded Ecologism in Canadian Foreign Policy

In assessing how well NAFTA's trade-environment regime has worked for Canada, it is necessary to specify first what Canada wanted and needed from this new NAFTA regime. This is best done by identifying the Canadian state's declared formal overall foreign policy priorities designed to endure over the medium term, and Canadian society's enduring, inclusive distinctive national values, as revealed in mass public opinion about Canada in international affairs. To this fixed foundation, more specific and changeable preferences about the NAFTA regime in its construction and operation can be added.

In contrast to its two NAFTA partners, the Canadian state has long given, in its overall foreign policy priorities, a growing importance to environmental protection, to equalizing and integrating environmental values with those of economic growth through trade. In June 1970, *Foreign Policy for Canadians* listed "economic" growth as the first-placed priority, but added for the first time a "harmonious natural environment" and put it in sixth place (Canada, 1970). The new Mulroney government's 1985 "Green Paper," *Competitiveness and Security*, demoted economic growth to the fifth position, while keeping "the integrity of our natural environment" in sixth place (Canada, 1985). Its 3 April , 1989 Speech from the Throne, inaugurating its second majority mandate, specified two co-equal objectives: "an economy fully competitive among the world's trading nations" and a commitment to "give firm leadership and support to international efforts to overcome the environmental threat to our planet."

The Chrétien government, which inherited and accepted the NAFTA agreement and environmental side agreement negotiated by Mulroney, took the final step in its 1995 foreign policy statement, *Canada and the World* (Canada, 1995). Here it put "the promotion of prosperity and employment" in first place, but added sustainable development as a cross cutting imperative that would govern how all three priorities would unfold. The *Statement* also listed the environment as a component Canadian value under the third priority, "the projection of Canadian values and culture."

This expression of Canada's embedded ecologism is confirmed by the data on Canadians' mass public opinion preferences about Canadian foreign policy. From the late 1980s onward, virtually all Canadians, virtually all the time, have with virtual unanimity placed "environmental protection" as their first preference in Canadian foreign policy as a whole. Trade liberalization always places well down on the list. Indeed, when confronted contextually with a clear choice, Canadians have preferred environmental protection over trade liberalization. Their rising and now strong support for NAFTA, with its strong environmental provisions (relative to the previous Canada-U.S. FTA) is consistent with this preference pattern (Kirton and Maclaren 2002b: 5). Indeed, by the autumn of 2003, a majority of Canadians, along with a majority of Americans and Mexicans wished to have environmental policy made at the regional, rather than the national level (Graves, 2003).

Environmental Regulatory Protection and the NAFTA Trade-Environment Regime

NAFTA's trade and related investment liberalizations were particularly important for smaller firms from smaller countries such as Canada, which depend increasingly on access to the larger U.S. market for much of their trade and GNP. Yet in moving to take advantage of the newly-opened NAFTA market, such firms and their governments were confronted with a new array of barriers and vulnerabilities, produced by the emerging conditions of "complex institutional responsiveness" (Esty and Geradin, 1997; Rugman and Kirton, 1999). The result was an upsurge of cases of "environmental regulatory protection" (ERP). Now, however, the new NAFTA institutions were available to help firms and governments solve the conflicts and seize the co-operative solution.[1] From 1980 to mid 1998, there were 84 cases

1 Environmental regulatory protection is defined as government action, at the subfederal, national or international levels, that is directed at affecting trade liberalization or environmental protection, but that has clear, direct, substantial and recognized implications for activities and values in the other domain. It thus embraces activity aimed at environmental protection that affects trade, as with national regulations that impede (or enhance) market entry for foreign firms, or international action to create region-wide environmental regulations (at any level) that lower transactions costs and thus facilitate trade. Furthermore, it embraces activity aimed at trade liberalization that affects environmental protection and quality, in either positive or

of such intergovernmentally managed ERP involving at least two of the three North American national governments or their subfederal units. An examination of these cases suggests several trends (Rugman, Kirton and Soloway, 1999).

First, there was a post-NAFTA upsurge in ERP. As Table 2.1 indicates, there have been substantially more trade-environment issues arising in the five years since NAFTA took formal effect, than in the five years when the FTA operated (1989–1993), and in the preceding five years when the three countries of North America could look only to the distant General Agreement on Tariffs and Trade (GATT) for international relief.

Second, there has been a similar post-NAFTA expansion in the range of ERP, seen in the broad range of sectors that have been affected by it. Such issues abound in the automotive sector at the heart of the North American manufacturing economy, in the environmentally rich natural resource sectors of agriculture, fisheries and forestry, in other manufacturing industries and service industries such as trucking and, paradoxically, in the new sector of environmental services.

Third, this upsurge took place in the long opened U.S.-Canada relationship as well as in the newly NAFTA-opened U.S.-Mexico one. Indeed, there are good reasons for expecting that in open relationships, characterized by high degrees of intra-industry trade, trade liberalization will lead individual firms to seek protection ever more strongly, including through different and higher environmental regulation (Gilligan, 1997; Weintraub, 1994; Leyshon, 1992). This administered protection dynamic leading to an environmental regulatory "race to the top" appears to be alive and abundant in the Canada-U.S. relationship of the NAFTA age. It confirms other analyses which show that NAFTA has produced no geographic or regulatory race to the bottom (Mahant, 2001).

It is a challenging task to identify how firms and their governments actually respond to this dilemma of rising ERP, when and why they use the new international institutional instruments offered by NAFTA, and when and why these institutions are successfully employed to produce balanced benefits.[2] Nonetheless, after a decade of

---

negative ways. Such cases can be initiated by government action at the subfederal, national or international level. In the later case, it embraces initiatives taken by the secretariats of intergovernmental institutions themselves. Such government action may arise in response to firm behaviour or pressure, or at independent government initiative. Moreover, such cases can encompass the full spectrum, from those marked by high conflict to those embracing full co-operation. The research universe thus runs the range from reactive, conflictual cases, in which new environmental regulations create trade barriers, to proactive co-operative ones, where governments actively create region-wide environmental or trade rules in advance of any conflicts occurring. Finally, unlike the original Keohane-Nye conception, which was limited to conflict cases that reached the attention of the U.S. president, the current study includes cases from the high political to the low functional level (Nye, 1976; Keohane and Nye, 1977).

2 The NAFTA regime has been in operation for only a short time. Many of the cases dealt with under it are still in progress. Some of the issues resolved immediately prior to NAFTA taking formal effect were done so in anticipation of and thus under the influence of

operation of the NAFTA regime, there is a sufficiently strong empirical foundation for confident judgments about the emerging patterns to be made.[3]

As Table 2.1 indicates, 50 of the 84 cases have come to an effective resolution where such outcomes can be scored. Ten have done so in the pre-NAFTA period, and 40 have done so in the post-NAFTA period or in the immediate lead up to and under the conscious anticipation of NAFTA. At first glance, the bigger winner of the ERP "battle" appears to be the U.S.A., which wins 58 percent of the time. Of the 50 cases effectively resolved by mid 1998, the United States and its firms won 29, Canada eight, and Mexico seven, while eight were resolved to the mutual benefit of two or three of the North American partners. Such a pattern would appear to be a further testament to the realist presupposition that in this bargaining domain as in so many others, the United States with its overwhelmingly superior power (based on having at least ten times as much economic capability as Canada and at least 20 times as much as Mexico) is bound to prevail.

However, this conclusion requires immediate qualification. For the impact of complex institutional responsiveness is largely to equalize outcomes in a trade-liberalizing and environmentally enhancing manner. First, the U.S., with 87 percent of the regional GDP, wins far less than its relative economic weight suggests it should. Second, in keeping with an issue-structure model, the degree of U.S. success varies widely across issue areas, according to the relative size of the home-based firms that dominate each (Keohane and Nye, 1977).[4]

---

the NAFTA, as a calculated consequence of how countries and firms would be better off by moving to particular solutions. Most importantly, in many of these cases several instruments worked together to produce an outcome, making it somewhat artificial to single out and score each in operation alone.

3 To begin this analysis, it is necessary to score the outcome of those cases that have been resolved, under NAFTA's influence or not. In keeping with the initial Keohane-Nye conception for scoring outcomes of Canada-U.S. disputes, and variants based on it, outcomes are scored as to whether these cases, once resolved, conform more to the initial preferences of each of three countries (Nye, 1976; Leyton-Brown, 1976; Norton, 1998). However, in an extension of this method, they include the co-operative, positive-sum possibility of joint or mutual gains, in which outcomes reflect the initial preference of both or all parties (as distinct from the original Keohane-Nye "compromise" possibility of "tied" outcomes equidistant between the initial preferences of each). A further extension allows a scoring of cases according to whether the positions, interests and values of the transnational trade or environment communities were realized in the outcomes.

4 Thus, the United States enjoys complete success (prevailing in all nine cases) in the area of automotive emissions and fuels, an area dominated by the U.S.-owned Big Three (including Daimler-Chrysler) assemblers and U.S.-owned parts suppliers. It has a success rate of 75 percent in manufacturing recycling and 67 percent in fisheries conservation. But it has only 60 percent in agricultural inspection, where the Canadian and especially Mexican industries (based on home-based exporters) loom relatively large. Moreover, the United States has a success rate of only 33 percent in forestry conservation, an area where Canadian companies are particularly strong. It is worth noting that these natural resources sectors of

Third, in many of the cases, notably in automotive emissions, U.S. dominance arises because of its national environmental leadership – it is the first to recognize an environmental problem and take regulatory action. Canadian and Mexican compliance with these regulations is not a case of acquiescence after significant resistance but a case of these two partner countries coming to support the initial U.S. action to produce an environmentally superior result. While this process involves the exercise of structural and other forms of power, it is best seen as a form of beneficent rather than coercive hegemony, based in part on the superior scientific resources of the United States. In some cases, more mutually balanced adjustments arise as an evidence based "share and compare" process points to which national regulatory approach is best able to solve common environmental problems and serve similar environmental preferences across the region as a whole. In other cases, where new environmental problems emerge, the NAFTA institutions and CEC operate in a world where states do not have fixed preferences and entrenched domestic interests but acquire their interests through the process of NAFTA-inspired and -guided interaction. Propelling this process is the dominance of U.S.-owned transnational multinational enterprises (MNEs), and an empowered North American public demanding better environmental solutions. This has led to a process of environmental regulatory leapfrogging, especially in the automotive and related air-quality domains, where Canadian jurisdictions have moved to introduce new environmental regulations and standards that are more stringent by many measures than those of neighbouring U.S. states and the U.S. as a whole (Kirton, 1998a; Kirton, 1999).

Fourth, in the domain of trade-related environmental cases there is an almost perfect equality of outcome, and a complete absence of U.S. dominance. In contrast to the environmentally related trade issues, where the United States is successful in 64 percent of the cases, in the domain of trade-related environmental cases it prevails in only 25 percent. In this latter realm, success is shared equally among the U.S. with 25 percent, Canada with 38 percent, Mexico with 25 percent, and all three with 25 percent. This sharp shift toward balanced outcomes can be attributed to two factors. The first is the superior ecological capability of Mexico and especially Canada, manifested in a vulnerability for the United States that has been expanded by NAFTA economic liberalizations. To contain this new vulnerability, the United States is forced to co-operate and accept balanced outcomes, as the cases of pesticides and environmental information suggest. The second is the presence in the trade-related environmental area of a strong international institution – the CEC – which, unlike those in the trade area, possesses an international organization with a single secretariat, substantial budget and staff, and considerable powers of autonomous investigation (Kirton, 1997; Housman, 1994).

The autonomous power of international institutions is further seen by examining the outcome of the cases according to their non-NAFTA or NAFTA-affected resolution. The NAFTA era makes an equalizing difference. As Table 2.3 shows,

fisheries and forestry (along with agriculture) are the ones where environmentalists are most concerned about the stress on ecosystems, and of trade and NAFTA's environmental effects.

in the ten resolved pre-NAFTA cases (with the U.S. directly involved in all), the United States prevailed in eight cases or 80 percent of the time. Canada, directly involved in ten, won in two, for a success rate of 20 percent overall and 20 percent in the issues of direct engagement. Mexico was not directly involved in any. This distribution is very close to the overall distribution of economic capability in the region, with Canada's somewhat larger than predicted score (20 percent rather than 10 percent) traceable to the presence of the bilateral FTA. Mexico's score reflects a still relatively autarkic Mexico, carefully choosing the issues on which it ventured to confront the United States. Equally striking, in this pre-NAFTA era none of the cases resulted in an equal outcome.

In sharp contrast, in the much larger set of 40 cases in the NAFTA era, the distributions are dramatically different. The rate of success for the United States alone, directly involved in all cases, has dropped from 80 percent to 50 percent. Canada's has remained relatively constant, moving from 20 percent to 13 percent in all cases and 19 percent in the 26 cases in which it is directly involved (as a disputant or through the NAFTA trilateral institutions). Mexico's has strongly increased to 18 percent over all cases and to 23 percent in the 30 issues in which it is directly involved. And outcomes that benefit both or all of the countries and their firms involved have risen from zero to 20 percent. Indeed, 57 percent or over half of the cases involving all three NAFTA countries are resolved according to the preferences of all three.

From these figures it is clear that the NAFTA era still works for the United States. It still wins half (50 percent) of the issues in the region. It further shares in the additional 20 percent of joint gains, to produce an overall success rate of 70 percent. But the NAFTA era also works for Canada, as its success rate holds at 19 percent in the issues in which it is directly involved, and it records an overall success rate of 39 percent. The greatest beneficiary of the NAFTA era, however, is the region's weakest member – Mexico – whose success rate rises to 38 percent overall. Over the dramatically expanded number of issues in which it is directly involved, relative to the pre-NAFTA period, it records a success rate of 23 percent against a still much stronger United States, with which it is now much more intensely involved. Above all, the NAFTA era works for the common North American community, as all three members benefit equally in 20 percent of the issues, and do so in 50 percent of those in which all three are directly involved. The world of three competitors struggling for relative gains in a zero sum game is clearly giving way to a single integrated community in which all members equally participate and profit.

The importance of the NAFTA era can be further seen by examining the outcomes of those resolved cases in the post-NAFTA era which have been importantly dealt with through the NAFTA institutions. Here it is clear that the NAFTA institutions make an equalizing difference. As the data in Table 2.4 show, of the 40 resolved cases in the post-NAFTA era, the NAFTA institutions attracted almost half the traffic. Nineteen or 48 percent were resolved through the NAFTA institutions (even if other instruments of firm strategy ultimately proved decisive in securing particular outcomes). Of these 19 cases, the United States prevailed in 47 percent, Canada in

22 percent, Mexico in 21 percent and all three countries equally in 21 percent. These are still clearly the United States' NAFTA institutions, as it is the sole beneficiary of their use to a greater degree than the other partner countries. Indeed, taking its individual and collective gains together, the United States wins through the NAFTA institutions 68 percent of the time. However, the autonomous impact of international institutions is evident in the greater equality of outcomes when issues are processed through the NAFTA bodies. Here Canada's success rate rises from 19 percent to 32 percent, and Mexico's from 18 to 21 percent. Most strikingly, when individual and common gains are taken together, the NAFTA institutions deliver a distribution of outcomes that is vastly more equal than power ratios among countries in North America: United States 68 percent, Canada 53 percent, Mexico 42 percent.

The remaining imbalance points both to the legacy of U.S. power and its highly active environmental movement, but also to Canada's particular historic skill at diplomacy through international institutions. However, the autonomous importance of international organization and the environmental intervulnerabilities that underlie it are again apparent. The NAFTA environmental institutions make a difference that does more than create an equal or common community. In the 11 cases where NAFTA's trade institutions served as a nest for resolution, the outcomes were distributed United States 55 percent, Canada 18 percent, Mexico 9 percent, and all 18 percent. In the eight cases where NAFTA's environmental institution – the CEC – served as the nest, the outcomes were Canada 38 percent, the United States 25 percent (including the joint win with Canada on Cozumel), Mexico 25 percent, and all 25 percent.

At the level of the firm, the importance of effective international institutions is again seen in the particular form in which the NAFTA bodies were fashioned. Of particular importance is the open architecture, allowing firms to have direct access to, and involvement in, the work of these institutions. Firms are involved in the CEC through the Joint Public Advisory Committee (JPAC) and many CEC working groups. This direct industry involvement was a critical element in producing the mutually beneficial outcomes through regulatory convergence in the Trilateral Working Group on Pesticides. Within the NAFTA trade institutions, industry involvement is less direct. The mechanism for industry involvement, through the joint meetings of the Committee on Standards Related Measures (CSRM) with trilateral industry bodies, is a facilitator of success (Clarkson et al., 2005; Kirton and Fernandez de Castro, 1997).

NAFTA Chapter 11

The NAFTA regime's provisions for civil society participation went much beyond the architecture of the JPAC and trilateral working groups. Indeed, perhaps the most innovative aspect of the NAFTA's regime's trade-environmental architecture were the rights it created for firms and environmentally concerned organizations and individuals to initiate and pursue processes of dispute settlement over trade-related environmental regulations, without having to face the barrier of first securing often unavailable or unenthusiastic home government support (von Moltke, 2002). This was a prescient as well as pioneering step, given the subsequent crescendo of demands for, and Canadian government support for, improved civil society participation in global governance (Graham, 2002). For firms that felt discriminated against by government environmental and other regulations in a foreign NAFTA country, including regulatory action that was "tantamount to expropriation", NAFTA's Chapter 11 offered the ability to take their claim for compensation to one of two multilateral dispute settlement mechanisms (Gal-Or, 1998). The NAAEC's Article 14-15 citizen submission process, in a balancing provision, allowed NGOs and citizens to pursue claims that national and subfederal governments were not adequately enforcing their own environmental laws and regulations.

Each innovation was the subject of considerable criticism, hope and speculation about their impact at the time of their birth. Many critics charged that Chapter 11 privileged private commercial interests over public environmental ones (Tollefson, forthcoming; Trebilcock, forthcoming; Mann and Araya, 2002; Mann, 2001; Mann and von Moltke, 1999). Others responded than in its actual judicial application, the Chapter 11 dispute settlement mechanism maintained the state's police power intact, and did not prevent bona fide effective environmental regulation from being introduced and applied (Soloway, forthcoming; Gaines, 2002; Soloway, 2002). Now, after ten years in operation, it is possible to identify empirically what the actual record, and its probable effect on regulatory behaviour, has been, judged against the inspiration for their initial creation and inclusion in the regime.

The inclusion of the Chapter 11 direct access dispute settlement mechanism was clearly a United States initiative directed against both Canada and Mexico (Price, 2000). In the case of Mexico, the inspiration for the U.S. demand was the memory of the widespread nationalization of U.S.-owned oil firms in the 1920s, Mexico's continuing closed one-party PRI dominated political system, and Mexico's reluctance to open its constitutionally protected oil and gas producing sector to foreign investment. In the case of Canada, the inspiration was the more recent 1980 memory of the National Energy program (NEP) with its discriminatory procurement and back in provisions, and the Chrétien Liberals' continuing caution about NAFTA's energy provisions. This was despite the subsequent Mulroney government's reversals of Canadian policy in regard to FDI policy and energy supply, the latter embedded in the bilateral FTA. Canadian NAFTA negotiators could look in relaxed fashion at the American proposal for Chapter 11 direct access, calculating that it was directed primarily against Mexico, that it might be useful to "lock-in" the Mulroney era liberalizations, and that by binding Canada, it would convince investors that Canada was an equally good place within the NAFTA area to place their new NAFTA-producing plants. No-one in Canada, or its partner governments, felt that government environmental regulations would be a primary, or even particularly relevant, target of Chapter 11 actions.

In the later regard, everyone was soon surprised. As Tables 2.2 and 2.3 show, from 1995 onward, there was a steady succession of new Chapter 11 cases initiated, declining only in 2003-2004 with environmental regulations being the subject of actions in every single year (excluding 2004). Indeed, the first major case, that of Ethyl, saw a U.S. firm sue the Canadian government over its core environmental regulations relating to a gas additive, with the Canadian government declaring defeat and making an out of court settlement with a substantial payment before the case was even judged by a NAFTA tribunal.

Compounding Canadian fears were the fact that the number of new Chapter 11 cases escalated, from only eleven during NAFTA's first five years in formal operation (1994-1998) to 25 in its subsequent six (1999-2004). Moreover during the first five years, Canada was the target of five of the eleven cases, compared to five for Mexico and only one (in 1998) for the United States. A full four of the five cases initiated against Canada concerned environmental regulations. All four environmental cases were initiated by U.S. firms. The environmental regulations they challenged covered a wide range, embracing the media of air (Ethyl MMT 1996), water (Sunbelt, 1998), land (Pope and Talbot, 1998) and living things (S. D. Myers PCB 1998). In addition to the initial Ethyl MMT "surrender" in advance, the Canadian government ultimately lost at the Chapter 11 tribunals the S.D. Myers and the Pope and Talbot cases.[5] Although environmentalists adopting a full life cycle analysis of ecological impacts could claim that the S. D. Myers outcome was environmentally enhancing, those focused on the freedom of governments to regulate for environmental protection saw the first five years of Chapter 11 as a dirty half decade in which Canada and the environment lost.

It was thus little wonder that the Canadian government as the *demandeur* pressed its U.S. and Mexican colleagues for a new interpretive statement that would limit the scope of Chapter 11 claims. Both countries resisted, for fear that it would discourage investment in their territories, and that any opening of the agreement would lead other demands and a difficult negotiation to arise.

This surge of cases against the United States had a particular dynamic. Inspired by the U.S. Pope and Talbot claims against Canadian softwood lumber regulations, Canadian forest product companies began to also invoke Chapter 11 cases in retaliation for U.S. trade remedy action against Canadians exports of softwood lumber to the United States. The essential claim was that such action constituted a discriminatory and unlawful taking of Chapter 11-guaranteed property rights, and was thus tantamount to expropriation in that respect.

In the almost four years following 1998, however, the dynamic of Chapter 11 litigation, and the ensuing diplomacy, changed dramatically. The number of cases soon escalated, from two in 1999 to four each in 2000 and 2001 to seven in the first nine months of 2002. More importantly, the two cases initiated in 1999 were both against the United States, which was the target as well in every subsequent year. In

5 In Pope and Talbot, the Government of Canada lost in the sense that damages were awarded to Pope and Talbot arising from the government's behaviour during an administrative audit undertaken to verify the company's quota. However, on the question of whether there was an expropriation, Canada could be said to have been successful in the outcome.

the full period from 1999 to August 2002, of the 17 cases initiated, the U.S. was the target of eight, Mexico in five and Canada in only four. Of the eight cases against the U.S., five dealt with environmental regulations.

The attitude of Canada's NAFTA partners quickly shifted. At the 31 July, 2001 meeting of the NAFTA Commission, the trade ministers of the three countries adopted an interpretive agreement that clarified the meaning of certain Chapter 11 provisions relating to "access to documents" and "minimum standard of treatment." They also directed their trade officials to continue examining the operation and implementation of Chapter 11, and to develop recommendations for further change. It was especially paradoxical that it was under the new Bush Administration rather than the Clinton Administration that environmentalists' pleas to restrict the scope of Chapter 11's use by corporations were finally accepted. Yet 2001 was the first time all three governments were not those that had created the NAFTA regime in 1994. They were thus free from the sense of ownership that this experience may have brought.

Further change from the U.S. followed quickly. In the Congressional Act of August 2002 giving the U.S. administration its long desired Trade Promotion Authority, the administration accepted a Congressional demand that Chapter 11-like provisions were to be avoided in future U.S. trade agreements, but that NAFTA-like environmental and labour provisions were to be included in them all. While in part the necessary price the Bush Administration paid Congressional Democrats to secure the TPA the former prized, the evolving record of Chapter 11 cases under NAFTA made it easier for the administration to adjust. The Chapter 11 cases of Methanex against California's environmental regulations, and the softwood lumber cases that threatened to imperil the effectiveness of the U.S. trade remedy system were an additional spur (Andrews, 2002).

This clear case of American adjustment does not, however, conclusively point to Canadian success in the larger issues that surround the Chapter 11 debate. The first is the existence of a Chapter 11-inspired regulatory chill, under which governments in Canada and elsewhere hesitate to regulate for the environment for fear of being taken to and losing in a Chapter 11 court. The magnitude of any such chill appears unlikely, given the large number of MNC's and FDI in North America, the continuing increase in environmental regulation, the small number of successful company Chapter 11 challenges and the very small amount of the Chapter 11 awards (relative to FDI and government expenditure). However, it remains unknown how large a stimulus government regulators require to become aware of potential dangers and alter their behaviour as a result. Of greater danger is the threat Chapter 11 could pose to Canada's trade, as opposed to environmental interests. For while the most recent cases assist individual Canadian firms investing in the U.S., they compound the overall problem of process protectionism that traders have long faced. As the far more trade dependent economy, more dependent on the U.S. market, it is Canadian firms that would suffer the most should process protectionism reach a new stage.

Even with this record, there remains a respectable case for an interpretative statement and for greater transparency in the Chapter 11 proceedings (Hufbauer et al., 2000; Mann and von Moltke, 1999). It could be well directed at ensuring that Chapter 11 panels take full note of the preambular and other environmental provisions of NAFTA in their work. However, the burden of the reform effort should be redirected at replacing the inherited multilateral nests for dispute settlement (International Centre for the Settlement of Investment Disputes [ICSID] and the United Nations Commission on International Trade Law [UNCITRAL]) with a new, more permanent, all-NAFTA tribunal, perhaps with a new *stare decisis* rule. Such a NAFTA creation would be more sensitive to the trade and ecological conditions and regulations within the region, and the specific trade-environmental balance of the NAFTA regime.

NAAEC Article 14-15

In a second mechanism for direct access, the NAFTA regime created a provision under NAAEC's Article 14-15 for any interested party to initiate direct action against governments felt to be systematically not enforcing their own environmental regulations (Wilson, 2002; Markell, 2000; Winham, 1994). Intended as a balancing offset to NAFTA, the Article 14-15 mechanism has been a subject of ongoing controversy since the very start. Many claim it has been a failure, especially when juxtaposed against Chapter 11 and the other effective dispute settlement mechanisms in the NAFTA trade regime, and have criticized it for having a slow, cumbersome, government controlled process that produced at best a factual record rather than fines, other sanctions or action to solve the problems it had identified (Tollefson, 2002; Kibel, 2001; Raustiala, 1995). Others argue that even with it limitations, it has done considerable environmental good (Fitzmaurice, 2003; Alanis Ortega, 2002; Bowman 2001). Still others see it as a potentially valuable instrument, at least for the educated upper middle classes, but one that has become endangered by restrictive action on the part of NAFTA's member governments (Blair, 2003; Mahant, 2001).

More so than Chapter 11, Article 14-15 was a provision that Canada supported during the NAFTA negotiations for an environmental side accord. The Canadian government of Brian Mulroney joined Canadian environmentalists (and their U.S. counterparts) in wanting some legally-grounded process to ensure the effective enforcement of Mexican environmental laws, in large part to prevent a regulatory and investment race to the bottom that would harm the Canadian economy and environment alike. Yet unlike American environmentalists, the Canadian government wanted no mechanism that would end with any trade-inhibiting sanctions, should governments be found at fault. For these would take away from the trade-dependent Canadian economy the "guaranteed assured access" that the hard-won bilateral FTA had finally brought a few short years before. An Article 14-15 mechanism that gave governments some scope to stop the process short of a final determination, and that would yield only a sanction-free "Factual Record" if they did not, fit the Canadian approach very well.

With 49 cases since the start to August 2002, this mechanism has generated more activity than Chapter 11, and more than twice as much if only the 17 environmentally related Chapter 11 cases are included in the count.[6] Of the 49 Article 14-15 cases initiated, Mexico has been the target of 22, Canada of 18 and the United States of nine. The overall pattern is not highly unbalanced, and Canada in the middle, with about one-third of the cases directed at it, has not been particularly singled out. When one accounts for the likely capacity of the respective governments to effectively enforce their environmental regulations, it is hardly surprisingly that a relatively poorer Mexico would be the target of more cases than the richly resourced federal and state governments in the U.S.

The balance shifts when one considers the 11 cases that have proceeded all the way to the release of a Factual Record. It does so even more when the broader array of cases currently "ongoing" are considered, for here the distribution is Mexico seven, Canada seven and the U.S. only one. However, not all the ongoing cases need end in Factual Records. Nor is it clear how much consequential attention Factual Records receive, and how much environmentally enhancing and trade-inhibiting or enhancing change they produce. While the initial Cozumel case in Mexico points to significant environmental benefits at no long term cost to trade (Alanis Ortega, 2002), the majority of the cases in Canada have come out too recently for confident judgements to be made.

Article 14-15 operates, as intended, as an instrument for NGOs concerned with environmental quality and related social concerns. Most of the cases have been filed by NGOs, with a few by individuals. In 1999-2000, firms began to file actions, but the two they mounted were declined on the grounds that they were already the subject of action under NAFTA's Chapter 11. Article 14-15 has thus remained a pure instrument for environmental protection, rather than being mobilized by firms and foreign investors to forward their ultimately commercial concerns. It is also accessible to individuals, who have used it in conjunction with an NGO.

Of the 49 cases initiated, approximately twenty percent have concluded in a published Factual Record. Far more have been terminated, withdrawn, diverted (to an Article 13 investigation), or deferred. Moreover, the CEC's Council of Ministers has declined a CEC Secretariat recommendation that a Factual Record be prepared in one case, involving hog farming in Quebec. The production of only eleven Factual Records during the first decade, the long and lengthening time it has taken to produce those that have emerged, and the government's willingness to veto production of a factual record, all suggest that Article 14-15 is a less effective instrument to ensure environmental enforcement than had been intended. Yet these derogations do not arise as a result of regulatory chill. For the chill hypothesis would suggest a consistent pattern of the United States and Canada being litigated against

6 Here it is assumed that all Article 140-15 cases are trade-related, given the alleged sensitivity of mobile firms in an open North America to international differences in regulatory costs, the newly complex character of ERP, and the trade dependence of most Canadian firms.

by NGOs fearful that their firms would flee to (especially post-crisis) Mexico, and that their home governments would relax enforcement to keep them at home. In contrast, one observes the initial emphasis on the U.S. and Canada as defendant, being soon replaced by a focus on Canada and Mexico, and subsequently on the U.S. and Mexico. Moreover, in the cases generating a Factual Record, it was not the advent of NAFTA that caused the lack of enforcement that was highlighted. The Cozumel case featured tourism rather than trade in goods, and actions that predated the advent of NAFTA. Similarly, the Canadian B. C. Hydro case dealt with a pattern of enforcement behaviour that existed long before NAFTA took effect, and where any NAFTA competitiveness link was highly indirect (reduced costs for hydro that would benefit all firms and residents in British Columbia, and potentially, under deregulated electricity trade, U.S. and Mexican ones as well).

Although the Article 14-15 record suggests that regulatory refugee and chill behaviour is not at work, there remain good general and trade-related grounds for significantly improving the mechanism. At a minimum, as a basic matter of good governance, democratically elected governments and their citizens all have strong interest in ensuring that their existing laws and regulations are fully respected and enforced. Furthermore, the accumulating evidence suggests that both governments and their firms have a strong interest in moving rapidly to high environmental standards to reap the full competitive advantages offered by the NAFTA marketplace and to thrive as North Americans in the single global market that is rapidly emerging (Kirton, 1999).

Emergent Supranational Initiative under Article 13

Perhaps the leading NAAEC-codified instrument by which the Secretariat can operate independently is its top-down "roving spotlight" mechanism under Article 13 (Kirton, 2002a). This empowers the CEC Secretariat, on its own initiative, to investigate independently and report on any matter related to its extensive co-operative work program. In the initial NAFTA negotiations, Canada supported an Article 13 constructed in such a fashion, particularly in the face of those in the U.S. who wanted a more powerful and independent Secretariat prerogative (Winham, 1994). Since that time, Canada has become increasingly enthusiastic about the value of Article 13 as it has been used by the Secretariat. Canada has always, without question, favoured making such reports publicly available, even when discussions take place over issues regarding the Canadian response to the recommendations in the reports. The Canadian government has not been deterred by any fear that the "scientific" Article 13 instrument might move into broad policy and directly trade-related areas, where Canada's preferences could be hurt.

Thus far, as Table 2.6 shows, there have been five Article 13 cases initiated and five completed, for an average of about one every two years. The initiation of these five reports has been evenly spaced over the first nine years. There is no trend toward making more or less frequent use of this instrument. However, it can take longer than two years from the start of an investigation to the release of a final report. The elapsed time from initiation to public release is steadily lengthening.

The Article 13 studies have taken up difficult and complex issues that have consumed considerable time, effort, money and other resources, and have required the CEC to seek expertise well beyond its very limited in-house staff. Yet the studies have embraced all ecological media. Moreover, they have had a clear effect in giving greater attention to environmental concerns, mobilizing a broad array of stakeholders and stimulating action, and thus inducing ecologically enhancing changes in policy. In the first four, long-completed cases, where the impacts are now clear, the actual reports have been less important than the process of producing them.

Two of the five cases – on continental pollutant pathways and electricity – have been directly relevant to Canada. The case on electricity was a sole initiative of the CEC Secretariat, in that there were no stakeholders inviting the CEC to intervene to solve a particular local dispute. The electricity report went to the annual CEC ministerial council meeting in June 2002. It produced a CEC working program, with a large budget (in a CEC context) of 350,000USD per year. The report's recommendations served as the impetus for an agreement on co-operative work to look at the controversial subject of tradable emissions permits in North America. Having ratified the Kyoto Protocol on Climate Change, Canada pushed this initiative very strongly. The Bush Administration's EPA agreed. A small group met in Dallas to begin work on a "Kyoto parallel" policy of emissions trading between signatory and non-signatory countries. The case clearly shows how Canada effectively used the CEC Article 13 instrument to forward broader multilateral environmental objectives, which some Canadians feared could harm the country's trade, investment and competitive interests if no innovative implementing mechanisms were found.

Canada has developed a highly favourable view of the Article 13 mechanism. Canada accepts and values the role of the CEC as a supranational initiator, and the status of Article 13 as the area where the Secretariat's autonomy is complete. Canada, long generally supportive of the Article 13 work, has increasingly come to see the immediate direct and future strategic value of Article 13, as the reports have increasingly come to embrace priority Canadian concerns.

A Canadian official participated in the first Article 13 case, which was on Lake Silva. It served as the first proof of the concept that this new multilateral engagement would work. The second Article 13 report, on Continental Pollutant Pathways, is regarded as a good contribution, in part because it was supportive of the work on SMOC. The third report, on San Pedro birds, was a bilateral U.S.-Mexico issue, where the CEC's contribution was reported to be very constructive and useful.

The fourth study, on electricity, is regarded as an excellent, credible, useful and timely piece of work that directly advanced several core Canadian concerns, particularly in its relationship with the United States. This judgement is well justified on several grounds. First, the report has been used extensively within Environment Canada. Second, the report has served as a way to inject environmental considerations into the trilateral consideration of energy, especially after environmental departments and considerations had been excluded, at American initiative, from the North

American Energy Working Group (NAEWG) formed in 2001. It is thus a clear example of CEC processes engendering a move from primary national identities and conceptions of interest to transnational trilateral ones. It has provided a way, not otherwise available, for North American governmental environmentalists at the national level to react to the intergovernmental process on energy cooperation initiated at the most senior level, by heads of government and state. The pre-existing regional organization of the CEC, with the autonomy granted to the Secretariat through Article 13, has provided the only way for the trilateral environmental community to react to a highest-level, ad hoc intergovernmental economic development initiative in which environmental actors were, institutionally, entirely shut out. Because this environmental exclusion was an American initiative, and because Canada is the North American country where environmental values in foreign policy come first, this exercise of the CEC Secretariat's prerogative has benefited Canada most of all.

Third, the electricity study has inspired and supported emerging CEC work that Canada particularly values, notably that on renewable energy and air. The new work on renewable energy will require cutting-edge policy development to overcoming the barriers of a fossil fuel economy. The electricity report also confirmed, with publicity and precision and supported by an independent expert source, that the U.S. was transmitting a large amount of smog to Canada. Canada has been able to use the report to its advantage in its bilateral discussions with the U.S.

A further sign of Article 13's value to Canada is the Canadian government's desire, as part of its overall strategic vision, to use the CEC to do more Article 13-like studies modelled on the electricity study. Indeed, Canada has suggested that the CEC work on health data and its comparability, in order to do forward-looking assessments. This work would, *inter alia*, support such efforts in the areas of both children's health and air quality. More ambitiously, the Article 13 electricity study could give the CEC a much greater presence in the area of energy, on issues such as energy conservation, energy efficiency, and energy production and use, as a source of so many of the pollutants dealt with by environmentalists and the CEC.

The fulfilment of this Canadian preference, however, confronts the constraint of the limited budgetary resources available to the CEC. The current Canadian dollar cutbacks coincide with the ongoing reality that there is no regular budgetary allocation or staff at the CEC Secretariat to deliver the expensive and elaborate Article 13 cases. Resources must be taken from other programs.

Conclusion

The 1994 NAFTA and its accompanying NAAEC introduced an innovative, world leading regime for giving trade liberalization and environmental protection a more equal, integrated and mutually supportive place. As the tenth anniversary of the formal coming into force of the regime has passed, the regime has proven to be effective for Canada in securing its trade-environment preferences and managing its relationship in these fields with the U.S. Canada's national commitment to embedded ecologism has on the whole been successfully realized in the North American region through the 84 cases of environmental regulatory protection that have arisen from 1980 to mid-1998, the 36 cases under NAFTA Chapter 11 where firms directly challenge foreign government's environmental and other regulations, the 49 cases under NAAEC Article 14-15 citizen's submission process where individuals appeal directly to the CEC with allegations that governments are systematically not enforcing their environmental regulations, and the five cases under the Article 13 "roving spotlight" that allows the CEC to initiate investigations on any matter within its work program. On balance, the NAFTA trade-environment regime works relatively well, in balanced fashion, for its three country members and its trade and environmental communities. This is due in substantial part to the autonomous impact of the NAFTA regime and the work of the CEC. As one of the less powerful members, with important trade and environmental vulnerabilities, Canada has benefited substantially from the regime. However, Canada has often resisted efforts to have the existing regime given full expression, and seldom pushed to build on the still fragile foundation the regime and its CEC represent. Policymakers could usefully chart a program to develop the regime, to reap even greater Canadian advantage, in the years ahead.

Table 2.1 Cases of North American environmental regulatory protection to 1998

Case	Regulatory initiator	Challenger (supporter)	Outcome closer to objectives of instrument	International institution
A. Environmentally Related Trade Issues (65)				
Automotive Emissions (6)				
SO_x	U.S.	(Mexico)	U.S.	
NO_x	U.S.	(Mexico)	U.S.	
Ozone	U.S.	(Canada, Mexico)	U.S.	
Particulates	U.S.	(Canada, Mexico)	U.S.	
OBD Systems	U.S.	(Canada, Mexico)	U.S.	
INM	U.S.	(Canada)	U.S.	
Automotive Fuels (**5**)				
Lead*	U.S.	(Mexico)	U.S.	
MMT	Canada	U.S. (Ethyl)	U.S. (Ethyl)	NAFTA 11
Sulphur	U.S.	(Canada)	U.S.	
Benzene	U.S.	(Canada)	Ongoing	
Methanex (methanol)	Canada	U.S.	Ongoing	NAFTA 11
Agriculture Inspections (24)				
Apples, 1989–98	Mexico	U.S.	Mexico	NAFTA 19
Avocados, 1914–97	U.S.	Mexico	Equal	
Beef 1, 1991–98	U.S.	Canada	Ongoing	NAFTA SPS
Beef 2, 1994–97	Mexico	U.S.	Mexico	–
Blueberries, 1991–93	U.S.	Canada	U.S.	FTA
Christmas Trees 1, 94–98	Mexico	Canada	Ongoing	NAFTA SPS
Christmas Trees 2, 94–98	Mexico	U.S.	Ongoing	NAFTA SPS
Citrus Canker, 1991–97	Mexico	U.S.	U.S.	NAFTA SPS
Global Wheat Trade	All	All	Ongoing	NAFTA CAT
Mangoes, 1993–95	U.S.	Mexico	U.S.	NAFTA SPS
Pork, 1997	U.S.	Mexico	Mexico	NAFTA SPS

Potatoes, 1995–96	U.S.	Canada	Ongoing	
Poultry 1	U.S.	Mexico	Ongoing	
Poultry 2	Mexico	U.S.	Ongoing	–
Seed Potatoes	Mexico	Canada	–	NAFTA SPS
Sorghum. 1997–98	Mexico	U.S.	Ongoing	NAFTA SPS
Strawberries, 1996	U.S.	Mexico	U.S.	–
Stone Fruits, 1991–97	Mexico	U.S.	U.S.	NAFTA SPS
Supply Management	Canada	U.S.	Canada	NAFTA 20
Sweet Cherries, 1991–97	Mexico	U.S.	U.S.	NAFTA
Tomatoes, 1937–98	U.S.	Mexico	U.S.	NAFTA 19
UHT Milk, 1987–95	U.S.	Canada	U.S.	FTA 18
Wheat 1, 1995–98	Mexico	U.S.	U.S.	–
Wheat 2, 1995–97	U.S.	Mexico	Mexico	NAFTA SPS
Manufacturing Recycling (4)				
Newsprint*, 19	U.S.	Canada	U.S.	–
Beer Cans 1, 1988*	Canada	U.S.+EU	U.S.	GATT
Beer Cans 2, 1992*	Canada	U.S.	U.S.	GATT
Beer Cans 3, 1992	Canada	U.S.	Equal	–
Fisheries Conservation (6)				
Lobsters*, 1989–	U.S.	Canada	U.S.	FTA
Tuna*, 1979–82	U.S.	Canada	Canada	GATT
Herring-Salmon 1*, 1988	Canada	U.S.	U.S.	GATT
Herring-Salmon 2*, 1989	Canada	U.S.	U.S.	FTA
Pacific Salmon, 1998	Both	Canada	U.S.	–
Tuna-Dolphin, 1993	U.S.	Mexico	Mexico	GATT
Forestry Conservation (**6**)				
Lumber 1*, 1986–	U.S.	Canada	U.S.	
Lumber 2*, 1992	U.S.	Canada	Canada	FTA
Lumber 3, 1998	U.S.	Canada	Ongoing	–

Table 2.1 continued

B.C. Forestry, 1998	EU	Canada	Equal	–
Pope and Talbot (lumber)	U.S.	Canada	Ongoing	NAFTA 11
Ketchum andTysa (lumber)	U.S.	Canada	Ongoing	NAFTA 11
Environmental Services (7)				
PCB Exports*, 1995	Canada	U.S.	Equal	
Metalclad	U.S.	Mexico	**U.S.**	NAFTA 11
DeSona	U.S.	Mexico	*Mexico*	NAFTA 11
USA Waste (a)	U.S.	Mexico	**Waived**	NAFTA 11
USA Waste (b)	U.S.	Mexico	Ongoing	NAFTA 11
S.D. Myers (hazardous waste)	U.S.	Canada	Ongoing	NAFTA 11
Sun Belt Water	U.S	Canada	Ongoing	NAFTA 11
Dangerous Goods Transportation (5)				
Small Packages	All	(All)	Equal	CSRM
Large Containers	All	–	Ongoing	CSRM
HOC	All	–	Ongoing	NAFTA CSRM
Truck Spills (ERG)	All	(All)	Equal	CSRM
Rail Cars	All	–	Ongoing	NAFTA CSRM
Other (2)				
Asbestos*	U.S.	Canada	U.S.	–
Trucking	U.S.	Mexico	Canada	NAFTA FTCC
B. Trade-Related Environmental Issues (25)				
Pesticides (4)				
PCBs	All	All	All	CEC TWGP
DDT	U.S. (Canada)	Mexico	U.S. (Canada)	CEC TWGP
Chlordane	Canada (U.S.)	Mexico	Canada (U.S.)	CEC TWGP
Mercury	All	All	Canada (Mexico)	CEC TWGP
Environmental Information (1)				

NAPRI, 1997	CEC	All	Mexico	CEC
Environmental Science (3)				
Silva Reservoir	CEC	Mexico	Mexico	CEC13
LRTAP	CEC	All	Equal	CEC13
San Pedro	CEC	U.S.-Mexico	Ongoing	CEC13
Environmental Enforcement (17)				
Biodiversity, 1995	U.S.	U.S.	Terminated	CEC 14-15
Sierra club, 1995	U.S.	U.S.	Terminated	CEC 14-15
CPRN, 1996	Mexico	Mexico	Canada/U.S.	CEC 14-15
Tottrup, 1995	Canada	Canada	Terminated	CEC 14-15
Oldman River, 1996	Canada	Canada	Terminated	CEC 14-15
SW Biodiversity, 1996	U.S.	U.S.	Terminated	CEC 14-15
BC Fisheries, 1997	Canada	Canada	Proceeding	CEC 14-15
Rio, 1997	Canada	Canada	Proceeding	CEC 14-15
CQDE, 1997	Canada	Canada	Proceeding	CEC 14-15
CEDF, 1997	Canada	Canada	Terminated	CEC 14-15
Animal Alliance, 1997	Canada	Canada	Terminated	CEC 14-15
Oldman River, 1997	Canada	Canada	Proceeding	CEC 14-15
IDA, 1997	Mexico	Mexico	Proceeding	CEC 14-15
IDA, 1998	Mexico	Mexico	Proceeding	CEC 14-15
Martinez, 1998	Mexico	Mexico	Terminated	CEC 14-15
Planet Earth, 1998	Canada/U.S.	U.S.	Proceeding	CEC 14-15
Sierra Club, 1998	Canada	Canada	Proceeding	CEC 14-15

Note: *denotes non-NAFTA cases, defined as those effectively resolved prior to NAFTA and whose resolution was unaffected by calculations about the onset of NAFTA. Status of cases is as of mid-1998.

Table 2.2 Chronological list of known cases under NAFTA Chapter 11, December 2004

Case	Process dates (From filing of Notice of Intent)	Regulatory initiator (Defendant)	Challenger (supporter) (Claimant)	Outcome
1. Halchette Distribution System	Aug. 1995, not pursued	Mexico	U.S.	Not pursued
2. Signa S.A de C.V.	Mar. 1996, not pursued	Canada	Mexico	Not pursued
3. Ethyl Corp. (MMT)	10 Sep. 1996-1998	Canada	U.S.	U.S.
4. Robert Azinian (Desona)	16 Dec. 1996-1999	Mexico	U.S.	Mexico
5. Metalclad	2 Jan. 1997-2000	Mexico	U.S.	U.S.
6. Marvin Ray Feldman Karpa (CEMSA)	18 Feb 1998-ongoing	Mexico	U.S.	Ongoing (Mexico has appealed the decision at the Court of Appeal for Ontario)
7. Loewen Group	29 July 1998-2003	U.S.	Canada	U.S.
8. Waste Management (Acaverde) (No 1)	29 Sep. 1998-2000	Mexico	U.S.	Waived
9. S.D.Myers	21 July 1998-2004	Canada	U.S.	U.S.
10. Sun Belt Water	27 Nov. 1998- in abeyance	Canada	U.S.	Ongoing
11. Pope & Talbot	24 Dec. 1998-2002	Canada	U.S	Canada (Overall, the tribunal found that Canada had not violated NAFTA in its implementation of the Softwood Lumber Agreement but the claimant was awarded damages arising from an administrative audit undertaken to verify Pope & Talbot's quota.)
12. Mondev International	6 May 1999-2002	U.S.	Canada	U.S.
13. Methanex	3 Dec. 1999-ongoing	U.S.	Canada	Ongoing
Waste Management (Acaverde) (No 2) (resubmitted case following case 8)	27 Sept. 2000-2004	Mexico	U.S.	Mexico
14. U.P.S.	19 Jan. 2000-ongoing	Canada	U.S.	Ongoing
15. Adams et al.	11 Nov. 2000- ongoing	Mexico	U.S.	Ongoing

16. A.D.F. Group	19 July 2000-2003	U.S.	Canada	U.S.
17. Ketchum Investments Inc. and Tysa Investment Inc.	22 Dec. 2000- not pursued	Canada	U.S.	Not Pursued
18. Lomas Santa Fe Investment	28 August 2001- ongoing	Mexico	U.S.	Ongoing
19. Trammell Crow Company	7 Sep. 2001-not pursued	Canada	U.S.	Not Pursued
20. Canfor Corp.	5 Nov. 2001-ongoing	U.S.	Canada	Ongoing
21. Crompton Corp.	6 Nov. 2001-ongoing	Canada	U.S.	Ongoing
22. Francis Kenneth Hass	10 Nov. 2001-ongoing	Mexico	U.S.	Ongoing
23. Calmark Commercial	24 Dec. 2001-ongoing	Mexico	U.S.	Ongoing
24. Kenex Ltd.	14 Jan. 2002- ongoing	U.S.	Canada	Ongoing
25. Fireman's Fund	15 Jan. 2002-ongoing	Mexico	U.S.	Ongoing
26. Corn Products International	28 Jan. 2002- ongoing	Mexico	U.S.	Ongoing
27. Robert Frank	12 Feb. 2002- ongoing	Mexico	U.S.	Ongoing
28. International Thunderbird Gaming Corporation	22 March 2002- ongoing	Mexico	U.S.	Ongoing
29. GAMI Investment	9 Apr. 2002-2004	Mexico	U.S.	Mexico
30. Doman Industries	1 May 2002- ongoing	U.S.	Canada	Ongoing
31. Tembec	4 May 2002-ongoing	U.S.	Canada	Ongoing
32. Terminal Forest Products Ltd.	12 June 2003-ongoing	U.S.	Canada	Ongoing
33. Glamis Gold Ltd.	21 July 2003- ongoing	U.S.	Canada	Ongoing
34. Albert Connolly	19 Feb. 2004- ongoing	Canada	U.S.	Ongoing
35. Grand River Enterprises Six Nations Ltd.	10 March 2004- ongoing	U.S.	Canada	Ongoing
36. Contractual Obligation Productions	15 June 2004- ongoing	Canada	U.S.	Ongoing

Table 2.3 Outcomes of NAFTA Chapter 11 cases by Regulatory Initiator and date (environmentally-related cases)

Notice of Intent	Total	Mexico	Canada	USA
1994	0			
1995	1	1		
1996	3 (2)	1 (1)	2 (1)	
1997	1 (1)	1 (1)		
1998	6 (4)	2 (1)	3 (3)	1
1999	2 (1)			2 (1)
2000	4 (1)	1	2 (1)	1
2001	6 (2)	3	2 (1)	1 (1)
2002	8 (4)	5 (1)		3 (3)
2003	2 (2)			2 (2)
2004	3		2	1
Total	**36 (17)**	**14 (4)**	**11 (6)**	**11 (7)**

Table 2.4 Chronological list of NAAEC Article 14-15 cases, December 2004

Case	Date of filing	Regulatory Initiator (jurisdiction)	Challenger (country)	Status/Outcome (elapsed time in the process)
1. Spotted Owl (SEM-95-001)	30/06/95	U.S. (federal)	Biodiversity legal foundation et al. (U.S.)	Terminated— 11/12/95 (6 months)
2. Logging Rider (SEM-95-002)	30/08/95	U.S. (federal)	Sierra Club et al. (U.S.)	Terminated— 8/12/95 (4 months)
3. Cozumel (SEM-96-001)	17/01/96	Mexico (federal)	Comité para la protección de los Recursos Naturales et al. (Mexico)	Proceeded— factual record released 24/10/97 (21 months)
4. Aage Tottrup (SEM-96-002)	20/03/96	Canada (federal)	Aage Tottrup (Canada)	Terminated— 28/05/96 (2 months)
5. Oldman River I (SEM-96-003)	20/03/96	Canada (federal)	The Friends of the Oldman River I (Canada)	Terminated— 02/04/97 (13 months)
6. Fort Huachuca (SEM-96-004)	14/11/96	U.S. (federal)	The Southwest Center for Biological Diversity et al. (U.S.)	Withdrawn— 05/06/97 (7 months)
7. Río Magdalena (SEM-97-002)	15/03/97	Mexico (federal and subfederal)	Comité Pro Limpieza del Río Magdalena (Mexico)	Proceeded— Secretariat submitted a draft factual record to council for 45 day comment period. Comment period expired with no comment from Parties 15/09/03. Council released factual record 11/12/03. (81 months)

Table 2.4 continued

8. BC Hydro (SEM-97-001)	02/04/97	Canada (federal)	BC Aboriginal Fisheries commission et al. (Canada)	Proceeded— factual record released 11/06/00 (38 months)
9. Quebec Hog Farms (SEM-97-003)	04/04/97	Canada (subfederal)	Centre Québécois du droit de l'environnement (Canada)	Terminated— Secretariat recommended factual record but council denied 16/05/00 (37 months)
10. CEDF (SEM-97-004)	26/05/97	Canada (federal)	Canadian Environmental Defence Fund (Canada)	Terminated— 25/08/97 (3 months)
11. Biodiversity (SEM-97-005)	21/07/97	Canada (federal)	Animal Alliance of Canada et al. (Canada)	Terminated— 26/05/98 (11 months)
12.Oldman River II (SEM-97-006)	04/10/97	Canada (federal)	The Friends of the Oldman River II (Canada)	Proceeded— factual record released 11/08/03 (47 months)
13. Ortiz Martínez (SEM-98-002)	10/10/97	Mexico (federal)	Hector Gregorio Ortiz Martínez (Mexico)	Terminated 18/03/99 (17 months)
14.Lake Chapala (SEM-97-007)	09/01/98	Mexico (federal)	Instituto de Derecho Ambiental (Mexico)	Terminated— 14/07/00 (30 months)
15. Guadalajara (SEM-98-001)	09/01/98	Mexico (federal)	Instituto de Derecho Ambiental AC et al. (Mexico)	Terminated— 18/03/99 (14 months)
16. Great Lakes (SEM-98-003)	05/05/98	U.S. (federal)	Department of the Planet Earth (U.S., Canada)	Terminated— 05/10/01 (45 months)
17. BC Mining (SEM-98-004)	29/06/98	Canada (federal)	Sierra Club of British Columbia et al. (Canada)	Proceeded— factual record released 11/08/03 (62 months)

18. Cytrar I (SEM-98-005)	11/08/98	Mexico (federal)	Academia Sonorense de Derechos Humanos et al. (Mexico)	Terminated— 26/10/00 (26 months)
19. Aquanova (SEM-98-006)	20/10/98	Mexico (federal)	Grupo Ecológico Manglar AC (Mexico)	Proceeded— factual record released on 23/06/03 (60 months)
20. Metales y derivados (SEM-98-007)	23/10/98	Mexico (federal)	Environmental Health Coalition et al. (U.S. and Mexico)	Proceeded— factual record released 11/02/02 (40 months)
21. Methanex (SEM-99-001)	18/10/99	U.S. (federal subfederal)	Methanex Corp. (U.S.)	Terminated— 30/06/00 (8 months)
22. Migratory Birds (SEM-99-002)	19/11/99	U.S. (federal)	Alliance for the Wild Rockies et al. (Canada, U.S., Mexico)	Proceeded— factual record released 24/04/03 (47 months)
23. Nestle Canada (SEM-00-002)	21/01/00	U.S. (federal and subfederal)	Nestle Canada (Canada)	Terminated— 30/06/00 (5 months)
24. Molymex I (SEM-00-001)	27/01/00	Mexico (federal)	Rosa María Escalante de Fernández (Mexico)	Terminated— 25/04/00 (3 months)
25. Jamaica Bay (SEM-00-003)	02/03/00	U.S. (federal)	Hudson River Audubon Society of Westchester (U.S.)	Terminated— 12/04/00 (1 month)
26. BC Logging (SEM-00-004)	15/03/00	Canada (federal)	David Suzuki Foundation et al. (Canada)	Proceeded— Factual Record released on 11/08/03 (41 months)
27. Molymex II (SEM-00-005)	06/04/00	Mexico (federal)	Academia Sonorense de Derechos Humanos, Domingo Gutiérrez Mendívil. (Mexico)	Proceeded— factual record released 08/10/04 (54 months)
28. Tarahumara (SEM-00-006)	09/09/00	Mexico (federal)	Comisión de Solidaridad y Defensa de los Derechos Humanos AC (Mexico)	Proceeded— factual record ordered 22/04/03. (31 months)

Table 2.4 continued

29. Cytar II (SEM-01-001)	14/02/01	Mexico (federal)	Academia Sonorense de Derechos Humanos (Mexico)	Terminated— Secretariat recommended a factual record but Council voted against it 10/12/02 (22 months).
30. AAA Packaging (SEM-01-002)	12/04/01	Canada (federal)	Names withheld	Terminated— 24/05/01 (1 month).
31. Dermet (SEM-01-003)	14/06/01	Mexico (federal)	Mercerizados y Tenidos de Guadalajara, S.A. (Mexico)	Terminated— 19/10/01 (4 months).
32. Ontario Logging (SEM-02-001)	06/02/02	Canada (federal)	Canadian Nature Federation et al. (Canada, U.S.)	Ongoing— Secretariat recommended a Factual Record 12/11/02; Council decided to defer voting on whether to instruct the Secretariat to prepare a factual record 22/04/03. Council ordered factual record 15/03/04.
33. Mexico City Airport (SEM-02-002)	07/02/02	Mexico (federal)	Jorge Rafael Martinez Azuela et al. (Mexico)	Terminated— 25/09/02 (7 months)
34. Pulp and Paper (SEM-02-003)	08/05/02	Canada (federal)	Friends of the Earth et al. (Canada)	Ongoing— Secretariat recommended a factual record to Council 08/10/03, Council ordered factual record 11/12/03.
35. El Boludo Project (SEM-02-004)	23/08/02	Mexico (federal)	Arcadio, Leonico, Fernanda and Milagro Pesqueira Senday (Mexico)	Ongoing— Secretariat received a response from the concerned government Party and began considering whether to recommend a factual record. 09/01/03
36. Alca Iztapalapa (SEM-02-005)	25/11/02	Mexico (federal)	Mr. Angel Lara García (Mexico)	Terminated— 31/01/03 (30 day term limit for submissions expired before the committee received a submission that conformed with Article 14(1).) (2 months)

37. Ontario Power Generation (SEM-03-001)	01/05/03	Canada (federal)	49 Canadian and U.S. NGOs. (Canada and U.S.)	Ongoing—submission accepted, response requested from concerned government Party 19/09/03
38. Home Port Xcaret (SEM-03-002)	14/05/03	Mexico (federal)	Alfonso Ciprés Villarreal, president of Movimiento Ecologista Mexicano AC, on behalf of several ecological groups, two academic groups and one individual citizen (Mexico)	Terminated— 02/09/03 (30 day term limit for submissions expired before the committee received a submission that conformed with Article 14(1).) (5 months)
39. Lake Chapala II (SEM-03-003)	23/05/03	Mexico (federal)	Fundación Lerma-Chapala-Santiago-Pacífico A.C. et al. (Mexico)	Ongoing—submission acknowledged and under review 28/05/03. Secretariat requested response from Mexico 19/12/03.
40. Alca Iztapalapa II (SEM-03-004)	17/06/03	Mexico (federal)	Mr. Angel Lara García (Mexico)	Ongoing— submission accepted, response requested from concerned government Party 09/09/03. Response received 04/12/03.
41. Montreal Technoparc (SEM-03-005)	14/08/03	Canada (federal)	Three Canadian and two United States environmental NGOs (Canada and U.S.)	Ongoing—submission accepted, response requested from concerned government Party 15/09/03. Response received 14/11/03.
42. Cytrar III (SEM-03-006)	15/08/03	Mexico (federal)	Academia Sonorense de Derechos Humanos, AC and Domingo Gutiérrez Mendívil (Mexico)	Ongoing— submission accepted, response requested from concerned government Party 29/08/03. Response received 21/11/03.
43. Hazardous Waste in Arteaga (SEM-04-001)	27/01/04	Mexico (federal)	Genaro Meléndez Lugo y José Javier, et al. (Mexico)	Ongoing— initial submission rejected 20/02/04, revised submissions received 16/03/04.
44. Environmental Pollution in Hermosillo (SEM-04-002)	14/07/04	Mexico (federal)	Academia Sonorense de Derechos Humanos, A.C., and Domingo Gutiérrez Mendívil (Mexico)	Ongoing—submission under review.

Table 2.4 continued

45. Gasoline spill in Tehuantepec (SEM-04-003)	07/09/04	Mexico (federal)	Centro de Derechos Humanos Tepeyac del Istmo de Tehuantepec et al. (Mexico)	Ongoing—the Secretariat notified the submitter(s) on 07/10/04 that the submission did not meet all of the Article 14(1) criteria and the submitter(s) had 30 days to provide the Secretariat with a revised submission that conforms with Article 14(1).
46. Oldman River III (SEM-04-004)	10/9/04	Canada (federal)	The Friends of the Oldman River (Canada)	Ongoing—the Secretariat notified the submitter(s) on 14/10/04 that the submission did not meet all of the Article 14(1) criteria and the submitter(s) had 30 days to provide the Secretariat with a revised submission that conforms with Article 14(1).
47. Coal Fired Power Plants (SEM-04-005)	20/9/04	United States (federal)	Friends of the Earth Canada et al. (Canada, U.S.)	Ongoing—submission under review.
48. Ontario Logging II (SEM-04-006)	12/10/04	Canada (federal)	Canadian Nature Federation et al. (Canada)	Ongoing—response requested from the concerned government party 14/10/04.
49. Quebec Automobiles (SEM-04-007)	3/11/04	Canada (Quebec)	Quebec Association Against Air Pollution (Association québécoise de lutte contre la pollution atmosphérique – AQLPA) (Canada)	Ongoing—response requested from the concerned government party 06/12/04.

*NAAEC – North American Agreement on Environmental Cooperation
*LGEEPA – General Law on Ecological Balance and Environmental Protection (Mexico)
*NEPA – National Environmental Policy Act

Table 2.5 NAAEC Article 14 and 15 cases by regulatory initiator and date (number of factual records released – number of ongoing cases)

Date of Filing	Total	Mexico	Canada	USA
1995	2	0	0	2
1996	4	1	2	1
1997	7	2	5	0
1998	7	5	1	1
1999	2	0	0	2
2000	6	3	1	2
2001	3	2	1	0
2002	5	2	3	0
2003	6	4	2	0
2004	7	3	3	1
Total	**49 (10-15)**	**22 (5-7)**	**18 (4-7)**	**9 (1-1)**

Table 2.6 Article 13 reports

1. Silva Reservoir (1 October, 1995)
This report addressed the death of migratory birds at the Silva Reservoir. It concluded with recommendations for preventing future mass mortalities and offered lessons for the management of bird habitats in other areas of North America.

2. Continental Pollutant Pathways (1 January, 1997)
This report addressed the long range transport of air pollution in North America. It concluded by establishing links between pollutants and health issues, indicating major sources of pollutants, stating the need of effective monitoring, and emphasising the need for collaborative mechanisms between different parties within the North American region and among other regions.

3. Ribbon of Life (1 June, 1999)
This report addressed the preservation of the transboundary migratory bird habitat on the upper San Pedro river. It concluded with a number of suggestions for pragmatic actions aimed at balancing human activities with the preservation of important wildlife habitat along the upper San Pedro River.

4. North American Electricity Market (17 June, 2002)
This report addresses the ability to secure North Americas electricity supply without compromising environmental and health objectives. It aims to conclude by showing how it is possible to achieve ample electricity supply and simultaneously protect the environment through increased cooperation and collaboration mechanisms.

5. Maize (8 November, 2004)
This report addresses the potential effects of transgenic corn on traditional maize varieties in Mexico, and examines issues related to the conservation and sustainable use of traditional maize varieties.

Chapter 3

Ground-Level Ozone: A Multi-Faceted Approach

Debora VanNijnatten

Canada and the United States share a set of ecosystems that span the North American continent and the transboundary nature of environmental problems creates the need for cooperation between the two countries at multiple levels. Certainly, we have learned much over the past two decades about the binational environmental relationship, where federal officials in both countries seek to exercise influence through diplomatic channels and collaborate via joint mechanisms such as the International Joint Commission. Adding to the state of knowledge on Canada-United States environmental relations are the growing number of studies aimed at unearthing less prominent subnational cross-border linkages. Subnational interactions are more likely to take place within the realm of the "workaday," yet are just as important for the state of the overall environmental relationship as national-level diplomatic interactions. Our understanding of the trilateral environmental context is rather more recent, although it is becoming clear that the continental influence tends to operate through collaborative science and shared problem definition. As Alan Schwartz, a long-time observer of Canadian-American environmental relations, explains: "there is a complex web of interactions on many levels… which holds most issues at bay as minor, behind-the-scenes irritants rather than allowing them to develop into full-blown crises" (Schwartz, 2000:223).

To grasp the full complexity of the Canada-U.S. environmental relationship, one must employ a multi-faceted framework for analyzing cross-border interactions. This requires *both* a multi-level approach that takes into account interactions at the subnational, national and continental levels, *and* attention to different modes of cross-border interaction. More specifically, it is necessary to combine examinations of, first, formal relations or negotiations generally conducted by senior-level officials and, second, less visible, working relations among mid-level officials, experts and non-governmental organizations, which can lead to the development of likeminded epistemic communities.

The recent Canadian-American negotiations on the "Ozone Annex" to the *Canada-United States Air Quality Agreement* demonstrate that analyses ought not to focus on national-level interactions at the expense of subnational and supranational relations or, alternatively, concentrate on formal, high-level interactions at the expense of mid-level working relations. Certainly, the manner in which the binational negotiations unfolded over 1999-2000 is an important part of the overall story. However, the development of a transboundary network of officials, experts and nongovernmental actors at multiple levels during the 1990s was critical. Out of this network, a web of cross-border support for addressing ground-level ozone via specific policy instruments gradually evolved.

Framing the Analysis: Lessons From a Burgeoning Literature

During the 1980s and into the 1990s, many studies of Canadian-American environmental relations focused primarily on the efforts of federal officials in the two countries to coordinate domestic and cross-border political dynamics in order to further bilateral aims, much as "two-level game" theorists would. In Putnam's classic characterization, cross-border negotiations consist of, first, Level I negotiations, or bargaining between negotiators from different countries which leads to tentative agreement, and, second, Level II negotiations, or separate discussions with domestic interests about whether to ratify this tentative agreement (Putnam, 1988). Domestic politics is thus seen as unfolding alongside negotiations, but it exercises influence on these negotiations only at the highest levels – specifically, at the point of ratification, which is generally the preserve of national policymakers.[1] The first comprehensive, cross-case analysis of Canadian-American environmental relations, John Carroll's *Environmental Diplomacy*, exemplified this approach:

> Since only governmental officials at the federal levels in both countries are constitutionally authorized to negotiate or make decisions in this area, these federal actors are naturally the central focus of attention. This is not to say, however, that other governmental and private sector actors are not important (indeed they are often key players) and thus their role is also treated in some detail. Their official bilateral impact, however, is channelled through the federal actors in both countries (Carroll, 1983:5).

The focus on domestic ratification power inevitably drew analysts' attention to the disproportionate role of U.S. executive-legislative dynamics in determining both the nature of American environmental policy and the scope of Canada-U.S. environmental relations. Moreover, although expert debates and working level relations were included as contextual discussion, interactions at the highest echelons were emphasized. For example, studies of the Canada-U.S. acid rain dispute – which dominated the study of bilateral environmental relations in the 1980s and early 1990s – presented a picture of political asymmetry whereby Canadian policymakers were largely at the mercy of American domestic political outcomes. Schmandt and Roderick, as well as Park, in their acid rain studies, traced the development of efforts

1 Two-level game analysts have emphasized the role of ratification, or the decision point responsible for endorsement and implementation of transboundary agreements; domestic constituencies have power because they can determine the fate of an international agreement, by voting it down or failing to endorse it in some other way. R. Putnam, "Diplomacy and domestic politics," 436.

to conclude a binational agreement and found that Canada had very little influence on U.S. policy developments – despite agitation by successive prime ministers, cabinet ministers and other high-level officials (Schmandt and Roderick, 1985; Park, 1987). Munton's analysis of the air quality relationship was starker: "… the acid rain-related amendments to the [U.S.] Clean Air Act that emerged in late 1990s were the product of a domestic political realignment. Though it watched these events closely, Canada's role was minimal"(Munton, 1997:345).

In the 1990s, however, many analysts of Canadian-American environmental relations were looking beyond the domestic point of ratification and "downward" to the subnational and cross-border regional level, where an increasing amount of activity was taking place. One would have been hard-pressed to find studies specifically devoted to state-province interactions in the 1980s;[2] indeed, Carroll declared in 1983 that: "U.S. states are not accustomed to dealing across international borders. Thus they have little history and little expertise in this area" (Carroll, 1983:17). By 1995, however, Munton and Kirton were concluding as a result of their subnational research that there were more than 100 linkages between Canadian provinces and U.S. states on environmental matters alone (Munton and Kirton, 1996). Alper, in his examination of cross-border relations in the Pacific Northwest, reported in 1997 that, "environmental concerns play an increasingly important role in the binational and international activities of western provinces and states," which have established "more formal institutional linkages in the region" (Alper, 1997:359). This characterization is supported in a recent study by Smith, who has described subnational economic and environmental policy initiatives in the "Cascadia" region as "rational, high-level and intense" (Smith, 2002:130). Moreover, studies by Rabe on Great Lakes ecosystem management have focused on states and provinces as the locus of environmental decisions that have significant implications for transboundary cooperation (Rabe, 1997).

This work on subnational interactions strongly suggests that the Canadian-American relationship has a less visible but possibly more productive side, one that is grounded primarily in the realm of mid-level working relations. These studies show that, although subnational governments in the two countries do not have formal bilateral negotiating power per se, they interact via a multitude of collaborative agreements, working groups, and conferences that have emerged out of daily problem-solving. In the Pacific Northwest and the Great Lakes regions, for example, cross-border cooperation through the British Columbia/Washington State Environmental Cooperation Council and the Great Lakes Remedial Action Plan (RAP) process has encouraged shared problem definition, information sharing and coordination of action by officials across numerous agencies on both sides of the border. The Conference of New England Governors/Eastern Canadian Premiers (NEG/ECP) has little actual decision-making power, but the group's regular meetings

2 Two exceptions include Stein and Grenville-Wood (1984) and Reiser, Spiller and Vander Zwaag (1986). This latter study focuses on Nova Scotia and the Gulf of Maine region.

have spawned considerable cooperative data-gathering and policy collaboration in areas such as air quality management and energy issues, and, most recently, CO_2 emissions.[3]

These subnational cross-border analyses also indicate that the Canadian-American power game is more complex than a focus only on authoritative transboundary decision-making arenas would suggest. In contrast to Carroll's description of subnational governments as "minor actors on the scene" (Carroll, 1983:17) these more recent studies are in accord with Kincaid's contention that the cross-border activities of constituent governments are not necessarily "inferior, ancillary, or supplemental to the 'high politics' of nation-state diplomacy" (Kincaid, 1990:54-75). Leyton-Brown and Sands have argued with respect to the Pacific Salmon dispute that, "…it would be a mistake to suggest the U.S.-Canada relationship was the exclusive preserve of policymakers in Washington and Ottawa" as state and provincial governments "play an important part in defining the timbre of relations" (Leyton-Brown and Sands, 1997:163). Alper recounts the ongoing saga of the fouling of shared Washington State-British Columbia waters by municipalities in B.C., who are "clearly not impressed with the argument that they should follow the American approach because it was mandated in the U.S (Alper, 1997:369-70). Rabe, in his work on Great Lakes management, has revealed that, "states and provinces bear the brunt of responsibility for securing collaborative approaches that best represent the region" and yet subnational governments tend to go their own way with regard to water management, with the result that standards and enforcement activities "vary tremendously" (Rabe, 1997:430).

To add to the complexity, by the mid-1990s the Canadian-American environmental relationship was increasingly seen as also being anchored in a trilateral framework. Here, academic attention has focused on such issues as the effects of the North American Free Trade Agreement (NAFTA) on the environment and the influence of new supra-national mechanisms, including those established under the North American Agreement on Environmental Cooperation (NAAEC). As Kirton explains: "NAFTA and NAAEC promised to transform a hitherto almost exclusively bilateral relationship into a new trilateral community, by making many issues, processes, and institutions into a new trilateral structure, (Kirton, 1997:459). By the end of the decade, it was argued that the NAAEC's institutional offshoot, the Commission on Environmental Cooperation (CEC), had "brought trilateralism in an intense and permanent way to North America and to Canada-U.S. environmental governance" (Kirton, 1997:481) and, in 2002, the CEC was described by one close observer of the organization as a "highly successful" regional cooperation body (Winfield, 2002).

Yet, formal trilateral agreements such as the NAAEC and institutions such as the CEC represent only the most obvious side of continental environmental interactions. In fact, other than the NAAEC and CEC, there is very little supranational environmental institutionalization at the continental level. More important is the expanding network of professional interactions among officials and experts in the

3 See, for example, http://www.negc.org/negecp2001.html.

three countries working on similar policy problems. These interactions, in which nongovernmental stakeholders often take part, act as the connective tissue that makes trilateral cooperation possible and increasingly influential. Kirton notes with respect to the CEC that, although the organization's autonomous political impact is limited by its lack of formal policy advisory responsibilities, it has nevertheless exerted influence through "the scientific credibility it has commanded and the broader support base and epistemic community it is fostering through the many expert groups, study teams, and consultations it has created…" (Kirton, 1997:473).

Indeed, as Kirton suggests, an important prerequisite for environmental cooperation across the Canada-U.S. border – at all levels – is the formation of epistemic communities composed of experts and officials, governmental and nongovernmental, who agree on the nature of a problem and on the appropriate instruments for addressing that problem. Epistemic communities exercise influence in a subtle manner; individuals' professional authority, their cohesiveness as a group and their ability to manoeuvre through domestic decision-making channels can help to encourage consensus and spur action in cross-border political arenas (Haas, 1990; Newell, 2000). Although epistemic communities are not mechanisms for dispute resolution per se, they can help to ameliorate or even avoid disputes arising out of differing interpretations of the available science and different ideas with regard to appropriate policy choices. Surely one of the most important developments in North America over recent years has been the sharing of information and increasing linkages among experts and concerned actors both inside and outside of government,[4] which has resulted in higher levels of consensus with regard to a number of shared environmental problems.

The combined wisdom of two decades of study thus makes it clear that, given the spatial-institutional realities of political influence in North America, the Canadian-American environmental relationship is a truly multi-level one. Moreover, it also has become evident that the question of "who is influencing whom" – which is really part of a larger question about why certain cross-border policy choices are made – is answerable only to the extent that we know what is going on at each level, both in the sense of formal, high-level interactions and ongoing "working relations" out of which epistemic communities may emerge. While an understanding and investigation of formal ratification power and consequent interaction is important, many forms of cross-border cooperation are rooted in more informal understandings that cooperation is necessary and needs to occur regularly. This leads to discretionary frameworks for action in which the onus often rests with actors in the subnational or trilateral realm, who may see things differently from national authorities and who depend on personal interactions and problem-solving via a broad range of collaborative mechanisms.

---

4 For example, one need only perform an internet search using keywords such as "tropospheric ozone," "biodiversity" and "mercury" to see the growing number of fora for trilateral environmental discussions among government officials, experts and NGOs, an increasing number of which are located in Mexico.

The above discussion suggests a two-step approach to studying the Canadian-American environmental relationship, one that will help to account for multi-directional power relationships as well as the nature of the policies resulting from transboundary environmental interactions. First, it is necessary to locate the formal constitutional and legislative framework of responsibility that defines the domestic point of ratification in each country and then investigate the interaction between domestic political dynamics and cross-border high-level negotiations, as a two-level game analyst would. In addition, the analyst needs to look for other, less visible modes of interaction at different spatial-institutional levels in terms of mid-level working relations and the operation of epistemic communities. The two realms of interaction can then be combined to provide a more complete picture of the relationship. The remainder of this article applies this two-step approach to the case of Canadian-American negotiations over 1999-2000 on an Ozone Annex (or "Smog Treaty" as the popular media often called it) to the 1991 Canada-United States Air Quality Agreement.

Applying the Framework: The Case of Ground-Level Ozone

Ground-level, or tropospheric, ozone is a colourless and highly irritating gas that is produced when two air pollutants, nitrogen oxides (NO_x) and volatile organic compounds (VOCs), react with each other in the presence of strong sunlight. NO_x result from the burning of fossil fuels, especially coal, while VOCs include a diverse class of compounds resulting from fuel combustion and the evaporation of liquid fuels and solvents.[5] When ground-level ozone mixes with airborne particles (or particulate matter), the resulting chemical soup is known as "smog". Both ground-level ozone and particulate matter pose significant risks to human health, thereby providing a clear rationale for regulatory action.

The long-range transport of ground-level ozone precursors, especially NO_x, raises challenging questions about environmental cooperation across the Canada-U.S. border. High levels of emissions from older, coal-burning power plants concentrated in the upper Midwestern states of Ohio, Pennsylvania, and Indiana, are carried on prevailing winds (as far as 800 kilometres away from pollution sources) across southern Ontario and Quebec and into the northeastern states. The northeastern states have thus pushed for changes to U.S. national air quality legislation to reduce Midwestern emissions. Central and eastern Canadian provinces have an obvious interest in the outcomes associated with these efforts, as up to half of their airborne pollution originates in the U.S. Yet these provinces themselves contribute to pollutant loadings that are then carried into the U.S. Northeast, especially New

5 Refineries, chemical manufacturers, and dry cleaning and painting operations are sources of VOCs.

York.[6] In particular, Ontario's provincially owned coal-burning utility plants have been pinpointed as a major source of smog precursors.

In the Canada-U.S. Ozone Annex case, policymakers were attempting to conclude an agreement to reduce the flow of ground-level ozone across the Canada-U.S. border. When the 1991 Canada-United States Air Quality Agreement was signed, committing both governments to reductions in acid rain-causing emissions,[7] the Agreement had made provision for future negotiations regarding the control of all types of transboundary air pollution between the two countries. In the late 1990s, ground-level ozone became the next air quality issue to make it onto the binational agenda.

There are two different yet interrelated stories that help to explain the origins and course of these negotiations. The first focuses on cross-border interactions at the point of ratification and chronicles the intermingling of domestic political dynamics and bilateral negotiations. The second is more explicitly multi-level and examines the less formal realm of cross-border, mid-level working relations, along with the operation of epistemic communities. Both are explored below.

Two-Level Game Analysis

In the United States, the national Environmental Protection Agency (EPA) and Congress are the authoritative decision-makers with respect to air quality, in terms of both domestic reduction requirements and transboundary agreements. In both realms, however, Congress has the final "say," and it takes a particularly dim view of any international actions taken which are outside of an agency's domestic responsibilities and mandate.

The EPA sets standards for ambient air quality that are applicable to every jurisdiction in the country. The major federal legislation, the 1990 *Clean Air Act*, authorizes the EPA to set binding science-based, national standards for criteria air pollutants (National Ambient Air Quality Standards, or NAAQSs), to initiate a point source permitting program (for industrial polluters), and to set deadlines for pollution reductions. New Source Performance Standards (NSPSs) ensure that new facilities do not operate in violation of the standards and a Prevention of Significant Deterioration (PSD) Program works to prevent the deterioration of air quality in regions that are already in compliance with the NAAQSs. The EPA may and does delegate implementation to those states that demonstrate their ability to administer national air quality programs, although state implementation of national air quality

6 Pollutants also travel up the "Northeast Corridor" of the US into the southern Atlantic region of Canada, especially the Saint John, New Brunswick area. Smog incidences here are less intense and less frequent, however. Infoterra, "North American Commission Report Finds Ground-Level Ozone." Accessed at: http://www.ee/lists/infoterra/1997/11/0012.html.

7 The reductions were specified in the US Clean Air Act, the Canadian Acid Rain Program and new SO2 regulations in Ontario.

standards takes place under the watchful eyes of the EPA and Congress.[8] Formulation and implementation of vehicle emission standards are the preserve of the national decision-makers.

In comparison, Canada has a less uniform and less extensive set of mandatory air quality controls currently in place. The Canadian federal government can regulate fuel content and emission standards for new vehicles and other polluting equipment, and it is authorized to regulate toxic substances under the revised *Canadian Environmental Protection Act* (CEPA 1999).[9] The federal government also can regulate air emissions where the ministers of the environment and health believe these will contribute to air pollution in another country or result in environmental or health effects. It is the provinces, however, which establish ambient and point source air quality standards within their boundaries.[10] The federal government can encourage national action within intergovernmental decision-making forums such as the Canadian Council of Ministers of the Environment (CCME) – comprised of federal, provincial and territorial environment ministers – but it cannot force the provinces to comply through regulatory means. Thus, authoritative decision-making on air quality issues in Canada is shared between federal and provincial executives. In fact, the provinces hold veto power in some policy areas, that is, electricity generation and industrial sources, which are crucial sources of air pollutants. Although the Canadian federal government has the power to conclude treaties with foreign powers, in the air quality arena it is the provinces that would be responsible for actually achieving air pollution reductions.

Domestic Air Quality Politics

At the root of air quality politics in the U.S. is a provision in the country's 1990 *Clean Air Act* that exempted (or "grandfathered") many older, mainly coal-burning, power

---

8 States must develop "state implementation plans" (SIPs) that explain how a state will carry out its delegated responsibilities under the Clean Air Act. The EPA must approve the SIP and, if a SIP is not considered acceptable or if a state fails to follow through, the EPA can take over implementing the Act in that state. The delegation rate for federal standards promulgated under the Clean Air Act is the highest of all federal programs, at 84 percent. See R.S. Brown, "The States Protect the Environment." ECOStates (Summer 1999) Accessed at: http://www.sso.org/ecos/publications/statesarticle.htm 05/15/2000. In very few states, then, is the federal level of government actually operating air quality programs and generally it is state pollution-control agencies which negotiate and issue pollution permits as well as monitor and enforce pollution levels. See: Mazur and Welch, (1998).

9 The federal ministers will add a substance (for example, an air pollutant such as PM10) to the CEPA Toxic Substances List, first declaring a "Notice of Intent" to regulate, after which they are obliged to propose control strategies within two years. These strategies must then be implemented within 18 months.

10 The federal government does set National Air Quality Objectives (NAQOs), which are non-binding, science-based guidelines for ambient levels of "criteria" air pollutants (ozone, SO2, NO, VOCs, CO).

plants from meeting stringent new air emission limits. At the time, policymakers were assured by industry that these older plants would gradually be shut down. This did not prove to be the case, however, and almost 600 older plants continue to operate, each emitting up to ten times the amount of a new plant that meets *Clean Air Act* requirements.[11] Moreover, these older plants are concentrated in the Midwestern states of Ohio, Pennsylvania, and Indiana, where emissions are then transported on prevailing winds to the northeastern U.S. states (as well as to Ontario and Quebec).

Under the *Clean Air Act*, the EPA had been granted authority to establish multi-state "ozone transport regions." In 1995, the EPA and the Environmental Council of the States (ECOS) established a temporary, two-year multi-stakeholder mechanism – the Ozone Transport Assessment Group (OTAG) – consisting of the 37 easternmost states plus the District of Columbia. The goal of the multi-stakeholder OTAG process was to identify and recommend to EPA cost-effective control strategies for VOCs and NO_x to facilitate compliance with NAAQS and reduce the regional transport of pollutants (that is, from the Midwest to the Northeast). However, if no consensus were achieved, the EPA would use its authority under the *Clean Air Act* to require emission reductions by states (Parker and Blodgett, 1999). When it ended in 1997, the OTAG process had succeeded in enlarging the number of people (researchers, state and federal officials, industry) who accepted the reality of long-range transport, but its minimalist recommendations failed to garner the full support of the states, five of whom opposed the final resolutions (Keating and Farell, 1998).

The EPA's response was to issue new air quality standards for ozone and particulate matter. The new, more stringent standards were justified on health grounds and strongly supported by the downwind northeastern states. They were vigorously opposed, however, by the Midwestern states (including the five that had opposed OTAG's recommendations) and their industries, and these opponents mounted a legal challenge. In response to a suit brought forward by these interests, the Court of Appeals for the District of Columbia held that the EPA, in issuing the new standards, had exceeded its constitutional authority and that its proposal was "an unconstitutional delegation of legislative power."[12] The EPA then turned to higher courts for a review of the Appeal Court's decision. In 1998, the EPA forged ahead and proposed a new NO_x emissions reduction program for utility and large non-utility sources, which aimed to cut emissions by 28 percent starting in 2003. The program called on 22 eastern states to develop plans detailing how the reductions would be achieved – SIPs, or state implementation plans – within their jurisdictions.[13] The EPA's NO_x SIP Call also was immediately challenged in the courts by a collection of Midwestern and southern states, utilities and industry organizations. Northeastern

11 These older plants accounted for 51 percent of all SO_2 and 18 percent of all NO_x emissions in 1997. "US pollution loopholes hurting Ontario: Report by US Public Interest Research Group" Canadian Press Newswire, July 13, 1998.

12 American Trucking Association, Inc. v. USEPA, Nos.97-1440 and 97-1441 (D.C. Cir. May 14, 1999). Summary of Decision.

13 See footnote 21 re: state implementation plans (SIPs).

states intervened in the litigation in support of the EPA, as did environmental groups, specific utilities (that had already undertaken control improvements), regional state business and industry groups and, significantly, the province of Ontario.

In Canada, air quality politics were unfolding quite differently. The smog issue appeared on the political agenda in the mid-to-late 1980s when the high number of ozone exceedences alerted the public to the seriousness of the problem. As a result of increased public concern, the Canadian Council of Ministers of the Environment (CCME) undertook to address the problem of ground-level ozone and bring about some coordination in varying provincial approaches. The result was a three-phase NO_x/VOC Management Plan in 1990, developed in consultation with industry and environmental interests and containing 59 separate (but mainly nonbinding) initiatives to be implemented by 2005.[14] Under the plan, the federal government also initiated a scientific assessment of the ground-level ozone problem.

In the mid-1990s, as implementation of phase 1 activities bumped along rather unevenly, federal and provincial officials were unable to agree on what further actions should be taken under phase 2, and the federal government issued its own phase 2 Federal Smog Management Plan in 1997. This phase 2 plan outlined limited "next steps" to be taken at the federal level and also publicized the results of the 1996 NO_x/VOC Scientific Assessment, which set out the case for federal regulatory action on the basis of health effects. Shortly after the phase 2 plan release, the federal Commissioner of the Environment and Sustainable Development – Canada's environmental auditor – undertook an evaluation of the 1990 NO_x/VOC Management Plan as the major national smog policy. The resulting report noted that, whereas the plan initially had provided "sound strategic direction" for addressing Canada's smog problem, federal and provincial governments never reached agreement on the details of a framework for implementing it and the program had been a failure.[15] In any case, the CCME moved on in 1998 to developing "Canada-wide standards" for

14 During Phase 1 of the Plan (1990-94), a national prevention program was to be established, interim targets for NO_x and VOC reductions were to be negotiated, and studies on which to base final reduction targets were to be conducted. During Phase 2 (1994-97), caps on NO_x and VOCs would be established and additional remedial measures for ozone problems were to be identified. Final adjustments to the caps and remedial measures were to be made during Phase 3 (1997-2000). Then, the implementation tasks were to be shared among the agreement partners.

15 The Commissioner stated that, although governments agreed on an ultimate goal (consistent attainment of 82 ppb ozone across the country) and a general approach for achieving this, they failed to formally set out interim reduction targets, prevention, remedial and study programs, means for monitoring, and consequences for non-performance. Commissioner of the Environment and Sustainable Development, "Smog: Our Health at Risk," Chp.4 in 1997 Annual Report. Accessed at: http://www.oag-bvg.gc.ca/domino/reports.nsf/html/c004ce.html.

ground-level ozone and particulate matter under the new Canada-wide Accord on Environmental Harmonization.[16]

Throughout these activities, officials from the province of Ontario emphasized the regulatory dilemma they shared with the U.S. Northeast: even if the province completely eliminated its own emissions of smog precursors within the province, air pollutants blowing in from the U.S. Midwest would still create problems in Ontario. Yet as critics pointed out, Ontario was the largest smog producer in Canada and possessed the largest coal-burning power plant in North America. Elected on a deregulatory platform, Ontario's Progressive Conservative government had no plans to regulate, however. The province's 1998 Anti-Smog Action Plan (ASAP) relied on voluntary efforts by industry, rather than government regulations, to reduce NO_x and VOC emissions by 45 percent by 2015 (Brennan, 1998). In late 1999, Ontario's Environment Minister did announce that the government would match or exceed U.S. standards for NO_x emissions (Middlestaedt, 2000). It was not altogether clear, however, what this meant in terms of actual reductions. Although officials promised to establish an emissions trading system for NO_x and expanded mandatory reporting on emissions of all criteria pollutants, neither detailed implementation plans nor additional resources accompanied these announcements.

Significantly, the advent of David Anderson as federal Environment Minister after a cabinet shuffle in 1999 signalled a change in the tone of federal-provincial environmental relations. Anderson made it clear in his press statements that he was prepared to push provinces to address pollution if they chose to drag their feet. As a result, federal-provincial meetings under the auspices of the CCME were characterized by more disagreements, often expressed vocally to the press afterward. In particular, relations between Ontario and Ottawa, historically amiable, became increasingly difficult. The type of rancorous debate that had already been occurring in the U.S. for some time with regard to reduction responsibilities seemed to be just gearing up in Canada.

Binational Negotiations

The American and Canadian governments had first signalled their desire to jointly address the ground-level ozone problem three years before negotiations actually began. In April of 1997, the EPA Administrator and Canadian Environment Minister had signed a Joint Plan of Action for Addressing Transboundary Air Pollution. One year later, the Administrator and Minister met again to review progress on the Joint

---

16 The Harmonization Accord, signed by all federal, provincial and territorial governments (with the exception of Quebec) was designed to eliminate "overlap and duplication" in federal and provincial environmental decision-making and to facilitate cooperative standard-setting. Under the terms of the Accord, a Standards Development Committee, consisting of managers/directors from the federal government and the provinces, undertook to assess and integrate the existing scientific, technical and socio-economic data on ozone and PM, and then propose candidate measures for the pollutants using a "risk-based" framework.

Plan of Action and consider possible elements of an Ozone Annex to the Canada-United States Air Quality Agreement. Formal negotiations on an Ozone Annex began in February of 2000 and continued through to October.

The first meeting between Canada and the U.S. was described by the two governments as "cooperative and productive" (DFAIT, 2000). Discussions centred mainly on technical and organizational issues central to the negotiations, such as the timing and scope of the negotiations as well as the elements to be included in the actual Annex. Negotiators also set out a work plan for future meetings in the summer and fall. It was agreed that the Ozone Annex would be a "reciprocal arrangement" with commitments for emission reductions by both countries in those regions identified as upwind sources contributing to transboundary flows (Environment Canada, 2000). Separate reduction targets and timetables for achieving them would be negotiated for each region at these later meetings, with a formal agreement to be signed by the end of the year. The overall goal was to be a 45 to 50 percent reduction in emission levels.

In March of 2000, the U.S. Court of Appeals for the District of Columbia upheld the NO_x SIP Call and, shortly thereafter, the EPA was awarded another victory when the Appeal Court's decision on the new ozone and PM standards was overturned and the standards were upheld. Although there were some details that remained outstanding, including the implementation deadline of the NO_x SIP Call, negotiators could now assume that the new U.S. reduction requirements would have to be met. This likely solidified the consensus on the part of individuals on the U.S. negotiating team that getting comparable reduction commitments from the Canadians, especially Ontario, was necessary on trade competitive grounds.

Canadian officials and environmentalists, quite publicly and in various media, worried that Ontario's weaker air pollution policies might jeopardize the Canada-U.S. negotiations. The federal Environment Minister noted early on in the negotiations that, ". . .if we don't have Ontario doing as much as the Americans, the Americans are unlikely to listen to the Canadian government" (Sturino, 2000). Great Lakes United, an international coalition based in Buffalo, New York, announced that negotiators need look no further than North America's largest coal-fired power plant, in Nanticoke, Ontario, to locate a transboundary source of New York's pollution (Judd, 2000). Similarly, a spokesperson for the OntAIRio Campaign, a coalition of Ontario-based environmental groups, asserted that: "The key to Canada negotiating a reduction in smog coming to us from the United States is in our being prepared to impose the same technological cleanup on our coal-fired plants that the Americans are putting on theirs. . . The government of Ontario has refused to make that cleanup happen" (Sturino, 2000). Ontario, it seemed, had become the focus of Ozone Annex negotiations, from the perspective of both Canadians and Americans.

Directly prior to the second round of Canada-U.S. talks, the Canadian federal government in May of 2000 unveiled an "updated" Clean Air Strategy. Federal officials announced new restrictions on NO_x, a promise to declare particulate matter toxic under CEPA (which would force the government to regulate within two years), and an intention to seek tighter timeframes to reduce emissions from utilities and industrial sources in negotiations with the provinces (MacKinnon, 2000). The federal and provincial governments met shortly thereafter and, after difficult negotiations, governments agreed to implement differential reduction targets by 2010. Ontario was to reduce its emissions output by 45 percent (as per the ASAP, although the target date is five years earlier), Quebec by more than 20 percent, and Alberta and BC by 10 percent (Duffy, 2000). The overall goal was to reduce smog by 20 percent and to achieve a recently agreed upon "Canada-wide standard" of 65 ppb over an eight-hour period.

Although the new standard was more stringent,[17] there were no real penalties for provincial non-compliance and no specific reduction commitments for point or mobile emission sources. Yet the federal Environment Minister argued that the provinces were now "serious" about meeting the commitments. Specifically, federal officials claimed that the agreement was made possible because Ontario withdrew its objections to the accelerated timeframe (Seguin, 2000). An Ontario spokesperson stated that the province had moved on the issue because of its concerns about health effects and because "we think it will be helpful in terms of our negotiations with the Americans" (Seguin, 2000). Closer to home, however, Ontario was facing stiff criticism as a result of another set of environmental developments; in May, six people had died from e-coli contamination of water supplies in the town of Walkerton, Ontario and many blamed the province's deregulation of water testing.

The June and August Canada-U.S. negotiations yielded further progress on key elements of the Annex, although the most substantial discussions relating to emissions reductions were addressed in September and October. Both governments were committed to completing talks before the presidential election in November, as it was feared that a new Bush Administration would be less favourably disposed toward both bilateral environmental agreements and emission reductions programs. A number of issues arose in the joint negotiating sessions. One concern, a recurring one in Canada-U.S. environmental relations, was the more rudimentary state of Canada's emissions reporting system and inventories and, thus, the relative lack of publicly available emissions data to aid in setting targets and tracking actual reductions achieved. Point source emissions data is the preserve of the provinces, which have varying emissions data collection and reporting systems. Another issue related to the desire to see additional controls put on industrial emission sources in Ontario.[18]

In July, New York's Attorney General, Eliot Spitzer, took aim at Ontario. Spitzer wrote a letter to U.S. Secretary of State Madeleine Albright pointing to Ontario's coal-fired power plants as large polluters whose emissions were carried across the border and contributed to human health effects and environmental damage in the U.S. Northeast. He also noted that, as of 2003, all power plants located in the Midwestern and northeastern United States would have to comply with the EPA's new, national emission controls which would be three times as stringent as those applicable to

17 The previous suggested guideline was had been 82 ppb over a one-hour period.

18 Confidential interviews with the Canadian and American officials.

Canadian plants. Spitzer thus called for comparable actions by the Canadians. Having obtained a copy of the letter, Ontario's Environment Minister Dan Newman wrote a response to the Canadian federal Environment Minister, declaring that "50 percent of the smog that affects our province is generated in the United States." Newman noted that Ontario had already committed to a 45 percent reduction in smog emissions by 2010 (though this target was not binding on the government) and he urged federal negotiators to demand that American emitters commit to the same ambitious schedule. On the very same day, however, federal Environment Minister Anderson sent a letter to Newman, expressing his "deep concern about the lack of progress in converting coal-fired power generation plants in Ontario to natural gas or other less-polluting fuel sources." Anderson explained that additional efforts on the part of Ontario to control its emissions were "central to establishing our negotiating position with the U.S."

Further negotiations took place in the fall, with pressure being applied directly or indirectly on Ontario from all sides to address power and industrial emission sources in the province in a more targeted manner. Ontario, having made a commitment to match U.S. standards for NO_x reductions directly prior to the negotiations, was now pressed to define this commitment in more concrete, regulatory terms. In the midst of these final discussions, American officials made it clear to Canadian federal officials through more informal channels – specifically, at a diplomatic social event – that any agreement reached would require that Ontario address industrial emission sources.[19] Canadian federal officials, in response, turned up the heat on Ontario. In October, agreement was reached among all parties.

A final draft of the Ozone Annex to the 1991 Air Quality Agreement, along with appropriate amendments to the Agreement itself, was released on October 13, 2000. In both countries, defined "Pollutant Emission Management Areas" (central and southern Ontario and southern Quebec in Canada; 18 eastern states and the District of Columbia in the U.S.) were to make NO_x and VOC emission reductions. The U.S. agreed to reduce NO_x emissions by 35 percent by 2007, which would represent a 70 percent reduction in emissions from its power plants and other major industrial sources. For its part, Canada (that is, Ontario) agreed to place a cap on NO_x emissions from Ontario power plants of 39 kilotonnes (representing a 50 percent reduction) and five kilotonnes in Quebec (Minister of the Environment, 2000). Moreover, Canada agreed to harmonize its vehicle emission regulations with those of the U.S. Annual reporting of emissions from major source categories and joint analysis of transboundary transport (with attention to the adequacy of monitoring networks) were also features of the Annex. Finally, progress was to be assessed in 2004, with a view to negotiating further reductions.

Observations

A two-level game analysis of the Canada-U.S. Ozone Annex negotiations, which focuses on the interaction between domestic political dynamics and international

19 Confidential Interviews with the Canadian and American officials.

negotiations at the point of ratification, yields a story of binational cooperation on ground-level ozone that served the interests of federal officials in each country. On the U.S. side, the EPA's goal was to move forward with its new NAAQSs for ozone and particulate matter as well as the NO_x SIP Call, even in the face of ongoing litigation and opposition from Midwestern states. It was anticipated that placing the NO_x SIP Call in the text of an international agreement as a legal obligation would help to further solidify the new requirements, especially if there was a change of administration. A binational agreement mandating emission controls in Canada also would address any trade competitive concerns that might exist.

On the Canadian side, the stakes were higher. The federal government needed an effective interprovincial agreement to bring about ozone-related emission reductions within an accelerated timeframe, as it could not do so unilaterally. The Canada-U.S. negotiations provided an impetus for getting commitments from provinces to reduce emissions, especially Ontario. Entrenching domestic reduction regimes in a binational agreement – which the federal government would be responsible for implementing – was more likely to result in actual emissions reductions than earlier intergovernmental agreements that could not be enforced by the federal government.

The above narrative of the Canada-U.S. Ozone Annex negotiations seems to suggest that much influence operated in a northerly direction, with American political dynamics having considerable effect on Canadian policy, specifically in terms of the target and nature of NO_x controls. Moreover, American pressure appears to have been consciously channelled by Canadian federal officials in order to achieve concessions from domestic players, especially the province of Ontario, which appeared unlikely under domestic conditions alone.

Multi-Level Working Relations and Epistemic Communities

A two-level game analysis of the Canada-U.S. negotiations, which focuses primarily on high-level interactions, is a necessary but not sufficient step in terms of explaining how the Canada-U.S. Ozone Annex came into being. The discussion below shows that less visible modes of interaction at different spatial-institutional levels, particularly in terms of mid-level working relations and the operation of epistemic communities, were critical in laying the groundwork for the negotiations towards the late 1990s. Specifically, these cross-border interactions were key in setting out the scientific basis for a transboundary control regime, putting in place the technical tools to support such a regime and defining what emission control measures were appropriate and necessary, especially in terms of NO_x emissions.

Subnational Interactions

Interstate regional air quality organizations are well established in the northeastern U.S. and include mechanisms such as the OTC and OTAG, both discussed above.

The activities of these organizations have been aided by the Northeast States for Coordinated Air Use Management (NESCAUM), a non-profit organization created in the 1970s to aid Air Directors in the northeastern states. NESCAUM is the repository of considerable technical and policy expertise with regard to air pollution controls, and it has played a key role in helping the northeastern states make a convincing case for regional pollution controls. Over the past two decades, the sharing of air quality policy-relevant expertise and collaborative problem-solving in the region has been truly remarkable, and a well-developed network of government officials, experts, NGOs and even federal air quality officials has developed.[20] This northeastern epistemic community has advocated on behalf of tighter emission controls both within the Northeast and in the U.S. Midwest, from whence much of its pollution originates.

The northeastern air quality community is connected to Eastern Canada via the Conference of New England Governors and Eastern Canadian Premiers (NEG/ECP). A transboundary organization established in 1973, the NEG/ECP is a mechanism for cooperation among six New England states (Connecticut, Maine, New Hampshire, Rhode Island, Massachusetts, Vermont) and the five easternmost provinces. The Conference considers itself "a forceful advocate of environmental issues and sustainable development"[21] and it has been argued that "[no] other transboundary regional body in North America approaches it by any measure" (Rausch, 1997). The Conference is seldom covered in media reports and its work is mainly of a technical nature. Although it is Premiers and Governors that attend its annual meeting, the NEG/ECP's actual work is carried out by mid-level officials and experts via collaborative research projects, joint seminars (often for training air quality officials in the two countries) and the preparation of policy papers.

The NEG/ECP was an early and influential proponent of transboundary acid rain controls and it turned its attention to other air quality issues, including ground-level ozone, in the mid-1990s. The Conference was one of the first to call for the cross-border exchange of emissions transport data and, by 1998, had implemented a joint Eastern Canadian-U.S. "mapping-without-borders" project in order to provide seamless, animated Canadian and American ground-level ozone maps for the region. With the technical aid of NESCAUM and the Eastern Canada Transboundary Smog Issue Group,[22] not to mention the involvement of officials from the eastern provinces, northeastern states, the U.S. EPA and Environment Canada, the Conference's activities broadened the expert and political community concerned with and knowledgeable

20 See, for example, Miller and Grumet (1998).

21 For general information about the NEG/ECP see: http://www.negc.org/premiers.html.

22 The Eastern Canada Transboundary Smog Issue Group (ECTSIG) is a partnership among Environment Canada and the provinces of Nova Scotia, Ontario and Quebec. ECTSIG was formed to assist an effort to evaluate transborder smog transport in collaboration with the Commission for Environmental Cooperation (CEC) and NESCAUM.

about ground-level ozone transport. In particular, the NEG/ECP highlighted the role of the electricity industry in the Northeast's emissions profile.[23]

Binational Interactions

At the binational level, there was considerable behind-the scenes activity by officials associated with the Canada-U.S. Air Quality Committee (AQC) in terms of preparing the ground for negotiations, while the International Air Quality Advisory Board (IAQAB) also played an important role. These binational mechanisms had been in existence for some time and had already fostered a cross-border epistemic community of officials in both countries that viewed the ground-level ozone problem as one that would have to be dealt with jointly and using similar policy instruments.

Already in the mid-1990s, there had been discussions about the ground-level ozone problem among Canadian and American staff associated with the AQC. [24] Two subcommittees – a more policy-related Subcommittee 1 and a science-related Subcommittee 2 – engage in collaborative activities to fulfil the AQC's mandate. Many of the Canadians and Americans associated with the subcommittees – themselves officials or scientists working on air quality problems in their respective countries – had begun working together on the acid rain issue and had almost a decade's worth of experience collaborating with one another on a personal level. As their focus turned to the ground-level ozone problem at home, they also began to move their governments toward joint action via a new Ozone Annex to the Canada-United States Air Quality Agreement.

In 1996, a few key Canadian and American officials associated with Subcommittee 1 put together a work plan for moving the Annex idea forward. First, officials prepared the Joint Plan of Action for Addressing Transboundary Air Pollution focusing on ozone and particulate matter in time for a high-level meeting in April 1997 between the EPA Administrator and Canadian Environment Minister (USCAQC, 1998). For the one-year anniversary of the signing of the Joint Plan of Action, and in an attempt to encourage progress, AQC staff prepared another document which reviewed progress on the Plan of Action over the past year and committed the two governments to begin considering in broad terms possible elements of and a timeframe for negotiating an Ozone Annex.

Meanwhile, Subcommittee 1 of the AQC prepared a report entitled *Ground-Level Ozone: Occurrence and Transport in Eastern North America*. Released in early 1999, it reviewed the state of knowledge on ozone transport using Canadian

---

23 In 1997, the NEG/ECP also released a Resolution Supporting Cooperative Action calling on the CEC and federal, state and provincial government to assess the impact of electricity restructuring on both sides of the border on air pollution in the region.

24 The AQC is composed of six representatives from Canada and six representatives from the United States. The Canadian members all hold significant positions within Environment Canada, other federal departments, or provincial environmental agencies, while the American members are from the EPA, the Departments of Energy, Interior and Commerce, and the President's Council on Environmental Quality.

and American data to show transboundary flows and concluded that there were substantial transboundary regional benefits to controlling NO_x emissions through bilateral action. The report, put together using whatever resources, agency staff time and technical assistance that could be made available on both sides of the border,[25] indicated the major sources of NO_x and VOCs and where control efforts would make most sense, that is, at electric utilities (USCAQC, 1999).

At the same time, the International Air Quality Advisory Board (IAQAB) of the IJC also had been considering the transboundary implications of ground-level ozone. The IAQAB, composed of five air quality officials from each country, was formed in the 1960s to provide advice on air quality issues along the entire Canada-U.S. boundary.[26] In November of 1998, air quality managers associated with the IAQAB released the *Special Report on Transboundary Air Quality Issues*, which emphasized that "atmospheric pollutants recognize no border or boundary" and that "Canada and the United States must take a similar approach, namely the formation of Transboundary Air Pollution Transport Regions (TAPTRs) spanning the boundary region."[27] The Report regarded NO_x as a "pivotal pollutant" and it reiterated the Board's oft-stated position that identical standards for common air pollutants would be advisable, although binational cooperation in developing a common base of scientific knowledge for individual standard-setting was perhaps more realistic in the shorter term.

The technical work of both the AQC and IAQAB, then, was key in cementing the growing consensus on the nature of the Canada-U.S. ozone transport problem and moving the process toward a consideration of specific policy options, especially with regard to NO_x. AQC officials, moreover, were instrumental in creating a concrete framework, via the Plan of Action and Progress Report, within which these processes could occur.

Trinational Interactions

At the trinational level, newer but equally significant relationships also were being forged. Noteworthy is the fact that interactions at the trilateral level appear to represent an extension of the cross-border epistemic communities at the subnational and binational levels, as is evidenced by the overlapping memberships of the various mechanisms.

The CEC has attempted to define a role for itself in long-range air pollution, although its activities have related mainly to information sharing. Interestingly, the current Director of the CEC's Air Program is a former Director of NESCAUM. The CEC also can undertake independent research under Article 13 of the NAAEC

25 Confidential Interviews with Canadian and American officials.

26 For general information on the IAQAB, see http://www.ijc.org/boards/iaqab/iaqabres.html.

27 International Air Quality Advisory Board, Special Report on Transboundary Air Quality Issues. Accessible at: http://www.ijc.org/boards/iaqab/spectrans/exec.html.

and, in the mid-1990s, it initiated a study into the nature, extent, and significance of the pathways by which air pollutants travel to, from and within North America. The study involved an Expert Advisory Panel on Continental Pollutant Pathways, a group of over 30 North American air quality experts, which produced a "general consensus" report of the sources, pathways and effects of air pollution in North America. The CEC also enlisted the aid of a consultative group of interested stakeholders, a policy group of air quality policymakers from all over North America and the Advisory Groups of the CEC Air Monitoring and Modeling Project. Released in 1997, the report stated that long-range persistent air pollutants posed significant threats to human health and the environment on a continental level and that pollution prevention, achieved through cross-border cooperation, was the best strategy for reducing deleterious effects (CEC, 1997a).

The CEC coordinated another report released the same year. The result of a collaborative effort on the part of the CEC, the Eastern Canada Transboundary Smog Issue Group (ECTSIG) and NESCAUM, it aimed to assess the scientific methods being used to quantify transboundary transport between the northeastern U.S. and eastern Canada. The report added to the available weight of evidence showing the existence of transboundary transport and concluded that continuing, cross-border scientific effort was needed.

Air quality experts and officials were also interacting via the recently established North American Research Strategy on Tropospheric Ozone (NARSTO). In the mid-1990s, U.S. founders had enlisted colleagues in Canada and Mexico with the aim of creating a cross-border coalition for research on ground-level ozone. [28] In 1994, the founders set up a multi-stakeholder framework whereby government, industry and NGOs would interact with scientists in carrying out research. NARSTO's mission was "to coordinate and enhance policy-relevant research" (NSCT, 2000) through "state-of-the-science" assessments and by participating in cooperative research projects at a regional level, that is, in cooperation with NESCAUM in the Northeast. NARSTO also holds an annual conference, which rotates among the three member countries and is attended by both scientists and air quality officials in the three countries – many of whom are active in NESCAUM, the AQC, the IAQAB and the CEC.

NARSTO's Ozone Assessment, carried out in the late 1990s, reviewed advances in the chemical, physical and meteorological science of ground-level ozone. The Assessment was considered "state of the art" and spawned considerable cross-border cooperation among the scientific and policy communities in the three countries. Significantly, the Assessment confirmed that concentrated NO_x sources in the industrial Midwest create a permanent reservoir of elevated ozone levels and that wind flow moves this pollution from the U.S. Midwest to the Northeast region (see Miller et al., 1997).

28 The U.S. agencies driving NARSTO include DOE, NOAA, and EPA. For Canada, Environment Canada has taken the lead. From Mexico, the Environment Institute and the Petroleum Institute, both governmental organizations, take part in NARSTO.

Towards a Multi-Faceted Approach

Having examined *both* interactions at the domestic-binational interface *and* multi-level working and epistemic linkages in the case of the Canada-U.S. Ozone Annex negotiations, a more nuanced and complete picture of the Canada-U.S. environmental relationship emerges.

By 1999, both Canada and the U.S. had undertaken a variety of emission reduction initiatives, although these differed in important respects and the American regime included a broader set of regulatory controls. Domestic opposition in both countries – from Midwestern states and industries in the U.S. as well as the Ontario government in Canada – had slowed progress in building national reduction regimes. It was becoming evident to federal officials on both sides of the border that a bilateral agreement might enable them to achieve domestic emission reduction goals as well as further entrench the bilateral air quality relationship.

At the same time, officials and scientists, and in some cases NGOs, at the subnational, binational and trilateral levels were busily cooperating within a complex of cross-border mechanisms, building the case for a transboundary air control regime. Collaborative research confirmed the nature and extent of regional air pollutant transport; whereas earlier models of pollutant transport had been purely domestically defined, policymakers were now able to track pollutants across the Canada-U.S. border. This work encouraged an explicitly transboundary perspective on the ground-level ozone problem because of the reality of long-range pollutant transport, and it showed that joint, more stringent emissions tracking and monitoring was crucial. It also confirmed the major sources of the "pivotal pollutant" NO_x, particularly coal-burning power plants in the U.S. Midwest and Ontario, and made it clear that additional restrictions would have to be placed on these plants. The politically difficult question of "who is polluting whom" had been answered and the frame for debate could be shifted to the mechanics of actually reducing emissions. Indeed, in the glare of this more technical spotlight, directed at political actors engaged in the negotiations by epistemic communities at multiple levels, Ontario's more informal approach to emissions monitoring and reduction appeared increasingly inadequate.

In the absence of the multi-level cross-border technical and policy work, and the consensus for action emerging out of this work, negotiations would likely never have been initiated. The overlapping cross-border networks of air quality officials, scientists and environmentalists forged in the course of transboundary collaboration from the mid-to-late 1990s allowed for the operation of an epistemic community that was working both domestically and in a cross-border capacity to address the ground-level ozone problem. Fanning out across various levels in the two governments, this epistemic community acted as the supports for the bridge being built via the binational negotiations.

This analysis of the Ozone Annex demonstrates the usefulness of adopting a multi-faceted approach to examining the Canada-U.S. environmental relationship. Focusing primarily on high-level interactions between the two countries cannot provide us with a complete explanation of how power operates across the border and why bilateral agreements look the way they do. Instead, less visible modes of interaction at different spatial-institutional levels, particularly in terms of mid-level working relations and the operation of epistemic communities, are a key part of the Canada-U.S. environmental narrative.

Chapter 4

Transboundary Air Pollution: Dependence and Interdependence[1]

Don Munton

Introduction

The nature of the geophysics and ecosystems of North America leads inescapably to transboundary pollution flows. These flows in turn ensure air quality issues have been a prominent part of Canada-United States relations since pollution was discovered in the Great Lakes in the early 20th century and the Trail Smelter case erupted a decade later. Beyond these fundamental facts, however, what do we know about the essential character of bilateral ecopolitics? Is the environment simply a different case in Canada-United States relations, as often assumed? Are the attendant political-social patterns *sui generis*? Or do bilateral environmental relations display certain features of the Canada-United States relationship writ broad, and perhaps features of international relations in general?

The present chapter attempts to address these questions in the context of a survey of transboundary air quality issues since the late 20th century. This necessarily brief survey begins with the emergence of acid rain in the late 1970s and traces its development through the signing and implementation of the Canada-United States Air Quality Agreement in 1991. It then continues with ground-level (tropospheric) ozone, an issue that surfaced in the 1990s, and moves to particulate matter, which the governments officially, and perhaps belatedly, recognized as a bilateral air quality problem early in the 21st century. The chapter opens, however, with an attempt to sketch out some key concepts and theoretical relationships – in short, a model for Canada-United States environmental relations. And it ends with an assessment of the applicability of that model to acid rain, ozone, and particulates and some speculation about whether it might help explain other bilateral and environmental issues.

1 This chapter is part of a long-term research project on Canadian international environmental policy. Research assistance was provided at various points by Stephanie Campbell, Geoffrey Castle, Teresa Cline, Karen Dube, Carol Fletcher, Laura Hurst, Cheryl Loeb, Wendy Marks, and David Vogt. Funding and support for the research herein was provided by the Fulbright Fellowship Program, Dartmouth College, the University of British Columbia, and the University of Northern British Columbia.

The discussion here does not ignore but does not emphasize the role of transgovernmental relations and local politics, as do some other chapters in this book. Suffice it to say, these are longstanding features of ecopolitics. Long before environmental issues became prominent national and then international concerns, they were local concerns. Pollution control, whether smoke abatement or sewage treatment, was originally conceived as a municipal matter. Both have remained sub-national to some extent. For most of the 20th century Canada-United States environmental relations have also involved binational groups of technical experts operating under the aegis of such formal intergovernmental bodies as the International Joint Commission.[2] The focus in this chapter, however, is on the relationship between the two countries at the national and official bilateral level.

A Model for Canada-United States Environmental Relations

Twenty-five years ago I proposed the concept of environmental dependence as way of understanding the conflicts that appear in Canada-United States environmental issues (Munton, 1980-81). I failed to develop the concept, however, or to propose linkages that might flesh out a model of bilateral environmental relations. Belated though it may be, that task is begun here.

The familiar notion of economic dependence, or *dependencia*, explains underdevelopment in terms of the extent to which a country's economy is tied to foreign purchasers of goods and suppliers of capital.[3] The crucial factor, though, is neither mere linkage nor even the degree of concentration on a particular purchaser or supplier, but rather the existence of alternative opportunities, for exports, capital, and so on, and the costs of shifting to such new arrangements. If a state is economically tied to external sources *and* there are few alternatives, or shifting would entail high costs, then the level of dependence is high. Through most of its history, Canada has been dependent on a major power, first Britain and then the United States, for its markets and capital. Its position of economic dependence is the theme of a genre of writings, explaining not only the structure of Canada's economy but the nature of its foreign policy (for example, Levitt, 1970; Lumsden, 1970; Moffett, 1972; Hutcheson, 1978; Clarkson, 1982, Williams, 1983).

In a similar way, I argue, Canada is to varying extents dependent with respect to the quality of its environment. *Environmental dependence* refers to a situation in which the environmental quality and/or valued resources of a country are endangered by transboundary pollution, pollutants originating outside its territorial control. To the extent that physical and geographical features such as terrestrial, aquatic and atmospheric ecosystems are not easily altered, and they seldom are, or

2 For example, International Joint Commission, Final Report of the International Joint Commission on the Pollution of Boundary Waters Reference, Washington, DC, 1918.

3 For an overview largely, but not entirely, from an American social science perspective of a term and literature developed by Latin American scholars (for example, Cardoso and Faletto, 1979), see Caporaso, (1978).

that environmental policies do not mitigate existing transboundary flows, and they often do not, then the level of environmental dependence is high.

Environmental dependence is an issue specific phenomenon. Eastern Canada was (and is) environmentally dependent on the United States with respect to acid rain, while a part of the United States was affected by Canadian emissions in the famous Trail smelter case (Dinwoodie, 1971). The Canadian Arctic is impacted by the deposition of persistent organic pollutants (POPs) transported from thousands of miles away. And so on. Environmental (or economic) dependence can in some cases be mutual, if two neighbours both pollute the other, more or less equally. Such cases display environmental interdependence. Symmetrical or nearly symmetrical interdependence, however, seems rare; commonly, for a given issue, the transboundary flows are more asymmetrical than symmetrical, and one country or the other is thus environmentally dependent. This situation is a reasonably well-recognized one in the environmental area. When the degree of asymmetry is significant the source of the transboundary flows is often termed the "upstream" state and the recipient the "downstream" state. Another common phrase used, albeit more bluntly, is "throwing your garbage in your neighbour's backyard."

What are the consequences of environmental dependence? In other words, how is it related to interest construction, to policy choices and to outcomes? A preponderance of transboundary flows means that unilateral, "domestic" control actions by the dependent state are insufficient to deal with the problem, and thus ineffective by themselves. The rational pursuit of self-interest would suggest therefore that a country in a position of environmental dependence will seek to reduce the transboundary flows of pollutants, and thus to change that position. In short, it will be the *demandeur* in the relationship with others. It will therefore champion policy changes and the adoption of new norms, or the creation of a new international environmental "regime," to reduce the problem (Young, 1989, 1999). The more extensive the resources at risk in country X and the more importance afforded them, the more priority it will place on developing a new binational environmental regime and ultimately to reducing its level of environmental dependence on country Y. On the other hand, the less country Y is environmentally dependent on country X, the less priority country Y will place on transboundary flows, and the less responsive it will be to proposals for a new environmental regime. The more asymmetric the level of environmental dependence of one country on another, therefore, the less common the interests of the states involved and the greater the conflict between them.

Assume the countries eventually agree, after some period of discussion, on the desirability or need for a new international environmental regime on a given issue or set of issues. The reasons why they may be able to do so have been explored elsewhere (Munton, et al., 1999). In that case, the more asymmetrical the environmental dependence for these issues, the more limited and less rigorous the regime's rules will be. Moreover, country Y will be less likely to implement the corrective policy measures fully and expeditiously and the new regime will less likely be characterized by full compliance.

Environmental dependence is not an automatic and inevitable determinant of policies or outcomes. Dependent or "downstream" states do not always construct their interests so as to give priority to environmental issues, even ones where they are in a position of environmental dependence. And "upstream" states, however much they are inclined to ignore transboundary pollutants, do not necessarily fail to reduce them. These flows may diminish as a secondary effect of the "upstream" state addressing its own national pollution problems, for its own reasons – and these reasons may not include the impact its emissions have on its neighbour.

As should be clear by now, the environmental dependence model contrasts with at least one conventional picture of the Canada-United States bilateral politics, the view that relations are characterized by interdependence, similar interests, a problem-solving approach, and a fundamentally cooperative spirit (Holsti, 1971; Keohane and Nye, 1977).[4] This alternative model certainly has a place; the relationship involves both conflict and cooperation. The focus here will however be on the clashing interests and policies characteristic of environmental dependence.

Acid Rain and the Canada-United States Air Quality Agreement

What became popularly known in the 1980s as "acid rain" is a complex set of physical and chemical phenomena by which gases – especially sulphur dioxide (SO_2) and nitrogen oxides (NO_x)[5] – are created and emitted, mostly by industrial processes, transported through the atmosphere, transformed into acidic compounds, and deposited onto land and water surfaces, often with serious negative effects for aquatic and terrestrial ecosystems. Acidification of lakes and streams kills fish and other aquatic species. The impact is particularly strong during the spring run-off period when melting acidic winter snows produce an "acid shock" in streams. Acidification can cause long-term damage to some soils and has a deleterious effect on various crops and on the growth of certain species of trees, particularly at high altitudes.

The major sources of SO_2 in North America are electrical generation and metal smelting. Motor vehicles and various industries produce NO_x. America and Canada, however, differ dramatically in terms of sources. In the United States the bulk of SO_2 emissions came from coal-fired thermal power plants. For Canada, the largest sources were a small number of non-ferrous smelters, particularly two located outside Sudbury, Ontario, owned and operated by mining giant International Nickel and its smaller competitor Falconbridge. There were (and are) some coal-fired power plants in Ontario, Nova Scotia, New Brunswick and Alberta. The major source of SO_2 in

4 An early Canadian reference to the resolution of conflicts with the United States can be found in the famous Gray lecture, given by Louis St. Laurent in 1947 (www.dfait-maeci.gc.ca/department/history/keydocs/keydocs_details-en.asp?intDocumentId=22).

5 Nitrogen oxides (NO_x) include both nitric oxide (NO) and nitrogen dioxide (NO_2). Emissions of sulphur are most often in the form of SO_2 but can also include sulphur trioxide (SO_3) and even sulphuric acid (H_2SO_4).

western Canada is the oil and gas industry but the soils in that region are much less susceptible to acidification than the ecosystems of eastern Canada.

Scientists began to discover and document the impact SO_2 and NO_x emissions have on the environment in the 1950s and 1960s in North America and in Scandinavia (Gorham, 1955; Herman and Gorham, 1957; Gorham and Gordon, 1960, 1963; Odén, 1968; Beamish and Harvey, 1972; Likens, Bormann and Johnson, 1972; Likens and Bormann, 1974).[6] It was these scientists, not environmentalists, who first brought the acid rain problem to the attention of politicians in the 1970s. Two sets of studies particularly aroused Canadian governments. On one hand, research by Ontario government scientists showed lakes were being acidified in cottage country just north of Toronto, hundreds of miles away from the well-known Sudbury smelters (Dillon, Jeffries, and Schneider, 1978).[7] On the other hand, meteorological research being conducted by Environment Canada scientists indicated that the acidity in precipitation falling in eastern Canada was not due solely to domestic sources such as the Inco smelter. Transboundary flows, or the long-range transport of pollutants, from the United States, and chiefly from coal-fired power plants in the American Midwest, played a significant and often dominant role in the acidification problem in Canada (Summers and Whelpdale, 1976; Galloway and Whelpdale, 1979). The combined message from these studies was clear: Canada had a serious and widespread environmental problem, one that was binational as well as domestic.

Canada became the *demandeur* in 1977 when federal environment minister Romeo LeBlanc gave a historic speech in which he termed acid rain an "environmental time bomb." Noting that the sources of acid rain were to be found in both the United States and Canada, LeBlanc proposed immediate negotiations with the United States to "draw up new rules which could allow one nation to tell the other to turn off the pollution at the source" (Howard, 1977). In other words, he called for a new North American air quality regime.

Shortly afterward, a 1978 "sense of the Senate" resolution formally called upon the administration of President Jimmy Carter to negotiate a bilateral "cooperative agreement" on air pollution with Canada. This move, however, was less concerned with long-range transport of air pollution or with acid rain than with the potential impact on the United States of emissions from two Canadian coal-fired power plants planned for locations near the U.S. border. The resolution was quickly forgotten when Canada broadened the agenda to include long-range transport; the United States

6 The history of the science of acid rain is discussed in Cowling, 1982 and Munton, 1981.

7 The 1970s studies providing evidence of aquatic acidification in southern Ontario were not the first evidence of acidification of the province's ecosystems. There was in fact a lengthy history through the 20th century of scientific discovery and of not-so benign neglect of the problems associated with smelter emissions. Ontario government researchers, following on from Eville Gorham's work (Gorham and Gordon, 1960, 1963) observed lake acidification and fish loss in a wide area surrounding Sudbury in the latter 1960s (Munton, 2002, 2004). Scientific investigations in the 1930s during the Trail smelter case had come to similar conclusions about the long-range transport of SO_2 and acidification damage.

quickly realized that it was more the upstream than downstream state. America was, for the next decade, a most reluctant warrior in the battle against acid rain.

The two governments could only agree to form a scientific fact-finding committee, ungainly dubbed the Bilateral Research Consultation Group on the Long-Range Transport of Air Pollutants (BRCG). The expert group produced an interim report in 1979 and, after some disagreements, a final report in October 1980 (Canada-United States Research Consultation Group, 1979, 1980). The BRCG warned that acidification was widespread and doing "irreversible" damage to lakes, rivers and fish, and also pointed to possible damage to soils, high elevation forests and man-made structures. The report also confirmed Canadian suspicions about the major sources of the problem. Given the larger population and industrial base in the United States, American emissions of sulphur dioxide were five times greater than Canadian totals and the U.S. produced overall about 70-80 percent of the pollutants that moved across the boundary. Canada's contribution to acidic deposition in the United States was minor in comparison. In short, acid rain was a highly asymmetric problem.

In 1979, the United States and Canada joined a large group of European countries in signing the Convention on Long-Range Transboundary Air Pollution (LRTAP), negotiated under the auspices of the United Nations Economic Commission for Europe (UNECE, 1979). This Convention highlighted the problems of acid rain and acidification and called for cooperation but stopped short of requiring reductions in emissions or long-range transport. After Canada continued to press the United States for cooperative action, the two countries signed a bilateral "Memorandum of Intent" (MOI) in August 1980, in many respects a reflection of the LRTAP Convention. The MOI committed both countries to negotiating a transboundary air quality agreement (but not to any deadline) and to pursuing vigorous enforcement actions under existing statutes (but not to enacting any new measures in the interim).[8] At this point, however, neither country had air quality programs or legislation dealing explicitly with acid rain. Working groups under the MOI picked up where the BRCG had left off but proceeded slowly. A senior Canadian official subsequently charged that there was ongoing political interference by Reagan Administration political appointees in the scientific work (Robinson, 1982; BNA, 1982). The groups eventually produced reports (MOI, 1983), but the two sides had to agree to disagree on critical recommendations, particularly on the need for controls.

In early 1982 Canada proposed formally that SO_2 emissions be reduced by 50 percent in both countries. This target was designed to achieve a level of deposition in areas sensitive to acidification of no more than 20 kg of wet sulphate per hectare per year – an estimate of what was needed, not to solve the problem, but merely to avoid permanent damage to such areas. The Reagan Administration rejected the

8 While the 1970 and 1977 U.S. Clean Air Acts had led to a gradual overall reduction in SO_2 emissions across the United States (from 32 to 27 million tons during the 1970s), one unintended consequence may have been to increase long-range transport and thus acidic deposition through encouraging "tall stacks" at plants for the purpose of reducing local, ambient air pollution. The Inco "superstack" was one such measure.

proposal, firmly, arguing that any control action, let alone a 50 percent cut, was premature. For the rest of the decade, it consistently took the position that more research was needed on the acid rain problem before actions could be considered. Canadian patience wore thin. Following an unproductive negotiation session in June 1982, Canada's environment minister, John Roberts, accused the United States of "stalling" and adopting a "stuck in the mud stance." Shortly afterward, Canada announced it would withdraw from the negotiation process. Given the realities of North American transboundary pollution, however, Canada had no alternative but to keep pressing. Informal talks occurred off and on over the coming years.[9]

Stymied at the official bilateral level, Canada pursued its campaign on acid rain by somewhat unorthodox, non-diplomatic means. Ministers and officials, and some hired guns, made speeches to U.S. audiences, explaining the nature of the problem and urging action. Some of the prodding was less than gentle. The phrase "environmental aggression" found its way into at least one of these speeches (Roberts, 1980). The Canadian embassy in Washington also cooperated closely with such groups as the National Wildlife Federation on public information campaigns. The Canadian province of Ontario joined with some American state governments in legal action against the Environmental Protection Agency's (EPA) lack of enforcement of American air pollution laws. The "public diplomacy" was a distinct contrast to the old sacred cow of Canadian-American relations, "quiet diplomacy." The new tactics particularly annoyed EPA Administrator Anne Gorsuch and some other Reagan Administration officials.

Canada also doggedly pursued its bilateral acid rain agenda through multilateral channels, especially the 1979 LRTAP Convention. It did so despite the fact that the United States was opposed to action there as well. When an official Reagan administration report on acid rain released in 1987 downplayed the seriousness of acid rain (U.S., National Acid Precipitation Assessment Program, 1987) the Canadian environment minister roundly denounced it. And when Washington began promoting "clean coal" as an alternative to SO_2 emission cuts, Canada criticized that effort too. Meanwhile Canadian governments began developing a domestic, federal-provincial program of emission reductions.

The longstanding conflict was finally resolved only after George H. Bush assumed the White House. Domestic divisions within the United States over environmental policy and acid rain had stalemated Congress since the early 1980s, with no consensus on how to amend the aging Clean Air Act (CAA) last updated in 1977. Presidential candidate Bush broke that logjam; he promised during the

9 The two major exceptions to the pattern of negative rhetoric and impasse during the 1980s were an ill-fated 1983 proposal for a limited, first step, acid rain control program championed by EPA head William Ruckelshaus and the ultimately unsuccessful efforts of Canadian prime minister Brian Mulroney in 1985-87 to use his personal relationship with Ronald Reagan and summit diplomacy to move the United States toward acid rain controls. The "atmospherics" of Canada-United States relations improved during the Mulroney years, but the impasse was not broken. Reducing acid deposition remained Canada's objective.

1988 primaries to overhaul America's air pollution laws and, in particular, to adopt new SO_2 emission controls. The resulting CAA Amendments of 1990 aimed to reduce SO_2 emissions in the United States by about 50 percent – precisely the target Canada had proposed in 1982. The new Act thus provided the United States with both the legislation to deal with its own acid rain problem and the needed basis for the international agreement Canada had long sought. The two countries began in earnest in early 1991to negotiate what became the Canada-United States Air Quality Agreement (AQA) – eleven years after the 1980 MOI and fourteen years after Minister LeBlanc's first call for such an agreement.

The formal bilateral negotiations only took a few months, not long by the usual standards of international environmental diplomacy. The negotiators were greatly assisted by the fact that the two neighbours now had compatible domestic control programs. There were, however, differing views over the essence of what was to be negotiated. And, while a compromise was eventually worked out, the fundamental issue remained unresolved. The Canadian side wanted the accord to feature mutual *commitments* to reduce *transboundary* air pollution. The Americans, on the other hand, preferred a minimal agreement with statements by each country of what its domestic law required in terms of controls. The U.S. thus wanted no *mutual* commitments; neither the United States nor Canada would make promises *to the other* about anything. Under such a wording, each then would be free in theory to alter its domestic acid rain laws and policies without directly violating the bilateral accord.

Both sides eventually compromised. They agreed on a mutual exchange of commitments on reducing national emissions, reductions already required under their domestic programs. The Agreement thus came close to doing what Romeo LeBlanc had called for in 1977, establishing "new rules" for air quality, but it did not "allow one nation to tell the other to turn off the pollution at the source." The compromise also did not provide Canada with what it had sought throughout the 1980s: an American commitment to *reduce transboundary flows* of pollutants. Indeed, the AQA would barely mention this concept. Nor did it make any reference to reducing deposition in Canada, the main Canadian concern. The United States was not willing to make any commitments beyond the requirements of its new Clean Air Act nor to make any promises, or even set any objectives, about what might happen outside its borders.

The problem for Canada was that these CAA requirements might or might not actually reduce transboundary flows, depending on the locations of the plants that reduced emissions and the effect those sources had on transboundary flows. Canadian scientists called in to estimate the likely impact on Canada of Clean Air Act-mandated cuts were cautiously optimistic. Precisely how American industry would respond to the mandated reductions in SO_2 emissions was not certain, given that companies could offset higher than allowed emissions at some plants through the use of "allowances" gained from reductions at other plants or from the purchase of additional allowances (Munton, 1998). The flexibility built into the new CAA meant the plants that contributed the most to acid rain in Canada were not necessarily the ones that would cut their emissions. The Canadian scientists, however, made educated guesses as to where the emission cuts would most likely be made, geographically speaking, and then modelled how much these cuts would reduce the export of sulphur compounds into Canada. They concluded the likely emission cuts would reduce acidic deposition in Canada to some extent, if not perhaps to the degree required by the environment.

The Canadian negotiators thus accepted a wording that meant the AQA would not directly address the basic aims of the decade-long Canadian acid rain campaign – reducing transboundary pollution flows and reducing acidic deposition within Canada. At best those goals were implicitly addressed. It could also be argued, however, that the AQA implicitly set both goals aside. Canadians had to accept on faith that transboundary flows and acidic deposition in Canada would be reduced by the measures Washington adopted to deal with acid rain in the United States, measures crafted, not to reduce the extent to which American emissions affected its neighbour, but rather to minimize the costs to the United States of the mandated emission cuts. The AQA, as a statement of rules for North American air quality, thus fell far short of the basic bilateral norm for water quality articulated in the Boundary Waters Treaty, namely, that neither side should pollute these waters so as to cause environmental harm to the other.[10]

Implementing the Air Quality Agreement

Since 1991, the governments of Canada and the United States have consistently and stoutly insisted that all is well with their implementation of the AQA. Biennial reports and formal reviews of progress under the Agreement regularly find the governments' performances to be satisfactory, if not exemplary.[11] The 2002 review, for example, concluded that "Canada and the United States continued to successfully fulfill [sic] the obligations set forth in the Air Quality Agreement" (Air Quality Committee, 2002: VI:6) Curiously, environmental groups have rarely challenged these claims.

If the details in these official progress reports are examined carefully, however, they do not in fact support the rosy claims the governments have made. Indeed, the reports themselves provide a basis for arguing that implementation of the Agreement

---

10 The key article of the 1909 Treaty is Article IV which stipulates in part that "waters flowing across the boundary shall not be polluted on either side to the injury of health or property on the other." For the text of the Treaty see: www.ijc.org/rel/agree/water.html (accessed December 2005).

11 As required by the AQA, Canada and the United States, through a bilateral Air Quality Committee, have provided biennial progress reports since 1992, and have to date conducted two mandated five-year reviews of the Agreement's implementation, in 1996 and 2002. All these reports are available on the Environment Canada website: http://www.ec.gc.ca/pdb/can_us/canus_links_e.cfm . The latest progress report is also on the U.S. EPA website (www.epa.gov/airmarkets/usca/2004report.html) but EPA apparently does not keep earlier versions of the biennial reports on the web.

has been problematic in key respects.[12] A close examination shows clearly that Canada and the United States have not met all their self-imposed obligations. Space constraints necessitate but a brief summary of two main arguments here: (i) both parties have failed to meet commitments with respect to improving air quality, and (ii) both parties have failed to meet commitments with respect to scientific and technical cooperation.[13]

Initially, in both countries, SO_2 emission cuts proved relatively unproblematic and surprisingly cheap (Munton, 1998). The lower than "expected" costs were due in part to the market mechanisms built into the Act, but also reflected the inflated projections about control costs prevalent during the 1980s. Given that the Clean Air Act's emission reduction target of 50 percent was based on these inflated projections and on a political judgement about what level of costs was manageable, the mandated emission reductions were not in retrospect overly ambitious. Arguably, they could and should have been more stringent. Nevertheless, the early momentum of American cuts has not been maintained.

The implementation of U.S. acid rain controls has recently been slower and more inconsistent than in Canada. Over the 1980-1995 period, Canadian emissions of SO_2 decreased by 43 percent while U.S. emissions decreased by 26 percent. Between 1985 and 1995, Canadian emissions dropped by 28 percent as compared to American emission reductions of 19 percent (Environment Canada, 2001). Moreover, the American government missed an important AQA deadline to cut SO_2 by "approximately" 10 million tons by 2000 (Munton, 2005). Indeed, that target remained unmet in the subsequent three years and SO_2 emissions in 2003 actually increased over 2002 levels.[14] While Canada has met its SO_2 emissions target, it has failed to comply with another provision of the AQA, namely its obligation to

12 The fact that the biennial reports by the Air Quality Committee have been overwhelmingly rosy is perhaps not surprising. Both the progress reports and reviews have been carried out by the very same officials responsible for the implementation of the Agreement – individuals who are thus in the enviable position of reviewing their own work. There is no third-party expert review of these reports. Suffice it to say, as international accords go, this is not an agreement with a great deal of transparency.

13 The key commitments of the Agreement are contained in Annex 1 ("Specific Objectives Concerning Sulphur Dioxide and Nitrogen Oxides") and Annex 2 ("Scientific and Technical Activities and Economic Research"). For an elaboration of the argument that both Canada and the United States have failed to meet key commitments of the Air Quality Agreement, see Munton, 2005.

14 Total SO_2 emissions from electric power generation in the United States in 2000 were 11.2 million tons (Air Quality Committee, 2004, p. 3). Thus, the US did not meet the AQA target of a 10 million ton reduction from 1980 levels of about 20 million tons. The considerable difference of 1.2 million tons between the target and the actual emissions would not seem to lie within the normal realm of the term "approximately." Higher emission level figures for 1998 through 2000 are provided in the 2004 progress report than in the 2002 progress report (2002, p. 2 versus 2004, p. 3). The EPA acknowledged U.S. power plant emissions in 2003 were only slightly below what they were in 1995, and only 38 percent below 1990 levels (Air Quality Committee, 2004, Section 1, pp 2).

"develop and implement" programs to prevent "significant air quality deterioration" in pristine areas.

The other side of the acid rain problem is the somewhat more complicated question of nitrogen emissions and nitrate deposition. While the power generating and smelting industries in both countries account for most of the SO_2 emissions, mobile sources, especially cars and trucks, play a more important factor in NO_x emissions. Canada and the United States however committed themselves in the AQA to reducing NO_x emissions from stationary sources only. They promised to develop new control programs and new standards to cut mobile source emissions, but did not commit to achieving specific NO_x reductions from these sources[15] – a significant omission. In fact, overall U.S. NO_x emissions increased from 1980 to 1995 (Environment Canada, 2001, p 75).

The AQA also contains commitments to undertake scientific research related to acid rain and other air quality issues (in Annex 2). Stated briefly, the parties committed themselves to coordinate emission and ecosystem monitoring, and to cooperate on research programs with respect to atmospheric modeling, environmental effects (aquatic and forest ecosystems, visibility, human health, and others), control technologies, economic measures, and other aspects of transboundary air pollution problems. While both countries have attempted to create the impression they are meeting their commitments here as well,[16] a close reading of the available reports again indicates otherwise.

The governments engaged in adequate if not significant coordination of SO_2 and NO_x emissions data as well as of atmospheric model development, or at least they did up to 1995. There has, however, been little cooperation and little or no coordination on monitoring acidic deposition. The governments have exchanged information but done little or no cooperative research on the effects of acidic deposition on aquatic ecosystems, forest ecosystems, visibility or materials. Canadian and American scientists have done some coordinated and cooperative work on human health effects; the bilateral AQC recognized this work but provided no funding or support. The governments have not cooperated to any significant degree on control technologies or market-based mechanisms, and they report no consultation on mitigative measures.

The most significant commitments the governments have not implemented to any significant degree relate to deposition monitoring and ecosystem effects research.

---

15 Both governments "recognize that nitrogen emissions are an important part of the acidification issue" (Air Quality Committee, 2002, p. 1) and both have called for nitrogen critical loads. At the same time, while claiming to have met targets for emissions from stationary sources, the official reports have little to say about mobile sources (Roberts and Jones, 2003-4), the most troublesome aspect of this problem, and the governments have not explicitly called for further control programs beyond those specified in the AQA.

16 In 1996 their officials concluded that "the level of scientific and technical activities and economic research has been adequate to meet the reporting needs of the Agreement" (Air Quality Committee, 1996). The Parties also found that the Air Quality Committee was fulfilling the objectives of the Agreement because it was meeting annually and publishing biennial reports. That is one measure, to be sure, but at best a rather minimalist one.

Recent American studies have begun to provide a picture of declining acidic deposition in that country (Driscoll, et al., 2001). Canada however has nearly forgotten about acid rain research. It has neglected adequate monitoring of acidic deposition and effects for the past decade, not only a violation of the Air Quality Agreement but also a disregard of the scientific basis needed to assess the environmental response in Canada to emission reductions during the 1980s and 1990s and to assess the extent to which these reductions have accomplished the aims of the 1991 Agreement.

It would likely require another chapter at least to explain fully why the record of implementation of the AQA has been so poor. Suffice it to say, one key factor is government funding cuts in Canada and the United States during the 1990s at both the federal and state/provincial levels that have made the task of implementing the accord more difficult. These budget cuts reflect the low priority afforded to environmental problems in the 1990s.

Ground-Level Ozone and the Air Quality Agreement

Ground-level ozone (not to be confused with stratospheric ozone) is a so-called secondary pollutant that results from the reaction of NO_x and volatile organic compounds (VOCs) in the troposphere, promoted by sunlight and warm temperatures.[17] Ozone (O_3) has been known for decades to have deleterious effects on vegetation and on synthetic materials and textiles. Long-term exposure to ozone is linked to a range of human health problems, particularly asthma and reduced lung function.[18] (The impact of ozone in combination with other pollutants will be discussed later.) Since the previous chapter dealt with this issue at great length, a brief synopsis will fill our needs here.

In December 2000, Canada and the United States signed into effect an "Ozone Annex" to the Air Quality Agreement, with the stated aim of reducing the precursors to ground-level ozone – emissions of NO_x and VOCs.[19] The Annex refers to the

---

17 The term "volatile organic compounds" covers a wide range of carbon-based, highly reactive gases and vapours. VOCs include such normally indoor sources as paints and cleaners and such outdoor sources as fuels (for example, benzene) and dry cleaning establishments.

18 See, for example, the websites of Environment Canada at: http://www.ec.gc.ca/cleanair-airpur/Ground_Level_Ozone-WS590611CA-1_En.htm (accessed December 2005) and the American Lung Association, at: http://www.lungusa.org/site/pp.asp?c=dvLUK9O0E&b=35352 (accessed December 2005).

19 Ozone Annex, Annex III to the Canada-U.S. Air Quality Agreement: http://www.ec.gc.ca/cleanair-airpur/CAOL/air/can_usa_e.html (accessed November 2005). The document signed, formally "the Protocol between the Government of Canada and the Government of the United States of America Amending the "Agreement Between the Government of Canada and the Government of the United States of America on Air Quality," not only added the "Ozone Annex" but also amended the body of the AQA itself to a minor extent. As the events leading up to the agreement on this Annex are the subject of Chapter 3 of this volume, they will not be covered in any detail here. This section of the present chapter will focus on the implementation of the provisions of the Annex.

problem of transboundary ozone but does not specifically proclaim a goal of reducing transboundary flows or ozone concentrations – a weakness the Ozone Annex shares with the AQA provisions regarding acid rain. The Annex identifies and targets a limited binational region – a "Pollution Emission Management Area" (PEMA) – consisting essentially of southern Ontario and Quebec and the eastern United States.

Under the Annex, Canada promised to maintain existing emission control regulations in several areas and bring new regulations into force in others, generally to harmonize Canadian law with existing U.S. standards. With respect to stationary sources, the regulations will limit NO_x emissions from power plants[20] and VOC emissions from dry cleaning. With respect to other emissions, the governments say they will regulate emissions from new vehicles, off-road vehicles and small engines; set sulphur levels in fuels; and promote low-emission vehicles. Canada also promised to establish Canada-Wide Standards (CWS) for ground-level ozone by 2010, involving "a comprehensive, national multi-pollutant emission reduction approach."

The Annex has details, indeed details aplenty, about the laws, regulations, and other measures to be employed, all with the expectation of bringing about reductions of ozone precursors. These long lists of measures are however "subject to modification" – indicating that the governments are not necessarily bound to all of them. More significantly, while the Annex is long with respect to the *hows*, it is utterly silent on specifics regarding the *whats* and *whens*. In other words, despite the stated aim of reducing precursor emissions and the abundance of tactics, the governments set themselves no hard and fast *targets* to reduce overall NO_x and VOC emissions by specified amounts and, of course, no firm *timetables* or deadlines for achieving these cuts. In this respect, the Ozone Annex falls well short of the AQA's SO_2 control provisions.[21]

The only specifics in the Annex about future emission reductions are expressly provided "for illustrative purposes only." Lest there be any lingering uncertainty as to their status, these targets are mentioned in a section entitled "indicative reductions." And, for Canada, even such "indicative" and "illustrative" reductions are subject to "comparable United States reductions." In other words, if the United States does not reduce its emissions, Canada is off a hook that was but an "illustrative" one in the first place. The governments say they expect tropospheric ozone concentrations will not exceed either Canadian or United States ambient air quality standards, at

20 According to the Canadian government news release announcing the Annex, the measures described therein are expected to achieve a 35 percent decrease in overall summertime NO_x emissions in the U.S. (including a 70 percent drop in power plant NO_x emissions) by 2007 and a 44 percent decrease in Canadian emissions by 2010 (Environment Canada, 2000).

21 The Annex did set (separate) caps on emissions from fossil fuel power plants in the Ontario and Quebec parts of the PEMA. Given that plants in both provinces were well above those limits in 2004 (Air Quality Committee, 2004), they seem unlikely to meet their 2007 deadline.

some undefined point, but simultaneously qualify this near-promise as a "long term" (i.e., completely open) one involving a "stepwise" process subject to "scientific advances."

The Ozone Annex, in short, is not a statement of commitments to achieve emission cuts let alone to reduce transboundary flows or to effect environmental improvements. It is a highly qualified promissory note – an agreement on actions to be taken not on results to be achieved.

Bilateral implementation of the Ozone Annex since 2000 gives little reason for a more positive appraisal. The 2002 biennial AQA report notes "progress in meeting all of the commitments included in the Ozone Annex" (Air Quality Committee, 2002), but that phrasing evidently does not mean any commitments themselves had actually been met. The governments reported "progress" on vehicle and engine emissions standards and on fuel sulphur content regulations, but no agreement on power plant emissions. The 2004 report states both countries took further specific measures dealing with VOCs and NO_x and they expect these to reduce ozone in the future. Beyond that, the reports point to no significant achievements.

The Canadian government neglected, perhaps, to mention (in either the 2002 or 2004 biennial reports) that it had failed to provide data on ambient ozone levels – as required in the Ozone Annex. Canadian scientists were in 2006 still establishing baseline ozone concentrations for the most affected areas, and therefore had not yet begun to assess the impact emission reductions might have – a task that itself necessarily precedes making recommendations about new control regulations.

Particulate Matter and Transboundary Air Quality

Particulate matter is the emerging issue in Canada-United States air quality relations in the early 21st century. Particulate matter (PM) comprises airborne particles in both solid and liquid form. It can be a primary air pollutant, when the particles are released directly from sources such as coal-burning power plants, or a secondary pollutant, since sulphate, nitrate and ammonia particulates are created by gaseous SO_2, NO_x and ammonia reacting in the atmosphere.[22] These gases along with volatile organic compounds (VOCs) are the principal sources. What is colloquially known as "smog" results from the combination of ground-level ozone and particulate matter.

Particulate matter is not merely an air quality problem but also "an important [human] health concern" (AQC, Subcommittee on Scientific Cooperation, 2004).[23] Long-term exposure can cause serious cardio-respiratory disorders, especially exposure to the finer $PM_{2.5}$ (that is, airborne matter smaller than 2.5 micrometres). Particulate matter and smog can both lead to respiratory conditions including

22 Environment Canada website: www.ec.gc.ca/cleanair-airpur/defaultasp?lang=En&n=2C8B45C-0 (accessed December 2005).

23 The connection between air pollution and human health is one that has been debated for decades at least. The pioneering research in Canada was Bates and Sitzo (1983), a study, controversial in its time, but one that more recent research has basically confirmed.

asthma, emphysema, and chronic obstructive pulmonary disease as well as to cardiovascular and neurological conditions. The elderly and young children are particularly vulnerable. Health Canada currently estimates that every year almost 6000 Canadians in eight major cities alone die prematurely due to complications resulting from particulate and other air pollutants. Estimates of U.S. fatalities are far higher. Air pollution incidents also measurably increase hospital admissions and thus health costs.[24] To put a human face on these statistics, Prime Minister Stephen Harper, who briefly checked into hospital shortly after his election victory in January 2006, describes himself as a "life-long sufferer from asthma."

The atmospheric chemistry of particulates is much more complex than that of acid rain but the two have definite similarities in terms of sources and transport. Both, along with ozone, involve long-range transport and transboundary flows. The major sources of $PM_{2.5}$ are motor vehicles (particularly diesel) and coal-fired power stations, road dust and, on a periodic basis, forest fires. Total American emissions of particulate matter precursors are, generally speaking, approximately ten times Canadian emissions, reflecting differences in population and industrial output. The major exceptions are SO_2 and VOCs where Canadian emissions are higher in relative terms though still much smaller than American emissions (Environment Canada, 2001). Overall, Canadian anthropogenic sources contribute about 10-15 percent of all North American emissions. There is some seasonal variation in emissions, particularly for VOCs, which are much higher in summer. Back trajectories of major particulate matter episodes in eastern Canada demonstrate that these episodes typically originate in the midwestern United States.

Ongoing collaboration under the AQA, particularly a 1998 joint work plan, led to a bilateral scientific assessment of particulate matter (AQC Subcommittee on Scientific Cooperation, 2004) – an effort to "synthesize the current state of knowledge" on the problem. Briefly, the assessment concluded particulate matter was indeed a "problem" in the border regions. $PM_{2.5}$ levels in the eastern half of the continent exceeded existing standards in both countries. (Particulate levels were much lower in the western parts of both.) At most eastern Canada sites exceeding the existing national standards, the $PM_{2.5}$ concentrations were measurably greater as a result of air flow from unidentified "sources south of this region"; in Toronto, local production of particulates contributed about one-third of the total levels. The scientists also estimated that Canadian sources accounted for some (about 13 percent) of $PM_{2.5}$ at several U.S. sites.

The 2004 assessment acknowledges that present and planned Canadian and American air quality regulations would result, at most, in modest annual reductions of particulate matter precursors by 2020. Such emission reductions, however, would not bring ambient concentrations into line even with current, let alone more

24 For background, see Health Canada – Environment Canada (1998).

stringent, air quality standards. The experts suggest further cuts in sulphur dioxide (SO_2) emissions are the best option for reducing harmful $PM_{2.5}$.[25]

As of early 2006, the two governments had made no decision to develop a new particulate matter annex to the AQA. The virtual absence of discussion about transboundary air quality during the 2005-2006 Canadian election campaign indicated well the astonishingly low public profile of the health threat posed by particulate matter. On the other hand, Washington began taking national action in 2005.

After Congress stalled President George W. Bush's much criticized "Clear Skies" proposal to revamp – some said gut – the U.S. Clean Air Act, the EPA moved to strengthen and extend America's air pollution regulations by unveiling the Clean Air Interstate Rule (CAIR), a regional program to reduce ozone and particulate matter. The regulations will require 28 states east of the Mississippi to reduce power plant emissions of NO_x and SO_2 – two of the prime precursors of particulates. First issued in March 2005, the CAIR took effect in early 2006, but the mandated reductions will not be fully realized until 2015.

The CAIR employs the "cap-and-trade" system pioneered by the acid rain provisions of the 1990 CAA. The EPA will cap emissions and allocate allowances on a state-wide basis. The states will then develop a reduction plan and allocate the allowances to utilities. A utility that has reduced its emissions may sell or trade credits to another utility. By 2015, EPA expects emissions of NO_x will be cut by 60 percent compared to 2003 levels and emissions of SO_2 more than 70 percent.

The EPA anticipates substantial benefits from these reductions in terms of human heath and reduced medical costs. The Agency calculated that by 2015 the CAIR would significantly reduce asthma cases and premature deaths and save Americans up to $100 billion annually in health costs. Since the CAIR's focus is on SO_2 and NO_x, an added benefit will be reducing acid rain in the northeastern U.S. – and thus in eastern Canada.

While *The New York Times* described the CAIR as "one of [the Agency's] most ambitious efforts to control soot and ground-level ozone" (Janofsky, 2005), it is none the less not a radical proposal. That much is clear by the responses it generated. The politically powerful utility industry, one that vigorously defends its interests, praised the initiative. On the other hand, some American environmental groups criticized it, as did the American Lung Association. The CAIR "is better than Clear Skies," said John M. Stanton, a lawyer for Clear The Air, "but not as good as it could be. Tens of millions of people will still be breathing dirty air" (Depalma, 2005). Some of those millions, of course, will be Canadians, although this fact received no attention in the American media and little in the Canadian media.

---

25 Earlier reports by and for government governments have indicated a need to reduce SO_2 and NO_x emissions further in order to prevent further acidification (Environment Canada, 1997; Canada, 1997).

The government of Canada meanwhile had announced no similar program as of early 2006. Ottawa's strategy seems to be to wait, patiently and uncritically, for American cuts to deal with the particulate matter problem.

Summarizing the Issues, Applying the Model

On each of the three bilateral air quality issues discussed here – acid rain, ozone and particulate matter – Canada finds itself in a position of environmental dependence. The quality of the Canadian environment, as well as the human health of Canadians, is endangered by transboundary pollution, by pollutants originating outside Canada's territorial control, as well as by domestic emissions and often *more than* by domestic emissions. In each case, given the nature and extent of transboundary flows of pollutants, the level of dependence is high. While there is in each a modest degree of environmental *inter*dependence, the transboundary flows are much more asymmetrical than symmetrical. Canada is thus generally the "downstream" state.

In each case, unilateral "domestic" control actions by Canada would be insufficient to deal with the environmental problem, and thus ineffective by themselves. There is, moreover, no provision in international environmental law comparable to the right of retaliation in international trade law and practice. Canada's traditional stance in bilateral ecopolitics has been that of the *demandeur*, to seek reductions in the transboundary flows of pollutants. As predicted by the environmental dependence model, Canada thus sought a new international environmental regime to deal with acid rain during the 1980s, negotiated for the inclusion of tropospheric ozone within that regime in the 1990s, and is pursuing a bilateral approach on the particulate matter problem, albeit quietly. The United States, less environmentally dependent on Canada than vice versa, was initially unresponsive on acid rain and slower to act. After Washington eventually agreed to negotiate what became the 1991 Air Quality Agreement, the two countries produced a limited regime that failed to meet vital Canadian demands. Since then, they have at best unsteadily implemented the regime's acid rain commitments. The 2000 Ozone annex created few commitments, lacked firm targets and timetables, and has been unhurried in implementation, again as predicted by the environmental dependence model.

One difference between the acid rain years of the 1980s and the more recent efforts to deal with ozone and particulate matter has been a striking lack of conflict in the past decade of the sort marking the acid rain case. Far from reflecting the problem-solving, "quiet diplomacy" approach in Canadian-American relations, acid rain was *not* resolved, was politically high profile, and was often handled noisily through the 1980s.[26] In contrast, Canada's bilateral approach on ozone and particulate matter has been much closer to the classic "quiet diplomacy" model. Why? If Canada is environmentally dependent with respect to ozone and particulate matter as well as

26 The sometimes strong rhetoric used shows also that Canada's politicians rarely get themselves into domestic political hot water by criticizing an American impact on Canada. This fact is one of the domestic consequences of dependence.

acid rain, should we not expect Canadian governments, both federal and provincial, to define and pursue their interests in the same manner?

As suggested earlier, however, environmental dependence in bilateral relations does not automatically lead to conflicting interests and agendas. States (and provinces) do not always construct their interests giving priority to environmental issues; sometimes they are unaware of, or simply inattentive to, environmental problems even where they are the dependent one. The latter has been the case here. Neither the Canadian federal government nor the provinces, especially Ontario, have been affording high priority to the environment since the mid-1990s. Indeed, environmental agencies have been cut drastically, and no more so than with respect to environmental monitoring. On the other hand, while the United States, as the "upstream" state, was not worried excessively about transboundary flows into Canada, it was at least somewhat concerned about the domestic impact of its own emissions. Washington's current attention to tropospheric ozone and particulate matter thus stem from pursuit of its own self interests rather than from concerns about the impact its emissions have on its neighbour. The Canada government evidently has been satisfied with the present slow pace of action, perhaps assuming that American policies are moving matters in the right direction and perhaps calculating that progress toward these ends is at least as good as would be achieved by a more outspoken, assertive stance.

The environmental dependence model can also help explain Canada's policy on other bilateral environmental issues – its pursuit of the Great Lakes Water Quality Agreement in the 1970s (Munton, 1980-81), its opposition to the Garrison Diversion Project (Nossal, 1978), and its current concerns about potential water diversions from Devil's Lake, North Dakota (mentioned in Chapter 1). The model also provides insights into the pressures the United States placed on Canada to reduce air pollution from the Trail smelter in the 1930s, and into why Washington sought an agreement in the 1980s with Mexico on emissions of SO_2 from Mexican smelters, at the same time it was rebuffing Canadian pleas to deal with transboundary acid rain.[27] It also helps explain why acid rain was such a deeply divisive national issue within the United States, and why it pitted midwestern states with their high sulphur coals and large coal-fired power plants against the northeastern states that, like eastern Canada, were recipients of much of the SO_2 produced in the midwest and, again like Canada, had significant areas sensitive to acidic deposition.[28] Environmental dependence also certainly helps explain why it was the Scandinavian states that initially pushed the acid rain issue in the European context during the 1970s and

27 "Agreement of Cooperation between the United States of America and the United Mexican States Regarding Transboundary Air Pollution Caused by Copper Smelters on their Common Border", (Annex IV to the Agreement between the USA and Mexico on Cooperation for the Protection and Improvement of the Environment in the Border Area). Washington, 29 January 1987. The document was carefully worded so as not to contradict U.S. Administration positions on the "uncertainties" of long-range transport; instead, it focuses on environmental problems "along the common border".

28 While this political split was foremost in the domestic politics of acid rain in the United States, there were also other contributing factors (Munton, 1983).

1980s, as well as why the United Kingdom was a key opponent. Furthermore, to the extent that environmental and other types of dependence are common features not only of Canadian-American relations but of international and global politics, the model may prove more broadly useful.

Conclusion

Prior to the 1990 passage of the U.S. Clean Air Act and the negotiation of the Canada-United States Air Quality Agreement in 1991, acid rain was the dominant issue and a major conflict in Canada-United States environmental relations. Even though the SO_2 cuts mandated in both countries by 1990 were regarded by many as but a first step toward solving the acid rain problem, the issue largely fell off the bilateral agenda during the following decade. The transboundary ground-level ozone problem has been garnering more attention and, more recently, particulate matter is struggling to get onto the agenda. Conflict, however, has given way to quiet diplomacy rather than open disagreement on ozone and particulate matter, and to bureaucratization rather than politicization.

The conflict during the 1980s on transboundary air quality issues can be explained by the environmental dependence model, developed here, as can the inconsistent implementation of the 1991 Air Quality Agreement. The lack of a strenuous effort by Canada since the mid-1990s to deal bilaterally with ozone and particulate matter, despite its position of environmental dependence with respect to these problems, seems to be due to the lack of priority afforded them both by the government, its ministers and senior officials. Despite the switch in tone, the record of success on ozone and particulate matter seems no better and if anything more questionable than that for acid rain. *Plus ça change …*

Chapter 5

Canadian-U.S. Cooperation: Regional Climate Change Action in the Northeast

Henrik Selin and Stacy D. VanDeveer

Introduction

Climate change policy developments are expanding in North America.[1] Many of the most innovative of these policy efforts to combat climate change are taking place at regional and local levels. Several U.S. states and Canadian provinces are forging ahead with climate change action beyond requirements mandated by federal governments (Rabe, 2004; Pew Center on Global Climate Change, 2004; NECC, 2005). The most ambitious regional effort is under development in the northeast by the six New England states (Maine, New Hampshire, Vermont, Massachusetts, Rhode Island, and Connecticut) and five Eastern Canadian provinces (Nova Scotia, Newfoundland and Labrador, Prince Edward Island, New Brunswick, and Quebec). Public and civil society actors across these eleven states and provinces argue that addressing climate change at a regional level offers several advantages over individual state and provincial action. This case of regional climate change policy development is part of growing state-provincial environmental policy interaction (Tomblin and Colgan, 2004; VanNijnatten, 2003; chapters in this volume by VanNijnatten, Schwartz, Sanders and Stoett, and Boardman).

The New England Governors (NEG) and the Eastern Canadian Premiers (ECP) adopted a joint Climate Change Action Plan in August 2001 (NEGECP, 2001). Under this plan, states and provinces commit to reduce GHG emissions to 1990 levels by 2010, 10 percent below 1990 levels by 2020. The long-term goal is to decrease emissions to levels that do not pose a threat to the climate (no identified date). This would require a 75-85 percent reduction from 2001 emission levels, according to an official estimate (NEGECP, 2001). In addition, the plan contains action steps and policy recommendations of varying degrees of specificity toward the fulfilment of identified emission reduction targets and successful climate change adaptation.

1 Research for this chapter was supported by the Knut and Alice Wallenberg Foundation, the Department of Political Science, University of New Hampshire, and Boston University. Valuable research assistance was provided by John Shea and Katlyn Stillings. We also thank the many individuals in the United States and Canada who have allowed us to interview them as part of our research.

States and provinces are currently working to develop and implement more detailed state and provincial level policies in support of the regional goals.

This chapter analyzes regional NEG-ECP climate change action. In doing so, we draw on insights from the literature on transgovernmentalism and transnational relations as we focus on issues of regionalism. We begin by identifying regional contributions to and vulnerabilities of climate change. Next, we characterize regionalism and regional cooperation and institutions for climate change action. This is followed by an outline of regional climate policy and implementation. We continue with a discussion of the impetus for regional climate change action, focusing on three factors driving policy-making and implementation. Following this, we assess regional policy development to date using three perspectives. We conclude with brief comments on existing policy progress and its role in a federal and trans-national North American context.

This study is informed by reviews of official regional and state/provincial documents, as well as reports and other written material produced by research institutions, public stakeholder organizations, and political leaders in the region. In addition, we have conducted interviews with numerous officials, civil servants and NGO staff members working on the regional climate change action plan and its implementation. Lastly, we observed meetings related to regional and state/provincial level climate change issues and policy action.

Regional Emissions and Vulnerability

The regional political and ecological appropriateness and potential of climate change action in northeastern North America was noted several years before it was launched (Moomaw, 1992). There is a long history of political and economic cooperation and integration across the U.S.-Canadian border and the region contributes approximately $700 billion (USD) in gross internal product to the U.S. and Canadian economies (NEGECP, 2001a: 14). In federal political systems such as Canada and the United States, moreover, provinces and states can have significant ability to influence regulations and behaviour important to the release of greenhouse gas (GHG) emissions (Rabe, 2004; Macdonald and Smith, 1999-2000). The northeastern region, home to over 23 million people, would rank as the world's 13th largest economy if it were a single country (Hamel, 2003).

Only ten industrialized countries submitting emissions data under the United Nations Framework Convention on Climate Change emitted more GHG than the Northeast region in 2000 (NESCAUM, 2004). Some states and provinces emit GHG emissions equal to the amount of some countries. For example, Massachusetts with a population of 6.4 million emits GHG emissions roughly equal those of Austria (population 8 million), Greece (population 11 million), or Egypt (population 69 million) (Hamel, 2003). Moreover, between 1990 and 2000, regional GHG emissions increased from 332 to 367 million metric tonnes of CO_2 equivalent (NESCAUM,

2004). This increase, however, is less than the total national increase in both the United States (14.8 percent) and Canada (20.1 percent).

Because of recent emission increases, the NEG-ECP region must reduce GHG emissions by over 9 percent from 2000 levels simply to reach the 2010 target. Public officials and environmental activists frequently cite the fact that the region is a major contributor to global GHG emissions as a justification for action – there is seen to be a responsibility to act. A regional GHG emission inventory shows that approximately 84 percent of emissions come from burning of fossil fuels for transportation, electricity and heat (NESCAUM, 2004). The single most important regional source, by far, is transportation, which is more than double the second largest source, which is utility generation.

However, emissions from utility generation vary widely across states and provinces. For example, Quebec and Vermont rely heavily on hydro power and have few GHG emissions from utility generation. In contrast, utility generation is a major source in New Brunswick, Nova Scotia and New Hampshire (NEGECP, 2001a). Differing emissions profiles and economic bases between states and provinces make a "one policy fits all" solution less efficient and effective. As such, joint emission reduction targets coupled with a flexible menu of policy options intended to meet the goals allow each jurisdiction to choose policy actions most suitable to its circumstances and institutions.

Table 5.1 Population and Emissions within the NEG-ECP region (NESCAUM, 2004)

Region	Population (million)	Emissions 1990 (MMT CO_2 eq.)	Emissions 2000 (MMT CO_2 eq.)	Per Capita Emissions (MMT CO_2 eq.)
New England	13.9	199.88	224.01	16.11
Eastern Canada	9.8	132.70	143.51	14.64

Knowledge about regional climate change vulnerabilities has grown in recent years even though much about the specific effects of a changing climate is uncertain. A central climate related issue for the region could be changes in the timing of seasonal changes such as later frosts and earlier snowmelts in the spring, having both potential ecological and social ramifications (NEGECP, 2001a). Annual average temperatures in the region over the last 100 years have risen by two degrees Celsius with temperature increases most pronounced during the winter months (NAST, 2000: 40-1). Sea level rise could affect sensitive areas of coastal wetlands, salt marshes, sandy shorelines, and low and barrier islands, as well as increase the risks and impacts of storm surges.

Natural resource-based activities relating to fishing, forestry and agriculture are of regional economic importance and also have symbolic statuses that go beyond their economic value (NEGECP, 2001a). A warming climate could initially be positive for the growth in forests and result in a northward migration of tree species, but a changing and more variable climate may result in increased stress on regional biodiversity. A warming trend could result in a longer growing season, although possible changes such as later springs and early frosts may have negative effects on planting and harvesting. A warmer climate may also result in changes and increases of pests damaging to crops.

Coastal erosion and possible changes in the migration of fish species could affect people directly and indirectly connected to the fishing and sea food industry. Reductions in sea ice due to a warmer climate could benefit marine transportation and offshore gas and oil drilling in Atlantic Canada. Winter tourism and foliage tourism could be adversely affected by a warmer climate and changing seasons. In contrast, longer and warmer summers could make lakes and beaches more desirable, although coastal erosion from sea level rise and winter storms could have negative effects on coastal areas.

Lastly, a warming climate could lead to an increased frequency of tropical and sub-tropical diseases. Also, melting of permafrost in Arctic Quebec would adversely affect the traditional life styles of indigenous Inuit populations who rely on permafrost for hunting and fishing activities (ACIA, 2004; Huebert, this volume).

Regionalism and Institutions

Regional climate change cooperation in northeastern North America involves both transgovernmentalism and transnational relations (see Stoett and Le Prestre, this volume). Transgovernmentalism, direct interaction between agencies and governmental subunits acting autonomously from their central governments, is a central driver of regional climate change action as U.S. states and Canadian provinces develop joint goals and action plans ahead of what is mandated by the federal governments in Washington D.C. and Ottawa. Regional policy development moreover includes a large number of nongovernmental actors from, for example, regional research institutions and environmental NGOs. As such, regional climate action displays dynamic transnational relations, as well.

Traditionally, scholars of political science, international relations and economics have relied primarily on a combination of geography, administrative designations, and economic factors such as trade patterns, currency use, and/or capital or labour flows to define regions (Lauson, 2003; Vayrynen, 2003). In contrast, "new regionalism" scholarship focuses on more complex combinations of political, economic, social and cultural factors to define regions (Mittelman, 2000; Vayrynen, 2003; Tomblin and Colgan, 2004). This new regionalism includes interactions among "(1) ideas and their ties to institutions, (2) systems of production, (3) labor supply, and (4) socio-cultural institutions, all undergirded by power relations" (Mittelman, 2000: 111-2).

From this perspective stressing the social construction of regions, regionalism occurs at various levels (or scales), from a macro-level (often continental scale) to much smaller geographic areas. Different regions vary greatly with respect to the extent that constituting interactions involve shared decision-making organizations, identities, traditions, civil societies and so on. Moreover, there can be regions within regions. For example, "North America" denotes a large commonly recognized region, even as it simultaneously incorporates numerous geographically smaller regional areas such as "New England" and the Canadian "Maritimes" – two regions with which many people identify.

While regional identities such as that of New England and the Maritimes have broad political, social and cultural salience, the NEG-ECP region is clearly more administrative in origin, being defined primarily in terms of state and provincial membership in a transborder political organization. Nevertheless, factors such as the NEG-ECP region's long-standing and deepening economic integration and cross border interactions of all kinds, together with the common position of New England and eastern Canada as "downstream" receivers of continental air pollution of many kinds, offer multiple justifications that underpin the social construction of the NEG-ECP region.

In addition, administrative designations of "regionness" such as that promulgated by NEG-ECP cooperation also serve, over time, to influence the construction of regional connections and identity. For example, scientific and technical communities produce regional scale images and knowledge of particular aspects of the environment, economy, and society, including those depicting (or mapping) things like "regional" GHG emissions, pollution transport and deposition patterns, power grid structures, trade and investments trends, transportation of goods, and tourism (VanDeveer, 2004). These images and such knowledge help frame public and political understandings and debates in regional terms.

Groups of scientific and technical experts also design and build integrated regional environmental assessment models and regional monitoring and data gathering and interpretations systems. For these models and systems to have meaning, they must be embedded within professional communities and networks of individuals and organizations with shared understandings about scientific and technical research and its products. Scientific and technical assessment such as those related to climate change plays a large role in the creation of regional identity because it is a major source of knowledge about "regional level" environmental and anthropogenic interactions (VanDeveer, 2004).

Civil society actors such as major environmental NGOs also influence the stabilization of regional institutions and identities – in part by incorporating information produced by regional scientific bodies into their policy advocacy and public awareness campaigns. As will be illustrated below, a host of regional networks and communities of public, private and civil society are active and influential on climate change action.

Regional Institutions and Climate Change

Constructing institutional capacities needed for climate change action poses significant challenges to contemporary societies (Williams and Baumert, 2003). Climate change action in the Northeast is embedded in existing institutions and a larger, long-standing process of regional cooperation and integration. The New England Governors began holding annual meetings in 1937. In 1973, cooperation was expanded to include the five Eastern Canadian provinces. The New England Governors and Eastern Canadian Premiers work to coordinate policy, develop programs on cross-boundary issues, and to promote regional integration. The Governors and Premiers formulate policy goals in the form of voluntary agreements and action plans. Regional cooperation currently covers issues of economic development, transportation, energy, environment, and human health. Since 2000, climate change action has become important in NEG-ECP cooperation.

NEG-ECP activities are coordinated through the small Secretariat of the New England Governors' Conference, located in Boston, Massachusetts.[2] One full-time staff member works on environmental issues. The Secretariat prepares and issues progress reports. In Canada, the Council of Atlantic Premiers acts as a Canadian clearing house.[3] Issues are addressed in working groups and steering committees made up of employees from Governor/Premier offices and state/provincial administrative agencies. Proposals are worked out in these sub-groups, principally on the basis of consensus. As such, disagreements generally do not rise to the annual meetings of the Governors and Premiers, but are addressed beforehand by their staff members.

NEG-ECP addresses environmental issues through its Environment Committee, which is comprised of the commissioners of the state/provincial departments of environmental protection. Over the last decade, NEG-ECP environmental cooperation focused on acid rain, ground level ozone, mercury pollution and climate change issues. NEG-ECP climate change abatement increasingly necessitates participation and collaboration with the region's energy and transport officials (and the NEG-ECP energy and transport working groups). As such, NEG-ECP climate change efforts offer expanded opportunities for data gathering, knowledge sharing and the development of more effective policy responses than could be achieved by each individual state and province.

NEG-ECP staff works closely with the New England Regional Office of the U.S. Environmental Protection Agency and with officials from Environment Canada. Staff members at federal environmental agencies are generally encouraging and aid NEG-ECP activities through limited financial support and more extensive in-kind support by contributions of expertise and staff-time to, for example, draw up action plans, prepare reports and highlight successful pilot programs. However, federal agencies are often cautious in their support for regional goals that exceed those of

---

2 For more on the New England Governors' Conference, see www.negc.org.

3 For more on the Council of Atlantic Premiers, see www.cap-cpma.ca.

federal policy; they generally do not fund programs premised on regional goals that exceed national rules and regulations.

In addition, regional climate change activities involve environmental and business organizations from Canada and the United States. These groups often supply NEG-ECP staff with information and contact them for updates on regional activities and goals, but the regional organization is not the primary focus of either environmental or private sector lobbying.[4] Instead, most such efforts are directed at influencing state/provincial policy. Nevertheless, a host of environmental NGOs have institutionalized regional collaboration and advocacy work on the U.S. side of the border under the umbrella of the New England Climate Coalition. Groups within this coalition work with their Canadian counterparts, including Sierra Club and Lung Association chapters.

Institutionalizing Regional Climate Change Action

When the development of the NEG-ECP Climate Change Action Plan began in 2000, Canada had not yet ratified the Kyoto Protocol, which it did in 2002. The Bush Administration publicly renounced the Kyoto Protocol in the spring of 2001, just a few months before the regional plan was finalized. As such, the regional action plan and its goals largely outpaced national efforts in both countries when it was adopted. NEG-ECP climate change action continues to be at the North American policy frontier.

The Action Plan

In developing the regional climate change action plan, NEG-ECP participants relied extensively on existing cooperative institutions, particularly the connections and experience generated by earlier NEG-ECP action around acid rain and mercury abatement.[5] Based on a proposal by New Brunswick, NEG-ECP representatives met in Fredericton, New Brunswick, in March of 2001. This workshop focused on assessments of existing and potential impacts of a changing climate in the region and discussed preferred areas for joint policy action (NEGECP, 2001a). Based on the results from this workshop and intense discussions among state and provincial staff, the New England Governors and the Eastern Canadian Premiers adopted the Climate Change Action Plan at their twenty-sixth meeting in August of 2001.

Naturally, the plan's adoption occasioned many comments by the region's political leaders. Many of the region's governors and premiers noted their hope that the plan would encourage other policymakers to become more active and aggressive on climate change action. Premier Bernard Lord, New Brunswick, noted that "[w]e need to show that we are leaders in our own jurisdictions, in our own region. But as we lead the way, we need to pull others along with us, including our respective

4 Interviews with NEG-ECP participants, March-November, 2003.

5 Interviews with NEG-ECP participants, March-November, 2003.

federal governments in Ottawa and in Washington." Governor Jeanne Shaheen, New Hampshire, added, "This agreement sends a powerful message to the rest of the nation about the importance of working cooperatively to cut pollution and clean up the air."[6]

An action plan is only as effective as its implementation. Also adopted at the NEG-ECP 2001 meeting was Resolution 26-4. This resolution directed the NEG-ECP Environment and Energy Committees to "form a Task Force of energy, environmental and other appropriate officials from state and provincial agencies to develop specific strategies and oversee and coordinate the implementation of the Climate Change Action Plan" at state/provincial levels. The subsequent task force, the Climate Change Steering Committee, is made up of state and provincial civil servants and prepares reports and some recommendations for the governors and premiers. In addition, the Climate Change Steering Committee in effect sustains the regional network of climate change related civil servants.

The regional plan identifies several action steps for emission reductions and climate adaptation (NEGECP, 2001). Regional cooperation is directed toward state and provincial economies through "no regrets" measures, i.e. measures that both reduce energy use/costs and GHG emissions. These include measures to reduce GHG emissions through shifting to lower carbon energy sources and implementing actions that result in higher efficiency in the transportation of passengers and goods. In addition, regional efforts should aid states and provinces to adapt to an already changing climate and to take advantage of any benefits that might come from these changes.

The regional plan outlines three emission reductions targets. In the short term, states and provinces pledge to reduce regional GHG emissions to 1990 levels by 2010. The medium term target calls for reductions in regional GHG emissions by 10 percent below 1990 levels by 2020. These targets are less ambitious than Canadian and U.S. commitments under the Kyoto Protocol of 6 percent and 7 percent reductions (respectively) from 1990 levels by 2008-12 (because the United States has not ratified the Kyoto Protocol it is not subject to any international reduction commitments). The long-term NEG-ECP target, for which there is no set date, calls for regional emissions reductions that are sufficient to eliminate dangerous threats to the climate.

As a means for fulfilling set emission reduction targets and taking appropriate mitigating action, the regional plan outlines nine major general action steps:

1. Establish a regional standardized GHG emissions inventory,
2. Establish a plan for reducing GHG emissions and conserving energy,
3. Promote public awareness,
4. State and provincial governments to lead by example,

6 Citations from governors and premiers were taken from the NEGC web site, June 2003: www.negc.org.

5. Reduce greenhouse gases from the electricity sector,
6. Reduce total energy demand through conservation,
7. Reduce and/or adapt to negative social, economic, and environmental impacts of climate change,
8. Decrease the transportation sector's growth in GHG emissions,
9. Create a regional emissions registry and explore a trading mechanism.

To specify and illustrate policies pursuant to the implementation of these nine action steps, the plan contains in total 34 more specific recommendations for policy action for the participating states and provinces. Some of these action steps and their associated recommendations involve building shared institutions for regional policy-making and implementation review. Others call for continued policy-making efforts by states and provinces in support of the regional policy goals (including emission reduction targets). Finally, the plan contains provisions for outreach to private and public groups and the promotion of public awareness.

Initial Implementation

In the first four years after the adoption of the 2001 NEG-ECP plan, public sector actors largely have focused on two sets of implementation tasks: institution building and the launching of relatively small-scale abatement programs. New cooperative institutions at the regional and state/provincial level to enact, support and monitor the implementation of the NEG-ECP goals had to be established. For example, states and provinces generally lacked the ability to carefully assess and track their annual GHG emissions, and most did not possess extensive legal authority to regulate GHG emissions before the regional plan was adopted.

The NEG-ECP Environment and Energy Committees supervise regional policy development and implementation. Operating under these committees is the Climate Change Steering Committee, which meets several times each year and is charged with working toward implementation of the action plan. For example, in 2005, the Environment and Energy Committees were tasked with producing an Energy Efficiency and Renewable Energy Strategy for review at the 2006 NEG-ECP meeting. In addition, human, financial and technical contributions are provided by Environment Canada, the U.S. Environmental Protection Agency, the Northeast States for Coordinated Air Management (NESCAUM), Ouranos and other non-jurisdictional agencies (NEGECP, 2003). These organizations help to produce data and create and disseminate information about pilot programs, "best practices" and "success stories."

A major regional short-term policy goal is the development of a joint GHG inventory (NESCAUM, 2004). Such a regional inventory is seen as a necessity for taking additional effective and measurable policy actions to reduce GHG emissions. Development of the regional inventory is being led by NESCAUM. The effort seeks to harmonize the reporting and calculation of GHG emissions across the region, and serve as a foundation for both a regional emissions registry and a possible emissions permit trading scheme, for which there seems to be growing regional support (Aulisi et al., 2005).

NEG-ECP officials are sponsoring a university outreach program. The program seeks to challenge universities to initiate climate action measures of their own and increase climate-related research and education efforts on campuses. To date, over 110 colleges and universities have signed onto the program (NEGECP, 2004). While most of their universities are on the U.S. side of the border, a number of Canadian ones also participate in the programs. Consistent with the idea of "leading by example," universities are encouraged to complete and release GHG emission inventories, to stabilize and reduce their GHG emissions, and share their experiences with each other and with public officials, NGOs and citizens.

State/provincial level efforts and accomplishments vary substantially (NECC, 2003, 2004, 2005). Connecticut was the first U.S. state to enact global warming legislation (albeit quite vague) in 1990 (Moomaw, 1992). In 2003, Maine became the first New England state to write the NEG goals into its state law, mandating that government agencies work together to achieve the NEG-ECP's target reductions for 2010 and 2020. In 2004, Connecticut passed similar legislation. Bills addressing CO_2 emissions reductions were under discussion in 2004-05 in a number of the region's legislatures, including Connecticut, Rhode Island and Massachusetts. Four states have issued state-level climate change action plans designed to achieve NEG-ECP goals (Connecticut, Rhode Island, Maine and Massachusetts). Important progress can be noted, for example, in efforts to reduce CO_2 emissions from power plants in Connecticut, New Hampshire and Massachusetts.

Among the Eastern Canadian provinces, Newfoundland and Labrador was first to develop a provincial action plan, followed by New Brunswick. Several other provinces have issued climate discussion papers and launched stakeholder dialogues about possible measures. In general, the Canadian provinces have spent more public resources on programs designed to raise public awareness than have the U.S. states. Yet, the provinces have promulgated fewer specific provincial climate change regulations than many of the U.S. states (Rabe, 2004a, 2005). Canadian federal authorities, however, launched a national "One-tonne Challenge" campaign in 2004 to raise public awareness about GHG emissions and promote ways that individuals and households might reduce these.

Much climate change policy development in the region to date has focused on so-called "no-regrets" measures. Such projects include the use of more efficient light emitting diodes (LEDs) in traffic lights, promoting the purchase of Energy Star products in state and provincial governments, and switching to more energy efficient vehicles in the vehicle fleets of state and provincial governments. State officials cite public and private estimates of potential savings in terms of energy used, CO_2 emitted, and costs reduced of the many smaller programs in various stages of development and implementation. Such programs can save state and local officials millions of dollars annually (Hamel, 2003).

In addition to the growing activity at regional and state/provincial levels, many municipalities throughout the region are developing climate related policies. This action is not formally linked to the regional plan, but is driven by grassroots movements and strong local political leadership. Some cities in the region were participating in the Cities for Climate Protection campaign, sponsored by the International Council for Local Environmental Initiatives (ICLEI), before regional action began (Betsill, 2001; Bulkeley and Betsill, 2003).[7] State and provincial level officials are generally supportive of municipal action, which could greatly contribute towards the fulfilment of several regional goals, including increasing public awareness and stimulating changes in citizens' behaviour on energy use and transportation.

Another related effort, the Regional Greenhouse Gas Initiative (RGGI), remains in development. RGGI involves states from Maryland to Maine that seek to develop a cap-and-trade system for emissions from power generating facilities. Participants in RGGI hope to achieve agreement on a proposed "model rule" to guide this market for pollution permits by June of 2006.[8] In late 2005, while much had been agreed between state officials, outstanding differences remained. Along the West Coast, officials from California, Oregon and Washington are working to establish joint goals for GHG mitigation as part of a global warming initiative launched in 2003.

Driving Regional Climate Change Action

The NEG-ECP Climate Change Action Plan and subsequent policy actions result from concurrent top-down and bottom-up efforts. Elected officials, civil service staff and NGO personnel have framed climate change goals in regional terms, consistently pushing for "regional action" justified in terms of regionally shared risks and benefits. There are simultaneous and interacting political pressures and policy developments at regional and local levels driving more concrete climate change actions. This helps to explain the creation of the plan, as well as its shape and content. In addition, a continuing combination of top-down and bottom-up approaches to the further development and implementation of the plan form a foundation on which important policy achievements could be made.

Three interacting drivers are shaping regional climate action in the Northeast: (1) developments in international scientific and political debates about climate change; (2) changing political pressures and incentives for regional office holders; and (3) an advocacy coalition of active networking and leadership activities on the part of state/provincial level civil servants. Across the region, at various levels of governance, public and civil society actors use developments in international climate change research and assessment in conjunction with developing understandings of the region's GHG emissions and vulnerability to climate change to justify further action.

7 For more on ICLEI, see www.iclei.org.

8 For more on RGGI, see www.rggi.org.

International Scientific and Political Debates about Climate Change

The NEG-ECP climate change action plan draws heavily on assessment information and data from the Intergovernmental Panel on Climate Change (IPCC). Such data are seen to demonstrate the need for policy action on climate change (NEGECP, 2001a, 2001). IPCC assessments served as a strong impetus for creating the regional plan and the third IPCC report also specifically focused on regional vulnerabilities.

International commitments under the Kyoto Protocol acted as political stimuli for regional emission reductions, although the NEG-ECP emission reductions targets for 2010 are more modest. This is largely an expression of political realism – regional GHG emissions have increased since the adoption of the Kyoto Protocol making it harder to reach its target. In addition, the long term NEG-ECP emission reduction targets of reducing emissions to levels that no longer pose a dangerous threat to the climate is similar to the aim of the United Nations Framework Convention on Climate Change of "stabilization of greenhouse gas concentrations in the atmosphere at a level that would prevent dangerous anthropogenic interference with the climate system" (Article 2).

NEG-ECP climate change efforts also draw from national U.S. and Canadian assessments and action plans with regional bearing (which, in turn, often draw heavily on IPCC data and conclusions). In the United States, the National Assessment Synthesis Team of the U.S. Global Change Research Program presented a national report on potential consequences of climate change in 2000, one year before the regional plan was adopted (NAST, 2000). In part, this report addressed climate change and vulnerability in the New England region. A national Canadian climate change plan, titled Project Green, was released in 2005, building on earlier national action plans as well as a report from 2003 on Canada's changing climate (Government of Canada, 2002, 2005; CCME, 2003). Project Green outlines a broad strategy for implementing Canada's commitments under the Kyoto Protocol.

The active transfer of information from external sources such as the UN agreements on climate change, IPCC reports and national assessments often moves through regional intermediaries – or what Karen Litfin calls "knowledge brokers" – into regional reports and policies (Litfin, 1994). Such brokers or translators of external information on regional climate change action in this case include members of the NEG-ECP Climate Change Committee, other state and provincial officials working on climate related issues, and regional experts and researchers advocating policy actions. The importance of such information and data is visible in NEG-ECP reports and the Climate Change Action Plan, as well as expressed by state and provincial officials (NEGECP, 2001a, 2001).[9]

In addition, several well-respected regional research institutions generate regional data on climate change of relevance for NEG-ECP policy-making and implementation. Such regional institutions include Ouranos and NESCAUM. Ouranos, which was established by several Canadian government agencies and

9 Interviews with NEG-ECP participants, March-November, 2003.

universities in Montreal in 2002, is an interdisciplinary research institution that works on North American climate change and adaptation. The institution is led by a former co-chair of the NEG-ECP Climate Change Committee, which developed the 2001 Climate Change Action Plan, and produces regional climate data and modeling of relevance for the NEG-ECP climate change action. The Ouranos staff is well networked with provincial and ECP officials and their work is well regarded by policymakers.[10]

NESCAUM, headquartered in Boston, was created in 1967. It is an interstate association of air quality control divisions in northeastern United States. The organization works to exchange technical information and to promote the coordination of technical and policy issues regarding air quality. NESCAUM staff organizes air quality training programs and promotes research initiatives. They conduct scientific and technical analyses of air quality issues and policy-related questions under contracts from public officials and with funding from non-profit foundations. On the regional climate change action, NESCAUM is most prominently involved in the development of the regional emissions inventory and ongoing preliminary discussions on the shape and form of a possible emissions registry.[11]

Changing Political Pressures and Incentives

The federal governments in Ottawa and Washington D.C. have differing views on the need for international policy action on climate change and the Kyoto Protocol. Canada supports the Kyoto Protocol, while the U.S. has rejected it. The rejection of the Kyoto Protocol and the unwillingness to enact mandatory GHG reduction policy by the U.S. government has acted as in incentive for state level climate change action in New England and elsewhere (Rabe, 2004; Selin and VanDeveer, 2005). In contrast, Canada ratified the Kyoto Protocol in 2002. The Canadian government released a Climate Change Plan for Canada in 2002 and Project Green in 2005, outlining guidelines for the development of federal, regional and local action on climate change (Government of Canada, 2002, 2005). As such, the five Eastern Canadian provinces are guided both by federal efforts to reach the national target under the Kyoto Protocol and the NEG-ECP climate work. However, Canadian federal and provincial progress on GHG emission reduction has been mixed at best (Rabe, 2005; NECC, 2005).

In their efforts to institutionalize policies and practices aimed at reducing GHG emissions, federal Canadian efforts and NEG-ECP actions have the potential to be complementary. However, it remains unclear exactly how Canadian federal government agencies and provinces will work together on climate change action, as well as how federal and provincial agencies should act to best draw synergies from federal, regional and local efforts and avoid unnecessary and costly duplication

10 For more on Ouranos, see www.ouranos.ca.

11 For more on NESCAUM, see www.nescaum.org.

of efforts (Rabe, 2005).[12] This uncertainty includes regional and federal efforts to develop emission inventories, as well as future possible registries for regional and national emission trading schemes.

In New England, competitive races for federal and state-wide offices regularly include debate about environmental policy and candidates' environmental credentials. Nationally prominent environmental advocates within both U.S. political parties hail from this region and actions by a combination of Democratic and Republican Governors in several states have led efforts to regulate CO_2 emissions from power plants and lower emissions from public sector facilities and activities. Furthermore, it appears that the G.W. Bush Administration's stand on climate change policy and GHG emission reductions has helped to mobilize New England's (and Canadian) public officials and environmental groups.

In the 2003 U.S. Senate vote on the Climate Stewardship Action bill (also known as the McCain-Lieberman bill), eleven of the twelve U.S. Senators from New England were among the 43 who voted for the bill, which called for federal regulation of some CO_2 emissions. These eleven included four Republicans Senators, out of the six total Republicans Senators who voted for the bill. In addition, the Bush Administration's changes in the new source review rules under the U.S. Clean Air Act have been widely interpreted in the region as weakening U.S. environmental standards in ways likely to be detrimental to New England and Eastern Canada.

Officials in both New England and Eastern Canada often cite support from the public for climate change action as a motivating factor (Hamel, 2003). An expanding regional network of environmental NGOs, the New England Climate Coalition, has coalesced around climate change action.[13] The Coalition prepares respected assessment and policy reports, which are read by officials and decision makers and covered by the region's television news programs and newspapers, and coordinates NGO lobbying and public awareness campaigns.[14] NGO representatives lobby officials prior to and during NEG-ECP meetings and use NEG-ECP meetings to publicize their reports and positions.

More evidence of the public support for more stringent climate change goals and policies can be found in the fact that over 50 of the region's cities and towns have joined the "Cities for Climate Protection Campaign." Only the U.S. West Coast states have a similar concentration. Pursuant to the ICLEI goals, several New England municipalities are developing their own climate change action plans and are calling on state and regional leaders to take supportive actions on a larger geographical scale. In addition, many universities in the region have climate change action plans and

12 Interviews with NEG-ECP participants, March-November, 2003.

13 This network includes state Public Interest Research Groups (PIRGs), state chapters of Clean Water Action and the Sierra Club, dozens of local environmental groups, and relatively new organizations focused on climate change including Clean Air – Cool Planet and Environment Northeast.

14 See, www.newenglandclimate.org.

emissions inventories of their own. The NEG-ECP sponsored universities program has signed up over 110 U.S. and Canadian universities.

State/provincial and local pressures for more proactive climate change action are also expressed in numerous newspaper editorials and Op-Eds from local politicians, environmental activist and scholars in favour of stronger state and federal policy to mitigate climate change (Cohen and Murray, 2003). In fact, coverage of developments in climate change science and politics is rather extensive in the elite newspapers such as the *New York Times*, *Boston Globe* and the *Globe and Mail*.

Numerous private sector actors are also joining calls for climate change action and increasing their investment in "green" technology and renewable energy (Aulisi et al., 2004; Deutsch, 2005). On the Canadian side of the border, Hydro-Quebec can benefit from regional efforts to reduce CO_2 emissions from energy production and use from fossil fuels. Many New England power plants have also already been forced by state level policies to undertake measures to update technology and reduce emissions, including CO_2 emissions. As such, they often support efforts to have these more stringent standards applied to their competitors both inside and outside the region in other parts of the United States and Canada.

There are, of course, also opponents to regional climate change action and mandatory GHG reductions. Automobile manufacturers and dealers remain steadfastly opposed to increases in U.S. CAFE standards for automobiles, sport utilities vehicles (SUVs) and light trucks, and voters seem as opposed to increased gasoline taxes as ever. NEG-ECP participants agree that any move to tax gasoline, energy use or production or CO_2 content would engender staunch opposition from business associations across the region.[15] Some policy analysts also claim to oppose the NEG-ECP climate plan on principle. For example, researchers at the Maine Public Policy Institute refute data pointing to an increase in human influence over the climate, declaring that higher energy prices would be "death to New England" (Reisman, 2003).

State/Provincial Civil Servant Networks and Activism

No account of the development of the NEG-ECP climate action plan would be complete without including substantial credit for driving the creation and implementation efforts to a small network of state/provincial civil servants.[16] Two decades of NEG-ECP environmental cooperation have built an organizational structure for continuous environmental cooperation between the region's states and provinces. Many participating officials worked together on environmental issues for several years. All interviewed officials regard this cooperation – and their interaction with their colleagues – as generally successful and useful for participating individuals.

Officials have forged important professional and personal connections across states and provinces over time, which has aided the development of regional climate change action. These participants inhabit an active and influential policy

15 Interviews with NEG-ECP participants, March-November, 2003.

16 Interviews with NEG-ECP participants, March-November, 2003.

(or advocacy) network (Keck and Sikkink, 1998; Florini, 2000). Frankly, the other driving factors noted above would have been unlikely to produce either the NEG-ECP climate action plan, or the subsequent implementation efforts under it, absent the active network of state and provincial officials who repeatedly express interpersonal trust and professional respect and admiration for their colleagues in the network. As one influential long-term state official said, "We help each other bring the Governors and the Premiers along."

The officials' network did not simply spring up. NEG-ECP participants, like the region's NGO advocates and newspaper coverage of regional climate issues, often cite the New England region's history of cooperating with Canadian officials on environmental policy to combat acidification and tropospheric ozone and mercury pollution. The frequently "downwind" status of New England and Eastern Canada likely spurred action, as regional actors shared a common need to change national policy on both sides of the border (Moomaw, 1992). The successful efforts by regional actors to set high goals and to dramatically reduce mercury emissions – by more than 50 percent between 1998 and 2003 – served as an impetus for the formulation of regional GHG policy goals.[17]

In many ways, the impetus for mercury and climate change action was the same: A perception on the part of actors in the region that national policies, particularly in the United States, are not addressing environmental issues of critical importance to the region's citizens and officials. The shared interest in attempting to influence public debate and national environmental policy is expressed in the stated goals of the region's Governors and Premiers to lead by example around mercury pollution and climate change issues. Premiers and Governors have repeatedly called for increased national policy action by their respective federal governments to adopt more stringent policy measures, citing their own activities and accomplishments as evidence that such actions are feasible and affordable.

Assessing Regional Policy Development

Only five years into the 2001 Climate Change Action Plan, whose targets and timetable for GHG emissions reduction are focused on 2010, it remains too early for a definitive assessment of NEG-ECP climate change action. However, an initial assessment of regional climate policy development can be conducted by focusing on three perspectives. The first perspective uses a goal oriented notion of effectiveness: are state/provincial actions taken to date likely to achieve the targets in the Climate Change Action Plan? A second perspective takes a more institutional approach, asking if climate change concern and policy are being institutionalized in the region. A third perspective assesses possible implications of the NEG-ECP initiative: can NEG-ECP influence other regional and federal climate change policy in Canada and United States?

17 Interviews with NEG-ECP participants, March-November, 2003.

On Track to Meet the Goals?

Recent reports sponsored by the New England Climate Coalition conclude that, even if announced CO_2 (equivalent) reduction strategies of the New England states yield their maximum potential energy and emissions savings, the projects and policy changes launched to date will fall well short of the agreed emission reduction goals (NECC, 2003, 2004, 2005). If existing programs all yield CO_2 reductions at the top of their range, only one-third of the 2010 emissions reduction target would be achieved (NECC, 2003). Reacting to such reports, state and provincial officials stress that they have only just begun to take action, and that they are attempting to build on existing programs to develop new ones.[18] Nevertheless, it is clear that the measures adopted in the first three years after the action plan was finalized will not be enough to reach the NEG-ECP goals. Absent additional action, the 2010 target will not be met.

Important challenges to the action plan's implementation lay ahead, including a set of issues related to GHG emissions from the transportation and electricity generation sectors. In short, the 2010 targets cannot be met without reducing emissions from one or both of these sectors. Transportation generates approximately one-third of regional GHG emissions (NESCAUM, 2004). In fact, GHG emissions from the Massachusetts' transportation sector alone are higher than total emissions from more than half of the world's countries (MASSPIRG, 2003: 12). Increasing transportation related emissions alone make the goal for 2010 difficult to meet (MASSPIRG, 2003: 15). Because of the perceived public unpopularity of the available options to lower transport emissions, even the major environmental NGOs generally avoid transportation issues. Nevertheless, effective action to reduce GHG emissions will require greater attention to transportation.

The utility sector is the other major source of the region's GHG emissions. Several older oil and coal powered facilities remain in use and, for the region as a whole, renewable energy supplies only a small fraction of total electricity production. For example, reports by the research NGO Environment Northeast argue that emissions from oil and coal-fired power plants in Connecticut could be reduced by 60 percent if replaced by new, more efficient natural gas plants (Environment Northeast, 2003: 12). Even more dramatic cuts would be gained by increased use of hydro and wind generated electricity. While power from hydro facilities has increased in recent years, much of it from Quebec, proposed wind power projects have engendered frequent local and legal resistance and they remain slow to come online (Daley, 2004).

Recently, regional officials have begun to engage two initiatives with potential to influence emissions from the transport and utilities sectors. First, state officials express support for the California-based initiative to reduce GHG emissions from automobile fleets. Because Massachusetts, Connecticut and Rhode Island have adopted other aspects of the California emissions standards, these states are widely assumed to be among the most likely to adopt California GHG emissions requirements, should these enter into force. Second, all New England states participate in RGGI working

18 Interviews with NEG-ECP participants, March-November, 2003.

to develop a joint model rule for a GHG emissions permit trading scheme (Aulisi et al, 2005). At the request of New England state officials, representatives from Eastern Canadian provinces were invited to attend these discussions in the hope that the resulting RGGI program, and the regional GHG registry required to support it, will further the goals of the NEG-ECP action plan.

Is Climate Change Action Institutionalized in the Region?

The adoption of the 2001 Climate Change Action Plan, with the expectation of yearly progress reports given to the Governors and Premiers, has institutionalized some climate change concern at the regional level. Staff members in both NEG-ECP and Governors/Premiers offices suggest that incremental progress by the Governors and Premiers and government bodies should be expected in the years ahead.[19] Because the NEG-ECP Climate Change Action Plan only outlines general policy goals, participating states and provinces need to develop their own more detailed climate change polices for the fulfillment of those and other climate goals. Such policies are expected to (and do) differ across the states and provinces based on their main sources of emissions, energy needs, and vulnerabilities. Not surprisingly, states and provinces have made differing levels of progress in developing state/provincial climate policy.

Partially as a result of the NEG-ECP climate change effort, all Governors and Premiers have designated staff in charge of (at a minimum) coordinating state/provincial information about climate policy. To date, announced state/provincial climate change policies have been dominated by executive branch action. The issuance of state climate change action plans and individual executive orders are the most common policy tools. Likely the most comprehensive such executive order was issued in 2003 by Vermont Governor James Douglas (State of Vermont, 2003). It essentially mandates that state agencies and facilities meet the emissions reduction goals established by the NEG-ECP climate plan and it establishes working groups and periodic reports on progress toward the goals. Also, the Maine and Connecticut legislatures have both endorsed the NEG-ECP goals, calling for state action toward their implementation.

In general, U.S. states in the Northeast (and on the West Coast) have seen more institutionalization of climate change action than their Canadian counterparts (Rabe, 2005; NECC, 2005). States executive orders and legislative action regarding renewable portfolio standards, energy efficiency, public sector purchasing and, for a few, CO_2 emissions limits put them ahead of most provinces, where the issuance of climate change action plans and public education campaigns are the norm. In fact, environmental NGOs have begun to highlight and critique generally slow provincial policy development. Still uncommon is state/provincial legislation on climate change issues and/or climate change emissions. While debate about such issues is increasing in state/provincial legislatures across the region, little legislation has

19 Interviews with NEG-ECP participants, March-November, 2003.

passed and there appear to be few if any ongoing efforts between governors/premiers and legislative leaders designed to achieve such legislation. This will be necessary for deepened institutionalization in the region.

Potential Implications Beyond the Region?

Regional cooperation in the politically and economically important region of New England and Eastern Canada may have important spill-over effects on other regional and federal climate-related programs and policies in North America. Many regional political leaders also explicitly argue that the NEG-ECP should seek to lead by example.[20] At the 2003 annual meeting, Governor John Baldacci, Maine, stated that the NEG-ECP action on climate change and energy "cannot save the world, but send a ripple across the continent." Similarly, he argued that the NEG-ECP should seek to "raise the bar" for national policies in the United States and Canada on climate and energy issues.[21]

Climate change related policy development in the Northeast could have substantial influence on policy outside the NEG-ECP region as policy precedents in one geographical area often serve as models (explicitly or implicitly) for future initiatives. The explicit regional goal setting and development of emissions inventories, emissions registries, and trading schemes for emissions permits in the Northeast are "firsts" for multi-jurisdictional GHG policy-making on both sides of the U.S.-Canadian border. Advocates and opponents of climate change policy-making in various governmental and non-governmental bodies both within and outside the regional are likely to mine these efforts.

If GHG emissions reductions in the NEG-ECP region are achieved at little or no cost to economic growth – or in ways that increase such growth and economic efficiency – then the more extreme claims about the economic and social "disasters"from GHG emissions reductions made opponents of climate change policy would be undermined. This would likely feed into ongoing policy development on climate change in, among others, New York, New Jersey, California and Oregon, as well as increase pressure on federal policy makers (Rabe, 2004). For example, the Governors of New York and New Jersey repeatedly have called for more stringent climate change action at state and federal levels. Existing organizations and networks for state/provincial leaders and civil servants moreover facilitate the diffusion of lessons and experiences from the NEG-ECP region across both the United States and Canada.

20 Similarly, Connecticut, Massachusetts and Maine have filed suit against the US federal government over the Bush Administration decision to overhaul the "new source review" process requirements. Furthermore, the New Governors and Eastern Canadian Premiers adopted a joint resolution at their 2003 meeting expressing great concern with te EPA decision, urging US officials to fulfill the 1990 Clean Air Agreement between the U.S. and Canada that they believe to be endangered by the EPA decision.

21 Authors' notes, 2003 NEG-ECP Annual Meeting, Groton, Connecticut.

In addition, the NEG-ECP university program and the ongoing development of city and town climate action plans hold out prospects for similar horizontal diffusion of ideas and policy options beyond the boundaries of New England and Eastern Canada. For example, the University of New Hampshire's publication of it greenhouse gas inventory and the methodology behind it, aided by the NGO "Clean Air, Cool Planet," has been used as a model at over two dozen American universities. Many of these universities are outside the NEG-ECP region. There are also Canadian universities working with the NEG-ECP university program that may act as leaders among Canadian universities.

Another potentially important implication of the development of joint NEG-ECP climate policies might be to take advantage of economies of scale in designing and implementing climate change policies and programs. If, for example, the region's officials move more aggressively toward greater use of renewable energy development, and switch to more energy efficient appliances and office equipment and low emissions vehicles, the markets for these products would expand. This market expansion has the potential to push the price of existing and future technologies designed to lower GHG emissions lower, making them more economically competitive and attractive in regional and national markets.

Concluding Remarks

The New England states and Eastern Canadian provinces have much to do in order to meet even the relatively modest GHG emissions goal for 2010, as well as better assess their adaptation needs. Furthermore, NEG-ECP policy development has done little to violate a number of important taboos in North American politics. In particular, there is still little specific policy targeting reducing energy demand more broadly. Likewise, the transportation sector is the major regional source of GHG emissions, but regional political leaders, as well as regional NGOs, are highly hesitant about proposing gasoline taxes and levying other economic incentives to encourage citizens to drive more gas efficient vehicles and drive less. While U.S. state level officials struggle to meet the rather modest goals they have set with a host of relatively modest programs, Canadian provinces have done little beyond issuing rather vague climate action plans.

In addition, many drivers of GHG emissions cannot be substantially influenced by regional policy alone, but will require (at least) federal action in both Canada and the United States. Such drivers include automobile standards, energy production and use, and consumer trends. Moreover, public officials' and private sector groups' fear of putting the region's businesses and economy at a competitive disadvantage is likely to affect the stringency of state level regulations unless similar policies are institutionalized outside the region. At the same time, the NEG-ECP region is dependent on national and international emissions reductions in order to slow down future regional warming.

Yet, NEG-ECP climate change action is an interesting case of dynamic trans-jurisdictional policy development. Important regional steps have been taken to set common goals and raise the profile of climate change issues. Also, modest policy developments continue at state/provincial levels, as well as in a growing number of municipalities. The evolving regional institutionalization of climate change action may serve as a political foundation for more stringent policy in the future. One area where NEG-ECP action can be particularly important is in the development of a regional emissions inventory and possible registry that can serve as a model for other such efforts. NEG-ECP activities also have the potential to improve links between environmental and energy debates, particularly in the U.S., where climate change issues largely remain framed in terms of environmental (not energy) terms.

New England and Eastern Canadian state/provincial officials, civil servants and environmental NGOs have taken up knowledge about climate change science and policy from a host of intra and extra-regional sources. They have worked to frame climate change related risks, responsibilities, and policy opportunities in regional terms, with the expressed goal of eventually influencing policy outside the region on both sides of the U.S.-Canadian border. Furthermore, they have justified the regional framing by citing environmental imperatives, potential efficiency gains of joint action and the existing and deepening economic and policy integration across the region. These regional networks show dynamic transgovernmental and transnational interaction.

If the New England Governors, the Eastern Canadian Premiers and others who are supportive of regional climate change action are successful in their desire to lead by example and establish and promulgate policy ideas "up" to other states/provinces and their respective national governments, then future U.S. and Canadian federal climate change policies may display greater convergence than currently evidenced. If regional climate change action across New England and Eastern Canada proves effective – in terms of policy outcomes and costs – it may serve as an important justification and interesting model for future North American continental scale climate change policy.

Chapter 6

Canada-United States Environmental Arctic Policies: Sharing a Northern Continent

Rob Huebert

The American-Canadian Arctic relationship is a complicated, often baffling, one. This is particularly true with respect to the environmental elements of the relationship. In this context, most casual observers expect Canada to be pro-conservation and the United States to be pro-development. While this may be the case in some instances, such generalizations by no means capture the complete nature of the relationship. Instead, a much more complex picture emerges upon close examination of the northern dimension of North American environmental relationships. There are issue areas where American actions are more environmentally sensitive than those of Canada. For example, the United States' shipping regulations for vessels operating in Arctic waters are some of the most environmentally sensitive in existence. Furthermore, the policies of both countries that have a direct bearing on the north have been adopted and promoted for reasons that are directed more towards southern issues and interests.

A complicating factor in understanding this relationship is the very fluid nature of current developments. The north is facing a series of changes that may alter its very nature. These include the effects of climate change as well as the increase in resource development. Put simply, the American Arctic is in a state of flux. While previous assessments of the north have always counted on a large degree of stability, this is no longer true. Thus environmental issues are continuously evolving and the very nature of the geophysical and social landscape is changing as well.

This chapter will assess the nature of the Arctic environmental relationship between Canada and the United States. It will do so by examining the following issues: 1) the historical development of the relationship – strategic and economic; 2) the internationalization of the relationship; and 3) current and ongoing issues.

The Cold War and Environmental Impacts – the Strategic Relationship

It was only with the outbreak of the Second World War that the two countries began to take steps that affected the environment of their respective northern regions. Specifically, the development of the Alaskan highway allowed for southern incursions into the region (Alaska Highway, 1998). The construction of a year- round highway meant that for the first time it was possible to begin active development in the region.

The highway was intended as a means for providing armaments and other supplies to counter any Japanese attack or invasion of the American west coast. While the actual likelihood of such an attack was low, the Japanese invasion of the Aleutian Islands demonstrated that such concerns had some foundation. The Alaskan highway was also perceived as a possible route for supplying the Soviet Union. However, such a supply route was never developed during the war.

The highway was the first major northern joint development program between Canada and the United States. Given the urgency of its development and given the time period in which it was built, no real consideration was given to the environmental issues surrounding its construction. No studies were undertaken regarding its impacts on the local flora and fauna. In addition, there were no efforts to build the highway in an environmentally sensitive manner. This is not surprising as such practises did not exist at that time. Furthermore, due to the region's remoteness, waste produced in the construction of the highway was simply dumped at sites along the highway with little effort to remove it.

The end of the war did not see the end of joint development in the region. Rather, the subsequent outbreak of tension between the western powers and the USSR meant that the Arctic developed into an even more strategically significant region. An atomic bomb ended the Second World War. At that time and until the mid-1950s, its primary delivery system was by long-range bomber. As relations deteriorated between the USSR and the western powers, including Canada and the United States, the most direct attack route was over the Arctic region. Even as technology developed and the primary means of delivery shifted to ballistic missiles from aircraft, the Arctic region was still the most direct route for deployment of these weapons (Eayrs, 1972:320-2).

As a result of these threats, Canada and the United States began to develop means of detection and defence. Their core action was the development of the Distant Early Warning (DEW) line (Purver, 1995:85-7). This consisted of the construction of a string of radar sites along the most northern region of continental North America. It ran from the western most part of Alaska through to Greenland. These sites were constructed throughout the 1950s. As in the case of the Alaskan highway, little consideration was given to issues of environmental protection. This was due in part to the haste with which these were built, but also due to the then existing scientific information being unaware of many of the dangerous effects of the products being used. Thus, much of the electrical equipment such as electrical transformers were constructed using PCBs. Paints were used that stood up well to the extreme climate but contained large amounts of dangerous additives such as lead. With the remoteness of the radar sites, containers that were used to bring in building products and fuel were simply dumped close to the location of the various sites, rather than being removed (Myers and Munton, 2000:122-4).

The magnitude of the environmental problems created was not fully appreciated until the late 1980s when the first effort was undertaken to decommission some of the sites. One of the biggest challenges facing the two countries was determining who was responsible for the clean-up of the sites (Myers and Munton, 2000:124-6). The clean-up process was not simply a matter of tearing down the various buildings and moving on. In many instances, the PCBs in both the paints and electrical equipment had leached into the ground. Therefore it was not only necessary to dig up the contaminated soil, but it was also necessary to build a suitable storage facility to contain the contaminated soil. This was an expensive and time-consuming task. As Canada began to prepare for the restoration of some of its decommissioned sites, the issue of paying for the clean-up arose. The United States has maintained a policy of not paying for clean-up of its bases on foreign ground. It has contended that any such clean-up is the responsibility of the host nation. Thus, the United States initially refused when Canada approached the United States about assisting in the clean-up. However, the American government did eventually agree to provide $100 million USD in credit to future Canadian military expenditures on the basis that its relationship with Canada is special. In other words, while the United States was unwilling to directly contribute to the clean-up of its military bases on foreign soil, it was willing to provide some resources in an indirect manner. However, as Canada is discovering, the actual clean-up of the sites is more arduous and expensive than originally thought. Of the 42 sites of the original system, the 21 sites still being used were assigned to the Department of National Defence (DND) for clean-up. The 21 sites that have been decommissioned are the responsibility of the Department of Indian Affairs and Northern Development (DIAND) (Standing Committee on Foreign Affairs, 1997:91). To date only a small percentage has been cleaned up (Myers and Munton, 2000:126-30).

Another very significant environmental issue left over from the Cold War is radiological pollution. Various activities throughout the Cold War had or could have tremendous impact on both the Canadian and the American northern regions. The first was the use of Arctic waters as a major area of operation for nuclear powered submarines (Standing Committee on Foreign Affairs, 1997:93-98). One of the most important features of the development of weapons systems for both sides was the nuclear powered submarine carrying nuclear weapons. The Americans were able to install nuclear reactor on board their submarines. The power generated by the reactor enabled submarines to remain underwater for longer periods of time, limited only by human endurance factors. This meant that submarines could now pass under the ice cover of the Arctic Ocean. Since the Soviets' main naval bases were along the Murmansk Peninsula, the Arctic Ocean became one of the natural transit routes for Soviet submarines proceeding to locations off the North American coast. Conversely, American submarines also used the Arctic Ocean as one of its transit points to counter the Soviet submarines. Therefore, nuclear powered submarine traffic continuously increased in the Arctic waters.

Two main environmental effects resulted from the increased traffic. First, the nuclear powered submarines were involved in accidents. While these incidents are highly classified, thereby limiting the knowledge regarding the actual number and severity of these incidents, there is some knowledge of accidents occurring. The *Komsomolets* sunk off the northern coast of Norway on 7 April, 1989 (Nilsen, Thomas, 2000). It has been monitored by the Soviet/Russian and Norwegians and so far there is no indication of significant radiation leaks. However, concerns remain that there could be greater problems in the future. Should there be a break in the reactor, ocean currents would eventually carry some of the materials to North American waters (Norwegian-Russian Expert Group, 1995:94).

There is also the potential of even greater pollution posed by the large number of improperly disposed, decommissioned nuclear power submarines. Following the collapse of the Soviet Union, the new Russian Government drastically reduced the size of the former Soviet Armed forces. This included much of the Soviet submarine force. However, due to the new Russian Government's reduced financial resources, it did not take the steps necessary to completely dispose of the submarines (Bellona, 2003). While the submarines were rendered inoperable, they remain in harbour. Although the prospect of a melt-down of the reactors is unlikely, the possibility remains that one or more of the vessels could begin to leak. In the event that were to occur, it is expected that some of the contaminants will reach North American northern soils.

Since the end of the Cold War, the United States has provided substantial resources to the Russian Government to assist in the clean-up of the decommissioned submarines (NTI, 1999). This has been done through the *Nunn-Lugar Act* and through its membership in the Arctic Military Environmental Cooperation (AMEC) (Standing Committee on Foreign Affairs, 1997:92). AMEC is comprised of Norway, the United States and Russia. Canada was asked to join but declined.

The United States has also been a source of radiological contamination. It has conducted a small number of nuclear weapons tests in Alaska (Norris and Arkin, 2005). However, as there are few open sources on the tests and their environmental factors, it is difficult to know the full extent of the problem. The Americans also considered detonating a nuclear device/bomb to create a crater that would then provide a harbour. Operation Crescent was ultimately abandoned (Huntington and Spark, 2003:217). It is not clear how much radiological waste would have been produced, nor is it clear if any of these wastes would have entered Canadian waters.

The Pursuit of Energy – the Economics of Northern Development Arctic Shipping and Pipelines

During the Cold War, both Canada and the United States explored means of exploiting new energy sources from the north. These explorations had a profound environmental effect on the North American Arctic and on the relationship between Canada and the United States. The United States' pursuit of new energy sources resulted in the development of the oil and gas fields found along the north slope. The development of these fields required the U.S. to find means of transporting the oil to the south. This had environmental implications and contributed to ongoing tensions with Canada. In turn, Canada also examined the process of developing oil and gas resources in its offshore area. Like the United States, Canada also spent considerable effort to determine a means of transporting these potential resources to southern markets. But unlike the United States, Canada was never able to decide upon an actual course of action. It is only now that Canada may decide to construct a pipeline that could transport gas southward.

Once large oil and gas reserves were confirmed in the north slope of Alaska in 1968 (New York Times, 1968), the issue of how to transport it to southern markets became a challenge (Kirkby, 1997). Two options were considered. The first was that the oil could be shipped by tanker through the Northwest Passage directly to eastern markets. The second option was to build a pipeline across the state of Alaska from the north slope to the Port of Valdez and then ship the oil by tanker to ports along the American west coast. The first option had two main challenges. First the ice conditions of the Northwest Passage in the late 1960s and early 1970s made the development of an economically feasible summer shipment schedule difficult. Little use had been made of the Northwest Passage for commercial shipping simply because of ice conditions. Secondly, such shipments would require transiting waters deemed by Canada to be internal waters (Miles and Wright, 1978). The United States would have to ask for Canadian permission or risk a diplomatic dispute with Canada by not doing so. The issue was not that the United States did not want to ask Canada for permission. However, any such request could have serious ramifications on American navigation in other regions of the world. That is, any effort to seek Canadian permission would set a precedent potentially harming American freedom of international navigation (Dosman, 1976).

In order to test the viability of shipping the oil via the Northwest Passage, the decision was made to send a test shipment through it. The *Manhattan,* a super tanker of approximately 110,000 tonnes, was contracted to sail through the passage in 1969 and 1970. The ship was specially outfitted for the task. It was given an ice-breaking bow and its rudder and propellers were strengthened for ice conditions. Since this was a test, it carried only one barrel of oil (McRae, 1987).

The Canadian Government protested the American decision and issued its "permission" for the Americans to proceed. A Canadian icebreaker was dispatched to assist the super tanker and its American icebreaker escort. While it protested the voyage, Canada wanted to ensure that the voyage took place in as safe a manner as possible. The extent of this was demonstrated by the government's action prior to the sailing of the *Manhattan.* Just prior to the voyage of the *Manhattan*, a Canadian company's two barges, carrying aviation fuel, had sunk in the middle of the route through the Northwest Passage that the *Manhattan* was scheduled to take (Kennedy, 1988:12-4). Rather than using the sinking as a reason to ask the Americans to cancel the voyage, the Canadian Government dispatched divers from the Department of National Defence to ensure that the barges did not act as an obstruction to the *Manhattan*.[1]

The *Manhattan* experienced substantial difficulties in making the passage and likely would have become stuck in ice had the Canadian Government not dispatched icebreakers to assist. The Americans concluded that while the Northwest Passage could be used, it was not economically feasible to do so. The decision was then made to build the Alaskan Pipeline and to ship the oil through the southern Alaskan port of Valdez (Kirkby, 1997:500-2).

The American decisions had two major environmental ramifications. First, the Canadian Government viewed the test voyages as a significant challenge and decided to take action. These ultimately had international legal ramifications. Second, the decision to ship oil through Valdez set the stage for the grounding of the super tanker *Exxon Valdez* in 1989. This accident crippled the local environment and its effects are still being felt despite a massive clean-up effort (House Committee on Interior and Insular Affairs, 1990; Shelby, 2004). Of equal importance, subsequent to the disaster, the American Government passed legislation concerning ship safety that is amongst the most environmentally progressive in the world. These two events are seldom seen as being connected. Yet they have created one of the most significant paradoxes of Canadian-American environmental Arctic relations.

Following the voyages, the Canadian Government decided that it needed a means by which it could assert its sovereignty over the Northwest Passage, albeit in a manner that would minimize antagonizing the Americans. There were some members of the Canadian Government who advocated issuing a direct challenge against the American action. However, the Trudeau Government ultimately realized that such a challenge could be lost and that Canada-U.S. relations would be seriously damaged in the process (Head and Trudeau, 1995:37-48). The decision was then made to develop a response that would protect Canadian interests while at the same time minimizing friction with the United States. This was done by creating environmental zones in the Arctic that required international shipping to comply with special rules. Although Canada was not claiming total sovereign control over the Northwest Passage, it was claiming the right to protect an especially fragile environment. Through the *Arctic Waters Pollution Prevention Act (AWPPA)*, Canada claimed the right to unilaterally enact stronger environmental regulations in its Arctic waters.[2]

After enacting the legislation, Canada launched an initiative to gather international support for its action. Its first efforts were unsuccessful. But it was eventually able to gain international acceptance of its actions at the negotiations of the third United Nations Conference on the Law of the Sea. This ultimately led to the incorporation of Article 234, the ice-covered waters article, into the United Nations Convention

---

1 Since the barges were carrying aviation fuel they did not sink to the bottom of the Passage. When the barges had sunk about half way down, they achieved neutral buoyancy. This meant that the divers needed to secure chains to the barges and then winch them down to the ocean floor. As far as can be ascertained the two barges still remain on there to this date.

2 Arctic Waters Pollution Prevention Act 1970 (Canada).

on the Law of the Sea (UNCLOS). This article gave states with ice-covered waters the right to unilaterally enact special environmental standards to protect these waters as long as they were applied on a non-discriminatory basis. In this manner, Canada gained international acceptance for the *AWPPA* (Huebert, 2001).

The dispute between the two countries was responsible for extending the rights of coastal states to protect their maritime regions in the Arctic. While Canada has achieved important international acceptance of this principle, its own enforcement of the rules has not been robust. Canada has drawn up a set of regulations covering ship construction, ship safety and other environmental requirements. However, the weakness of the Canadian regulation is that while the *AWPPA* gives the appearance of being mandatory for all ships entering Canadian northern waters, it is not. A problem exists in the enforcement of the law. Canada does not mandate vessels entering Canadian waters to report that they are entering.[3] Only those that voluntarily report are subjected to the provisions of the *AWPPA*, but a vessel may choose not to report. Since Canada has limited surveillance and enforcement capabilities in the north, this means that any such vessel can sidestep the requirements of the *AWPPA*. Since reporting is not mandatory, there is nothing that can be done against any such vessel even if it is sighted in Canadian waters. This refusal to enforce the *AWPPA* hinders the Canadian claim to regulate environmental standards in the area.

Following the American decision to build the pipeline along the north-south axis of Alaska, oil began to flow by 1977 (Alyeska Pipeline, 2004). It proceeded without much attention until an environmental disaster occurred at the end of the 1980s. In 1989, the *Exxon Valdez* ran aground just outside the Port of Valdez after taking on a full load of oil. The resulting spill was disastrous for the marine flora and fauna. Despite the massive clean-up effort that followed, thousands of birds, seals, otters and other wildlife perished. Following this disaster, the United States passed some of the strongest environmental regulations governing ship construction and safety.

The reason why the United States is able to enforce such regulations for shipping in its waters is due to the Jones Act (Michele, 2004-5). This is a law which requires that goods shipped directly between American ports be only done so with American built and flagged vessels. This legislation is protectionist of the American ship building industry. There are continued efforts on the part of other shipping nations to have this act repealed, but none has ever succeeded. Since the shipment of Alaskan oil is to southern American ports, it can only be carried in U.S. flagged and built vessels. Following the *Exxon Valdez* disaster, the U.S. mandated that all such vessels had to be double-hulled and contain other safety and environmental protective features for vessels operating in northern waters.[4] Thus, all new tankers that are built in U.S. yards for this route must meet these standards.

Thus the paradox exists that while the United States has continuously rebuffed Canadian efforts to require international shipping to comply with stricter environmental standards for operation in its Arctic waters, it has effectively ensured

3 Interview with Coast Guard Official.

4 United States Congress, Oil Pollution Act 1990.

that ships in American waters follow stricter codes. In the 1990s, Canada launched another attempt to internationalize the regulations governing ship safety, construction and environmental standards in the Arctic. Referred to as the Polar Code, this effort was ultimately derailed by the United States. The intention was to reach agreement on an Arctic-wide set of regulations that all of the main Arctic states could agree upon. Once such an agreement was reached it was hoped to make them mandatory. The Americans refused to allow this to happen. While agreement was eventually reached on a set of voluntary guidelines to be followed by the industry, the final results fell short of the desired objectives (Brigham, Lawson, 1997).

While the United States wasted little time in the construction of its pipeline, Canada took a different route. As companies began to examine the potential for oil and gas development in and around the Beaufort Sea area, Canadian aboriginal and environmental groups began to argue against the construction of a Canadian oil pipeline running along the Mackenzie River valley. Partly due to the unsettled nature of aboriginal land claims in the area and partly due to the fear of environmental damage to the area, there were increasing public calls against any potential pipeline. At the same time, the Canadian energy industry pushed for permission to begin construction. In an effort to assess the problem, the Trudeau government commissioned Justice Thomas Berger to undertake a detailed assessment. While it had originally been granted a relatively narrow frame of reference, Berger very quickly expanded its mandate (O'Malley, 2004). The Commission eventually expanded to include general questions of aboriginal land claims negotiations. The final decision of the commission was to postpone the building of the pipeline until all land claims were settled. Ironically by the time the Commission issued its report, falling oil prices meant that industry's interest in the pipeline had dissipated.

The Internationalization of the Canadian-American Environmental Relationship – New Beginnings and Old Renewals

The end of the Cold War ushered in a new era of cooperation in the arctic region that had a profound impact on the environmental relationship between Canada and the United States. The collapse of the Soviet Union and the emergence of a democratic Russian Government meant that international cooperation now became a possibility. Perhaps equally important for the U.S.-Canada environmental relationship, the focus by the new Arctic international institutions were almost entirely based on the environment.

The first signs that cooperation was possible emerged with a speech made by Mikhail Gorbachev in 1987. In the speech Gorbachev called for greater international cooperation in the Arctic region. To facilitate this peace, he called for a zone of peace in which no military activity was to occur. However, this zone did not include the Soviet naval bases in Murmansk. Therefore this call for cooperation was viewed with a high degree of scepticism by the western states (Scrivener, 1989). However, the reforms that Gorbachev introduced soon resulted in the implosion of the USSR.

Even with the fall of the Berlin Wall and the dissolution of the Soviet Union, several of the western states did not want to take for granted the elimination of the Soviet threat. They wanted to incorporate the new Russian Government into a set of international cooperation that would hinder any efforts to return to the aggressive positions of the USSR. Specific to the Arctic, officials from Finland pursued the development of multilateral agreements to commit the Russian Government to international cooperation.

New Arctic Multilateral Environmental Initiatives: Arctic Environmental Protection Strategy

In cooperation with Canadian officials, Finnish officials launched an initiative that became the Arctic Environmental Protection Strategy (AEPS). The Finnish initiative was led by the Finnish diplomat Esko Rajakoski (1989). It brought together the eight arctic nations in a multilateral forum to discuss shared environmental concerns. At its creation the AEPS included three northern aboriginal groups that were given special status within the organization. It was designed to allow the members of the organization to come together to discuss shared environmental problems and to develop cooperative responses to these threats. While it did a good job of providing a cooperative forum to discuss and assess the international environmental problems, it had more limited success in devising responses. It was not provided with an independent source of revenue and could only take action on funds volunteered by its members.

AEPS developed the practise of meeting at the senior level once every two years (Scrivener, 1996). This would involve Government Ministers normally from either the foreign or environment portfolio. It was also decided that the chairmanship of the organization would also be rotated among the eight states every two years. The core of the work of the organization was accomplished through working groups and task force – Arctic Monitoring and Assessment Program (AMAP); Protection of the Arctic Marine Environment (PAME); Emergency Prevention, Preparedness and Response (EPPR); and Conservation of Arctic Flora and Fauna (CAFF).[5] AMAP was assigned the tasked of coordinating efforts, monitor and share information on Arctic pollutants. PAME focussed on examining environmental problems facing the Arctic marine environment. EPPR was tasked to develop shared response plans to environmental emergencies in the Arctic. CAFF was given a mandate to develop conservation policies for the Arctic plant and animal life. A subsequent addition to these was the Task Force on Sustainable Development (TFSD) (Arctic Environment,1993:3-4).

The Canadian and American responses to the development of AEPS were different. The AEPS was an internationalized version of a Canadian domestic programme called the Arctic Environmental Strategy (AES). While Finland is recognized as

5 Arctic Environmental Protection Strategy (hereinafter AEPS), (Rovaniemi, Finland June 1991) p. 2-3.

the state that led the effort to develop AEPS, the actual agreement was based on domestic Canadian policy. Obviously, the Canadian commitment and role have been substantial. On the other hand, the United States joined the agreement reluctantly. It was only Canadian lobbying that convinced the American Government to join. Even then, it remained a hesitant participant.[6]

A close comparison of the AEPS and AES will show that the founding documents are very similar. In fact, the same Canadian official drafted them. The AES was the Canadian effort to establish an Arctic element to its overall "green plan." During the first term of the Mulroney Government's mandate (1984-1988), the Canadian government attempted to develop a coherent environmental policy that would guide all Canadian policy. This effort ultimately was abandoned, but before this occurred, all government departments were asked to establish their own environmental priorities. Prior to this requirement, the Department of Indian and Northern Affairs had been dealing with the growing realization that the Canadian Arctic was not in a pristine environmental state. Beginning in the late 1970s and early 1980s scientific studies were increasingly finding pollutants accumulating in the Arctic. The most disturbing element of these pollutants was that they originated in areas a considerable distance from the Arctic. Now called transboundary pollutants, among others, these included persistent organic pollutants (POPs), heavy metals and radiological pollutants. POPs are found in a wide range of uses such as pesticides, and fertilizers and heavy metals are used primarily in industrial activities including power production from coal. Scientists with DIAND were finding that many of these pollutants were originating from as far as Asia (Huebert, 1998).

In order to properly assess and respond to the problem, DIAND established the Arctic Contaminates Programme. This was an inter-department committee that examined the problem of transboundary pollution in the Canadian Arctic. With a limited budget it also was mandated to develop a research programme to better understand the problem in order eventually to develop policies responses. This committee also included representatives from northerners, in particular, several of the main northern Canadian indigenous organizations. This model served as the template for AEPS. Thus the idea of equal participation of the northern people can be traced to Canadian initiatives.

The American position to AEPS was considerably different than the Canadian position. First and perhaps most importantly, at the end of the Cold War the United States was reluctant to join any new multilateral organization. There was a general sense within the United States that its own policy priorities could best be served outside of the creation of multilateral organizations. In part this was due to a growing frustration with the United Nations, but it also due to the recognition by some policy elites that American interests as the sole remaining superpower were better met through unilateral action or by taking action with targeted allies and friends.

As the AEPS was being created the United States remained uncommitted to the organization. They sent observers to the initial organizational meetings, but were

6 Confidential interview with Canadian official.

not enthusiastic participants. It was only through lobbying efforts by the Canadian Government that the Americans were brought on side. However, even once they became more active they still had major reservations about the nature of the organization. The United States was not comfortable with the development of the concept of permanent participants. They viewed this move as giving the members of the aboriginal groups double representation on AEPS. Their position was that since all members of indigenous organizations were citizens of one of the eight arctic nations, there was no need to provide them with special representation. In the end they reluctantly accepted the decision to keep this category in the new organization.

The Americans were also opposed to any effort to extend AEPS into a treaty-based organization. While they reluctantly accepted the need to create AEPS as an international body, they refused to consider the possibility of extending its mandate through a formal treaty. Related to this, the Americans also refused to allow AEPS to be granted a budget beyond what the members states were willing to contribute on a voluntary basis. In this manner each state would have direct control over any resources that were to be contributed. Finally, the Americans were also opposed to the development of an independent bureaucracy to oversee the actions of the AEPS. Once again they insisted that each member state had to be willing to volunteer directly its own officials to deal with the requirements of the programme.

AEPS has performed well given the operational limitations it faces, doing a good job of bringing together the Arctic states and indigenous people organizations to achieve a shared understanding of the environmental problems of the north. The effort of some of the working groups such as AMAP have been instrumental in achieving a shared understanding of the nature of the pollutants reaching the Arctic region. However, the work of AEPS was not reaching the highest political levels. As such, Canadian officials decided to lead an effort to develop a politically more powerful organization.

Arctic Council

The desire to create a politically significant arctic multilateral organization has been a topic of consideration among Canadian academics and Non-Governmental Organizations prior to the end of the Cold War. Both the Canadian Institute for International Affairs (CIIA) and the Canadian Arctic Resource Committee (CARC) examined the issue of creating such an organization (Standing Committee on Foreign Affairs, 1997:42-3). The need for some form of organization was based on the need to coordinate international Arctic policy in general. While environmental issues were seen as an important concern, there were not the only topics of consideration. The Canadian effort to develop the Arctic Council began by the early 1990s. However, when it became clear the Finnish initiative for the AEPS was gaining greater political acceptance, the push for an Arctic Council was placed in the background. Once the AEPS established itself as focussed almost exclusively on economic issues, Canadian officials began to push once again for the creation of an Arctic Council.

In order to facilitate the drive for creating such an organization, the Canadian Government created the position of Circumpolar Ambassador. Mary Simon formerly with the Inuit Circumpolar Conference (ICC) – the major international Inuit organization – was appointed to the position. Her main mandate was to push the development of the Arctic Council. There was resistance to the Canadian initiative. The Americans had the same concerns about the Arctic Council as they had for AEPS; there was also resistance from Finnish officials who worried that an Arctic Council would negatively affect the workings of AEPS. However, the Canadian initiative was ultimately successful. On 19 September, 1996 the Arctic Council was created.

American concerns influenced the final shape of the organization. As in the case of the AEPS, the Arctic Council was not to have a permanent secretariat or budget. Although it was hoped that the mandate of the Arctic Council would go beyond that of AEPS, it was specifically forbidden to deal with issues relating to military security. While it was hoped that the Arctic Council would advance beyond AEPS, the initial formation of the Arctic Council was little more that an amalgamation of the working groups of the AEPS into the Council. However, over time the Council has begun to expand beyond the AEPS. The main accomplishment of the Arctic Council has been the examination of the issue of climate change. Once again there are substantial differences between the Canadian and American Governments on this issue.

Climate Change

The position between Canada and the United States on the issue of climate change is quite different in general. The Canadian Government accepts that anthropic factors are the principle cause of the production of carbon gases causing climate change. The 2002 ratification of the Kyoto Protocol indicated the willingness of the Government to take policy actions to address this problem. Conversely, the American Government has made it clear that they do not accept the argument that climate change is being caused solely by human activity, have refused to participate in the Kyoto process, and will not ratify the treaty.

These differences are echoed on the Arctic Council. The Council was able to reach consensus to examine the question of climate change. This meant that the American Government was willing to engage on research on the subject. In order to facilitate the study of this issue, the Arctic Council created the Arctic Climate Impact Assessment (ACIA, 2004). This body commissioned a study by the world's leading experts to evaluate the impact of climate change on the Arctic. It did not develop new research, but synthesised and reviewed existing model and studies. The intent was to provide three main documents. The first document was to be the scientific review of the state of the science. The chapters within this study were subjected to extensive peer-review. This report of over 1,000 pages was released in 2005, along with Policy and Synthesis reports.

A second document that provides a concise synopsis of the report was published in November 2004 to coincide with the bi-annual meeting of the Arctic Council.[7] This makes it clear that the scientific community is unified on their assessment on the nature of the impact of climate change in the Arctic. There is agreement in the scientific community that the impacts of climate change are most pronounced in the Arctic. The report then summarized these effects. It is clear that the Arctic is literally being transformed as temperatures rise. While American policy-makers are not willing to acknowledge the causes of climate change, it is interesting to note that it is American scientists and their research that have played a major role in reaching the consensus on the severity of the problem. Furthermore, American scientists played critical roles in the drafting of the first two reports that established in stark terms the nature of the problem. A third report was supposed to be written that was to offer policy recommendations. However, this report was not produced because of opposition from the United States Government. It appears that the Americans were concerned that such a document could conflict with their opposition to the Kyoto treaty.[8]

It is clear that climate change will have a major impact on Canada and American relations, and this extends beyond environmental issues. First and most important, a warming Arctic will make the Arctic region more accessible to southern interests. This means less ice in the Northwest Passage and the Beaufort Sea, which will encourage more economic activities. As this happens the Canadian-American environmental relationship will become more complicated. This chapter will now examine the current state of this relationship.

Current International Issues

As discussed earlier, Canada and the United States have had a long-simmering dispute regarding the legal status of the Northwest Passage. It is possible that as its ice cover is reduced there will be an increase in ship traffic. If that occurs it seem likely that at some point the dispute will once again escalate. If shipping increases, there are no indications that the United States would change its position that freedom of the sea would need to be maintained. At the same time Canada has continued to maintain that the passage is internal waters and that it has the right to control the shipping that enters these waters. If there is an increase of shipping, there will come a point in which a ship attempts to enter the water without Canadian permission. In such a case, it is highly probable that the United States would act to defend the position of that ship and its owner. While the point for the Americans will remain the need to defend the principle of freedom of navigation, the Canadian position will be based on the need to defend its right to establish its control over environmental protection, construction standards, and safety requirements of the ships entering these

7 This is *Impacts of a Warming Arctic*.

8 The author was in attendance at Arctic Council meetings where this was confirmed by several officials who did not wish to be identified.

waters. While not all experts agree that such a conflict over the Northwest Passage is inevitable, there will be a need to reach agreement over the rules governing shipping in Canadian Arctic waters (see Griffiths, 2003, 2004; Huebert, 2003, 2004).

Energy and U.S.-Canadian Arctic Relations

A second problem is re-emerging as the Americans expand their search for resources in the north: the maritime border between Alaska and the Yukon. There has been a longstanding dispute between the countries over the boundary dividing the Beaufort Sea. Since the end of the 1980s, the two sides had managed the dispute largely by ignoring it. While neither side retreated from their position, neither took steps that could be seen as aggravating the dispute. This changed in August of 2003, when the United States Department of the Interior included the disputed zone as part of their call for development and then repeated this in October 2004. While no company put in a bid to explore these zones, this was the first time since the 1980s that the U.S. had included the disputed zone in their lease proposals. The following year, in 2004, the State of Alaska included the section of the disputed zone that is in its jurisdiction in its call for oil and gas development. As was the case the year before, no company put in a bid to search for oil in the disputed zone. Currently the American federal government has reopened its call for bids in these zones. The deadline is spring 2005. The actions taken by the two levels of American Government demonstrate their intention to actively push their claim (USDOI, 2004).

While it appears that the part of the renewed interest in northern development is being driven by the expectance of greater accessibility, a greater motivation for the Americans is the increasing desire to reduce their dependency on foreign sources of oil. The Bush Administration has made repeated statement on the need to develop energy security. One element of this strategy was to expand oil and gas development in Alaska (Hebert, 2003).

Complicating this effort was the location of some of the reserves. There are indications that substantial reserves lie under lands that are also important to caribou. These lands are located in the north-eastern corner of Alaska. Their importance to the caribou and other local fauna is such that the land was turned into a national wildlife refuge named the Arctic National Wildlife Refuge. While the Clinton Administration had resisted efforts to open these lands up to drilling, the Bush administration has been attempting to allow development of oil and gas resources in this region (Whitehorse Star, 2004). However, by a very narrow margin, the U.S. Senate has rejected this policy. It seems that with their ability to develop land-based sources prevented, the Americans are now looking to the offshore region (Calgary Herald, 2003). Thus the effort to develop in the offshore disputed area is part of this overall energy development and it is the move to the offshore that has re-opened the Canada-U.S. border dispute.

The core issue of the dispute is the resources that are expected/hoped to be found in the disputed zone. Thus, the problem comes down to the revenues that will be produced and the regulatory regime to govern the development of any gas and/or oil that is found. It is not inconceivable that the two sides would be able to resolve the issue through the development of a joint management scheme to address these two issues. However, there are no indications that serious consideration has been given to such a proposal. If such cooperation could be agreed to in principle, one of the most important issues that will need to be addressed is the manner of environmental protection. What will be the manner of environmental regulation to be put in place – American, Canadian or some mix of the two? Similarly, who will be responsible in the event of an environmental accident? If one were to occur on a large scale, the expenses for the clean-up would be substantial. Who would be responsible for paying? Once again these are not impossible issues to resolve, but they would need to be addressed before any further shared management arrangement could be agreed upon.

A complicating factor is the re-emergence of pipeline issues involving both states. Both Canada and the United States are developing plans for the building of new gas pipelines. The Americans are looking at the development of a new gas pipeline to follow the Alaskan highway to bring the new supplies being developed from the North Slope directly to southern markets (Cattaneo, 2004). This is based on an effort to increase the existing pipeline capability and to connect directly to the existing pipelines system that now extends to northern Alberta. At the same time there is a renewed Canadian effort to develop a gas pipeline along the Mackenzie Valley to bring Canadian gas being developed in and around the mouth of the Mackenzie River to southern borders (Howatt, 2003).

While the programmes are not necessarily in competition with each other, there is a concern that if construction of the American pipeline begins before the Canadian project, investor interest may recede, seriously jeopardizing the project. There is also a problem that if the two are built at the same time, the demand for steel will substantially increase the construction price of both. Thus there is a developing sense of urgency in commencing the Canadian line, despite potential environmental consequences.

One of the most interesting elements of the new effort to develop the Canadian pipeline is the position of the majority of the Canadian aboriginal organizations. As commented earlier, the effort to build a similar pipeline in the 1970s was stopped in part by the opposition of aboriginal groups. With the exception of the Deh Cho First Nations, all of the major aboriginal peoples whose land would be used are now in support of the project (MacNamara, 2004). This is a direct result of the settlement of almost all land claim issues with the exception of the Deh Cho. The other Canadian aboriginal organizations have become important partners in economic development. They have formed a company that will have a direct equity role in the ownership of the pipeline if it is built. The Aboriginal Pipeline Group is an aboriginal company that will play a key role in the ownership of the pipeline (Aboriginal Pipeline Group, 2004). The development of this capability indicates a very important advancement in the role that is now being played by the Canadian northern peoples. It is no longer an issue of deciding how to allow others to use their land but how to actually play an ownership role in the businesses that are using the land.

On the American side the main issue that is facing the development of the American pipeline is cost. There have been efforts underway to provide federal funds to support its construction. Prior to the American presidential election of 2004, it appeared that American support would not be forthcoming. However, after the election, the U.S. Senate approved a substantial assistance programme (Whitehorse Star, 2004a).

There are three key environmental issues that arise from the development of either or both pipelines. The first involves the actual construction of the pipelines (Weber, 2005). There is no doubt that the construction of these pipelines will entail considerable effort. Both proposals will require environmental assessments before they are given approval. Both will attempt to minimize the dislocation that they will produce.

The second and more serious impact will be due to the additional development that either pipeline will facilitate. Once the pipelines are in place, the development of other smaller gas fields will become economically feasible. As that occurs the roads constructed to build the lines connecting these smaller fields to the main line will allow for the exploration and development of other resources. This in turn triggers further development to be undertaken. Thus the initial pipeline promotes a continuation of further development that on its own would not be feasible, the cumulative impact of which is difficult to predict and control.

The third environmental impact of the construction of both or either pipeline is the continued reliance it will provide on the use of fossil fuel. The gas that will be shipped south will be used and will ultimately contribute to the continued North American production of greenhouse gases. In this manner the pipeline will play a role in the problem of climate change. This has to be balanced against the need for the gas for North American consumers. Since a large percentage of the gas will be used for such needs as heating houses, it is clear that the gas is needed. But its utilization will continue to add to the problem of greenhouse gases accumulation. Since the Arctic is particularly sensitive to the impacts of climate change, the argument can be made that the pipelines from the north are playing a direct role in the continued warming of the Arctic. The pipelines are of course not the only factor nor will their addition to the build-up be that large of a percentage, but the point remains that pollutants produced by the gas brought south by the pipeline will be contributing to the problem.

Any effort to respond to this problem is complicated by the fact that the United States and Canada have adopted a different position on the issue of climate change. As mentioned earlier, Canada has signed and ratified Kyoto while the United States has not. Since both pipelines will be travelling through both countries and the gas shipped south will be used by both countries, it is not at all clear how either country could effectively attempt to respond to the pollutants produced. How can Canada attempt to meet its goal to reduce greenhouse emissions as the gas comes on market from these pipelines?

Conclusion

It is apparent that understanding the Arctic environmental relationship between Canada and the United States is complicated. Both countries share many of the same problems. However, owing to a large number of reasons, it is equally clear that both countries have often responded to these problems in ways that have actually created additional complications in the overall relationship. Furthermore, it is also clear that many of the problems facing the north will continue to grow. While there are signs of increased international cooperation in responding to these problems, there are also signs that differences between the United States and Canada on the importance of acting in a multilateral basis will continue to challenge policymakers as they look to answers in responding to these problems. What then can be observed about these problems?

First the issue of sovereignty will continue to challenge both states. It is clear that the real issue is one of control. Canada wants to be able to control the actions of other states as they enter Canadian waters. Specifically, this is based on the desire to ensure that the northern environment is protected. The United States is equally determined to prevent Canada from exercising this capability. It is not that the United States is opposed to the specifics of the Canadian effort, but it does not want the precedent set. What is interesting about this issue is the manner in which the United States has addressed this issue for its own Arctic waters. It too has acted in a multilateral fashion to enact legislation governing ship standards. But rather than do so through international routes, it has used trade law to protect its waters. Since it is possible that climate change will open up the Canadian waters to more shipping, it is entirely possible that this issue will soon re-enter the political agenda between the two countries.

A second theme that appears continually throughout the relationship is the manner in which multilateral organizations are used in the Arctic. Keeping with a theme that is consistent with Canadian foreign policy since the end of the Second World War, Canada has attempted to pursue its agenda through the development of international organizations. However, the United States prefers to limit the powers of these organizations and would prefer to deal with arctic issues on a bilateral (or unilateral) basis. While Canada has had some success in enticing a reluctant United States to join the main post Cold War organizations, this success has been tempered by the limited resources that are made available to these organizations. It is perhaps most telling that the issue areas that have been the focus of these new institutions are centred on the environment. Both AEPS and the Arctic Council have made important strides in allowing Canada, the United States and the other Arctic nations to come to a shared understanding of their shared problems in the north. However, there is no indication that the resources needed to deal with these problems will be made available in the foreseeable future.

Finally, it is clear that resource development in the North American north will emerge as the central environmental issue. Even if a warming Arctic were not making the resources of the region more accessible, the oil and gas riches would be leading to more development. There is a need to ensure that the exploitation of these resources be done in a manner that takes the interests of both states into account, but more importantly is done in an environmentally sustainable fashion. Given the lack of cooperation that has existed in the past and given that there are no indications that thought is being given to future cooperation, the hope for cooperation seems misplaced. Canada and the United States are not working together to develop their pipelines and instead appear to be in mild competition. The re-opening of the Beaufort Sea boundary issue only serves to illustrate the unilateral nature of American action in the north. Even though NAFTA made North America a unified energy market, it is clear that the development of energy supplies is still a competitive unilateral activity.

In conclusion, environmental issues between Canada and the United States will continue to dominate the sharing of the north of the continent. There is the possibility for increased cooperation. This makes sense, but the record is not encouraging.

Chapter 7

The Management of Shared Waters: Watershed Boards Past and Future

Alan M. Schwartz

Introduction

The host of real and potential environmental issues between Canada and the United States led to the creation of a special dispute resolution mechanism over ninety years ago. The *Boundary Waters Treaty* of 1909 established the International Joint Commission (IJC) to implement the treaty, with six members, three to be appointed by the government of each country. While the IJC was given standing authority to regulate transboundary water levels, as well as the standby capability to, when asked, act as an arbiter between Ottawa and Washington, its most important function, resulting from both the treaty and practices that have evolved, has been to study and make recommendations on transboundary environmental issues referred to it by both governments (Spencer, et al., 1981).

This chapter reviews the century old efforts of Canada and the United States to manage shared waters with an emphasis on the Great Lakes. A review of the Great Lakes Water Quality agreements of the 1970s is followed by a discussion of recent proposals of the International Joint Commission to create Transboundary Watershed Boards across the entire Canada/U.S. border. The chapter seeks to address if these boards will revolutionize the future management of shared waters and why progress in this regard whiled hailed by environmentalists will be slow in coming.

It is important to emphasize that the IJC cannot act as an environmental advocate or watchdog on its own initiative. The IJC can only study environmental issues that have been referred to it by Ottawa and Washington. The Commission maintains small separate staffs in Ottawa and Washington and Windsor, and "borrows" public servants, especially scientists, from the EPA and Environment Canada to work on specific topics.

While the IJC's recommendations have not always been received warmly in either Ottawa or Washington, and while the slowness with which it has acted has often been frustrating to some, the Commission has nonetheless won widespread respect for its careful scientific work and for the bipartisan approach to problems taken by both the commissioners and their staffs. Most noticeably, the commissioners very rarely split their votes along national lines.

The usefulness of the Commission has been a subject for periodic scholarly debate for years (Carroll, 1981; Munton, 1981; Schwartz, 1981). Some critics point to the long delay between references and final IJC reports and the fact that Commission recommendations have often been ignored. They conclude the IJC in its present form is not all that useful to Canada and the U.S. Some argue for substantial reform to the point of making the Commission a supranational decision-making body for all transboundary environmental issues. Even those who would like to see this happen realize that it is almost unthinkable that either nation would give up its own sovereignty and transfer environmental authority to an appointed Commission. Indeed, if this could happen the apolitical nature of the Commission would surely be eliminated and the Commission's work would be greatly politicized. Others, looking at the same evidence, conclude that the Commission has played an extremely important role in environmental dispute resolution, that its recommendations have been instrumental in protecting environmental resources, and that the Commission should be used as a model for environmental management for other countries throughout the world (Legault, 2000). The reality is complex and may vary greatly depending on the specific issue under discussion. Those who think the IJC is a positive model most often point to its long role in management of the Great Lakes, while others are less impressed with the Commission's ability to prevent or resolve conflicts regarding the transport of air pollutants.

When one looks at all the environmental issues between the U.S. and Canada that have arisen over the years, a clear trend emerges. All issues can be contentious, especially ones that have significant economic implications. However, if there is some convergence between the interests of both nations, problems are easier to resolve. Thus when the waters of the Great Lakes are polluted or proposals arise to remove water from the Great Lakes, it is in the mutual interest of both nations to mitigate or resolve the problem. On the other hand, if there is divergence, whereby one country receives the majority of the benefits from a project or a policy, while the other country receives most of the detriment or pollution, that problem is going to be much more difficult to resolve. Thus, when acid rain was perceived to be an issue of the U.S. having to pay for most of the clean-up and the benefits of that clean-up accruing mostly in Canada, little progress was made. Only after the problem was recast as each side bearing responsibility for the environmental problems of itself as well as its neighbour, and both sides having to share in the prevention of future pollution was progress initiated (Munton, 1997).

The Commission's work begins when both governments of the U.S. and Canada agree to send a reference, or question for study, to the Commission. Although the Boundary Waters Treaty allows for one country to send a reference without the concurrence of the other, this has never happened. Since the Commission depends on financial resources from both countries to carry out the reference and since the final recommendations of the Commission are not binding, a unilateral reference would be foolish and counter-productive. The IJC can and has in the past played a useful role in studying and making recommendations about contentious transboundary environmental issues. The Commission when studying an issue puts together working groups of scientists from both countries to analyze data. A reputation for sound unbiased science has been a hallmark of the Commission's work for over 90 years. When governments are less than eager to solve an environmental problem they have found that giving a reference to the IJC allows for getting the issue off the front burner while the Commission does its studies. Recommendations are often delayed for years, perhaps even beyond the term of elected officials who were in office when the study was first requested.

From its creation in 1912 until 1972 most of the IJC's work centered in Orders of Approval for water level issues. Here the Commission had the authority to issue water level regulations which are binding on both parties. In issues of environmental quality (as opposed to water quantity) the IJC could not investigate a problem without an express question, called a reference, being presented to it by both federal governments and there were relatively few of those (Carroll, 1981). This situation changed with the signing of the Great Lakes Water Quality Agreements (GLWQA) in 1972 and 1978. In these agreements the Commission was given a "standing reference" on the Great Lakes. The IJC now continually monitors the progress of both nations in implementing the GLWQA and makes public reports on this progress or the lack thereof. In 2004 the Commission published its *Twelfth Biennial Report on Great Lakes Water Quality*.

Management of the Great Lakes

In 1970, with public support for environmental improvement in both the U.S. and Canada at an all time high, the IJC issued a report on pollution of the Great Lakes. Both governments, feeling the pressure of a growing public concern for the environment, pledged themselves to a massive Great Lakes clean-up by signing the 1972 Great Lakes Water Quality agreement.

"The 1972 agreement was, with the exception of the Boundary Waters Treaty itself, the most comprehensive environmental agreement ever reached by the two countries" (Jockel and Schwarz, 1984:242). Water quality objectives were established for each of the lower lakes. Although the Commission's authority was not expanded beyond its investigative function, it was given a permanent watchdog role in Great Lakes matters; it would no longer need a reference to investigate any Great Lakes problem. It would have the responsibility for the

> tendering of advice and recommendations to the Parties and to the State and Provincial Governments on problems of the quality of the boundary waters of the Great Lakes System, including specific recommendations concerning water quality objectives, legislation, standards, and other regulatory requirements, programs, and other measures and intergovernmental agreements relating to the quality of those waters" (Agreement Article VII, section 1C).

To accomplish this, the Commission created two permanent standing Boards. The Water Quality Board, composed of agency staff from both governments, would advise the Commission of the status of water quality. The Science Advisory Board, composed primarily of academics, defined the research needs that provided the information the Commission required to fulfill its mandate.

The 1972 agreement was to last for a period of five years. Because of the failure to meet established deadlines, and equally important, the discovery of new problems of toxic substances in the Lakes, both governments decided it was in their best interests to renew the agreement. After much debate, an agreement was finally concluded and signed in 1978. It was designed to restore and maintain the integrity of the waters of the Great Lakes:

> The changes in the 1978 agreement from that of 1972 were striking. Formal deadlines of 1982 for municipal pollution abatement and 1983 for industrial pollution abatement were set. New, more stringent, overall phosphorus loading reductions were established. A long list of hazardous polluting substances was to be banned from the lakes. New tougher standards for radioactivity were established. Perhaps most significantly, the concept of an ecosystem approach was developed by the inclusion of sections dealing with airborne pollutants, and pollution from agriculture, rural forestry, and other land use activities. Article VII of the 1978 agreement continued the permanent watchdog role that the Commission first spelled out in the 1972 agreement. The new agreement held out considerable hope that a renewed committed effort on the part of both countries was to be made in cleaning up Great Lakes water quality. The IJC was generally pleased with the new agreement (Jockel and Schwarz, 1984:243).

In meeting the goals of the agreement, the IJC published biennial reports on the progress, or lack thereof, made by governments. After years of writing geared toward complimenting governments where some progress was made and trying to nudge governments where progress was lacking, the IJC reports in the 1990s became more strident in their criticism of a lack of follow through by governments. This accomplished two things for the IJC. First, it raised the profile of the Great Lakes in the eye of the public. Interest groups such as Great Lakes United widely publicized the Commission reports, chastising governments for lack of action and therefore putting human health at risk. At the same time the Commission's criticism and push for a new initiative led the IJC to become, in the words of Ian Jackson, "the official nagger" for the Great Lakes. Thus being the constant watchdog for the Great Lakes was a useful role, but one that governments did not always appreciate. This watchdog role was exclusive to issues of Great Lakes and the IJC still needed a reference before issuing reports on any other environmental issue.

How the IJC Reinvented Itself

In April of 1997, the Canadian and United States governments charged the Commission to address how the "Commission itself might best assist the parties (governments) to meet the environmental challenges of the 21st century . . ." (IJC, 1997, Annex A, p.41). In this question, governments made clear that they "reaffirm their commitment to the IJC and its important role . . ." (IJC, 1997: Annex A, 41).

They made two matters clear in their charge to the Commission. First, they did not want the Commission to tinker with the Boundary Waters Treaty; second, they did want a more effective Commission.

Why would governments raise such a question with the Commission? It was virtually unprecedented for governments to ask such a broad open-ended question. Thus, how serious were they about reform and what was the motivation behind this reference? President Clinton and Prime Minister Chrétien were preparing for their summit meeting that was to take place in April 1997. Once Clinton's staff members decided that one of the items at the summit would be some agreement on the environment, both governments had to produce tangible results, or, in the terms of governmental jargon, "deliverables." The first thing considered was a new reference to the Commission to give it a new piece of meaningful work. There were many items of mutual cross border environmental concern so surely choosing one should have been easy. Not so; no agreement could be found on the specific issue that would have formed the basis for a reference.

Canada, through the urging of Environment Canada, wanted air quality to be the subject of the next reference. Canada was deservedly pleased with its progress in many areas of air quality and thought that a reference on this subject would result in a report that would have larger consequences for the U.S. The U.S. was not interested in a reference on air quality, instead preferring to work through the Air Quality Committee that was operating under the Clean Air Agreement of 1991. This group was low key, generated little publicity, and was making progress on several issues. It did not push very vigorously for new and expensive programs; it was fairly obvious that the Republican Congress was not about to approve new laws regulating air quality. The U.S. did not want a new reference concerning air quality.

The U.S. on the other hand was more interested in questions dealing with the Great Lakes especially water diversions. The Canadian federal government was not only opposed to water diversions from the Great Lakes, they were opposed to talking about diversions. This was a non-starter as far as a potential reference to the Commission. Other issues were studied but no agreement was forthcoming and time for the April summit was quickly approaching. The give and take discussions yielded no concrete results. Finally, civil servants in Foreign Affairs and the State Department landed upon what most involved thought was a brilliant idea; ask the IJC itself what it should do in the next century to make the bilateral environmental relationship smoother and the Commission more efficient. The final text of the question for the IJC was completed only days before the President and Prime Minister met.

Surely, there were benefits to examining an organization that appeared to be suffering from a bit of stagnation and underutilization. However, there were also risks in asking the question and then receiving answers that were unpalatable. Ironically, a primary reason for asking the IJC to renew itself was a disappointment with recent IJC performance.

In addition to this recent dissatisfaction with the Commission's work, the arrival of Lloyd Axworthy as Minister of Foreign Affairs in Canada played a role in the charge to the Commission. Axworthy was a firm believer in institutional mechanisms to prevent disputes and, even though the IJC was often held up as a model for the rest of the world in transnational ecosystem management, he felt there were simply too many environmental irritants crossing his desk. He wanted a mechanism that better matched the rhetoric of the IJC's original mandate of problem prevention.

Another reason to reinvigorate the IJC was the concern by some civil servants in both countries that the IJC did indeed play a time tested useful role and that if it were not reinvigorated, a newer organization, The Commission on Environmental Cooperation (CEC), would move to the forefront of transboundary environmental dispute resolution and marginalize the IJC even more. In order for Clinton to get the North American Free Trade Agreement (NAFTA) through the Congress, several compromises were made including the creation of an environmental "side agreement" known as the North American Agreement on Environmental Cooperation. This agreement created the CEC, the Commission on Environmental Cooperation, a ministerial commission, to examine North American environmental issues related to NAFTA. While the role of the CEC is beyond the scope of this paper, it could be argued that although the CEC was to look at trade-related environmental issues, there is hardly an environmental issue that could not potentially be included in its mandate. While the thrust of the CEC was intended to be trilateral (to include Mexico), the potential for it to involve itself with bilateral Canada/U.S. issues, such as the sale of water, or other areas of IJC concern was real. In addition, while few in Congress know anything about the IJC, the CEC is much better known and much better funded.

Those in government who focus on the Canada/U.S. environmental relationship and who believed that the IJC plays a valuable role in that relationship were not anxious to see a new organization such as the CEC with a broader focus and no track record supplant the activities of the Commission. Thus, while the rush to have a "deliverable" for the Clinton-Chrétien summit played a key role, the appreciation of the value of the IJC by those individuals in Foreign Affairs, the State Department, the EPA, and Environment Canada should not be underestimated. There was a real consensus that the IJC should be made a more efficient 21st century institution and not be allowed to become marginalized and peripheral in environmental transboundary environmental issues.

After the IJC received the request from government to examine its mission it convened a rapid response strategy. It commissioned a number of papers from scientists and other academics, who had prior involvement with, or interest in, the Commission's work. It asked for comments from other academics and government employees, especially those associated with existing IJC boards. Although there was some consultation between Foreign Affairs and the State Department, in reality their involvement was minimal. Indeed, the governments were not privy to the content of the report until only weeks before its release and the Commission made it obvious at this time that the fundamental structure of the report was set.

The absence of an active role of foreign affairs officers in both governments could be explained at least in part by the time constraint that the Commission faced. Governments had set a six-month deadline for a response, in part because if something were going to result from the study, chances would be greatly reduced if the report came after a change in administration in either country. The IJC was also fully aware of previous government dissatisfaction with the long lag time between the submission of questions to the Commission and the responses received. This was one report the IJC commissioners knew had to be finished on time.

Time, however, was not the only reason for a relative lack of government involvement. The Commission has always prided itself at being an independent body; the commissioners' responsibility is to the Boundary Waters Treaty and not to the government that appoints them. The Commission chairs viewed too much involvement of government officials before the report was released as tantamount to self-censorship. They knew well that both Foreign Affairs and State would have ample opportunity to make significant changes to their document, or even ignore it entirely; there was no need in their view to limit the Commission's thinking this early in the process.

Given the six-month deadline it is not surprising that most of the report was shaped by dialogue between the Commissioners and the staff. Indeed, many long-term staff members had thought long and hard about these issues in the past and IJC wish lists were easy to develop.

In November of 1997, in conjunction with its biennial meeting on the Great Lakes, the Commission met its six-month deadline and published *The IJC and the 21st Century*. After reviewing past IJC successes and the new environmental challenges facing both countries the report made five specific proposals:

Proposal 1: Create ecosystem-based international watershed boards from coast to coast. These boards would be responsible for "monitoring, alerting, studying, advising, facilitating and reporting on a range of transboundary environmental and water-related issues."

Proposal 2: Initiate broad studies on water quality and quantity and air quality along the entire border.

Proposal 3: Review existing IJC orders governing levels and flows of transboundary water resources.

Proposal 4: A reference from governments requesting the Commission to examine nuclear pollution.

Proposal 5: Biennial reports on the state of the transboundary environment. (IJC 1997, P. 2-3)

The first proposal of the report for ecosystem based watershed boards across the entire Canada/U.S. border would be a dramatic change in the role of the Commission. It would, in short, give the Commission the powers it has in the Great Lakes along the entire 8,000 km border. Canadian Foreign Minister Axworthy and Secretary of State Albright met in March 1998. Minister Axworthy noted that, "We have also received a report from the International Joint Commission, which recommended a major reformation of that institution, in terms of being a proactive or preventative body, and we have asked them to go forward and begin looking at how they could establish a pilot project to deal with cross-border water problems . . . to do a Watershed Board system that allows to do planning (sic) the various water areas" (Axworthy, 1998). Secretary Albright echoed Axworthy's remarks: "We are asking the International Joint Commission, which manages our trans-border water issues, to recommend the creation of a new Watershed Board. This will begin an effort that we hope will allow us to work together for the sound management of all the watersheds that feed the lakes, rivers, and streams along our common border" (Albright, 1998).

The other proposals of the *21st Century Report* were all ignored. This may be because governments were only prepared to respond to the first proposal or because the other proposals were less appealing. The IJC's third proposal, a review of existing IJC orders governing water levels, is a proposal that is already under way and needs no government approval. The other proposals are more problematic. The general consensus of government officials was that the nuclear review proposal was dead before it was ever submitted. The IJC commissioners knew this, but many staff members thought it was an issue that needed discussion and the independence of the Commission required that this proposal be included in a list of problems that lie ahead. Including this recommendation in the *21st Century Report* would be keeping with the Commission's role in informing the public about potential problems. The second proposal about water and air quality studies is also not likely to go very far unless the United States changes it views about IJC involvement in air quality issues. This is not likely to happen anytime soon. Thus, for the foreseeable future the only result likely to come from the IJC *21st Century Report* is the creation of a pilot watershed board outside of the Great Lakes Basin, but that alone could be considered to be potentially very significant.

Prospects for the Creation of New Watershed Boards

The potential power of these proposed boards elicited resistance to their creation from many quarters. Interestingly, the first actors to express reservations about the creation of these boards, and a reason for the delay in the IJC's receiving a formal reference from government to investigate this possibility, were the U.S. Environmental Protection Agency and Environment Canada, the federal agencies charged with environmental protection on both sides of the border. In both the U.S. and Canada, these agencies have been required to create their agendas and implement their priorities with increasingly scarce resources. The creation of IJC boards across the entire border would, indeed, have the potential to raise public awareness and result in a call for more attention to problems that are discovered. But a call for specific effort on a particular watershed might not be accompanied by additional resources. In that case, the agencies realized they might lose control over their priorities and their agenda.

Another major concern the IJC has uncovered in discussing the creation of boards with both provinces and states is the worry that the Commission would represent unwanted federal involvement. This view is certainly not uniform; New Brunswick was interested in the possibility of a board on the St. Croix River, while Maine was less than enthusiastic; Washington State was quite interested, while British Columbia was initially hostile to the entire concept. Another issue that has been raised wherever the idea of a watershed board has been broached is the duplication of efforts with the existing IJC control boards or water quality boards. Boards to regulate the level of water or to investigate water quality trends, or both, are in place on many transboundary rivers. Water quantity boards exist on the Niagara, Souris/Red, St. Croix, and St. Lawrence Rivers. Quality boards also exist on the Red, Rainey, and St. Croix Rivers (IJC, 1997:45). The existing boards, which are made up almost exclusively of government officials and, in the case of water level boards, engineers, have not necessarily welcomed the idea of the amalgamation of existing boards or the creation of new boards with broader citizen membership.

Some believe that the only pragmatic way to begin this effort is to use existing IJC boards and slowly broaden their mandate. Others believe that the only way to begin to fulfill the vision of the *21st Century Report* is to include already existing regional interest groups, and influential citizens in addition to the membership of IJC boards. Also, a central question regarding the autonomy of these boards needs to be resolved. There is currently no indication that there is a consensus on either of these issues in the Commission staff or among the commissioners themselves.

All of these problems might be considered minor compared to the issue of defining the operating principles of such boards. All existing boards, with the exception of the Great Lakes boards, have specific and somewhat limited charges. In contrast, the IJC has vigorously maintained that the only way to deal successfully with Great Lakes water quality issues is through an ecosystem approach. An ecosystem perspective means that one does not look simply at a particular body of water to define solutions to water quality problems, but rather looks at the entire ecosystem (water, air, land and human activities) and the interrelationships between all the components of the ecosystem to devise problem solutions. Indeed, this issue, the scope of the boards' charge, may well represent the greatest problem for the Commission in establishing these boards. The single biggest strength of these new boards would be the ability to view issues within watersheds from an ecosystem perspective. This is indeed the hallmark of the Great Lakes effort.

However, it is the ecosystem perspective potential that is the most threatening to some subnational governments. This means that a broad investigation into the problems of water quality in the Red River might make recommendations about farming practices that result in runoff or airborne industrial emissions that originate hundreds of kilometres from the river. The real potential for addressing environmental quality results in the biggest threats to entrenched interests.

Progress on this initiative has begun. In December 2000 the Commission issued its first progress report *Transboundary Watershed*. Although the Commission found interest and support in some quarters for watershed boards, it was forced to conclude that it had neither the widespread support nor the resources to create international watershed boards as proposed. It did, however, state that interim measures to "move the concept forward" were being implemented. The Commission amalgamated pre-existing boards with water resource and water quality responsibilities in two watersheds, the Red and the St. Croix, and directed them to adapt an ecosystem approach for carrying out their responsibilities. An ecosystem approach would almost certainly mean broadening the membership of the boards beyond the current federal, state, and provincial members who represent various agencies, to include local citizens. This has not yet happened and is an idea not embraced by all the members of the boards. The IJC has asked governments to support this work by approving the new amalgamated International Red River Board as a pre-pilot effort and providing funding to develop this board as such. Funds requested would enable the board to maintain liaisons with in-basin stakeholders, organize meetings, produce a web site, coordinate research and data collection, and fund minimal new scientific studies. Although the funds requested for this board were only $165,000 (U.S.) there has yet to be a response by governments. This is perhaps the best *prima facie* evidence that government enthusiasm for such boards is lacking.

The IJC has spent a good deal of time testing the waters regarding board creation all over the border. The variation in response is interesting. The Governor of Alaska wrote to the U.S. Deputy Secretary of State requesting a reference on the Tulsequah Chief mine in B.C. and noted with interest the Commission's watershed initiatives. Likewise the Flathead Basin Commission, created by the State of Montana, invited the IJC to establish an international watershed board in the Flathead Basin. British Columbia, a necessary partner in both of these potential initiatives, has stated it does not support the establishment of IJC boards anywhere in the province. BC views the IJC as an extension of Ottawa and an eastern intervener in its affairs. However, with the appointment of Jack Blaney as a new Commissioner in 2003 things might change. Blaney, in addition to being from B.C. and past President of Simon Fraser University, was Chair of the Fraser Basin Council. This council has brought together all stakeholders including First Nations so that they may address sustainability questions in the Fraser River Basin. This is exactly the experience and skill needed to move the concepts of watershed boards forward.

The IJC had hoped to announce Rainey as the first new watershed board. They proposed that the new board would combine the existing International Rainey Lake Board of Control and the International Rainey River Water Pollution Board. The International Rainey Lake Board of Control was established in 1941 to regulate water levels in the Rainey Lake and the International Rainey River Water Pollution Board was created in 1966 to monitor water quality in the Rainey River including compliance with water quality objectives approved by the governments. This new board would be the first to meet the objectives of a more integrated basin approach with water quantity and water quality issues being linked. The new board was to be known as the International Rainey Board and have a very broad mandate. Included in this mandate was the charge to monitor the water quality and the aquatic ecosystem of the boundary waters of the Rainey River, maintain awareness of developments and conditions which might affect the water quality and ecosystem health of these boundary waters, and alert the Commission to any existing or potential boundary waters issues and recommend appropriate strategies. This would make the board potentially powerful. The board was not only to report to the Commission in written annual reports, but also produce reports for public release. To make the transition easier, the membership of both boards were to be combined to establish the new board. This plan is now stalled due to resistance from several quarters. Not only are members of existing boards resistant to bringing on new individuals whose interest could differ considerably from those now on boards (engineers), and resistant to potentially more work (these are part time folks who have full time jobs), but the power company and local pulp and paper companies have also played a strong role in resisting this merger. In December, 2003, a more modest step of adding two non-engineers to its International Rainey Lake Board of Control was announced. These members were added to give a stronger voice to local communities within the basin.

Although the potential contributions of watershed boards are significant, the progress will be slow. No one should expect an instant metamorphosis of these boards into new "super boards" utilizing ecosystems perspectives. Indeed, the incorporation of citizen input will be a slowly developing process; experts do not like to complicate their lives with elaborate citizen involvement mechanisms. However, the workings of these first boards will be watched closely to see if benefits derived from them surpass the problems of creating them. It is certainly not a positive sign that as of the beginning of 2004, IJC's 2002 report on Transboundary Watershed Boards is not yet published. There may simply not have been much progress since the release of the 2000 report.

Conclusions

As long as two decades ago, scholars, such as Carroll, and many environmental activists longed for a more proactive IJC. Even though most realized that a commission with decision-making authority across a wide range of environmental issues was not possible, they advocated for an IJC that could, at the least, initiate investigations anywhere along the entire boarder and make recommendations to governments without being asked. While the transboundary watershed boards proposed by the Commission in its *21st Century Report* seemed to be an answer to these wishes, it is not likely that these boards will spread very far or very fast. The reasons for this pessimism are numerous.

First, the motivation for governments asking the IJC about reform was questionable. There was not a truly pressing need or question where both sides felt a convergence of interest on an issue that needed a solution. Governments asked the IJC to conduct an exercise in self reflection knowing full well that implementation of any forthcoming recommendations was optional.

Secondly, a myriad of pitfalls faces the creation of new watershed boards starting with the federal bureaucracy and including resistant provinces, existing boards, and serious resource constraints. Any change in bureaucratic structure creates winners and losers. In this case many of the potential losers wield influence, as in the case of existing boards, or have *de facto* veto power, as in the case of the provinces. Although there is pressure in some quarters for progress, even then tight financial constraints are sure to limit progress.

It can be argued that the IJC has a track record of success on past issues and therefore they should be successful in implementing these reforms. However, past IJC success is focused on issues where solutions were truly desired on both sides, such as issues involving Great Lakes water quality, or specific localized issues both governments truly want off the agenda, such as the controversy of a mine dumping wastes into the Flathead River. In other words, the IJC succeeded where there was a convergence of interests. These conditions do not seem to apply to these proposed reforms.

Even on issues such as the Great Lakes, the Commission's ability to write biennial reports without needing further reference did occasionally cause discomfort in agencies of government responsible for implementing the Great Lakes Water Quality Agreement. It is highly questionable that governments want the "official nagger" for the Great Lakes to become an official nagger for environmental quality of all types along the entire border.

There are also risks for the Commission pushing for strong watershed boards. The limited resources allocated for the Commission's other work might be diluted weakening the Commission's effectiveness. Alternatively, the prestige of the IJC would be damaged by the creation of watershed boards that became boards in name only and did not tackle tough issues or use an ecosystem approach. Ineffective transboundary watershed boards might be worse than the status quo.

Perhaps even more worrisome for those that understand the strengths of the IJC as they exist today is the possibility that boards are created, and they do accomplish just what environmental advocates desire. Boards active along the entire border could raise issues governments did not want to elevate as issues in the public mind, issues that were beyond the resources of the states and provinces to address, or issues that were simply not government priorities. In these instances it is very possible that the IJC would be viewed as an entity creating transboundary environmental disputes rather than mitigating them. For an independent commission whose budget is totally dependent on the goodwill of both governments, this could mean disaster. The governments would not have to abolish the IJC to make it totally ineffective (that would not be likely because the Commission was established by treaty); they would just have to ignore it.

Chapter 8

Can the Great Lakes of North America Survive Globalization?

Mary Durfee and Mirit Shamir

The Great Lakes of North America – indeed, the whole of the Canada-U.S. border – have long represented a textbook case of the peaceful resolution of disputes between nations. That very long peace, coupled with nature's bounty, provided the basis for both the wealth and the continuous democratic development of the two nations. International peace and prosperity was predicated on bilateral treaties between the U.S. and Britain/Canada and helped along by other, failed, efforts to use treaties as a basis for solving economic and shared resource issues. Recently, however, continental and global trade treaties have put considerable pressure on the bilateral relationship. Nowhere is that pressure clearer than in the binational management of the Great Lakes. The crucial issue explored in this paper is whether the 1909 Boundary Waters Treaty and, hence, the International Joint Commission, can stand up to the pressures posed by NAFTA and the WTO.

In their 1999 Final Report on the Reference on Water Uses, the International Joint Commission noted: "the achievement of a coherent and consistent approach to water conservation and management in the Great Lakes Basin – an approach clearly grounded in environmental policy – would be an important step in addressing any trade-related concerns with respect to the use of Basin waters." Such management entails ecosystems, water levels and quality, air-borne toxics, as well as a dramatically improved understanding of ground water. Yet the connection between trade and environment remains highly fluid. To some degree, then, the central problem in the relationship of Great Lakes management to trade is in the dynamism of the trade-environment nexus. If trade law could be harnessed effectively to environmental management and protection, there would be powerful means for improving on human impacts on the environment. The problem of getting the "costs" of goods and services right, rather than just the price, could be advanced. That would help correct for the problem of treating the environment as an externality. But, at present, international trade law is rapidly growing in scope and "hardness," and the rules there remain incoherent relative to long-standing patterns of environmental cooperation, especially in the Great Lakes.

The Boundary Waters Treaty (BWT) covers all waters that flow between the two countries and is thus certainly not limited to the Great Lakes. Yet a particularly complex and old relationship holds in the lakes, one that predates even the BWT. The relationship begins at the initial creation of the U.S. borders after the Revolutionary War. It continued, critically, through the 1817 Rush-Bagot agreement (never a formal treaty) that demilitarized the Great Lakes, as well as Lake Champlain. Other border treaties, efforts to delineate the boundary, cope with fishing issues, trade, and electrical power further deepened the relationship. The 1909 treaty, however, marks the point were the U.S. firmly moved its relationship with Canada out of the realm of conflict and into the realm of cooperation. Originally, the U.S. was going to have the War Department handle the agreement – and War did handle the boundary treaty signed in 1908. But the Boundary Waters Treaty, at Secretary of State Elihu Root's request, was assigned to the U.S. State Department. The treaty also created the International Joint Commission, an international organization created by the two countries to solve disputes before they become so large that the peace eroded. As the Canadian negotiator for the treaty, (Sir) George Gibbons, put it: "If we get the treaty through…it would simply mean that these two people could not get up a decent sized row if they wanted to."[1] And, unlike the commission between the U.S. and Mexico that predates it, it has been fully functioning since its inception and has considerably greater powers assigned to it.

Few people know of the BWT or of the International Joint Commission, though probably more Canadians know of it than Americans. But it has had its successes all along the border in maintaining water quality, reviewing requests for water diversions for power purposes, and balancing competing water needs by the two sides. Despite the modest successes of the BWT and the IJC, newer international agreements and recent U.S. Supreme Court decisions may weaken this older pattern of cooperation, with uncertain results for the U.S.-Canada border and relationship. In particular, bilateral treaties are more likely than multilateral ones to constrain a nation's behaviour, even if that nation is the United States. These treaties are deemed largely self-enforcing, as representing the direct will of two parties to achieve a particular outcome; multilateral treaties are not accorded such a presumption. That said, treaties with economic rules tend to trump "softer" rules in the realm of the environment – a point even illustrated by the BWT where the IJC is very effective at balancing the economic interests associated with water levels but less so in the environmental arena. Third, U.S. courts assume that the treaty or statute "most recent in time" is the dominant approach and may interpret other agreements in light of the new agreement. Taken together, continued protection of the Great Lakes based on the success of nearly a century of the Boundary Waters Treaty can only be assured if the two nations take vigorous steps to affirm the status of the IJC and to weave the precautionary principle into matters of trade.[2] Efforts in both U.S.

1 Sir George Gibbons, Letter Book, AC.

2 At the 2005 Biennial IJC meeting on the Great Lakes Water Quality Agreement in Kingston, ON, a Canadian IJC commission member expressed considerable satisfaction with the legislation emerging in both Canada and the US limiting water diversions. Durfee agreed that this was exactly the kind of governmental behavior needed, but suggested that it was only one part of solving the water/trade nexis.

and Canada to limit water diversions from the Great Lakes and to renew efforts to finish the clean-ups begun over 30years ago suggest a willingness to moderate the impact of multilateral trade agreements. Similarly, the IJC's recent efforts to treat all the boundary water systems as ecosystems – with the permission of the U.S. and Canada – suggest an emergent principle of management of natural resource systems.[3] Even more optimistically, it is possible that the sound patterns of conflict resolution and protection of ecosystems on the Canadian-U.S. border can finally be brought to bear on the U.S.-Mexico border via reform of NAFTA. But the changes are still diffuse and ill-connected to the trade regimes of WTO or the even more restrictive NAFTA.

Let us explore some problematic dimensions of the management of the Great Lakes. Two central questions guide the discussion. First, can conflict resolution devices established over the past 95 years between the Canada and the U.S. and exemplified by the IJC and the BTW operate effectively in the light of new dispute resolution options found in WTO and NAFTA? Second, will science continue to ground policy for the Great Lakes, particularly since the expert networks and policy assumptions of NAFTA and the Great Lakes rarely overlap?

Conflict Resolution in the Great Lakes

Ours is as close to a perfect model of peaceful resolution of conflicts and joint problem solving as any two nations have ever achieved. It grew out of international law and is based on bilateral treaties and executive agreements. Indeed, the entire rationale for the Boundary Waters Treaty was to force prior consultation on water diversions and to prevent transboundary pollution. The IJC was given the power – which it still wields – to approve works that would change the water levels of the lakes (and other boundary waters not in the scope of this chapter). The treaty clearly states a hierarchy of uses for the boundary waters: health and sanitation, navigation, industrial and agricultural. That hierarchy predates by decades the modern principles of international environmental law. Yet, in a recent ruling by the International Court of Justice, the emphasis on human health comes through clearly. "The environment is not an abstraction but represents the living space, the quality of life and the very health of human beings, including generations unborn. The existence of the general obligation of states to ensure that activities within their jurisdiction and control respect the environment of other states or of areas beyond national control is now part of international law relating to the environment."[4]

Through references to the IJC, the U.S. and Canada have solved a range of issues and established quiet forms of on-going management. As the hierarchy suggests, trade is important, as is economic development. But the first priority must be human health. Indeed, in 1919 the IJC was asked to write a Treaty of Pollution, following

---

3 Note, however, Schwartz's caution in this regard, as seen in the preceding chapter.

4 See Legality of the Threat or Use of Nuclear Weapons, Advisory opinion, ICJ Reports 1996, pp. 241-242.

the results of Reference #4 on pollution of waters from the Rainey River through the international Great Lakes and to the St. John's River between Maine and New Brunswick. It would have assumed that pollution on one side cause pollution on the other – the first use of a precautionary principle in a treaty. While the treaty was never perfected, the stage was set early to think about what we now call ecosystems. As scientific understanding of the Great lakes grew, so too did understanding that human health is exquisitely tied to ecosystem health and so management of the Great Lakes has moved, however imperfectly, in that direction.

No such set of values attends NAFTA. This agreement was signed in 1994 and it creates a free trade area between the U.S., Canada and Mexico. This agreement seeks to stimulate economic growth, to raise standards of living for people and to tighten the relations between all three countries. But in reality it restricts these three countries from passing and enforcing their own strong domestic environmental standards and from protecting public health. Not surprisingly, the impact has been to weaken the close ties between the U.S. and Canada on issues long-managed through other means.

The most likely source of conflict between export products control measures and trade discipline arises under Article XI of GATT, which is also common to NAFTA and WTO. This provision imposes a blanket prohibition against the use of quantitative export controls on any product destined for the territory of any other contracting party. There are exceptions in the GATT agreement that Canada and the United States may use if they wish to protect the ecosystems or public health.[5] However, in reality it is not as simple as it sounds to use these exceptions. Several trade cases have considered the application of these provisions to import controls concerning endangered species and hormone treated beef.[6] In each case domestic import restrictions were deemed to violate Article XI of GATT. In other words, it is difficult to have product export control measures that would not violate article XI of GATT, unless the countries, which are members to the GATT, will impose an export duty or tax as opposed to ban or embargo to control product exports. Canada or the United States, however, cannot use this technique on each other because they abandoned this option under NAFTA.[7]

The IJC in its final report in 1999 stated, "The Commission believes it is unlikely that water in its natural state (e.g., in a lake, river, or aquifer) is included within the scope of any of these trade agreements since it is not a product or good." However, the United States Supreme Court ruled that ground water is an article of commerce.[8] In the El Paso case the United States Supreme Court ruled, "The conservation and

5 The Article XX (b) and Article XX(g).

6 See United-States – Import Prohibition of Certain Shrimp and Shrimp Products, AB-1998-4 and WTO Reports of the Appellate Body on U.S and Canadian Complaints on European Communities – Measures Concerning Meat and Meat Products (Hormones), WT/DS26/AB/R, WT/DS48/AB/R.

7 See Articles 302, 309.2 and 314 of NAFTA.

8 See Sporhase v. Nebraska 458 U.S. 941 (1982).

preservation of water is of the utmost importance to the citizens of New Mexico … Nevertheless, the New Mexico ground water embargo violates the commerce clause of the U.S. constitution."[9] If ground water is a commodity, it is at least plausible that the United States Supreme Court will rule that surface water is also an article of commerce and therefore all the provisions in GATT and NAFTA apply. Moreover, the belief that water in its natural state does not fall within the definition of a good under GATT/WTO rules probably will not hold regarding NAFTA.[10] The NAFTA agreement is stricter than the GATT agreement due to chapter 11, which contains a variety of rights and protections for investors and investment in NAFTA countries. One of these rights is "National Treatment." Chapter 11 specifies that each party shall accord to investors of another party treatment no less favourable than it accords, in like circumstances, to its own investors.[11] Once Canada or the United States allows water to be withdrawn from its natural state for various purposes such as industrial use and domestic consumption, the same right must be accorded to foreign investors. Furthermore, chapter 11 of NAFTA is not limited in its application to trade in commodities. Thus the rules in this chapter concerning investors and investments would extend to water, whether water is considered a commodity or not.[12] In other words, if Canada lets investors from Canada use water from the Great Lakes, it has to give the same opportunity to investors from the United States if they wish to do the same. These new rights and protections are unprecedented in power. NAFTA allows companies to sue the national government of a NAFTA country in arbitration tribunals if they feel that a regulation or government decision affects their investment and conflicts with these new NAFTA rights for investors and investment.[13] While considerable activity has taken place since 1999 to limit the prospect of major water diversions from the Great Lakes at the IJC, national and state/provincial levels, a host of questions have yet to be resolved ranging from triggers of removals, the emphasis to be given the return flow to the system versus total gallons diverted, and how to treat groundwater issues relative to surface waters.[14]

A further complicating factor for continued conflict resolution between the U.S. and Canada derives from U.S. Supreme Court treaty and statute interpretation. The Most Recent in Time rule shapes the court's decision-making in deciding what statute or treaty should be used as the initial grounds for interpreting U.S. policy.

---

9 See El Paso v. Reynolds, 563 F. Supp. 379 (1983) near [*392].

10 The June 2005 Congressional Research Service report, Great Lakes Water Withdrawals: Legal and Policy Issues, says that the "extent to which water can be regulated by trade agreements…has yet to be resolved" p. 18.

11 See Article 1102 of NAFTA.

12 See Article 1138 of NAFTA definition of investment.

13 See Section B Settlement of disputes between a party and an investor of another party of NAFTA.

14 See the final report of the IJC on a reference concerning the uses of water http://www.ijc.org/php/publications/html/finalreport.html#8. Presumably if U.S.-Canada investors in the Great Lakes must provide a return flow to the Great Lakes for all their diversions, then California investors would need to do the same.

Fortunately, both the U.S. and Canada have continued to use the more ancient methods of the BWT to resolve disputes, notably the governments sent a reference on water uses to the IJC in 1999, suggesting that the "most recent in time" interest is to continue the use of the IJC.

Furthermore, there is also a mechanism in NAFTA that its members can use when they wish to protect the environment and public health.[15] Article 1114 of NAFTA states that each party to the NAFTA agreement can adopt, maintain and enforce its domestic environmental standards, despite the investors and investment rights. Moreover, Article 1114(2) states "The Parties recognize that it is inappropriate to encourage investment by relaxing domestic health, safety or environmental measures." The NAFTA countries agreed to protect the environment and public health and none of these countries can waive environmental measures just to encourage investors. In other words if investors' activities may cause damage to the environment or public health Canada or the United States may issue rules that make sure that these activities will take under consideration environmental issues. But the "soft" language in Article 1114(2) alone would not be a strong defence against developments such as bulk water exports.

Expert Networks and Science-based Decision Making

In the Great Lakes, the IJC has encouraged cooperation by local, state, provincial and federal agencies. Through its use of public consultations, it facilitated widespread adoption of various public health technologies in water and sewage treatment. A study of pollution completed between 1914 and 1919 ultimately improved public health. Several years later, an official of Ontario's Public Health Service told Charles Magrath, Chair of the Canadian section of the IJC, that the IJC's efforts were "yielding splendid results along the boundary. It has brought home to the various health organizations, both provincial and state, that they have certain duties" in the area of preventing pollution (Magrath, 1924; Chacko, 1932:264-272). Similarly, conference papers by municipal civil engineers as late as the mid 1920s used the IJC study conclusion on sewerage needs. Later, its efforts to monitor of the anoxic area in Lake Erie led to action in the 1970s and 1980s to cope with cultural eutrophication.[16] The vast expansion of scientific understanding of ecosystems, of currents, or climate change relative to the region was at least partly driven by the efforts of the IJC to recommend research needs to the two governments. In sum, over the nearly 100 years of the Boundary Waters Treaty, various levels of governments have invested billions into infrastructure, and into clean up of water, as well as into fundamental science. A community where policy, scientific, technical experts talk to each other and to the public emerged.

15 See Article 1114 of NAFTA.

16 For a discussion, see William McGucken, *Lake Erie Rehabilitated: Controlling Cultural Eutrophication, 1960s-1990s*, University of Akron Press, 2000.

In contrast, NAFTA and WTO are dominated by legal, economic and business experts, not engineers, doctors, and natural scientists. Even in the realm of law, where one might imagine consonance over water issues, there are problems: at the U.S.-Mexico border, most of the law is based on western water rights law, rather than the riparian law used in the Great Lakes. Little consideration seems to have been given to the mismatch between the community experts in the two, overlapping settings. If there were an equally strong pattern of scientific and political cooperation over shared waters between the U.S. and Mexico (and Mexico is increasingly interested in water conservation and preservation), the mismatch might not matter. The Commission for Environmental Cooperation of NAFTA is still young and building the scientific basis needed for better decisions, but a commonly expressed view in the Great Lakes is that it "interferes" with the IJC's work, and thus encourages venue shopping by aggrieved parties rather the continued building of community.[17] Even if that were not true, the CEC has no meaningful dispute resolution powers, quite unlike those assigned to the IJC via the Boundary Waters Treaty.

If this assessment is correct, then a further problem arises between the old BWT system and the new NAFTA system. Policy in the Great Lakes, at least sometimes, has been science-driven; the same is not likely to be as true for NAFTA. This could have devastating consequences for the U.S.-Canada borderlands. If one looks at projects of the CEC under NAFTA, one finds few ecosystem projects (though considerable interest in biodiversity), but a number of sustainability, hazardous waste air pollution tracking projects. These issues appeared first in the Great Lakes, but the relative emphasis on them in NAFTA illustrates the quite different networks of experts and their trade-related concerns. Now, there are some ways in which seemingly intractable problems for the Great Lakes might be aided by the continentalization of decision-making. Our countries have been hard pressed to handle invasive species – which is costing billions upon billions to industry and municipalities and incalculable loss to ecosystem functioning (see Chapter 9). This transboundary issue may be easier to manage in a continental frame than in a regional ecosystem context. The CEC is working hard on this issue. Similarly, the binational air toxics strategy was going nowhere for years in the Great Lakes.[18] NAFTA's CEC could play an important coordinating role in this complex issue, as it seems to be doing.

Curiously, the CEC has not apparently developed a major project on water uses, which could be because the particular water treaties between the nations hold, or could reflect the parlous state of legal affairs relative to water uses. What matters in our view is how difficult it could become to control water diversions if ecosystem-based science declines along the Canada-U.S. border. Out-of-basin diversions

17 Informal discussions with Great Lake United individuals, a former IJC member, and some government personnel with Durfee. See also Schwartz in this volume for a similar observation.

18 Personal observation: Durfee was five years a member, 2.5 years as US Co-chair, of the Lake Superior Binational Forum. Air toxics was a recurring agenda item where "no progress" seemed to be the governments' report.

destroy multiple ecosystems by adding or removing the water (and could worsen the problems with invasive species, assuming that the problem could get any worse). Yet, the U.S.-Mexico border has too little experience and interest in this issue compared with the Great Lakes. If the governments will clearly and repeatedly set the IJC over the CEC in such matters, we might be able to harness the experiences from the Great Lakes better to the needs of basin ecosystems along the U.S.-Mexico border. But the gaps in conflict resolution techniques and in expert networks make this difficult, if only because of a physical reality: considerable research shows that conflict over a shared water resource can lead to cooperation. But the U.S. boundary waters with Mexico and with Canada are not shared water resources and so conflict could grow, especially if there is no reasonable means of conflict resolution in place and if ecosystem-based policy attenuates in importance.

In sum, we think the highly successful patterns of conflict resolution established in part via the BWT and the IJC are under severe pressure. Direct attention to the problem of preserving the gains made along the border and to the extension of our experiences to NAFTA and perhaps WTO must be on the agendas of both nations. The concluding section outlines legal and institutional ways to preserve the strengths of the long-standing Great Lakes management regime, while enhancing environmental concerns within NAFTA.

Keeping the Best, Improving the Rest

The incoherence between environmental and trade law in many ways is predicated on the uncertain understanding of the relationship between ecosystem science and economy. The IJC treats the Great Lakes water system as an ecosystem, while the trade agreements, particularly NAFTA, have more emphasis on economic achievement. Pursuing these economic goals makes it difficult for Canada and the United States to have strong domestic environmental standards. Nevertheless the U.S. and Canada can advance several legal arguments to preserve and even extend protection to the Great Lakes.

If only one nation sought to preserve the current managerial approaches to the Great Lakes, then one of these arguments is necessity. In the case concerning the Gabcikovo-Nagymaros dam project[19] the International Court of Justice (ICJ) stated that the state of necessity is a ground recognized by customary international law for precluding the wrongfulness of an act not in conformity with an international obligation. For a claim of necessity to be successfully invoked by a country, however the nation has to prove that a real grave and imminent peril existed at that time and that the measures taken by the country were the only possible response.[20] The chance that the ICJ, much less the U.S. Supreme Court, will accept this argument for water diversion or negative impact on ecosystem is very small. Most of the environmental

19 See Hungary v. Slovakia ICJ judgment of 25 September 1997, General List No. 92.

20 See supra note 5 near paragraph 54.

consequences are not an imminent peril but rather have the character of being a major long term impact.

Another argument that either Canada or the United States may claim in order to gain back their sovereignty in environmental and public health matters is based on Article 64 of the Vienna Convention of the Laws of Treaties. According to this article if a new peremptory norm of general international law emerges, any existing treaty that is in conflict with that norm becomes void and terminates. In the Hungarian case[21] the ICJ said that new peremptory norms of environmental law had emerged. These new norms include protecting public health and nature. Peremptory norms, called in Latin *jus cogens,* could be changed by the whole international community. This norm enjoys the highest status within international law and no state alone may change this norm.[22] The ICJ also stated that these new norms have to be taken into consideration, and such new standards given proper weight, not only when states contemplate new activities but also when continuing with activities begun in the past.[23]

It is mainly in the last two decades that safeguarding ecosystems at various scales has come to be considered an important interest of all states. In the Hungarian case the ICJ did not get into the legal question of whether the new peremptory norms regarding the environment may terminate a treaty that was signed before these norms arrived, because none of the parties brought up this argument before the court. But the ICJ did mention that the new developed norms of environmental law are relevant for the implementation of a treaty and told Hungary and Slovakia to use the dispute resolution mechanisms within their treaty to address the new norms. If there is a treaty mechanism to solve conflicts, the ICJ says to use it.[24] The Hungarians and Slovaks took this to heart and visited the IJC for advice on how to cooperate better. Thus, it would be best if Canada and the U.S. used the robust cooperation processes embedded in treaty law first and extended them as possible to the trilateral relationship in NAFTA. Another principle that may help Canada and the United States to tighten their relations and still continue to enjoy the benefits of a trade agreement between them is the precautionary principle. [25] The concept of the precautionary principle was formally introduced in Europe in the early 1970s. This approach was intended to provide environmental risk managers with a tool for decision-making with regard to extraordinary environmental threats.[26] It has since been inserted into a variety of environmental regulatory policies

21 See supra note 5 at pp.

22 See supra note 8 at p. 678.

23 See supra note 5 paragraph 112.

24 See supra note 5.

25 The precautionary principle would enjoin us to prevent some kinds of environmental harms even when conclusive scientific proof is not available. The simple idea here is that this approach would protect both humans and ecosystems from potentially catastrophic danger. If the danger is real we have acted correctly; if the danger never materializes we can at least claim prudence.

26 See Mansour M., "Excessive 'precaution' threatens food consumers and foreign trade," *Legal Backgrounder* Vol. 16 No. 44, p.1.

and is embedded in the regulations of the EU and several international environmental agreements.[27] Precaution in general is certainly integral to responsible business practices and serves as a foundation for most contemporary health and environmental regulation. In situations where science cannot yet provide a full or appropriate response to concerns about the significant or irreversible impacts of a certain activity or technology, precautionary action is appropriate.[28]

In recent years, the precautionary principle has emerged as perhaps the most controversial of all international environmental law principles.[29] Recent controversy has erupted between the United States and Europe regarding beef hormones. Precaution has probably always been an element of both the United States and European environmental and health policy, but a strong World Trade Organization now provides for the first time an opportunity to challenge or advance this principle. This principle requires those states that accept it to regulate activities that may be harmful to the environment even though there is no conclusive scientific evidence of their harmfulness available yet.[30] Supporters of the precautionary principle have argued that all states should adopt this principle as a matter of international law in several environmental and public health areas such as pesticides, food safety, the transport of radioactive waste on the high seas, sustainable development, genetically engineered food, and the use of certain synthetic hormones in beef.[31] Critics however take the stand that this principle is vague and uncertain and will be used by states as a restraint on trade.[32]

The use of the principle in international environmental agreements has experienced dramatic growth since 1980,[33] (for example in the 1985 Vienna Convention on Ozone Depleting Substances, at the Second International Conference on the protection of the North Sea, and in the Bergen Declaration of the United Nations Economic Commission for Europe on sustainable development).[34] Moreover, this principle can now be found in the rules governing international trade, such as the Cartagena Protocol on Biosafety, which regulates trade in living modified organisms.[35]

Furthermore, the precautionary principle is increasingly being invoked at the national level. For example, Germany has adopted this principle as broad guidance for its environmental policy.[36] This principle has also begun to appear in domestic

---

27 See supra note 13.

28 See supra note 13.

29 See Hunter et al., "International Environmental Law and Policy", 2nd ed, Foundation Press, p. 407.

30 See Weintraub, B.A., "Science, International Environmental Regulation, and the Principle: Setting Standards and Defining Terms", N.Y.U. ENVTL. L.J, pp. 173, 181 (1992).

31 See supra note 20.

32 See supra note 17.

33 See Woolcock. S., "The Precautionary Principle in the EU & Its Impact On International Trade Relations", CEPS Working Document No. 186, October 2002, p. 21.

34 See supra note 26 at pp. 21-22.

35 See supra note 26 at p. 22.

36 See supra note 20 at p. 410.

and international judicial decisions. For example, the Ontario Divisional Court used the precautionary principle in a case involving the proposed filling of a ravine with a small creek.[37] The International Tribunal for the Law of the Sea applied this principle in the bluefin tuna case. This case involved a claim by Australia and New Zealand that on the grounds of precaution, unilateral experimental fishing of bluefin tuna by Japan was inconsistent with Japan's obligation under the Law of the Sea.[38] In addition, the European Union has incorporated this principle into its regional policy.[39] The European Court of Justice has accepted precaution as grounds for allowing trade restrictions under Article 36 of the EEC.[40]

According to several scholars, among them Professor Van Dyke, customary international law today includes a precautionary principle.[41] On the other side there are scholars who claim that there is no room to adopt the precautionary principle as a matter of international law in trade due to its vagueness, uncertainty and use by states as a restraint of trade.[42] Even though we would not accept the argument that the precautionary principle is customary international law – much less *jus cogens* – it seems reasonable to argue that this principle has been raised to a level of general principle due to its acceptance in many legal areas including international environmental and trade agreements. International and national courts do use general principles of law when there is a lacuna in written law and they need to fill it up. Therefore, it would be wise to assert this principle for both the Great Lakes, perhaps using the precautionary language from the unperfected Pollution Treaty of 1920 written by the IJC. Article IV of this draft treaty provided that any instance of pollution from one country flowing into the waters of the others would be assumed to have impaired the uses of the water for the receiving state "until the contrary is proved." This provision was consistent with the IJC's arguments at the time that some transboundary pollution was sure to cause harm, but not be directly traceable to a source. As they put it, where pollution exists on both sides, no matter how small in extent it is on one side, "it may be difficult to trace positively the source of pollution, and to say with certainty what pollution originated on one side and what on the other. This difficulty is enhanced by varying winds and currents."[43]

---

37 See supra note 20 at p. 410.

38 See supra note 26 at p. 23.

39 See C-393/01 France v. European Communities.

40 See Danish brown bee case - European Court Reports II 3051 (1996).

41 See Van Dyke. J., "Applying the precautionary principle to ocean shipments of radioactive materials, 27 Ocean & INT'LL. 379 (1996) and Cameron. J., "The Precautionary Principle in International Law", in O'Riordan et al. (2001).

42 See Weinberg, M.S., "Technical Barriers to Trade (Non-Tariff Measures)", Metro. Corp. Couns., October 1999, p. 48.

43 Ibid. 711.42155/411.

Conclusion

Due to the uncertain interface between international environmental and trade law, it may be best for the governments of the United States and Canada to use a version of the precautionary principle in their relationship through an increased reliance on ecosystem-based policy to manage shared water resources. Even in the Great Lakes there is much to be done. For example, the BWT covers surface waters, yet most of the ecosystem science and management has concerned only the quality and quantity of surface waters. Little is known about groundwater systems. Many communities along the Lakes use groundwater for sanitation and drinking, and the aquifers are petering out or declining in quality. There is evidence that some of the recharge of the lakes, at least for Lake Superior, comes from artesian springs and other groundwater-related mechanisms. As the U.S.-Mexico border can well illustrate, loss of groundwater has devastating effects on surface waters and habitat. While matters are not as desperate, the IJC thinks this a critical issue for understanding the Great Lakes. Like the U.S.-Mexico border, however, groundwater needs to be managed locally, but more attention to ecosystem science could enhance that management – and perhaps even change the concept that ground waters are "goods" in ways surface waters may or may not be. A policy-diplomatic precautionary principle of this nature would help speed effective management of continental water resources and could only contribute to the long-term economic well-being of the NAFTA partners.

Concurrent with the use of science, should be more use of the precautionary principle as a means to bridge two different treaty systems, multilateral trade and bilateral environmental. As discussed above, it is a general principle of international law and thus provides a robust means of managing the current tensions between the two issue areas. That such a convergence of science, economy and law might arise through U.S.-Canada cooperation in the Great Lakes seems appropriate and sound. That bilateral relationship has led the way for the world in so many ways – legal, economic, environmental, and political – that success in the Great Lakes could eventually better harmonize international rules on trade and environment.

Chapter 9

Extinction and Invasion: Transborder Conservation Efforts

John Nick Sanders and Peter Stoett

Introduction: From Species to Habitat to Ecosystem

In the 1960s and 1970s, the near disappearance of numerous emblematic species, such as the bald eagle, gave rise to increased awareness of wildlife conservation needs. A spate of legislation was passed, including the U.S. Endangered Species Act (USESA), the (U.S.) Wilderness Act, and national provisions to enforce the Convention on International Trade in Endangered Species of Wild Flora and Fauna (CITES), while other state and provincial measures followed (see Boardman and Beazley, 2001). The Nahanni National Park Reserve was protected by Pierre Trudeau in 1972 and declared a World Heritage Site in 1978 (Parks Canada, 2004), and Jean Chrétien, building his own green legacy, named ten new national parks during the 2002 World Summit on Sustainable Development (CBC, 2002). Even with these legislative protections, species continue to become extirpated or extinct. In some cases, species are threatened directly by poaching, but the broader threat to habitat viability is caused by land conversion, poor extractive and management techniques, road construction and subsequent habitat fragmentation, and degraded water and air quality. A myriad of economic incentives discourage environmental stewardship (Soulé and Terborgh, 1999), and climate change and invasive species provide further threats as well.

This chapter will focus on Canadian-American efforts to manage species whose distributions are inevitably crossborder in nature; the broader theme is the provision of environmental security. We will range from efforts to reintroduce threatened species and provide crossborder corridors matching their natural distribution patterns to efforts to stop the spread of invasive ones. Such efforts are subject to a number of critical perspectives: they are arrogant attempts to further control nature; they are apologetic policies scrambling to compensate for disastrous policies in the past; they are futile efforts to stem the tide of industrialization and preserve the image of a benign and bountiful natural world that never actually existed. No doubt, there is some truth to all of these.

Yet, much more is happening, and much more is at stake, with transborder wildlife conservation and invasive species policies alike. As the case studies selected for this chapter demonstrate, there have been considerable efforts to bring cases to public light, from environmentalists and animal welfare activists, economic stakeholders, wildlife agents, biologists, and politicians. Economic threats posed by both conservation efforts and invasive species are sure to rouse the slumbering political machinery. Cooperative management between the U.S. and Canadian governments concerning biodiversity dates back to the Migratory Birds Treaty of 1916 (see Boardman, this volume), and continues at low levels, focusing primarily on cooperative species management and recovery plans. However, the inclusion of many non-state actors in these case studies suggests that transborder species management issues are indicative of the movement away from transgovernmental to transnational relations in Canadian-American affairs. Since Canadian First Nations and American Indians have a fundamental link to the land and its inhabitants, their participation is as inevitable as it is advantageous, but other hunters, trappers, fishers, farmers and tourism-providers colour the political landscape, as do large-scale loggers, agri-business, fisheries companies, and others. Regulatory activity falls mainly within the jurisdiction of state and provincial agents, but the federal agencies (the U.S. Fish and Wildlife Service, the National Marine Fisheries Service and its Canadian counterparts, the Canadian Wildlife Service and Fisheries and Oceans) play a significant role. Moreover, contemporary conservation efforts take place largely within the context of international organizations, such as CITES, the CBD, the IMO, and many others. In the North American context the role of the CEC is of course important, but the International Joint Commission (IJC) is of equal significance, especially regarding aquatic habitats (see Kirton, Schwartz, and Durfee and Shamir in this volume).

To better understand the development of the conservation movement and its cross-border implications, it is essential to understand the key actors involved in advancing and implementing the agenda. Three main actors have fuelled the entire conservation movement: state or provincial agencies, federal agencies, and the NGO community. The conservation NGO community in particular has dominated the generation of science and progressive agenda setting through legal action, community building, and the development of long-range visions for ecoregional conservation. Not only do conservation NGOs monitor agency actions, especially in the U.S., they have also compelled governments to act, in the case of citizen suits described below, and introduced compromise policies to placate opposition fears. Anti-conservation actors are discussed only tangentially in this chapter, as these groups generally oppose programs that restrict access to resources (minerals, energy, timber, or grazing allotments) or promote biodiversity. However, when economic interests are clearly at stake, such as in the case of debilitating invasive species, industrial actors are often the most vocal proponents of government action.

Regional organizations are also important players. We discuss the IJC when we deal with invasive species below. The NAFTA-based CEC has provided a facilitative forum for the protection of species across borders by initiating cooperative programs for both species-based management (North American Conservation Action Plans) and complementary programs working at the landscape and ecoregional level found in the *Strategic Plan for North American Cooperation in the Conservation of Biodiversity*. The CEC's role in enforcement is minimal (see Citizen Submission provision, Articles 14 and 15 of the NAAEC) due to potential impositions on national sovereignty. Accordingly, the CEC acts as a cooperative body, attempting to align stakeholders towards management actions that are agreeable to all parties. The approach borders on impossible, as a result of the reliance on the national and regional governments for implementation and a lack of serious action by these actors, but there has been limited success. In 2004, a pilot program for the first continental species management plans was established for the humpback whale, leatherback turtle, and the pink-footed shearwater (Trio, 2004) and the commission has developed ecoregional maps of North America and identified priority conservation areas and a list of common species of conservation concern. The effect of these and subsequent action plans remains to be seen, as budgetary and enforcement restraints may lead to poor or no implementation of these action plans; a result common for the CEC (see Markell and Knox, 2003).

This chapter will juxtapose two vital efforts to preserve the American and Canadian natural heritage. One involves saving species in danger of extinction because of habitat destruction, while the other involves saving the biodiversity of habitat from an invasive species of central European origin. This will allow us to look at both sides of the contemporary conservationist coin from the perspective of Canadian-American cooperation. We conclude that this is yet another issue-area where state-province collaboration is necessary, if insufficient, and where past efforts have taught us that sustained public attention is necessary to keep the issue-area on the agenda. In one case we deal with the protection of a land-based ecosystem, rangelands for the Yellowstone wolf, and two cross border ecoregional conservation case studies, the Yellowstone to Yukon Conservation Initiative (Y2Y) and the 2 Countries, 1 Forest (2C1Forest) initiative in the Northern Appalachians. The other case involves the zebra mussel infestation of the Great Lakes, where it is too late to reverse the invasion, but where future preventative efforts are vital. We argue that in both cases, whether one seeks to prevent extinction or prevent invasion, a movement from concern with individual "keystone"[1] species, to protection of their immediate habitat, to an ecosystemic approach, is evident in the field of wildlife biology and conservation. This is why it is increasingly absurd to even contemplate a non-transborder approach to such issues. Meanwhile, the complexity of actors involved, while a good thing for participatory democracy, makes the ultimate implementation of progressive policies increasingly difficult.

From Parks to Species

Concern with environmental destruction and biodiversity loss first surfaced in North America 150 years ago with the writings of Thoreau, followed by other visionaries such as John Muir, Teddy Roosevelt, Gifford Pinchot and Aldo Leopold (Soulé and

1 For an interesting discussion on the cultural value of "keystone" species, see Cristancho and Vining, 2004.

Terbourgh, 1999). Their focus fell on saving large game and the great landscapes: Yellowstone, Yosemite, Jasper and Banff, Algonquin and Katahdin (Maine). Their work led to the establishment of National Parks, both as a means to preserve these areas and to encourage economic development and tourism. This movement "evolved into the wilderness movement" committed to preserving areas of natural beauty and "the creation of National Parks dedicated to protecting particular charismatic species: these parks include Wood Buffalo and Antelope National Parks" (Soulé and Noss, 1998:21).[2]

Legislation was passed in both countries and parks and wilderness continue to be established. Unfortunately, these pockets of wilderness have had only limited efficacy, and complete assemblages of natural communities could not be sustained (Soulé and Noss, 1998). For example, one of the largest parks, Yellowstone, seemingly wild, was missing a key element, the wolf; "*Canis lupus* used to be the top predator in this ecosystem and is the only missing member of Yellowstone's native fauna" (McNamee, 1997:13). Wolves had been extirpated by the 1930s from the Greater Yellowstone Ecosystem through intensive government-supported hunting and trapping campaigns, and Minnesota possessed the only viable population south of the Canadian border (Mack and Holyan, 2004). Without the wolf, all the other species' movements and interactions changed; in particular, ungulate populations (such as deer) were unregulated. In addition, the coyote population had exploded and the

> hyperabundance of moose in areas of the Greater Yellowstone Ecosystem without wolves and grizzly bears (*Ursus arctos*) ha[d] reduced neotropical migrant bird populations [as] aspen overstory recruitment ceased when wolves disappeared from Yellowstone National Park. Wolves are a significant predator of elk (*Cervu elaphus*), and wolves may positively influence aspen overstory through a trophic cascade caused by reducing elk numbers, modifying elk movement, and changing elk browsing patterns on aspen (Miller et al, 2001:205).

The loss of this keystone species affected forest composition, and in order to re-establish the ecological community, the reintroduction of the wolf and protection of the grizzly bear was a necessary imposition. Protection of the lands within the park was not enough to maintain biodiversity and a species-based approach was necessary to remedy this faunal deficiency.

Species-based Conservation

The U.S. and Canada have pursued two basic approaches to species-based conservation programs. The first approach is multilateral, and finds international

---

2 One ideological split apparent in these early approaches is between conservationists, who would advocate "wise-use" policies of resource management, and preservationists, who would argue some areas should be entirely off-limits to human intrusion. See Norton, 1991; and Attfield, 1991.

articulation in the CITES, and functions by regulating poaching, smuggling, and the sale of endangered species. Both countries are also party to more specific treaties aimed at special species, such as the Circumpolar Agreement on the Conservation of Polar Bears. The second approach is national, consisting of the various approaches established in the myriad state, provincial, and federal endangered species laws that restrict or prohibit killing endangered species and protect designated habitat in order to promote species recovery.

CITES, which went into effect in 1975, focuses on reducing market demand for species in order to reduce exploitation. It is by all means a regime based on self-regulation by states, which must impose restrictions on poachers, smugglers and brokers of endangered species through national enabling legislation. The U.S. and Canada are two of the largest CITES-related markets; the U.S. is the "world's largest wildlife consuming country in the world and a centre of commerce for the world's animals and plants" (TRAFFIC, 2004). The billion-dollar black market for endangered species continues, and the U.S. continues to import numerous species listed under CITES, including species of mahogany, tigers, turtles, and sharks. In response the Fish and Wildlife Service has passed labelling and enforcement regulations in order to reduce market access for these products (TRAFFIC, 2004).

CITES has three levels of protection (appendices I-III) and as the species status becomes more endangered, the import/export provisions are increasingly stringent. For example, for species listed in Appendix I, CITES "generally prohibits commercial international trade in specimens of these species. However trade may be allowed under exceptional circumstances, e.g. for scientific research" (CITES, 2004). Both the U.S. and Canada include all species from the CITES listing appendices on their national endangered species lists.[3]

The second approach has focused on habitat protection and the protection of specific species populations, federally the realm of the U.S. Fish and Wildlife Service and the Canadian Wildlife Service (see Burnett, 1999). In Canada and the U.S., overconsumption of species has become less of a threat due to hunting restrictions and the removal of state sponsored bounties, while habitat destruction has become the greater threat to at-risk species and at-risk communities (Ray, 2000). Key provisions in the USESA require management agencies to use the best available science to determine critical habitat and design a prescriptive management approach that does not create deleterious impacts to the species' critical habitat. Most provincial measures have similar, but generally weaker, policies regarding the protection of endangered species habitat. The Canadian *Species at Risk Act* (SARA) has a habitat provision, but it is incredibly weak, covering only the species' "residence" on federal lands[4] (see SARA sect. 33). During the 30 years since the passage of the USESA, numerous

3 There are many controversies associated with the CITES approach; see Stoett, 2004, for an overview. For example, though the U.S. has delisted the grey whale from the ESA, it refuses to support efforts to move it from Appendix I to Appendix II at CITES.

4 From Species at Risk Act C-29, 2002 "residence" means a dwelling-place, such as a den, nest or other similar area or place, that is occupied or habitually occupied by one or

species populations have been stabilized, and in some cases recovered to the point of delisting. The American alligator, bald eagle, peregrine falcon, and piping plover are all "success stories" within the context of the USESA and demonstrate the efficacy of protecting habitats, restricting hunting, and reducing external habitat impacts (i.e. DDT in the case of the bald eagle and peregrine falcon).

This approach does have its limitations. Both government inaction and political listing processes have limited the scope of endangered species protections. In addition, the myriad endangered species laws have not been as effective in recovering less visible or charismatic species and protecting critical habitats from external environmental threats. Enforcement of the USESA and other conservation related laws (National Environmental Policy Act, Federal Environmental Assessment Review/Canadian Environmental Assessment Act) has also been a problem due to local antipathy and federal intransigence. Lengthy delays in species listings, poor protection of critical habitat, agency impediments to listing and a lack of funding have reduced the efficacy of species at-risk legislation (Suckling et al, 2004). This has led to numerous non-tortious lawsuits brought by environmental groups to compel governments to enforce environmental provisions.[5] The citizen suit provision is fully established in the U.S. in the USESA and NEPA (among other laws), and it is partially enshrined in Canada under the *Environmental Protection Act* (sections 39 and 40). Indeed, the citizen suit provision of the USESA has been indispensable in its continued efficacy under a regime that provides little high-level support for species conservation; for example, "[e]very listing of an endangered species in the last decade in Arizona and New Mexico, with only one exception, was the result of a citizen suit or petition against the U.S. Fish and Wildlife Service" (Defenders of Wildlife, 2000:10). Without this avenue, concerned stakeholders would be forced to rely on expensive, long-term campaigns aimed at embarrassing governments to act (Center for Biological Diversity, 2000). Critics of this approach cite expensive court costs and burdensome bureaucracy, but the

> ultimate goal, of course, is not to file lawsuits, but to protect wildlife and other natural resources. Without the opportunity of citizen enforcement, however, we believe environmental protection will suffer. Although we will remind the government to honour its commitment to serve as the trustee for biological diversity and all environmental values, only the public in the end can ensure protection of the public's interests (Defenders of Wildlife, 2000:5).

---

more individuals during all or part of their life cycles, including breeding, rearing, staging, wintering, feeding or hibernating.

5 Another avenue of recourse within the Canadian and US is found in NAFTA, under the Citizen Submission provision, Articles 14 and 15 of the North American Agreement on Environmental Cooperation, NAFTA's environmental side agreement. There are no mechanisms to compel enforcement of environmental laws, but a full investigation into government action or inaction is completed and this record can be utilized to pressure governments to act. The record has been mixed. See the chapter in this volume by Kirton.

The disparity of reach between the U.S. and Canadian citizen suit provisions results from the differing strengths of the federal governments and the respective separation of powers. U.S. federal law supersedes state law and the federal government has full jurisdiction on federal lands, thus citizen suits and subsequent judgments based on federal provisions supersede any local authority. Canadian provinces, on the other hand, have jurisdiction over natural resources and wildlife on Crown lands and the federal government rarely trumps provincial authority. The decentralized Canadian context encourages such action at the provincial level; the litigation concerning the Oldman River Dam and Rafferty-Alameda projects are examples of lawsuits brought using public interest standing in Canada (Hazell, 1999).[6]

The use of *indicator species* for monitoring and *focal species* adds another layer of protection to species inhabiting protected habitats, providing additional biodiversity benefits by affording an umbrella of protection to other species. The Nature Conservancy targets numerous types of species for conservation planning, including endangered or threatened species, species of conservation concern, focal species that are either keystone or wide ranging, species groupings that have similar habitat needs, or large aggregations of species (Nature Conservancy, 2003). These groupings provide a basis for delineating habitat and connectivity requirements, while using the targeted groups as proxy indicators for monitoring ecosystem health.

Grizzly bears and wolves act as indicator and keystone, or "umbrella", species within their large ranges. Reintroducing these species in the northern Rocky Mountain region of the U.S. has re-established "the regulatory roles of large predators" and is a part of a process referred to as "rewilding" (Soulé and Noss, 1998). These species act as indicators of ecosystem health due to their habitat requirements and their wide-ranging nature (Miller et al., 2001). Noss and Soulé (1998) note that there are three "major scientific arguments [that] constitute the rewilding argument and justify the emphasis on large predators":

> First, the structure, resilience, and diversity of ecosystems is often maintained by "top-down" ecological (trophic) interactions that are initiated by top predators ... Second, wide-ranging predators usually require large cores of protected landscape for secure foraging, seasonal movement, and other needs; they justify bigness. Third, connectivity is also required because core reserves are typically not large enough in most regions; they must be linked to insure long-term viability of wide-ranging species (Soulé and Noss, 1998:22).

The use of indicator and focal species is a vital component of ecoregional conservation, since land use planning and resource extraction must minimize habitat destruction, encouraging the establishment of transborder corridors (Poiani and Richter, 1999),

---

6 In Canada, most environmental regulations do not contain citizen suit provisions, but citizens or groups may be conferred standing if the case passes the following tests: "(1) is the matter justiciable? (2) is the matter serious? (3) is the person directly affected genuinely interested in the litigation? (4) is there an alternative means of challenging the validity of the Act or action at issue?" (Sossin, 1999:205).

and encouraging Canadian-American cooperation. For example, separate grizzly bear management plans for the Northern Cascades and the Rocky Mountains have been drafted through cooperative, but low-level joint meetings. In 1997, a meeting between Environment Minister Sergio Marchi and Secretary of the Interior Bruce Babbitt spawned the *Framework for Cooperation Between the U.S. Department of the Interior and Environment Canada in the Protection and Recovery of Wild Species at Risk*. Agency cooperation included more than research and management; it promoted the use of source populations for crossborder species reintroduction. Canada has received swift foxes from Colorado, South Dakota, and Wyoming, while the U.S. has received Albertan and British Columbian wolves and grizzly bears to re-establish populations in the Northern U.S. Rockies (EC and USFWS, 2001). Similar cooperative actions regarding habitat protection have occurred with wide-ranging avian migratory species, specifically the whooping crane and piping plover.

Perhaps the most publicized transfer involved the reintroduction of the wolf in Yellowstone National Park in 1995, a milestone in North American conservation and one of the most combative, confrontational conservation projects carried out under the USESA.

The early management of Yellowstone, founded in 1872, was meagre, and hunters "slew Greater Yellowstone's elk and bison by the thousands, always sure to leave behind a few carcasses laced with strychnine to poison wolves (and any other meat eater that happened by – eagle, coyote, raven, bear). By 1886, the carnage in Yellowstone had become a national scandal, and the U.S. Cavalry was sent in to protect what was left of the "good" wildlife, a category that did not include wolves" (McNamee, 1997:31). The remaining wolves began to prey on livestock and calls for government-sponsored eradication campaigns were answered by bounties and predator control programs (McNamee, 1997). By 1926, wolves had been persecuted to extirpation in the region (Smith et al., 2004).

As mentioned above, the Yellowstone ecosystem, including forest composition, had been significantly altered by the wolf's disappearance (Miller et al., 2001). The initial concept of wolf reintroduction surfaced during the crafting of the USESA during the Nixon Administration, but the process only started in 1987 as conservation groups threatened to sue the USFWS for not complying with federal law (McNamee, 1997). A series of impact assessments, critical habitat designations, and legal battles ensued. National Park policy requires reintroduction of species that can be reintroduced with a chance of succeeding and if the species' disappearance was a result of human action (Smith et al., 2004). However, without sustained efforts by the NGO community and a sympathetic Secretary of the Interior, Bruce Babbitt, wolf recovery would not have proceeded.[7]

The ranching community in the Greater Yellowstone Ecosystem was, generally, opposed to reintroduction of the wolf, but the extreme stance of the state Farm Bureaus further radicalized much of the ranching community, setting the stage for

7 Bruce Babbitt served as Secretary of the Interior during both terms of the Clinton Administration, (1993-2001).

an acrimonious reintroduction.[8] National support for reintroduction was strong, but "the greatest political power would be wielded by those who had something to lose, or thought they did. As general public enthusiasm for the wolf was rising, so was the pressure brought by livestock interests on their congressional delegations to scuttle the proposal" (McNamee, 1997:36). In 1995, after numerous lawsuits attempting to stop wolf reintroduction had failed, fourteen wolves trapped in Alberta were transported to holding pens in Yellowstone, and after a period of acclimation, released. Subsequently, seventeen additional wolves from British Columbia were transported and released.

By 2003, wolf reintroduction had occurred in Central Idaho and the populations had reached recovery targets that could allow for delisting. The Yellowstone population numbered 174, after fewer than ten years, and the ecosystem had already begun to revert back to pre-extirpation characteristics, including regulation of the elk and deer populations. Currently, management is posed to be devolved to the state level, as part of the delisting process, but only Montana and Idaho have had their management plans approved by the Fish and Wildlife Service. The state agencies have continued to oppose wolf protections due to the perceived impact on the ranching community and restrictive habitat safeguards imposed on the timber, energy and mining interests (Defenders of Wildlife, 2004; McNamee, 1997). The lack of support and commitment of the state agencies have forced NGOs to continually monitor, and threaten lawsuits for management prescriptions that countervail the USESA and wolf recovery management plans.

Ecoregional Conservation

Ecoregional conservation is instituted at the regional, ecosystem, and landscape scale. Each management scale is interlinked to provide a solid foundation for biotic communities to sustain themselves (Nature Conservancy, 2001; CBD, 1996, 2003). The basis for this approach is the concept of functionality within each scale. Conservation programs must be implemented along ecoregional boundaries, not political ones, representing all ecosystems within an ecoregion that cover the "group of interconnected natural communities on land or water that are linked together by ecological processes" (Nature Conservancy, 2001:5). Lastly, functional sites and landscapes form the cogs of this approach by providing areas with high potential for conservation; these include protected areas and corridors connecting these core areas (Nature Conservancy, 2001, 2003). This moves quite beyond the foundational "island biogeography" approach often favoured in the past, and encourages the development

8 Importantly, prior to the actual reintroduction, Defenders of Wildlife created a fund, the Bailey Wildlife Foundation Wolf Compensation Trust, to reimburse ranchers that lose livestock to wolf depredation. The fund has expanded to include proactive funding measures that assist ranchers to implement best management practices to reduce the potential for wolf or grizzly induced livestock or property damage (Defenders of Wildlife, 2004; Mack and Holyan, 2004).

of large, connected networks of protected and managed areas that are functional and, as much as possible, contain complete assemblages (plants, herbivores and predators). (Groves et al., 2000; Nature Conservancy, 2001; CBD, 1996, 2003).[9] The approach uses a holistic vision to implement

> far-reaching strategies [to] identify biodiversity goals and targets. They propose representative systems of conservation areas of sufficient size, condition, and connectivity to maintain even the most sensitive species and ecological processes … These features strengthen the conservation community's credibility in predicting the consequences of different resource-use scenarios and its bargaining position during negotiations with stakeholders for whom conservation is a lower priority (Olson et al., 2002:3).

This approach focuses on the entire ecosystem, the natural and anthropogenic processes, biotic and abiotic communities, and cultural or economic uses. Ecosystem conservation is centered on the creation of a network of protected areas, or biologically functional landscapes, connected by a matrix system of corridors and buffer areas (Nature Conservancy, 2001). This ecoregional management framework is found within the CBD and has been incorporated into NGO strategies for the past ten years. The CEC's *Strategic Plan for Biodiversity* promotes the same ecoregional management framework. The strategy calls for biodiversity gap analysis, threat identification and biodiversity monitoring, conserving species of common conservation concern, identification of priority areas for conservation (i.e. biodiversity hotspots), sustainable utilization of resources, alignment of management regimes, and cooperative cross border action in order to promote both sustainable development and reduce or halt biodiversity loss (CEC, 2003). On paper, the strategy appears to be an effective mechanism in developing cooperative conservation programs and initiating stakeholder dialogue, but its efficacy and reach relies on how it is implemented, the resources dedicated, and the level of priority it receives by the national and state or provincial governments.

The buffer areas consist of rehabilitated landscapes and areas subject to resource extraction. Riparian areas are protected by buffer zones, with the width depending on the size and biological importance of the watercourse (CBD, 1996). Resource extraction and use mimics natural disturbance by limiting road construction, soil compaction, and impacts to sensitive wildlife populations (CBD, 1996).

---

9 E.O. Wilson's concept of island biogeography provided the foundation for this holistic, adaptive, and integrative approach that attempts to reassemble and connect functional landscapes. Governments had developed systems of protected areas and wilderness, but many of these sites were isolated and incomplete; the focus on wilderness preserves provides half of the solution. "The science of conservation biology has shown that the island strategy, by itself, is inadequate to the formidable challenge of conserving most living species. The evidence, that isolated reserves gradually lose native species, especially large mammals and carnivores, is overwhelming" (Soule and Terborgh, 2000:4). Thus the phrase "big is good, but linked is better" (Dearden, 2001:88).

The implementation of ecoregional conservation uses the "three C's" of conservation: cores, corridors, and carnivores (Noss, 2003). Core protected areas provide the basis for conservation, while buffers provide protection from edge effects of resource use. Corridors allow species to range and intermix between core protected areas. Core areas cover the range of biotic and abiotic elements within an ecosystem and provide key habitat for focal species and other biotic assemblages. Corridors are "linear habitat[s], embedded in a dissimilar matrix that [connect] two or more larger conservation areas on the ground [to] enhance or maintain the viability of specific wildlife population in the habitat blocks [cores]" (Beier and Noss, 1998:1242). Importantly for Canadian-American relations, there are several cases where this approach demands crossborder organization and mutual commitment.

The *Yellowstone to Yukon*, and the Northern Appalachian *2Countries, 1 Forest* (2C1Forest) initiatives implement ecoregional conservation planning as a means to preserve functional landscapes and provide core and connective habitats for wide-roaming endangered species (specifically grizzly bear, wolves, and lynx).[10] These networks developed through the realization that local efforts were effective in preserving small landscapes and ecosystems, but their work had limited efficacy within an ecoregional context, and their site-based conservation efforts needed to be connected. The driving force behind these initiatives has been various coalitions of NGOs; while state and federal agencies contribute, they have little impact on defining the conservation vision. In fact, NGOs not only initiated the promotion and implementation of these initiatives, they have driven the development of the science that supports the conservation network designs. The Nature Conservancy and the Wildlands Project have invested significant resources into developing science-based action plans and conservation designs. These resources have not been available to government agencies and these NGOs have filled the conservation void created by the intransigence of federal agencies on both sides of the border and the inability of local agency bureaucrats due to fiscal and management restraints.

The Yellowstone to Yukon ecoregion covers the northern section of a mountain corridor stretching from Mexico to Alaska, and it swathes a stretch of land 3200 kilometres long and 200 km wide from southern Wyoming to the Peel River Basin in the Yukon and west near the Alaska border (Y2Y, 1998). The Y2Y Conservation Initiative developed out of a common understanding within the NGO community that connected areas across the border were imperative in order to provide substantial habitat for wide-ranging predators, most significantly the grizzly bear. This common understanding drives the conservation agenda in a region generally dominated politically by the energy, mining, forestry and livestock industries. The Initiative has been the driving force behind the development of conservation science and has created enough community support to allow the U.S. Fish and Wildlife Service to realize the reintroduction of grizzly bears and wolves. Y2Y's inception in 1993 was

10 Other examples of cross-border conservation initiatives include the Algonquin to Adirondack (A2A) in Ontario and New York and the Baja to Bering (B2B), covering the West Coast of North America.

led by a group of scientists and conservationists interested in applying conservation biology principles over the U.S. and Canadian Rockies (Y2Y, 2004). The network formalized in 1996 and includes over 800 local and national NGOs, foundations, and scientists that effectively collaborate on developing a network of protected areas and connective corridors with the goal of providing "the foundations for long-term economic sustainability, community vitality, and the quality of life we associate with mountain living" (Y2Y, 2004).

The Y2Y network has coordinated programs across the border that government agencies have yet to accomplish. At the outset, the mapping capabilities of network members had to be harmonized in order to produce suitable conservation assessments and to determine potential wildlife corridors, buffers, cores and potential ecological stresses. Where thematic or geographic gaps existed in the data, agreements were developed for data-sharing and a data framework was established (Y2Y, 2000). The outcome of this mapping exercise was a conservation areas design that incorporated accurate data concerning habitat requirements for various indicator species, roads, land use, human population density, vegetation, resource extraction (forestry, mining, grazing and so on), hydrology, climate, land ownership, and altitude. The myriad agencies managing the lands within the ecoregion did not have this mapping resource, and similar government sponsored cross-border mapping programs were not planned (Pedynowski, 2003). The driving force behind the data harmonization was the network of NGOs, who, through the creation of this ecoregional assessment, effectively set the conservation agenda by highlighting areas of critical importance, potential wildlife corridors, and land use and other human-induced stresses. Low-level agency representatives were involved, but their participation was not mandated through agency directives. The harmonization of these data sets allowed the member organizations of Y2Y to map areas suitable for protection across the entire ecoregion and target specific connective barriers. In addition, potential human stresses were identified using integrated land use mapping system, and as means to remedy poor development, the network developed a land use planning program (Y2Y, 2004). The network has also worked to remedy economic conflicts in the region and to institute sustainable natural resource extraction programs (Gailus, 2000).

A study of a subsection of the Y2Y, the Crown of the Continent (COCE), conducted in 2002, provides a good example of the regulatory impediments that continue to be erected by agency bureaucracies and how these can limit ecoregional conservation. Interaction across the border between the seventeen management agencies has focused largely on crisis management, for example the wildfires of 2000, and land managers do not have funds to allocate to cross-border conservation (Pedynowski, 2003). After initial "crisis" interaction, demands for resources to be allocated for cross border conservation increased, but allocating resources to such initiatives was not a priority. Steps to formalize cross-border conservation, such as a joint declaration similar to the 1997 Babbitt/Marchi Framework, could be implemented in order to ensure the activities are prioritized and funded, but a bilateral agreement within the current political context is highly unlikely; both federal and state/provincial governments are not "friendly" towards conservation initiatives. The management agencies in the region continue to be years behind the NGO community in conservation planning and management, and they do not have the flexibility to modify their management mandates. "For jurisdictions to develop, and subsequently implement, common policy goals, it is necessary to identify transboundary issues that require attention, formulate common values and goals with neighbouring jurisdictions that have similar concerns, and prioritize action (with requisite resources) to act on transboundary concerns" (Pedynowksi, 2003:1266). Regulatory bureaucracy has inhibited this development.

Another example from eastern North America is focused on the Northern Appalachian/Acadian ecoregion, stretching from the Adirondacks of northern New York, across northern New England, into the Eastern Townships and Gaspé Peninsula of Québec, and across all of New Brunswick and Nova Scotia. It is the most densely populated region of North America, and the population pressure in the region's hinterlands continues to intensify. On the other hand, the Northern Appalachian ecoregion represents a unique opportunity in terms of the conservation of biodiversity, as its myriad forests, decimated in the first 300 years of European inhabitation, have slowly regenerated, albeit with a different community composition, over the past century (Foster and Motzkin, 1998). In 2001, conservation groups from across the region convened and decided to work within a coordinated work plan; the *2 Countries, 1 Forest Initiative* (2C1F) was formalized in 2003.

The nascent, NGO-driven initiative began as numerous individual programs and projects began to overlap. The Wildlife Conservation Society and wildlife agencies at the state, provincial and federal levels were assessing the potential to coordinate regional recovery efforts of the Canada lynx, while the Wildlands Project and the Nature Conservancy were developing individual regional conservation area designs. All three provincial governments were, and continue to be, in the process of developing protected areas networks as required in the CDB. Biodiversity planning within the GAP Analysis program of the United States Geological Survey (USGS) was ongoing or complete in all of the states. Much of the privately held timberlands in Maine were being sold, with portions purchased for conservation, but many of the lots were subdivided with the intention to build cottages and second homes in the region. Cross-border relations between agencies continue to be limited, but the increasing sophistication and coordination of NGO activities within the ecoregion are creating a vision for ecoregional conservation and regional identity.

Constructing a regional identity, similar to the Y2Y, was a difficult initial step due to misperceptions pertaining to a lack of knowledge concerning cross-border connections and the idea of the existence of a Northeastern Wilderness (Ray, 2000). To overcome the notion that conservation and restoration could be conducted in a landscape that is far from pristine, the initiative has worked to build an image of eastern wilderness. Meso-predators (medium) like the lynx, bobcat, marten and foxes all inhabit the region and all face increasing human-induced habitat stresses and the 2C1Forest program of work is attempting to establish a conservation network, based on sound conservation science, to protect these focal species, while implementing sustainable development programs in the ecoregion.

Both the Y2Y and the 2C1Forest initiatives indicate that conservation NGOs have effectively taken the lead in setting the agenda in these regions due to a combination of government inaction, agency capture and political antipathy towards conservation. Both of these initiatives were established by conservation NGOs; these groups grasped the necessity of developing connections between core protected areas as a means to preserve wide-roaming species. Lower level bureaucrats became involved on both sides, but the federal governments have remained largely on the sidelines, while state/provincial level cooperation has also been minimal. Governmental declarations on cross border cooperation have been few, but cooperation between NGOs has evolved to become highly sophisticated. Federal governments on either side of the border have been subject to political paralysis – in Canada, due to weak federalism and a lack of jurisdiction over natural resources; and in the U.S. due to the funding starvation of U.S. federal bureaucracy successive Republican congresses have caused. In addition, political accounting has misjudged the value of both ecological services supplied by wildlands and the provision of intergenerational goods to successive generations. As state actors have betrayed their effectiveness, non-state actors filled the void. Sanderson's (2002) pessimistic view echoes this concern: "[s]o long as national governments and the intergovernmental system are solely responsible for global conservation policy leadership, better results cannot be expected" (166). Both the Y2Y and 2C1F initiatives have developed, and are in the process of implementing, conservation area designs and have highly technical capacity for research, mapping, and communication that government agencies are unable and unwilling to contribute. Perhaps not surprisingly, we find more muscular government response when dealing with the case of an invasive species that threatens economic interests.

Invasive Species: *Dreissena polymorpha*[11]

First noted by German naturalist Peter Simon Pallas in the Caspian Sea and Ural River in 1769, the zebra mussel (*dreissena polymorpha*) is very small: a full-grown adult is about 50mm long, roughly the size of an average human fingernail. Yet it more than makes up for a lack of individual size by its collective mass, and is well known as a voracious consumer of particulate matter including phytoplankton and even smaller forms of zooplankton. It is found in freshwater (which made its sudden spread in North America, an entire salt-water ocean away from the original donor system[12] in southeastern Europe, all the more curious), and reproduces when temperatures rise to 54°F. Most *dreissena polymorpha* have distinctive brown stripes, which gives them the "zebra" label.

Problematically, the mussels adhere to hard surfaces; young larvae will die if they do not secure themselves to a hard surface at an early stage in their development.

11 Special thanks to Cristina Romanelli for research assistance.

12 Specialists refer to the origin ecosystem of invasive species as "donor systems," and newly colonized areas as "recipient systems."

They prefer (unfortunately, as we will see) to latch onto other shelled species, but can certainly make do with anything from wood to rock to steel. Their average lifespan is four to five years. Mature females produce several hundred thousand eggs per reproductive season, which are externally fertilized by males; females can release up to *five million* eggs per year. The eggs turn to *veligers*, free-swimming larvae, and they drift in river/lake currents until they find a suitable space to adhere and grow their shells. The majority do not find one and are eaten, but – depending on the ecosystemic characteristics in which they are born – hundreds, or even thousands, do survive. Because of the improvement of water quality in the Great Lakes in the 1970s and 1980s, this became suitable habitat. The fact that veligers are free-swimming is central: mussels endemic to the Great Lakes are dependent on species of native fish to serve as hosts for larvae, whereas the zebra mussel does not exhibit this population-balancing necessity.

Ships have long been conduits for species distribution. The colonization of North America brought smallpox and other deadly microbes to the native population, and re-introduced the horse, changing the technological landscape. But the advent of transoceanic sail power also spread many other species across the globe, such as the European shore crab, which by the mid-1800s could be found in North America, Asia, and South Africa (see Carlton and Cohen, 2003). Worms in the wooden hulls and organisms found in fishing gear would provide the nutrients necessary for long-distance survival. More importantly, half-empty ships would use soil or sand as ballast (to even the keel), and this would be ejected after arrival. In this way untold numbers of plant species and insects were unknowingly transported around the world. In fact the *purple loosestrife*, an invasive plant native to Eurasia and now found throughout North America, was probably introduced in this manner (see White, et al., 1993: 38-44). However, freshwater bivalves such as zebra mussels could never survive a two to three week journey through saltwater. Another innovation would in fact increase the possibility of transoceanic marine biological invasions: the use of *water* as ballast in large cargo ships and oil tankers. Ballast refers to water taken on board purposely, in large tanks designed for this purpose, in order to provide greater stability for a ship.[13] If, for example, a cargo ship is half-full, the discrepancy in weight will cause serious navigational problems (imagine loading an anvil on one end of a canoe). Ballast tanks are filled to even out the ships weight distribution. Further, empty ships will float too high above the waterline for proper navigation, so they too are filled with ballast in order to lower the ship in the water. This act of delicate balancing is essential to large-scale ship transport today. Since seawater is heavier than freshwater, boats tend to take on ballast when they are near freshwater ports, and thus intake indigenous aquatic species at that point, only to jettison them into the local water where they are loading/unloading.

---

13 In the case of oil tankers, the actual oil tanks are filled with water to provide ship stability. When these tanks are emptied into the sea, they deposit residual oil as well as invasive species. This is in fact the single greatest source of oil pollution at sea, not the more photogenic oil spills that capture public attention. See Mitchell, 1994.

It is believed that in this manner the zebra mussel made its maiden voyage from a European port to the Saint Lawrence Seaway and up to Lake St. Claire between Lakes Huron and Erie, in 1988 (Hebert, et al., 1989). Shipping on the Great Lakes was one of the building-blocks of North American industry, from early fur extraction in the 1700s, to the construction of the Erie and Welland Canals and the shipment of iron ore to the great steel towns of Cleveland, Buffalo, and Hamilton, to the age of modern bulk cargo carriers and oil tankers making their way from far-off ports through the St. Lawrence Seaway and into the heartland.[14] Overseas shipping was an economic mainstay long before concerns with invasive species were realized (see, for example, Kochan and Schenker, 1970). According to one estimate, since the completion of the Seaway in 1959 at least 43 non-indigenous species have been established in the Laurentian Great Lakes, with over 65 percent of these attributed to ballast water from commercial ships (Grigorovich, et al., 2003).[15]

The zebra mussel itself was no stranger to navigation, having spread throughout Europe with the canalization of the major waterways there. They were found in the Hungarian slice of the Danube River by 1790, and Great Britain as early as 1824. But they have been particularly adventurous of late, not only populating all of the five Great Lakes (Ontario, Erie, Michigan, Superior, and Huron), but surrounding estuaries and rivers as well as river system and lakes in Northeast Nebraska and Ohio. They have been found far south also, along the Missouri River, in El Dorado Lake in Kansas, and in a quarry near Haymarket, Virginia. Specialists assume this was achieved by adhering to large coal and steel barges making their way south. Even more impressively, zebra mussels have been found as far west as California. In these cases it is believed they latched onto boats being transported, over American highways, to dock on the west coast (they can survive an out-of-the-water experience, provided they are adults, close their shells immediately, and get back in water within several days).[16] While it is clear that the initial intake and transport stage of the invasion was the result of transoceanic shipping and the use of ballast water in particular, the spread stage is facilitated by barges, infiltrated pipe systems, personal and fishing boats, and even the automobile. In short, the zebra mussel found a perfect landing point, equipped with all the transport afforded by mass industrialization.

---

14 It was the construction of the final phase of the Welland Canal, in the 1920s, which permitted the invasion of the ectoparasitic sea lamprey – previously stumped by Niagara Falls – into Lakes Erie, Michigan, and Huron, with disastrous consequences for the fishing industry.

15 Perhaps the most infamous invader swam its way to the Great Lakes from the Atlantic Ocean: this was the sea lamprey, a predacious parasite that killed millions of native fish, wiping out the bluepike, shortnose cisco, walleye, and other species. The U.S.-Canada Great Lakes Fisheries Commission was established in 1955 primarily to address this threat, which it has: elaborate "lampricide treatment", which continues today, has reduced the lamprey population by up to 90 percent.

16 For more on contemporary species distribution, including a helpful interactive graph charting the spread of the species, see the United States Department of the Interior's Geological Survey, at: http://cars.er.usgs.gov/Nonindigenous_species/ZM.

Post-invasion: Impacts and Responses

Although there have been mixed results, the Canada-United States Great Lakes Water Quality Agreement of 1972 has certainly improved the quality of lake water, reducing excessive nutrient-loaders such as phosphates which threatened to lead to the premature eutrophication of Lake Erie in particular. Its expansion in 1978 to cover all five lakes and other harmful pollutants has also led to the creation of action plans for some 43 "areas of concern", monitored by the IJC (see Sproule-Jones, 2002). However, some worry that all this progress will be in vain because of the impact of the zebra mussel invasion. This may be somewhat alarmist, but there is certainly cause for sustained concern.[17]

The most evident biological impact is on other unionid bivalves, such as clams and other mussels, native to the newly-colonized area (see Schloesser and Nalepa. 1994). Zebra mussels will, if possible, adhere to living shells, and then rapidly begin the process of adhering to one another. Needless to say this is life-threatening to those species at the bottom of such a pile, in terms of their reproductive, locomotive, respiratory, and feeding functions. Indeed up to 10,000 zebra mussels can cling to a single native mussel, and some 140 species are at risk, especially in the Ohio and Mississippi River Basins. (Another invader in the Great Lakes, the quagga mussel (*Dreissena bugensis*) does not prefer unionids as substrates, and is therefore less threatening to local ecology.)

As the population inevitably increases in size, so does its collective appetite, reducing the amount of phytoplankton and zooplankton available for other species. Ironically, these voracious filtering devices also remove other particulates from the ecosystem, and this can have the effect of partially clearing contaminated water; for example, parts of Lake Erie are much clearer than before the invasion, allowing more ultraviolet rays to penetrate the bottom and increasing plant growth and thus fish nesting grounds (see Hebert, et al., 1991). Of course, whatever toxins the mussels ingest end up back in the ecosystem, as they excrete, decay at death, or are eaten by other species, including birds. The overall ecological impact is still being evaluated.

There is less debate, however, over the economic impact, which is quite significant. Beyond possible harm to fish and mussel stocks and thus local fisheries, the reason they are considered such a nuisance is because of their opportunistic adherence to a wide variety of substrates. They can colonize entire pipes, restricting water flow used in heat exchangers, condensers, fire-fighting equipment, and air conditioning systems. This can also affect public water supply and sewage plants, and hydroelectric plants as well. One power plant in Michigan reported a density as high as 700,000 per cubic meter in its pipes (though the average density of 30,000-

17 There is ample concern also that the large numbers of introduced salmonid fish stock in the Great Lakes – in excess of 745 million fish between 1966-1998 – have also fundamentally altered the recipient ecosystems; see especially Crawford, 2001.

70,000 is more usual).[18] At least twelve nuclear power plants have been affected, and it costs nearly one million dollars per year to conduct the needed cleaning operations for each of them. In the words of one analyst, the clogging caused by zebra mussels is akin to "an acute hardening of industrial arteries" (Bright, 1998:181). Analysts have suggested losses of over five billion dollars in revenue can be attributed to the invasion (Wittenburg and Cock, 2001).

They are perhaps most notorious for their impact on boats: they cling to hulls, slowing down boat speed, destroying engine cooling systems, and fouling fishing gear. Their weight can even sink marker buoys, presenting dangers for navigation. Far more than the ecological impacts, these economic threats cutting across several industries in the Great Lakes region have induced governments – national and state/provincial – on both sides of the Canadian-American border to take a vivid interest in the invasion. However, there are few viable options to eradicate the zebra mussel from colonized areas, and we can only make strong efforts towards post-invasion containment.

Clearly, invasive species are an international problem – so much so that it was customary until recent decades to even define invasive species according to the criterion that they had effectively crossed borders. It is no surprise, then, that there have been notable multilateral efforts to publicize and deal with the issue in general, perhaps most famously with the SCOPE Ecology of Biological Invasions Programme, begun in the 1980s, and now referred to as the Global Invasive Species Programme (see Ruiz and Carleton, 2003). This represents an effort to catalogue and recommend remedial action for thousands of invasive species identified so far, zebra mussels amongst them (see also CBD, 2001).

Regarding the latter, perhaps the most active role has been taken by the IJC, which was established by the *Boundary Waters Treaty of 1909* and advises both Canada and the United States on furthering the goals of the 1972 *Great Lakes Water Quality Agreement* (see Sproule-Jones, 2002; Bilder, 1972). In the summer of 2004 the IJC saw its recommendations come to life when the Army Corps of Engineers began construction on a permanent Asian carp barrier on the Chicago Ship and Sanitary Canal; however it was slow to react to the zebra mussel issue. The IJC did release a report in 2004 relating to zebra mussels, but there are little concrete actions that can be taken at this stage.[19] The prevention of further invasions is the main goal.

The immediate problem is with ballast water travellers. Indeed, zebra mussels are but one problematic invasive species that have been specifically linked to ballast water discharges by the International Maritime Organization, Global Environment Facility, and UN Development Programme, which have together instituted an international Global Ballast Water Management Programme. The others include cholera, the Cladoceran Water Flea, various sources of toxic algae, and the self-

18 This is according to the U.S. Geological Survey, op. cit.

19 Officials fear the Asian carp would devastate the $4.5 billion (U.S.) Great Lakes fishery if it is introduced via ships using the canal for ballast purposes. Press release found on ijc-announce@listserv.ijc.org, 12 July, 2004.

fertilizing hermaphroditic North American Comb Jelly. Many of these species have literally criss-crossed the globe as a consequence of the expansion of trade, secure in fresh-water ballast tanks, and emptied in awaiting ports.

The Management Programme provides a list of concrete (though invariably costly) measures both ships and port authorities can take to limit such marine bio-invasions. These include providing crews with relevant training; avoid ballasting in areas known to be of risk; keeping ballast tanks free of sediments; undertaking ballast water exchange at sea; and maintaining related and accurate records.[20] Improved intake filters and cleaner ballast tanks are essential. Port state measures include the designation of a lead agency (such as a national task force); conducting awareness campaigns; requesting ship information from logs; carrying out risk assessments for each port; conducting periodic monitoring in ports so as to alert; and providing shore-based ballast water treatment facilities where practical and cost-effective.[21] This may be the most comprehensive effort at advocating preventive measures, and both Canada and the United States have taken such recommendations seriously, stunned by the swift spread of the zebra mussel. Canada adopted the *Great Lakes Ballast Water Control Guidelines* as early as 1989, and the United States the *Nonindigenous Aquatic Nuisance Prevention and Control Act* in 1990 (this voluntary regulatory regime was expanded to the entire American coastline with the 1996 *National Invasive Species Act*) (Kolar and Lodge, 2000; Baskin, 1996). There are still international co-ordination problems and, as the history of oil tanker regulations demonstrates, it is hard to engender a policy context conducive to cooperation in the highly competitive political economy of transoceanic shipping (see Mitchell, 1994). The U.S. has yet to ratify a special IMO Convention on ballast water, since the convention would give port states authority over American ships.

The larger problem, however, is that the zebra mussel is already here. Containing it seems the only option now, because eradicating it would take a mammoth campaign of possibly ecocidal proportions. In areas where they are highly concentrated and the technology permits, colonies can be eradicated. This involves using chemical agents (known as molluscicides), freezing and boiling (through steam injection), acoustical vibration, electrical currents, and the introduction of biological agents (such as predators, parasites, and disease). All of these techniques present obvious problems for the greater aquatic environment, and may in fact cause more problems than they solve. As van Driesche and van Driesche remind us, "no examples of successful biocontrol of aquatic invertebrates exist" (2000:74).[22] Manual removal is possible for small boats, but presents an enormous challenge (in terms of safety and manpower)

---

20 Ballast exchange at sea is controversial. It does not eliminate sediment, which falls to the bottom of the tanks; for this they must be flushed out and cleaned. Furthermore, it is quite dangerous to eject ballast when not in port, especially in rough waters. See Wittenburg and Cock, 2001, 64.

21 For more information on the Global Ballast Water Management Programme, see http://globallast.imo.org.

22 There is greater hope, however, that "anti-fouling agents" can be used to repel mussel adhesion. See de Lafontaine, et al., 2002.

for large ships and underwater pipelines. Reporting the sighting of mussels in non-contaminated areas is vital, so that protected areas (such as clam grounds along the Mississippi River) can receive immediate attention. For this it is apparent that public education is necessary. But there will be no large-scale eradication programme. Like the purple loosestrife, the zebra mussel is here to stay.

Though a technical solution may be possible in the future, it would seem more reasonable at this point to suggest that there are no serious options for the complete elimination of the zebra mussel from North American waters. Environmentalists point to the impact of dams and slow-moving rivers engineered by humans as a major casual factor in the invasion, but it is unlikely there will be sufficient political pressure to deconstruct hydro dams and managed waterways. However, through constant vigilance by mariners, corporations, and other aquatic stakeholders, we can ensure that new colonies are quickly discovered and perhaps stopped before the population reaches an unmanageable mass. Ultimately, this can only be made possible with visible awareness campaigns and international policy co-ordination. This applies to all invasive species with deleterious impacts, not just those in the aquatic realm. If globalization[23] and global warming[24] are increasing the likelihood of similar invasions, then it is up to individuals, corporations, and governments to learn as much as possible about the process of identifying and reducing them before their spread becomes irreversible. Canadian-American cooperation will be instrumental in this regard, as will the participation of non-state actors.

Conclusion

This chapter has examined the question of transborder species management, from a conservationist perspective as well as that of responses to invasive species. In both cases we found that non-state actors played instrumental roles, especially when it came to the development of nature corridors and species reintroduction programmes. We have seen that there is a pronounced contemporary movement toward approaching both species loss and invasion from an ecosystemic perspective, as complicated as this is from a political vantage point. Meanwhile, government response to crisis is much more noticeable in the case of the zebra mussel invasion, which threatens a

---

23 One author has referred to invasive species as "pathogens of globalization" (Bright, 1999).

24 There is evidence that warming trends will induce species migration northward, and this raises concerns about disease and threats to native species (see Hughes, 2000). However, such "unassisted migration" will prove difficult for rare species of plants and trees, and adaptation or extinction are as likely (see Iverson, et al., 2004). In the case of zebra mussels we might see northward migration as the appropriate reproduction temperatures are more common. Flooding could also expand zebra mussel territory even further. On the latter, it is believed that "…climate change will affect the incidence of episodic recruitment events of invasive species, by altering the frequency, intensity, and duration of flooding … by allowing aggressive species to escape from local, constrained refugia" (Sutherst, 2000:224).

multi-billion dollar fishing and shipping industry, than the ecosystemic impact of the loss of wolves or grizzlies in the Rocky Mountain ranges. Of course, this is not in any way surprising: governments are more likely to respond to security threats that can be easily converted into financial resource loss, and they are more likely to co-operate with other governments if mutual economic advantage is anticipated. But by largely sitting on the sidelines during the establishment of transborder nature reserves, governments may be missing a golden opportunity to become more involved, thus strengthening relations between Canada and the United States, promoting scientific progress in monitoring the impact of global warming and other ecoregional threats, and thus enhancing the ability to confront future threats posed by invasive species as well.

Chapter 10

Multi-Level Environmental Governance in North America: Migratory Birds and Biodiversity Conservation

Robert Boardman

Arrangements for conserving North American wild bird populations, including regulation of hunting practices in the case of some species, evolved gradually during the twentieth century. This history has also been punctuated by bursts of political activity directed towards reform and restructuring. A focus on renovation of the institutional arrangements with a view to broadening the coverage of species, emphasizing the importance of habitat protection, thinking through the significance of processes of continental economic integration, enhancing transborder cooperative links, constructing wider networks of partnership links among multiple actors at multiple levels of governance, and facilitating the participation of Mexico within traditionally U.S.-Canada frameworks, has been a characteristic feature of developments since the mid-1980s.

Regimes at and across various levels of government in North America reflect diverse meanings of key terms such as conservation and biodiversity. In policy terms, issues of bird conservation revolve around two divergent but overlapping categories: discourses and actions related to sustainable development, or the management of species for hunting and related ends; and those centred on inherent values of protection, regardless of the utility of a species. Other policy questions presented by birds include the economic value of species in relation to national parks and birding and other recreational activities, the role of wild birds in the spread of diseases, public health issues presented by the abundance of some species in urban settings, such as Canada geese, and the workings of crop protection programmes. Wild birds also serve in some scientific assessments as indicators of the ecological health of landscapes.

A concern with mounting threats to bird species and habitats forms a common thread through many of these complex governance activities. Globally, many bird species are increasingly threatened by a variety of factors. These include pressures that contribute to wetlands and other habitat deterioration, such as agricultural developments, forestry, urbanization, industrial practices, and changes resulting from the management of rivers and coastlines, and the effects of hunting, invasive species and chemicals (Youth, 2003). Climate change is likely to become increasingly significant, for example through its effects on vegetation. In the U.S. the federal Fish and Wildlife Service has identified 131 bird species, or 12 percent of all native species, as "of conservation concern" (USFWS, 2002: Table 49).

These diverse factors affect species in different ways. Whereas some species depend for their survival on natural disturbances to habitat, for example the rare Kirtland's warbler on forest fires in northern Michigan (Askins, 2000:41-48), and although other species are adaptable in various ways to landscape changes brought about by human activities, anthropogenic habitat alteration has exerted profound effects on many species and populations. Forest fragmentation has had significant consequences for populations of neotropical migratory birds, many with ranges or migration routes in Mexico and the southern United States (Robinson, et al., 1995; Burton, et al., 2003:24). Species such as owls and woodpeckers are especially vulnerable to threats from logging operations because of their dependence on undisturbed features of the Canadian boreal forest (Imbeau, et al., 2001). There are also natural factors at work. These include prevailing temperatures during migration and the body mass of birds; such factors probably account for most of the high mortality rates of young greater snow geese in their migration between sites in Nunavut and Quebec (Menu, Gauthier and Reed, 2005). Conservation politics is also fuelled by growing appreciation of the local and national economic significance of activities such as ecotourism and birdwatching (Bibby, 2002:27-29).

Governance in this area is characterized by dense thickets of non-governmental organizations, the engagement of governments at multiple levels, and diverse sets of partnership and other relationships among these. Civil society groups are crucial actors in continental governance arrangements because of the roles many play in relation to land management and species conservation, either autonomously or in collaboration with government wildlife or parks agencies. Governance arrangements derive from and reinforce both cooperative impulses on the part of actors and also cleavages grounded in different framings of the core policy problems. The resulting multi-actor and multi-level complexity nonetheless springs from an underlying governance question: What is the most effective way to promote continental bird biodiversity?

In this chapter continental arrangements for the conservation of bird biodiversity will be viewed in terms of the intersections between and cross-linkages among four arenas. These are, first, developments in the migratory bird treaty system that initiated government activity in this area in the early 1900s, particularly through the North American Waterfowl Management Plan since 1986; secondly, the impact on continental arrangements of the cumulative growth in governmental and NGO species-at-risk programmes and broader mandates of protection of wild species of flora and fauna, which since 1996 has incorporated Mexico in the Trilateral Committee system; thirdly, the important effects on bird conservation practices of NAFTA, and the North American Agreement on Environmental Cooperation (NAAEC), for example through the involvement of the Commission on Environmental Cooperation (CEC) in birds-related issues, and the development of the North American Bird Conservation Initiative (NABCI) since 1999; and finally, multi-actor and multi-level species and habitats networks centred on or critically incorporating non-governmental conservation organizations.

The Classical Model: Migratory Bird Management

Governance arrangements for much of the 20th century were largely a product of frameworks initiated in the early 1900s (Boardman, 2006:Ch. 3-4). The Canada-U.S. Migratory Birds Treaty of 1916 was a pioneering agreement in the field of transboundary wildlife conservation. Its origins lay in the conservation group politics of that period, and the rising concerns about national parks and the protection of wild spaces. The growth of data sets on wild birds from civil society groups, fledgling government agencies, and the U.S. Biological Survey (Hawkins, 1984:2), accelerated these efforts. The convention set up a framework for an evolving transboundary regulatory system centred primarily on migratory species of game birds. Washington and Ottawa specified various regulatory instruments to achieve these objectives, including demarcation of hunting seasons and limits, for example by means of a ban on hunting in the spring designed to ensure survival of game species. Some species of migratory game birds thought to be seriously at risk from excessive hunting, including species of swans and cranes, were protected by a ten-year moratorium. The convention and subsequent measures by the two governments also created a permits system, and brought in specific rules in relation to harm to nests and eggs. Also set in motion was a protected-area system of bird sanctuaries for species regularly crossing the Canada-U.S. border (Juillet, 2000a:104-6). As such the convention reflected the wildlife conservation consensus of the early 1900s. Juillet describes it as "resolutely an early twentieth century development, embodying a utilitarian approach to the conservation of nature" (Juillet, 2000a:106).

Key elements in this system became increasingly controversial in subsequent decades, particularly with the growth of the environmental movement from the late 1960s, the rise of aboriginal governance issues in both Canada and the U.S., and continuing pressures from the core hunting constituency. There were intensified debates on the specifics of annual seasons and bag limits regulations. Many hunters continued to see the regulatory system in general and the specific transborder form it had taken as a violation of basic rights. Duck-hunting and other groups objected to the emerging system of flyway councils from the 1940s and early 1950s on the grounds that these implied differential privileges for hunters in different jurisdictions (Day, 1949:87-88). The four main flyway councils were innovative governance developments that have formed the basis for much state regulatory activity, in association with NGOs and federal wildlife bodies. Rising pressures from environmentalists and broad-spectrum nature conservation groups led to advocacy of a shift away from game birds and towards inclusion of other species within a protected system. (In implementing the convention the two governments omitted species such as hawks and crows which were thought enemies of rather than desirable targets for bird conservation (Burnett, 2003a:29-30).) Critics increasingly pointed to a relative lack of emphasis on the habitat protection needs of wild birds, despite the commitment of both governments to a migratory bird sanctuary system.

Aboriginal hunting rights, based on the spiritual as well as the material value of harvested species, proved a particularly difficult obstacle for the evolution of the migratory birds system. There had been recognition in the convention of some aboriginal exceptions to hunting rules to allow the taking of some seabirds, but such provisions were of marginal significance to the regime. Thus Northern communities in Canada and Alaska resisted the spread of the new regulatory regime from the south. A particular concern was the spring-hunting ban, an issue that continued to dominate relations between governments and aboriginal communities. Many bird species were present in northern regions only during months when hunting was banned. Negotiations among actors aimed at meeting some of these concerns led to a controversial Protocol signed in 1979. This provided for a limited, needs-based, system of aboriginal hunting in the spring. This compromise generated heated opposition in the U.S. from hunters' organizations, leading environmental groups which were influential in the Congress, such as the National Wildlife Federation, and state wildlife agencies. By 1984 it was apparent that the planned change would not get through the constitutional hurdle of the U.S. Senate's Foreign Relations Committee (Juillet, 2000b:131-34; Juillet, 2000a:244-82). A successful change negotiated later, the 1995 Protocol, defined aboriginal peoples' access to migratory bird species and among other things updated the list of species identified in the convention.

Three sets of factors contributed to more fundamental change in the workings of the system from the 1980s. First, by this time the convention was being influenced by shifts in wildlife conservation philosophies and politics generally in North America. In particular, the convention was increasingly being viewed by environmental organizations as excessively restricted in terms of the species listed, the criteria for their inclusion, and the regulatory approach embodied in the agreement and its subsequent implementation. The habitat protection arrangements associated with the convention were widely criticized as inadequate. The migratory bird sanctuary (MBS) system was criticized in an Ontario study which concluded that only three or four of the 13 MBSs in the province could be justified. The report produced a litany of complaints about practices inside sanctuary boundaries that included the operations of a nickel smelter and a gypsum plant, residential subdivisions, and the caging of migratory birds for public display (Levesque, McCullough and Mohr, 1984:2). More generally, major factors contributing to habitat transformation or degradation were not addressed directly in the migratory birds system. This gap became critical as conservation approaches in the U.S. and Canada increasingly moved away from species-centred to more broadly defined habitat or ecosystem strategies.

Secondly, waterfowl populations (duck, geese and swan species) were undergoing serious threats and were responding in different ways to pressures on their habitats during the 1980s. While some species such as wood ducks had clearly benefited in terms of numbers by Canada-U.S. cooperation under the migratory birds convention framework, waterfowl populations generally suffered severely from the prairie drought of the 1980s and from other factors affecting wetlands habitats, such as draining for agricultural development and urbanization. Some goose populations continued to flourish in agricultural areas and city landscapes, but many duck species were reaching unprecedentedly low numbers and appeared headed for chronic decline.

A third influence on the system was the geographical and political broadening of scope resulting from the expanding participation of Mexican agencies and groups in North American governance arrangements. This followed the growth of knowledge of the pathways of many species, particularly in the context of the 1936 U.S.-Mexico migratory birds agreement, and the bilateral committee on Wildlife and Plant Conservation set up in 1975. The upshot was a *de facto* if not a formal tri-national framework covering key waterfowl migratory routes. Canada and Mexico did not sign a corresponding bilateral agreement (though cooperation on birds expanded), nor were the two bilateral agreements codified into a trilateral convention. Even so, it was increasingly evident that North American waterfowl conservation objectives could not be achieved on the basis primarily of cooperation between Canadian and U.S. actors.

The North American Waterfowl Management Plan put in place in 1986 (and which Mexico joined in 1994), was an attempt to reverse species population trends and to recover levels of the 1970s, especially the high numbers reached by duck populations in the early 1970s. The NAWMP recognized that "the maintenance of abundant waterfowl populations is dependent on the protection, restoration and management of habitat. The persistent loss of important waterfowl habitat should be reversed… The loss and degradation of habitat is the major waterfowl management problem in North America" (USFWS 1986:2, 9). Central to these overall goals was the emerging principle of trilateral cooperation among governments and agencies in the U.S., Canada and Mexico. At the same time – and in line with the political atmosphere of Washington in the 1980s and 1990s – there was widespread acknowledgment that governments, whether federal or state and provincial, were only one constituent of a governance system, and that there were clear limits to what regulatory, or top-down, strategies from governments could achieve. Waterfowl conservation programmes had to be "generally beneficial or neutral with respect to agricultural activities and industrial land uses. The efforts required to maintain and enhance waterfowl habitat in North America are beyond the capability of public natural resource agencies alone. Long-term solutions will require the coordinated action of governments, private organizations, landowners and other citizens" (USFWS 1986:11).

The work of NAWMP gathered momentum from the late 1980s, with revisions in 1994 and formal updates to the Plan in 1998 and 2003. Funding for waterfowl conservation projects became more institutionalized, though not guaranteed, with passage of the U.S. North American Wetlands Conservation Act (NAWCA) in 1989. The central work of NAWMP continued to be centred on data-gathering in relation to key species and the monitoring of bird habitat conditions, such as the continuing degradation of coastal habitat by urbanization and industrial developments affecting sea duck populations. Activities were expanded and integrated as a result of the impact of the North American Bird Conservation Initiative (NABCI) from the late 1990s.

Following its inception, NAWMP activities and species interests became in effect part of a broader continental conservation strategy, and the joint venture approach became increasingly central both to traditional waterfowl conservation planning as well as to the wider range of projects on non-game-bird species and habitats. U.S. wetlands legislation of 1989 and the resultant continent-wide availability of funding for wetlands projects also drove this process of change.

Shared-species Trilateralism

A broadening of the scope of continental bird conservation activities beyond core NAWMP concerns thus developed out of the discussions of the 1980s and 1990s aimed in part at bringing about greater participation by Mexico in the North American system, in other words at nudging arrangements into a more formalized trilateral direction. Attention to bird species beyond the range of those traditionally focused on in continental governance arrangements followed logically from these developments. It was reinforced by activities springing out of the NAFTA environmental side-agreement (discussed in the next section), continued and deepening interest on the part of U.S. actors in neo-tropical migratory birds, and pressures from environmental and conservation groups for change in the migratory birds framework.

In 1988, the three governments had created a tripartite committee linking their federal wildlife agencies – on the initiative of Mexico – which was designed to protect migratory birds, broadly defined, and their habitats. Discussions on the future of the 1988 committee, which was arguably redundant after 1994 (when Mexico joined the NAWMP), prompted a Canadian initiative to restructure it with an enlarged wildlife conservation mandate. The result was the Trilateral Committee for Wildlife and Ecosystem Conservation and Management, which was created by a Memorandum of Understanding signed at Oaxaca in 1996. This was given a wide mandate "to facilitate and enhance coordination, cooperation and the development of partnerships among the wildlife agencies of the three countries, and with other associated and interested entities, regarding projects and programmes for the conservation and management of wildlife, plants, biological diversity and ecosystems of mutual interest" (Trilateral Committee, 1996:2).

Bird conservation questions have been a significant part of this bigger picture. The main work is based on activities undertaken by each of the countries' government wildlife agencies, with in practice a tilt towards focusing on questions arising from endangered-species lists and recovery programmes. Thus birds questions arise primarily in two of the sub-committees (or Working Tables) of the Trilateral Committee, those respectively on Wetlands and Migratory Birds, and on Shared Species. In these forums and in the annual meetings of the Trilateral Committee, officials from each country raise species and conservation issues felt to require consideration at a tri-national level (Jewell, 2000:26). Joint discussions of members of the shared species and migratory birds working tables at the 2002 annual meetings in Nuevo Vallarta reviewed the status of 11 bird species and conservation activities related to each of these. All were targets of continuing national or bilateral research or recovery projects (Shared Species Table, 2002). The value of tri-national cooperation is thus particularly evident where species have either a transborder range or migratory routes crossing national jurisdictions. Protection of the habitat of the piping plover, a high-priority species for Canada, is enhanced as a result of these kinds of exchanges by greater knowledge of its wintering grounds in the U.S. and Mexico; and protection of the thick-billed parrot similarly requires transborder cooperation because of threats to habitat in its range in the southern U.S. and Mexico. A closely related development was the framework agreement signed by the U.S. and Canada in April 1997 on the protection and recovery of species at risk (or so-called borderline species). This aimed to formalize and strengthen cross-border cooperation between officials of federal and state and provincial wildlife agencies on species monitoring and recovery projects. These forms of cooperative ventures already had a lengthy history in U.S.-Canada relations, and historically have been important in the case of birds for recovery of populations of the whooping crane and piping plover. The 1997 agreement drew also on increasing attention to the overlaps and complementarities between the U.S. and Canadian lists of species at risk: 33 of the fauna and flora species on official U.S. lists (under the Endangered Species Act) are also present in Canada, and 125 of those on the Canadian list of species at risk are also found in the U.S. (U.S.-Canada Framework for Cooperation, 2003:2). The borderline species agreement thus provided greater opportunities for the promotion and sharing of expertise and data between the two countries, including discussions on the potential harmonization of the processes of identification and monitoring of species confronting varying degrees of risk. The whooping crane, piping plover, and marbled murrelet were initial targets of concern in the conservation efforts promoted through this framework.

Towards an Integrated "All Birds/All Habitats" Approach

The North American Agreement on Environmental Cooperation (NAAEC), the environmental side-agreement of NAFTA signed in 1993, envisaged a broad range of objectives across the environmental policy agendas facing the U.S., Mexico and Canada. These were to be the responsibility of the Commission for Environmental Cooperation (CEC), encompassing a Council consisting of the environment ministers of the three countries, a secretariat based in Montreal, and the Joint Public Advisory Committee. The wide-ranging set of objectives set out in Article 1 of the NAAEC included several of particular relevance to biodiversity and bird conservation issues (Glicksman, 2003). The goals were stated to be among other things to "increase cooperation between the Parties to better conserve, protect, and enhance the environment, including wild flora and fauna" (Article 1[c]), and to "strengthen cooperation on the development and improvement of environmental laws, regulations, procedures, policies and practices" (Article 1[f]). In addition the general formulation of the monitoring role of the CEC as stated in Article

1(g) – to "enhance compliance with, and enforcement of, environmental laws and regulations" – also implied a potential role in relation to bird conservation insofar as protection measures were embodied in legislation or government regulations. Articles 14 and 15 of the NAAEC defined a process whereby citizens' groups could make submissions to the CEC regarding the alleged failings of a government to enforce its own environmental legislation, and the circumstances in which the CEC could generate a factual record related to such submissions.

As indicated earlier, the mid-1990s were a time of restructuring and a broadening of the scope of bird conservation efforts beyond the traditional waterfowl management issues. The CEC quickly became a major player in these developments in two ways: it sought a facilitating or catalytic role in relation to integration and enhanced cooperation among existing bird conservation organizations, and it also responded on bird-related questions in its fact-finding (or quasi-judicial) role following submissions by non-governmental groups.

Its presence on the continental scene coincided with one of the many crises that have historically triggered environmental policy law and policy developments in North America. During the winter of 1994-95, an estimated 20-40,000 waterbirds died in the Silva Reservoir in Mexico, an important wintering ground for many migratory species such as ruddy ducks, eared grebes and the American coot. The Silva incident was widely reported in the media as one with significant implications for the NAFTA environmental machinery, especially since migratory birds issues were already defined as part of the CEC's work programme for 1995 (De Palma, 1995). In June, the U.S. National Audubon Society and two Mexican groups formally petitioned the CEC to investigate and report on the incident. The conclusions of the expert panel set up by the CEC secretariat focused on botulism as the cause of the bird deaths, with contributing factors being the high levels of chromium found in reservoir sediment, a result of local industrial activities, and untreated sewage. The panel also emphasized, however, that the outbreak was not exceptional, and that it should be seen in the context of other mass deaths of birds – including one of 60,000 waterbird deaths in Alberta in the summer of 1995 – that had been relatively frequent during the 20th century and which had a variety of anthropogenic and other causes. The CEC secretariat in its report pointed to the wider relevance of the Silva incident for trinational environmental policy relations and put forward a set of options (though not "recommendations") in relation to the reservoir and its surrounding area for the consideration of Mexico (CEC Secretariat, 1995a: Pt I, 27-30, 69; Dillon, 1995). The Council later announced that it would develop a "rapid response system" to deal with future outbreaks of disease affecting migratory birds (CEC, 1996).

Submissions from groups involved the CEC in other bird protection issues during the 1990s. In a submission of November 1999 a group of nine U.S., Mexican and Canadian environmental organizations maintained that the U.S. federal government was violating the Migratory Birds Treaty Act (MBTA), the U.S. implementing legislation based on the 1916 and 1936 conventions with Canada and Mexico respectively, by allowing logging to take place in areas throughout the United States in such a way that nests, eggs and birds were threatened. Particular problems were noted by the groups filing the submission in relation to practices in Arkansas, Georgia and California. The submission also argued that the "unwritten policy" of federal wildlife officials in relation to the MBTA was that no action would be taken in relation to logging operations if these resulted in harm only to "non-endangered, non-threatened migratory birds and/or their nests" (CEC, 2003d:14).

The U.S. federal government was asked to respond, and after considering the response the CEC secretariat found central questions to be unresolved. The Council in November 2001 authorized it to prepare a factual record (following the procedures defined in Article 15 of the NAAEC), but in relation only to two California cases. The first of these involved logging by a private landowner in 1996 that destroyed great blue heron nests; the second centred on the burning of trees by a logging company on private land in 1995 and the associated destruction of an osprey nest. This restricted scope was significantly narrower than the enquiry the groups had been seeking (and also narrower than the CEC Secretariat itself thought justified). For example, data on the effects of U.S. logging activities on the numbers of migratory birds taken was outside the scope of the investigation. The central question, following NAAEC principles, was whether the U.S. had failed to enforce its own legislation, and not, as some environmentalists had hoped, whether these laws met conservation criteria. Accordingly, specific issues in the CEC investigations were concerned with the exercise of discretion in relation to MBTA enforcement, for example in the way in which allocation of enforcement resources to higher-priority matters was decided, and with the relations between federal responsibilities and the forestry and wildlife law and practices of state authorities in California (CEC, 2003d:7-22, 46-63).

The factual record produced by the CEC secretariat failed to cite evidence that the submitting organizations could use as part of their wider political campaign against logging threats to wild bird habitats in the United States. In relation to the osprey case the report found that it was "an open question whether destruction of an osprey nest in a prescribed burn would violate the MBTA, absent evidence that a migratory bird or egg was killed or destroyed as a result" (CEC, 2003d:13). The disappointing situation for environmental groups appeared to be confirmed with a later submission, in February 2002, by a group of nine Canadian and U.S. environmental organizations that alleged violations of migratory bird protection responsibilities in relation to logging operations in Ontario. The CEC Council response, in April 2003, was that there was insufficient basis for it to proceed with a factual record process (Wilson, 2003a:12-15).

This investigative activity has been only a part of the CEC's work in relation to conservation and wild birds issues. The Commission has also taken a leading role in identifying bird conservation as a central issue on continental environmental agendas, and in promoting a restructuring of trinational institutional arrangements to better pursue conservation objectives across the continent.

The main push for change came from a CEC Council decision in Toronto in 1996 to work towards the development of a continental bird protection framework. This led to the creation of the North American Bird Conservation Initiative (NABCI) at the Banff meetings of the Council in June 1999. As noted above, the1995 Council meeting, in Oaxaca in October, released the Secretariat's report on the Silva reservoir migratory bird deaths. CEC bodies were also at this time working on ways to protect continental biodiversity more generally, including strategies for greater protection of key habitats both for their ecological value and more specifically because of their role in relation to migratory species flyways. The CEC was already moving significantly beyond the migratory waterfowl emphasis of the traditional arrangements that were at this time being restructured under planning for the NAWMP. Growing habitat threats to migratory songbirds were being identified, and the CEC was also moving to build conservation networks with non-governmental bird protection organizations in the three countries to gather better data on habitats and flight paths (CEC, 1995a:3).

NABCI, as the new flagship bird conservation enterprise, was thus designed to be comprehensive. Included within its mandate were cooperative actions to engage in "all bird/all habitats" protection. It rested on working principles of multi-level cooperation among federal, state/provincial and territorial levels of government, and groups in the non-governmental sector. Significantly too, its work on bird species was linked with the wider ecological work on biodiversity, especially on regions, that the CEC was also promoting as part of its continental environmental enterprise. While it built on the habits of several decades of cooperative activities among the U.S., Canada and Mexico on migratory birds, that is, it aimed to have a much broader mandate in terms of participating actors, bird species, and ecological concerns, it also aimed to encourage practical integration of existing bird conservation efforts based on particular bird species or groupings of species. Further, since other programmes already existed – including particularly the recently launched NAWMP and its species and habitat joint ventures, and a multiplicity of government-based and non-governmental bird conservation actors – NABCI participants emphasized that it was "first and foremost a facilitating effort, and not a directing and controlling organization" (NABCI, 2001:9).

The NABCI ethos was defined largely at a key meeting of officials and experts from the U.S., Canada and Mexico in Puebla, Mexico in November 1998 and a specialized follow-up meeting in early 1999. A broad-ranging set of objectives for the Initiative were discussed in the context of the overall goal of promoting improved trinational coordination and cooperation and "all bird/all habitat" conservation initiatives. These objectives were defined as pursuing sustainable diversity and bird abundance; data-based and effective conservation and management of birds; ensuring that land-use practices took note of birds needs; capacity-building, including the strengthening and expansion of bird conservation legislation; developing an agreed continental framework for bird conservation efforts based on partnerships; and increasing public awareness and involvement in bird conservation (NABCI, 1998; NABCI, 1999).

Ecological and species-based data gathering continued as a central concern both of the bird-related activities of the CEC Secretariat and the emerging NABCI networks in each of the three countries. From the mid-1990s the CEC, in conjunction with leading continental bird conservation organizations, actively supported the broad project of identifying Important Bird Areas (IBAs) in North America. The

IBA concept originated in work by European non-governmental organizations, in conjunction with the European Union and Council of Europe, in the 1980s, and had grown into an ambitious international enterprise. This overlaps with non-governmental activities designed to identify Endemic Bird Areas (EBAs), that is areas that include important groupings of bird species that do not exist anywhere else, for example much of the coastal region of California and, in Mexico, the north Yucatan coastline, central marshland areas, and southern Baja California (Stattersfield, et al., 1998:96-130). Based on data produced in collaboration with individuals and groups connected with the new NABCI framework, the CEC published its initial survey, a detailed inventory of 150 North American IBAs, in 1999 (CEC, 1999a).

This effort both drew on and fed into related CEC and NABCI activities aimed at scientific consensus on the identification of ecological and bird conservation regions. The first of these, as developed by the CEC in 1997, drew directly or indirectly on the scientific work of Omernik (1995) in the U.S., Wiken (1986; Wiken, et al., 1996) in Canada, and others, and provided a solid scientific foundation for a variety of continental conservation tasks. The second led to the development of an adaptable classification of bird conservation regions (BCRs) in North America. The bird conservation regions are each distinct, and defined as having similar bird communities and habitats and therefore similar conservation and management problems. The approach was envisioned as flexible and open to periodic updating as new data and ecoregion knowledge grew. The NABCI meeting in Puebla in 1998 took the decision to ground the BCRs specifically in the ecological regions classification already developed by the CEC secretariat, with differences reflecting the particular ecological circumstances and conservation needs of bird species. The listing of the 66 BCRs was designed to facilitate conservation planning, and "provide the bird conservation community with a convenient scale for priority setting, planning, and evaluation" (NABCI, 2002: 4-5). The criteria for the delineation of regions in either of these senses were explicitly ecological rather than political or jurisdictional. Different parts of Canada, for example, fall within 12 distinct BCRs, but of these only three encompass ecosystems falling exclusively within Canada (Burnett, 2003b:2). More commonly, regions straddle different national or other jurisdictions, such as the Northern Pacific Rainforest (covering all or parts of British Columbia, Alberta, Washington, Oregon and California) or the Lower Great Lakes/St. Lawrence Plain (Ontario, Quebec, Ohio, Pennsylvania, New York and Vermont).

These various developments were also significant influences on the work of the U.S. Fish and Wildlife Service from the 1980s. Particularly through its migratory bird division, the agency became increasingly committed to a broad range of bird conservation programmes. In its plan for migratory birds for the period 2004-2014 the FWS identified three main emphases: the degradation and disappearance of migratory bird habitats; the spread of scientific data on migratory bird populations; and the building and expansion of multi-actor partnerships for "comprehensive bird conservation" (USFWS, 2004:6-7).

The logic of ecological thinking on conservation on a continent-wide base thus increasingly confronted multi-level governance issues, and in particular the requirement of building science-based conservation programmes and projects around consensus among many types of actors and involving multiple jurisdictional levels. This brings us to the final dimension of North American bird conservation arrangements.

Multi-actor/Multi-level Linkages for Species and Habitats

So far we have been looking for the most part at bird conservation arrangements connecting federal government wildlife and species protection agencies, and the extensions of these into state and provincial government domains. Many of these are in practice elements, or lead actors, of wider conservation networks. Multiple North American actors with a stake in bird conservation and the protection of wild bird habitats have forged working links and frameworks. These include relations with and among governments at different levels, and non-governmental organizations and the private conservation and land-use sector. The complexities stem from the nature of the conservation problems, the multiplicity of actors and the incentives for the spread and growth of links, the key roles which many NGOs have historically undertaken in relation to continental bird conservation issues, and the core requirements of funding and the nurturing of constituencies. As the NAWMP recognized, waterfowl conservation "had its roots in international treaties, but the resources to support it would have to come from the private, state, provincial, and federal sectors" (NAWMP, 1998:11). The resulting diversity and complexities raise difficult questions for continental conservation strategies. While this pluralist setting encourages defences by conservation actors of their own distinctive places in traditional and emerging arrangements, it has also stimulated calls for simplification, rationalization and harmonization – what NABCI participants in the U.S. have called moving towards "one layer of carpet" in bird conservation.

First, state and provincial governments have some claims to be regarded as the primary conservation actors because of their constitutional and statute-based roles in relation to the environment and natural resources. The U.S. states and the Canadian provinces have extensive links both with their counterparts and with federal agencies. Provincial environment ministers and heads of wildlife agencies meet regularly in Canada; other key forums include the annual federal-provincial-territorial wildlife meetings of officials and experts. Provinces and states have also been sensitive to problems of what is sometimes seen in both Canada and the U.S. as excessive or unproductive federal interference. In New York State, for example, state wildlife officials have periodically viewed cormorants as a species threatening fish populations, but have been prevented from implementing control measures because of federal protection rules governing the species. There are also important international aspects. The government of Michigan has pursued its protection of the Kirtland's warbler in part by developing cooperative links with agencies and groups in Central and South America. State and provincial governments make their own listings of bird species as part of endangered species legislation. Governments at this level vary in their willingness, ingenuity and capacity to take on bird protection and broader environmental conservation roles, and also in their ability to move flexibly within a wider federal system.

Secondly, there has been growing recognition of the need for broader participatory arrangements involving private landowners in the making of critical conservation decisions (Wise, 2004). Without them conservation goals may remain unreachable. According to the CEC, biodiversity is protected "according to its perceived value. A considerable proportion of priority ecological areas in the North American region is in private hands. Having the owners of those lands or waters participate in [NABCI] will thus be crucial for the conservation of North American species, their habitats, and other natural phenomena" (CEC, 2001:33). The spotted owl and other political controversies that have periodically surrounded U.S. endangered-species legislation from 1973, particularly those stemming from the designation of species on private lands, were signals of these unavoidable complexities and constraints. In Canada, federal moves to create endangered-species legislation stumbled for much of the 1990s through issues that included problems of species protection and recovery on lands – private as well as provincially controlled – over which the federal government had little or no authority. Private or common land is the norm in Mexico, so as NAWMP has noted "it is especially important that residents play an active role for conservation to be effective" (NAWMP, 1998:4).

Thirdly, civil society groups are in practice crucial players in North American bird conservation strategies. Some of these also face the constraints typically confronted by government wildlife agencies, such as reaching accommodations with private landowners. Many nature trust or conservancy groups in the U.S. and Canada, including bird-related organizations, have extensive programmes for the direct acquisition and management of lands for conservation purposes, or other methods such as easements which allow protection of a habitat on the basis of agreement with the landowner. Ducks Unlimited has extensive ownership and management responsibilities in relation to North America's wetlands, including, since the mid-1990s, wetlands and other habitats of the boreal forest (Wilson, 2003b:32-36). The leading groups, such as the American Bird Conservancy, typically have their own international programmes, particularly in relation to Central and South America (ABC, 2004).

Conservation groups, that is, should not be seen only, or even primarily, in terms of the conventional political-science language of interest groups or pressure groups. The lobbying of governments at various levels may be part of a bird or nature conservation group's mandate, within the constraints of the rules set out in various jurisdictions for charitable or not-for-profit status. But some also participate directly in government-led frameworks, as World Wildlife Fund-Canada has traditionally done in the species-listing work of the Committee on the Status of Endangered Wildlife in Canada (COSEWIC). Some broader networks of bird organizations are primarily centred on non-governmental organizations, and either initially or gradually bring on board officials of wildlife agencies in different ways. Within the broader environmental conservation area, bird issues are distinctive too because of the traditionally data-centred nature of many issues. While government agencies and programmes have their own and population-monitoring activities in relation to defined bird species, non-governmental conservation groups, including groups centred around particular species or habitats, have in practice been essential parts of this wider data-gathering task. Examples include the 50,000 volunteers taking part in recent annual bird counts organized by the National Audubon Society (Youth, 2003:41). Groups also engage in the essential tasks of conservation education on which effective planning is based.

This wide range of types of actors in continental governance arrangements produces considerable diversity in partnership and other relationships among these. Some multi-actor/multi-level arrangements focus on particular sets of species or regions, such as the Western Hemisphere Shorebird Reserve Network, formed in 1985. Partners in Flight, set up in 1990, incorporates U.S. federal, state and local government wildlife agencies as well as NGOs such as the American Ornithologists' Union and the National Audubon Society, and private-sector economic actors (Beissinger, et al. 2000:549-60). The grouping has among other things aimed to extend key concepts and lessons from the migratory bird convention record to other species (occasionally under the odd-sounding slogan "Birds are just like ducks"). In other words, "If waterfowl populations across North America could be stabilized via science-based management plans coordinated across government agencies and the private sector, why not apply the same approach to land bird populations?" (Fitzpatrick, 2002:908). The focus, at first, was on neotropical migratory land birds, an important priority of many U.S. bird conservation organizations, but this grew to incorporate landbirds generally as well as marine and coastal species that have land habitats.

There has also been several decades of transborder cooperative experience not only of the migratory birds convention frameworks linking the U.S., Canada and Mexico, but also of more bottom-up conservation approaches such as the flyway councils. These grew out of expanded exchanges from the mid-1940s between federal and state wildlife officials in the U.S., in association with hunters' and other private groups. Particular species threats requiring federal-state and other frameworks were identified, such as deterioration of eel grass habitat for black duck populations along the Atlantic coast. Although much state activity at this time was devoted to waterfowl data and management questions, it was evident that often coordination among them was lacking. This gap was compounded by other problems, such as the diversion of conservation funds for partisan or political-reward purposes in many states. The Pacific, Central, Mississippi and Atlantic flyways regimes were established in the 1950s to promote more effective cooperation among state agencies in collaboration with the FWS and non-governmental groups (Jahn and Kabat, 1984:376, 381-83).

A pragmatic approach to the concept of joint ventures has also given rise to various multi-actor/multi-level enterprises. As developed by the NAWMP, this covers both critical habitats, such as prairie habitat, and species. In Canada partnerships between the Canadian Wildlife Service and NGOs have been the basis for NAWMP joint ventures on Arctic nesting geese, black ducks and sea ducks, with funding from both Canadian and U.S. federal government and other sources. The Arctic goose joint venture for example, founded in 1989, has varying forms of participation from among others the CWS and the U.S. Fish and Wildlife Service and the Mexican government, groups and agencies from Ontario and the Northwest Territories, Ducks Unlimited, and the Atlantic, Mississippi, Central, and Pacific Flyway Councils (NAWMP, 2002:8). A variety of bird species other than or overlapping with traditional waterfowl definitions, such as pelicans, puffins, murres and whooping cranes, are included in the waterbird conservation objectives of the North American Waterbird Conservation Plan. This also promotes cooperative and continental conservation planning among government agencies at different levels in the U.S., Canada and Mexico, and private sector groups, in close association with the trinational NABCI network (NAWCP, 2002:7-8, 56).

Towards a Continental Bird Biodiversity Conservation System?

The many inter-governmental and multi-actor conservation frameworks that characterize bird conservation efforts in North America occupy an uncertain ground on the spectrum between autonomous actions on the one hand, and genuinely continent-wide integration on the other. The record discussed in this chapter, and especially the quickening pace of organizational restructuring efforts in the last two decades, nonetheless focuses renewed attention on the question of continentalism. The economic context of deepening North American economic integration has brought related issues into sharp focus. Would a more fully integrated continental system better serve conservation goals and priorities? Is such a system achievable? What trade-offs would have to be made to secure this, and would these costs be worth paying?

In practice, processes of formulating bird conservation objectives and action plans have often rested at some point on broader continentalist thinking. The efforts of NABCI, and the scientific reasoning underlying directions taken by the CEC secretariat in this area, typify this kind of approach. In a sense this follows naturally from scientific work in biological conservation, the classification of ecological regions, and, more specifically, in data collection and monitoring related to bird species. From such perspectives, the significance for scientific enquiry or the identification of species conservation objectives of national or sub-national jurisdictional boundaries can be discounted. The protection of species and habitats in protected areas requires extensive rules governing human activities in surrounding areas, and such areas may fail to promote goals of ecological integrity and species population goals if they are not effectively linked by wildlife corridors (Askins, 2000:238-39). Advocacy of planning based on these principles naturally transcends different jurisdictions. The pursuit of research or species recovery objectives in relation to particular bird species also has an inner dynamic that promotes the spillover of activities among jurisdictions, as in Canadian links with U.S. wildlife experts on the piping plover. To some extent, then, institutional responses to the problem of implementing plans based on transboundary scientific consensus on the recovery or management needs of a species or critical habitat have operated functionally in such a way that species or habitat needs are drivers of policy processes. The major continental flyway councils are perhaps the best historical examples of this pattern. In these, state or other agencies and non-governmental groupings are brought into the multi-actor mix depending on a geographically based definition of functional requirements. Similar patterns are evident in the habitat protection joint ventures initiated through the NAWMP and other groupings oriented around broad classes of bird species such as waterbirds.

Yet institutional arrangements are also respectful of national, and other inter-jurisdictional, differences. These differences are evident in the way governmental mechanisms for designating targeted bird species are structured, the relations among government and private organizations, the rationales for conservation that animate them, the impact of differing constitutional principles governing federal-state/provincial relations and the respective conservation powers of different levels of government, the uneven spread of administrative and financial resources available to agencies and NGOs for pursuing bird conservation objectives, and the degree of interest on the part of different actors in taking part in broader coalition-based activities.

Bird conservation issues are embedded, moreover, in governance frameworks that are shaped by larger political and economic contexts. The federal governments of each of the three North American countries face considerable constraints in the design and implementation of conservation strategies, in view of both the political realities of federal structures and also the problems presented by species occurring on private lands. There are complexities too within these governments: about a dozen U.S. federal agencies have direct or indirect responsibilities relating to birds or bird habitat issues. Yet conservation actions are also determined in the context of discourses that may downplay these limits.

The framing of bird biodiversity issues by different actors is subject to wide variation. As in other scientifically grounded environmental resource and conservation enterprises, as Ludwig has argued, research tends to be highly technical, and is often based on unrealistic expectations that the results can easily be translated into policy (1994:112).

There is no easy answer to the question of how centralized or decentralized federal systems should be in order to serve the interests of effective conservation. The traditional advantages of the heavily decentralized Canadian system are that this increases sensitivity and responsiveness to local species and habitat requirements, and that multi-stakeholder formats can as a result be more energized and better able to secure the elusive optimal balance among competing economic and conservation priorities. However, the limited capacities of federal agencies to manœuvre within and among provincial fiefdoms poses serious constraints on the making of coordinated national biodiversity plans, especially where provincial political cultures and economies are resistant to conservation pressures. In such settings, bird conservation advocacy is steadily weakened by a chronic, and less media-friendly, process of the replacement of specialized bird species as a result of habitat change, for example in the forestry sector, by more generalized and adaptable species. In relation to environmental policy generally, some critics have maintained that the relatively greater powers of U.S. federal authorities translate more readily into enhanced capacities for effective national decision-making. Rabe goes further, and argues that the constitutionally larger federal environmental policy role in the U.S. does not cramp state effectiveness, but on the contrary that it serves directly to stimulate or support policy innovativeness on the part of state governments (1999:289, 304).

One implication of this observation is that shifting conservation policy levels "upwards" in the governance hierarchy to that of the continent may thus reinforce and galvanize conservation efforts at "lower" levels. However, this is likely not a viable option. Its practicality and appeal decrease to the extent that top-down styles of decision-making, as opposed to European-style notions of subsidiarity, are envisaged. The record of the NAAEC seems to indicate that the CEC is not equipped to play a more full-fledged quasi-judicial role in monitoring and ensuring compliance with the spirit as well as the black-letter law of environmental rules in the U.S. and Canada, and indeed that the necessary political will to bring this about is lacking on the part of the three governments. These states moreover do not have comparable conservation policy resources. Growing Mexican participation in North American bird conservation arrangements has underscored the significance of economic disparities among actors in such frameworks, even down to the mundane level of the funding of delegates' travel to technical committee meetings. Apart from the constitutional realities and the continental division into three states, there is the simple political or cultural reality that some important conservation players will always engage more enthusiastically at local, regional or national levels. This is especially so since, as with the whooping crane or bald eagle, some protection issues are inter-mixed with political symbolism, and, as often in Canada and even more so in Mexico, continentalist or transborder regional solutions are routinely trumped in public debates by nationally constituted environmental discourses.

A more likely outcome is thus continuation of the trend of enhanced biodiversity continentalism outlined in this chapter, but without a concomitant dilution of governance efforts at other levels. If this is true, then the emerging core tasks of conservation governance in North America lie not so much in the design of new continental architecture, but rather in the creative forging of more robust trans-level and inter-actor linkages.

The problems associated with these tasks cross conventional divides between the political, scientific, technical, and managerial arenas. Critical tasks include the harmonizing of the various regional classifications – for example of North American ecological regions, Bird Conservation Regions, Important Bird Areas, and Endemic Bird Areas – and the integration within policy communities of changing ideas on wildlife and habitat management. The drain on the time and resources of active participants in continental governance processes is increasingly evident, as are cross-pressures; to cite one example, very few Canadians attended the key 1999 Trilateral Committee sessions in Manzanillo, Mexico, because these were scheduled at the same time as COSEWIC meetings (Jewell, 2000:27). Finally, because of the migratory habits or large ranges of some species, some difficult management and organizational issues are also connected with the relations between continental and wider international bird conservation efforts, as well as with links to the south and the north – respectively to the Caribbean and Latin America, and to the circumpolar bird conservation arrangements associated with the Arctic Council. The nature of the continental conservation problem bears repeating: birds have little respect for the political and geographical boundary lines that humans like to cultivate.

Chapter 11

The Pacific Salmon Dispute and Canada-U.S. Environmental Relations

Samuel Barkin

Introduction: the Salmon Dispute

In July of 1997 some 200 small Canadian fishing boats blockaded a huge U.S. passenger ferry in the port of Prince Rupert, British Columbia. The fishers took this action to protest what they saw as overfishing of Pacific salmon by U.S. fishers, and the inability of the U.S. and Canadian governments to come to an equitable agreement on quotas in the fishery (Wilkinson, 1997; Williams and Gilmore, 1997). This blockade followed several months of escalation in the dispute over the quotas, which included a policy by Canadian fisheries authorities of harassing U.S. fishers passing through Canadian waters by enforcing rules that had never been enforced before (Henton, 1997), and an attempt by the government of British Columbia to expel the U.S. Navy from a facility in Nanaimo that it had been using to test torpedoes (Morrison, 1997).

In the end, the escalation of the dispute was limited by the context and norms of the Canada-U.S. relationship. Nobody was hurt, the ferry was allowed to leave Prince Rupert once the point had been made, the U.S. fishing boats detained were released when the mandated fines were paid, and the U.S. Navy was permitted to stay in Nanaimo. The two national governments finally came to an agreement, and the dispute faded from public view. This particular dispute, however, did not follow the normal pattern of behind-the-scenes negotiation and compromise that characterizes most of the hundreds of bilateral environmental agreements between the two governments. It also highlights weaknesses in some of the predominant theories of international environmental cooperation.

What was it about the Pacific salmon fishery in 1997 that turned recurring quota negotiations governing a fishery of declining economic significance into front-page news? Several factors combined to popularize the issue. For both cultural and biological reasons, salmon are more important to the Pacific Northwest, British Columbia, and Alaska than the economics of the commercial fishery might suggest. The decline of the fishery itself was a partial cause of the escalation of the issue at that particular point in time. The politics of salmon quota negotiations highlight the difficulties of negotiations between governments in a federal system, when the two national governments do not have full authority over the issue, and where the distribution of authority between national and sub-national governments is different in the two countries. And finally, the case points to tensions in the interaction between imperatives that governments face on the one hand to cooperate on international environmental issues and on the other hand to represent the expressed desires of their populations.

This chapter will use the negotiations over Pacific salmon quotas in 1997 as an example both of some of the difficulties faced in the Canada-United States environmental relationship, and of some of the issues faced by students of this relationship in applying theories of international environmental politics to this relationship. It will begin by giving some context for the dispute, and by tracing both its evolution and resolution. It will then put the dispute in the context of theories of international environmental regimes and negotiation.

The Pacific Salmon Fishery

The Pacific salmon fishery is actually a relatively minor industry in the Province of British Columbia, and in the States of Washington, Oregon, and Alaska. In British Columbia, where the popular visibility of the crisis was greatest, the industry in 1997 was worth about $400 million a year. Not only did this represent less than 1 percent of the provincial economy at the time, it was less than the value to the economy of the tourism associated with the non-commercial salmon fishery (Steele, 1997). A government following the tenets of economic rationality should not then choose to make a major issue of the commercial industry – British Columbia as a whole may in fact be better off closing the industry altogether, thereby saving on regulatory costs and subsidies, and allowing greater scope for the salmon-related tourism industry. So why was this dispute allowed to escalate to the extent that it did? Three reasons acted in concert: culture, industry decline, and federalism.

Salmon is more important to the culture of the Pacific Northwest, Alaska, and British Columbia than it is to the economy. Not only is it a keystone species, and thus a good indicator of the health of the regional ecosystem more generally, salmon have also historically been important to the region's identity. This is true both of native cultures, for whom salmon are an important cultural and artistic motif, and of European colonists, many of whom came originally to participate in the salmon fishery and cannery. This cultural importance tends to give the politics of salmon a greater visibility than would be suggested by the contemporary economics of salmon.[1]

But these contemporary economics are themselves part of the problem. The commercial fishery is in long-term decline relative to the economies of the relevant states and province, and long ago ceased to be a primary motor of the regional economy. The industry has also faced a long-term decline in commercially viable salmon stocks. But beginning in the mid-1990s this long-term decline was complemented by a precipitous drop in the market price of salmon, driven largely by

1 For a general political background to the politics of Pacific salmon, see Barkin and Moseley, 2003.

the growth of the salmon farming industry. For example, the average price of Pink Salmon in Alaska declined from near fifty cents a pound in the late 1980s to between 10 and 15 cents a pound in the mid-1990s (Alaska Department of Fish and Game, 2003). While the combination of decline in stocks and decline in prices made the fishery less important to the overall economy, it made the issue of quotas all the more important for individual fishers. General economic models suggest that as prices decline, some producers will simply exit the industry. This will decrease supply and increase prices for the remaining producers. But in an industry, such as commercial fishing, with high barriers to exit, decreasing prices can act simply to make producers more desperate, and force them to try and increase production (Barkin and Mansori, 2001). Decreasing prices can therefore have the effect of making the issue more politically salient because of the increasing desperation of the producers, rather than less politically salient because of its increasing economic marginality. It is precisely this sort of desperation that drove 200 salmon fishers to use their boats to blockade the American ferry in Prince Rupert.

The third reason that the dispute escalated to the extent that it did is the federal political structures of both the United States and Canada. Both federal governments remained more or less committed throughout the confrontation to principles of international law, of scientific management of the fish stock, and of negotiation and due process. Both federal governments saw the salmon quota negotiations as embedded in a vast network of agreements between the two countries, covering both environmental and economic cooperation, and both seemed loath to endanger that cooperation over an issue that was of little national economic import and that had limited cultural resonance in Washington or Ottawa. The relevant state and provincial governments, however, saw things differently. They governed populations for a significant proportion of whom the issue was politically salient. At the same time, they could afford to play popular politics with the issue without as much concern for the political ramifications as the federal-level governments – the state and provincial governments knew that the federal governments were there to moderate conflict escalation and to absorb any political fallout, providing the sub-national governments with a security net that the national governments themselves did not possess.

The situation was confused further by different divisions of political authority between national and sub-national governments in the two countries. In Canada, while the provinces have the authority to regulate with respect to many resource issues, it is the federal government that has the authority to regulate all ocean fisheries. In the United States, conversely, state governments have the authority to regulate fisheries within state waters, while the federal government has the authority in the United States' Exclusive Economic Zone, meaning that the salmon fishery comes under both jurisdictions.[2] This means that in any U.S.-Canadian negotiations over fisheries within territorial seas, the Canadian government can agree to a quota

2 United States Congress, Magnuson-Stevens Fishery Conservation and Management Act, Public Law 94-265, as amended through 11 October 1996, sections 3 (11) and 101 (a); Government of Canada, Fisheries Act, R.S. 985, c-14 (Ottawa: Department of Justice Canada,

on its own authority, but the U.S. government needs to seek agreement from the relevant state governments. International relations theory suggests that this difference should give the U.S. government increased bargaining leverage with respect to the Canadian government, because the former faces greater audience costs and more veto players than the latter.[3] As we shall see, the eventual resolution of the crisis bears out this prediction. But at the same time, the difference and the ensuing bias in the bargaining structure goes a long way towards explaining the resort by both the provincial government and by fishers in B.C. to attempts to apply pressure outside of the existing negotiating structure.

This existing negotiating structure was (and remains) defined by the 1985 *Treaty Between the Government of Canada and the Government of the United States of America Concerning Pacific Salmon*.[4] This treaty is in many ways a model international fisheries treaty. It creates a body, the Pacific Salmon Commission, that is tasked to provide (among other things) unbiased scientific estimates of the state of the fishery stock and of its maximum sustainable yield. From these estimates the Commission is supposed to recommend total quotas for the various species of Pacific salmon.[5] The treaty also provides a clear rule for the allocation of the quotas; each country is supposed to get a proportion of the quota equal to the proportion of the salmon that spawn in its territory. This decision rule is based on the idea that a salmon that spawns in one country's rivers belongs to that country and that it is fair that each country should benefit from the salmon fishery to the extent that it is contributing "its" salmon to the overall fishery.[6] The intention of the rule is to prevent the quota politics that plague some fishery agreements by taking the politics out of the decision-making process, and replacing it with a clear rule, based on a fairness principle, that is not subject to political interpretation.

Taking politics out of the decision-making process in an environmental issue like this one is important because it is in part a directional issue rather than a commons issue. High seas fisheries are usually thought of as commons resources. In a commons issue those using the resource are assumed to have a similar level of interest in achieving a cooperative outcome, because they all have similar levels of access to the resource. But salmon do not just swim about randomly on the high seas, they swim in a particular direction, and this direction has political implications. They hatch in rivers, grow and mature at sea, then return to the river of their birth to spawn. At sea, Pacific salmon swim in a clockwise pattern. This means that Alaska salmon return from the high seas directly to Alaska. But B.C. salmon swim through Alaska

---

Consolidated Statutes and Regulations, 31 December 2003), section 2. Viewed at http://laws.justice.gc.ca/en/F-14/index.html, 7 May 2004.

3 These theoretical approaches will be discussed below.

4 Treaty Between the Government of Canada and the Government of the United States of America Concerning Pacific Salmon, 17 May 1985. Viewed at http://www.psc.org/Treaty/Treaty.pdf, 6 May 2004.

5 Ibid., Article II. See also Pacific Salmon Commission, "The Pacific Salmon Commission," viewed at http://www.psc.org/Who/WHO.HTM, 6 May 2004.

6 Treaty, Article III, paragraph 1 (b).

waters on their way back to B.C., and Washington and Oregon State salmon swim by both Alaska and British Columbia first (DeSombre and Barkin, 2000). This pattern gives Alaska fishers, and Washington and Oregon fishers fishing in Alaska waters, an advantage over B.C. fishers – they can catch what they want first, leaving B.C. in a position of having to decide between bankrupting the fishing fleet or overfishing the stock. This advantage, in turn, should give the United States a negotiating advantage in discussing quotas, an advantage that is negated by the terms of the Treaty.

The Treaty seemed to work more or less as designed until 1992. But after that year the process broke down. The Commission continued to gather and analyze data, and to make recommendations. But the U.S. and Canadian governments failed to agree on, and to formally accept, the quotas recommended by the Commission. The absence of agreed quotas was not immediately critical, as the relevant governments continued to regulate their fisheries in ways that prevented major year-to-year changes (Morrison, 1997). But by 1997 two things had happened that brought the two federal governments back to the negotiating table. The first was the accretion of minor year-to-year changes that was resulting in catches well above levels that were sustainable at that time. The other was the crash in prices for wild salmon, increasing pressure on fishers to catch more fish in order to stem the decline in their incomes. In particular, increasing catches in Alaska of salmon spawned in B.C. rivers, and the resulting stresses, both on the Canadian fishery and on breeding stocks in those rivers, put pressure on the Canadian government to get the U.S. government to the negotiating table (Seattle Times, 1997; Henton, 1997a; Williams and Gilmore, 1997).

The position of Canada at these negotiations, supported by the government of British Columbia, was that the terms of the Pacific Salmon Treaty should be the terms of the negotiations (Williams and Gilmore, 1997). In other words, the Canadian government went into the talks trying to get U.S. fishers to cut back their take of Canadian salmon.[7] The U.S. government was caught between on the one hand a desire to stick to its international commitments and deal with the issue in a business-as-usual way, and on the other hand pressure from the relevant state-level governments to allow their fishers to continue to fish at or near their current levels. The U.S. government's position was further complicated by the federal division of authority – it could not determine fixed quotas without the acquiescence of the relevant State governments.

The U.S. government had not resolved this contradiction in its negotiating priorities before negotiations began. As such, the U.S. delegation to the negotiations did not have the authority to commit the government to specific quotas or concessions. The U.S. government had failed to inform the Canadian government that the talks were exploratory rather than binding, and the latter was caught by surprise when, after the negotiations had already begun, the negotiating team discovered that its U.S. counterpart was not authorized to make binding commitments. The Canadian

7 The phrase "Canadian salmon" has two meanings in this context – it refers both to Canada's share of the general catch, and to salmon that spawn in Canadian rivers, particularly specific runs the survival of which was threatened by overfishing.

government pulled out of the talks in protest, which marked the beginning of the escalation of the conflict (Ottawa Citizen, 1997).

In order to put pressure on the U.S. government to return to the negotiating table with the authority to make a deal, the Canadian government began a policy of what amounted to legal harassment of U.S. fishing boats; it began enforcing rules long on the books but never enforced, such as a rule that boats must notify the Canadian Coast Guard upon entry into Canadian waters for purposes of passage. The Canadian and B.C. governments also started discussing imposing a transit fee on U.S. boats passing through Canadian waters on the way from Washington State to Alaska and back (Financial Times, 1997). The government of B.C., seeing the potential to make political capital of the issue, jumped on the bandwagon with the threat to kick the U.S. navy out of the Nanaimo testing range (which, as it turns out, the B.C. government does not have the authority to do). The politics of dispute escalation were also to be found on the U.S. side, with members of Congress protesting the detention of U.S. fishing boats and the relevant State governments playing to their coastal communities by taking hard lines on the issue (Henton, 1997, 1997a).

In the end, the Canadian government prioritized conservation over economic equity. It cut back on various salmon quotas sufficiently to make up for U.S. overfishing. At the same time it resumed negotiations with the United States on U.S. terms, giving up the assumption of quotas distributed according to proportion of national origin. This decision sat well neither with the government of B.C. nor with the coastal communities in B.C. most involved in the commercial salmon fishery; it was this decision that led to the blockade of the ferry in Prince Rupert. It also sparked a personal feud between the Premier of British Columbia, Glen Clark, and the federal Minister of Fisheries and Oceans, David Anderson, that was to last for over a year. In the end, however, Anderson was able to sell conservation to the national audience, and to the average British Columbian, better than Clark was able to sell confrontation (Bryden, 1998).

No agreement was reached in 1997. The publicity surrounding the issue gradually died down after the ferry incident, as salmon season ended and as it became clear that the Canadian government was not likely to back down from its conservationist quotas. The Canadian government began negotiating with individual State governments as well as with the U.S. federal government, a reasonable response to the division of authority on the issue in the United States. This strategy began to show returns in 1998 when the Canadian government signed an agreement with the government of Washington State. The agreement covered only chinook and coho salmon, and did not address issues that involved Alaska or Oregon, but it was the first tangible sign of progress on the issue in half a decade. The agreement restarted the public feud between Anderson and Clark, but in this round Anderson seemed to be the clear winner (Bryden, 1998).

Continuing negotiations finally resulted in an agreement in June 1999 that amended the Treaty via an exchange of diplomatic notes. The agreement backed away from the idea that each country had ownership of salmon spawned in its waters, and divided up quotas on some Canadian fish, particularly those from the large Fraser River salmon run, according to a formula that gave Canadian fishers a majority of the catch but also gave U.S. fishers a significant proportion. At the same time, the agreement necessitated a significant reduction in actual catches by U.S. fishers.[8] In other words, both sides made concessions, with Canada backing away from its demand that international law as written be enforced, and the U.S. backing away from a *status quo* in which it could more or less do what it wanted. The quotas agreed to in 1999 were slated to last for a decade, until 2008. To this point both governments seem to be honouring their commitments under the amended Treaty.

Pacific Salmon and International Relations Theory

What does this case have to say about theories of international environmental cooperation? There is a limit, of course, to how much one case can tell us about general theory, but the case does lend support to some theories of cooperation, and point to the limitations of others. Two particular areas of theory will be discussed here; negotiating theory and neo-liberal institutionalism. The case tends to support some theories of international environmental bargaining and negotiation, but not others. At the same time, it points to some issues with neoliberal institutionalism as applied to some international environmental issues.

At first glance, negotiation and bargaining theory suggests that this case should not have generated difficult or contentious negotiations. In fact, by many measures, negotiations over a salmon quota should have been relatively easy and uneventful. Keohane and Nye (2001:145), for example, use the Canada-U.S. relationship as an example of complex interdependence, when negotiations about specific issues should not be expected to escalate. Some of the earliest insights into regime theory suggest that both agreeing to and enforcing an agreement should be easier the smaller the number of countries involved and the more iterated the negotiating environment. In this case the number of countries involved is as small as it can be in an international negotiation, and the context of the negotiation is highly iterated, both in terms of the country relationship (Canada and the United States are involved in a vast array of concurrent and ongoing negotiations) and in terms of the issue type (which requires some renegotiation annually in perpetuity).

At the same time, there are reasons to expect that the structure of the environmental issue should not have been particularly contentious either. Bargaining theory tells us that agreement is easier when there are clear agreement points that are obvious to all parties (Schelling, 1960), and such an agreement point was built into the original Pacific Salmon Treaty in the form of the national origin rule for dividing the catch. Theories of international environmental cooperation suggest that agreement is made easier when there is little scientific and informational uncertainty (Young, 1989:12), and when there is a source of scientific input, such as maximum sustainable yield estimates, that all of the parties involved accept as unbiased but which have been

8 Treaty, "Diplomatic Notes: June 30, 1999," pp. 83-88.

challenged (Susskind, 1994:71-3). They also suggest that cooperation is most likely to succeed when there is clear concern for the environmental good in question, and when state capacity to enforce agreements is high (Keohane et al., 1993). All of these conditions were met to a fairly high degree in this case.

And yet negotiations were fraught, lengthy, and acrimonious. Does this suggest that these theories are wrong? Not necessarily, for two reasons. The first is that the negotiations were ultimately successful in reaching an agreement that fulfilled the primary environmental goal (fishing quotas that do not exceed maximum sustainable yield), and that seems to have survived its first half-decade intact. The second is that the counterfactual may indeed be worse. In other words, had negotiations over a similar resource taken place among more countries, in a less iterated environment, with greater uncertainty and more biased science, and in the face of lower levels of environmental concern or state capacity, agreement might never have been reached, and cooperation might never have succeeded.

This suggests that the negotiations over the Pacific Salmon Treaty in the mid-1990s were inherently more difficult than the first cut at negotiating theory might suggest. Why? Two types of issues complicated the application of bargaining theory to this case. One involves the political structure of the negotiations, the other the structure of the environmental good. The key complication in the first case is the federal structure of both countries, and the key complication in the second case is the different shadows of the future of the two countries.

The idea that the Pacific Salmon Treaty negotiations should have been a relatively easy case of international cooperation, according to bargaining theory, was premised on the notion that it was a bilateral negotiation. It did involve two countries. But it was also not strictly bilateral, in that both countries are federal. Bargaining theory often begins with the assumption that countries will follow an exogenously given national interest, or that national leaders will reflect the preferences of the median voter. In federal systems, however, it will often be the case that the national interest will differ from the provincial/state interest, or that the preference of the median national voter will differ from that of the median provincial/state voter. This was clearly true in this case; both national governments stressed conservation and bilateral cooperation more, and the interests of the commercial fishery less, than the various state and provincial governments. In a way, this observation supports both the idea of complex interdependence and the idea that iteration is good for cooperation – the federal governments are involved in a much more deeply embedded pattern of cooperation than are the state and provincial governments.

The existence of a federal structure of government in both countries was further complicated by the fact that the division of powers was different in each country. In the United States state governments had much more legal authority over the issue in question than did the relevant provincial government in Canada. The government of British Columbia could create political awkwardness for the government of Canada if it opposed a particular deal, but it could not ultimately prevent the deal from being implemented. The governments of Alaska, Washington, and Oregon, on the other hand, could legally prevent any deal from being implemented (although, of course, the federal government was not without effective means of persuasion should it choose to use them). Two particular bargaining theories speak to this difference in authority; two-level game theory and veto player theory. Both theories make the same prediction, and do so for similar reasons. They both predict, somewhat counterintuitively, that the country where the federal government has less authority will ultimately get the better deal in negotiations.

Veto player theory posits, among other things, that the more veto players there are in a polity, the more constrained that polity will be in negotiating and enforcing international agreements (Tseblis, 2002). A veto player is any political actor, whether an individual or an organization, that can unilaterally veto a political outcome. This veto can be official, as in the U.S. Senate's veto over treaty signing, or unofficial, if particular political leaders, governmental bureaucracies, or lobby groups have a functional ability to prevent a national executive from taking a particular action. A country can only effectively engage in cooperation on terms acceptable to its own domestic veto players; if there are no terms acceptable to all veto players, then the country cannot effectively engage in international cooperation at all.

The application of veto player theory to this case is straightforward – state governments have veto power over U.S. decisions with respect to cooperation over Pacific salmon, but provinces do not have a symmetrical veto over Canadian decisions. To the extent that the short-term wellbeing of the commercial fishery defined the interests of state/provincial governments more than the interests of national governments, the veto power of state governments, and the lack of such powers on the part of provincial governments, meant that any final agreement needed to reflect the short-term interests of U.S. commercial salmon fishers, but not those in Canada.

Two-level game theory posits that national leaders, and national negotiators, face two audiences simultaneously while they are engaged in international negotiations. They face their opposite numbers from other countries, and at the same time they face a domestic audience that will ultimately need to ratify the deal, either legally or practically, if it is to work. They should only make a deal with their opposite numbers if there is a coalition of interests domestically that is sufficiently big that it will get the deal ratified. The domestic politics level of the game defines what the country's win-set will be, while the international level of the game determines if there is any overlap between the win-sets (Putnam, 1988).

One of the ancillary hypotheses of this theory is that the country with the smaller win-set, the one in which negotiators are more constrained by the demands of domestic politics, will have greater bargaining power than the country with the larger win-set, because the country with the smaller win-set can more credibly threaten that any given agreement will fail to be ratified and therefore will fail to yield a successful cooperative outcome (Putnam, 1988:440). In one sense, this hypothesis is saying exactly the same thing as the veto player hypothesis. A veto player can be defined as an actor that is necessary for domestic ratification. State governments were necessary, the relevant provincial government was not. But in another sense, this construction allows for a more reflective look at the construction and definition of interests in this case.

To the extent that we say that the United States better achieved its interests in the negotiations, we are assuming that the relevant interests are maximizing the share of the total quota reserved for a country. But there was another interest that both countries held in common, an interest in long-term salmon conservation. There are ways in which the Canadian government had more particular conservation needs than the U.S. government, because it was seeking moratoria on certain salmon stocks, whereas the United States was not. In the end, Canada failed to get what it wanted on quotas, but succeeded on conservation issues. In two-level game terms, the U.S. government won on those issues in which it was more constrained by domestic politics, but not on those issues in which it was not. This supports the two-level game hypothesis, but with the caveat that national interests in international negotiations are not unidimensional; they are often not about winning or losing per se, but trade-offs in which different countries win on different issues. It also supports another of the seminal hypotheses of bargaining theory, that cooperation will be more successful the greater the scope for issue trade-offs and side payments (Oye, 1986:9-11).

The discussion to this point has been of political structure, but bargaining theory in the international relations literature also discusses the effects of issue structure. Two different aspects of issue structure are relevant here, the way in which the physical characteristics of the environmental good itself interact with political structures, and the way in which the political actors value the good. One way in which different environmental issues have been characterized in the study of international environmental politics, as discussed above, is to distinguish between commons goods and directional goods. A commons good (or common pool resource) is one for which there is open and equal access by a group of actors. A directional good is one that is available to actors sequentially, first to those that are upstream or upwind, then to those downstream or downwind. A good example of this distinction is the difference between lakes and rivers. Lakes are typically commons goods; pollution put into an international lake by any coastal states affects all of the coastal states more or less equally. Rivers, on the other hand, are directional; pollution put into the river by an upstream state affects downstream states, but pollution put in by downstream states does not affect upstream states (DeSombre, 2002:17-8).

International fisheries are usually thought of as pure commons issues, because fishing on the high seas is open to all, and there are generally no directional aspects to fisheries issues (Peterson, 1993). Pacific salmon are an exception to this generalization, because they swim in such a predictable directional pattern, and because they are usually caught inside national waters rather than on the high seas. But they nonetheless retain commons characteristics; overfishing by either country affects the stocks available to both countries. In directional issues, the upstream state is usually assumed, other things being equal, to have predominant negotiating power. In commons issues, the structure of the issue does not impart negotiating power to one country over the other (although the way the countries value the good does, as will be discussed below).

In this issue, the matter is confused further by the fact that the United States is both the upstream country, because of Alaska, and the downstream country, because of Washington State and Oregon, while Canada is the middle-stream country. Furthermore, boats from the two downstream states often fish in Alaskan waters. In the end, the behaviour of U.S. states was consistent with what the theory would predict if they thought of themselves as upstream actors. But this interpretation is clouded by the political structure of the issue, as discussed above, in which key U.S. negotiators (at the state level) cared relatively more about the health of the commercial fishery, while key Canadian negotiators (at the federal level) cared relatively more about the health of the stock. In other words, the outcome seems overdetermined, making it difficult to tell whether the outcome was being driven by issue structure or political structure. In short, the Pacific salmon case suggests that not all international fisheries issues are commons issues, but the upstream-downstream relationships can be too complicated for the logic of directional environmental issues to be of clear explanatory or predictive value.

The difference in concern between negotiators on the U.S. and Canadian side can be expressed as concern with different issues, the health of the commercial fishery versus the health of the stock. But it can also be expressed in terms of time horizons, as the difference between primarily shorter-term and longer-term interests in the stocks of the various Pacific salmon species. This observation connects the case with a part of the bargaining literature in international relations theory and international environmental politics that looks at the effects on negotiations of different time horizons, different shadows of the future (Barkin and Shambaugh, 1999). This literature suggests, among other things, that when dealing with environmental issues shorter time horizons imparts bargaining power. In other words, it suggests that, other things being equal, the country that cares relatively less about the long-term health of the environmental good (and more about short-term economic extraction) will be relatively more able to achieve a bargaining outcome closer to its preferences (Barkin and Shambaugh, 1999a:12-14).

The logic of the theory is that the country with the shorter time-horizon should be willing to hold out in negotiations longer than the country with the longer time-horizon, because the former is focusing more on the short-term gains of overconsumption, while the latter is focusing more on the long-term costs of the damage being done by the overconsumption. As such, the country with the longer time-horizon is likely to cave in first and accede to the demands of the country with the shorter time-horizon, as long as those demands are consistent with the long-term health of the environmental good. Another way of phrasing this argument in a language specific to fisheries issues is to speak of substitutability. The more easily one party to a negotiation over the management of a fishery can substitute for specific fish stocks, the greater its bargaining power. The ability to substitute for the specific stock under negotiation means that that party has less concern with the long-term health of that particular stock, and a more credible threat to overconsume it in the absence of an agreement, because it is more able to make use of other fisheries (DeSombre and Barkin, 2000:339-360).

The Pacific salmon case supports both the conclusion of this theory and its logic, whether the theory is stated in terms of time-horizons or substitutability. For the U.S., the stocks in question were more substitutable than they were for Canada; Canadian negotiators were thinking in terms of the health of specific salmon runs, while U.S. (federal and state) negotiators were thinking more in terms of the aggregate catch. In other words, for U.S. negotiators, specific runs were substitutable for other specific runs, whereas for Canadian negotiators they often were not (DeSombre and Barkin, 2000). The U.S. bargaining advantage, which led to substantial Canadian concessions on the question of access to Canadian stocks by U.S. fishers, was gained largely by a willingness to hold out longer in negotiations while salmon stocks were fished out.

The final body of theory that will be discussed in the context of this case is neoliberal institutionalism. This theoretical approach argues that the primary purpose of international regimes is to improve the contractual environment of international cooperation. This can be done by clearly specifying the rights and responsibilities of all of the actors involved, improving flows of relevant information, and by decreasing the costs of participating in cooperative ventures (Keohane, 1982). As applied to international environmental regimes, this approach suggests that the role of cooperative agreements should be to make clear what the rules are, to provide generally available and credible information both about the science of the environmental issue and about state behaviour relative to the issue, and to routinize negotiations so that details that need to be respecified annually, such as quotas, can be agreed upon with a minimum of fuss (Keohane et al., 1993).

Another way of phrasing the improvement of the contractual environment is to speak of improving transparency; the elements of improving the contractual environment generally boil down to making information on both rules and behaviour clear and available to all interested parties (Mitchell, 1988). The Pacific Salmon Treaty was a sound treaty from a neoliberal institutionalist standpoint. It made property rights clear, by specifying that countries own those salmon that spawn in its territory. It improved flows of information, by creating the Pacific Salmon Commission to generate and analyze needed data. And it routinized negotiations over annual quotas so that they could be managed largely by technical experts, with a minimum of political input. In other words, the Treaty created exactly the sort of transparent environment for international cooperation that neoliberal institutionalism calls for. This environment, however, fostered successful cooperation for only a handful of years before it began to fail, at first quietly then increasingly publicly. From this theoretical perspective the question is, what went wrong?

The answer is domestic politics. The goal of transparency in international regimes assumes a clearly identifiable national interest. Whether that interest is determined by the state apparatus for its own reasons, is reflective of the interest of the median voter, or is the result of the give and take of domestic interest group politics, neoliberal institutionalism assumes that once a government gets to the international negotiating table it represents some exogenously given national interest.

Transparency in international regimes then makes that interest easier to achieve. But when that interest is not exogenously given, when the domestic politics of the issue continue after attempts at international cooperation have begun, transparency plays a more complicated role. It improves the contractual environment for cooperation within the specific terms of the international regime, but at the same time it can contribute to patterns of domestic politics that undermine the regime.

Transparency has the effect of preventing disagreement and inefficiency among those people already involved in a cooperative process, given exogenously defined interests. But when interests change, transparency can contribute to increasing the politicization of the issue, which in turn can contribute to more intractable negotiations than would otherwise be the case. Transparency means creating a rules-based system of international cooperation in which the rules are clear to all. But by making information more broadly available, increased transparency can bring people into political processes with respect to an issue who would otherwise not be there. To use the terminology of two-level games, this popularization of the issue can have the effect, by increasing the number of domestic players in the ratification game, of decreasing the size of a country's win-set, and therefore of decreasing the potential for overlap among the win-sets of the different countries involved.

In the Pacific salmon case, the transparency of the international regime meant that information both on rules (property rights) and the relevant marine science was available to all. Canadian fishers could point to the property rights enshrined in the treaty and demand what they saw as fair by those terms. U.S. fishers could point to the analysis that said that if they overfished, Canada would bear a disproportionate ratio of the costs. Absent that information, it is much less likely that salmon quota negotiations would have become front-page news in British Columbia and the Pacific Northwest. Had the negotiations been run throughout as back-room deals based on private information and political expediency, there would not have been equivalent points on which the issue could gain traction in the popular imagination. The outcome might well have been similar, although if it would not it would probably have differed in the direction of Canadian preferences, for many of the reasons discussed above, not least of which is that state governments in the United States would have been less likely to wield their vetoes in the absence of prospects for political gain from the issue. But even if the outcome were similar, the process of getting there would have been much less contentious.

This should by no means be taken to suggest that backroom deals are preferable to transparent ones. Rather it should be taken to suggest that the basic argument of neo-liberal institutionalist theory, that transparency makes cooperation more efficient, is not universally true. Transparency can have the effect of popularizing and politicizing issues, and the process of politicization can itself change the national interest that a country brings to the table. This is equivalent to the arguments critical of open diplomacy Endogenizing the preferences that neo-liberal institutionalist theory exogenizes makes for a much messier theory. But the messiness is something that needs to be taken into account in designing international regimes in the first place. Negotiators should recognize that transparency can affect perceptions of interests, and plan regimes accordingly. Sometimes such planning might involve less transparency when more transparency would lead to greater politicization. In the Pacific salmon case, an original treaty that was less clear in specifying property rights might have led to more flexible negotiating stances in follow-up quota negotiations, and prevented several years in which there were no agreed-on quotas.

Conclusion

There are a number of elements in the discussion of U.S.-Canadian Pacific salmon negotiations in this chapter that relate to themes that run throughout this volume. This case highlights especially the difficulties when the division of powers among levels of government with respect to the environment differs between the countries. It indicates the indeterminacy of the power relationship between the United States and Canada, and the need for nuance in the reading of that relationship. And a comparison of this case, which caught the popular attention in both countries, with some others in this volume in which environmental cooperation largely happened between governmental bureaucracies and out of the public eye, suggests that the interrelationship in bilateral ecopolitics between intergovernmental diplomacy and popular politics provides a useful direction for future research.

This chapter also points to the utility of theories of international environmental cooperation in understanding the U.S.-Canadian environmental relationship. These theories can give us context for understanding particular relationships, and can help us identify the ways in which the politics of particular environmental issues differ from the norm. They can also help us in extrapolating from individual cases to identify patterns in bilateral ecopolitics more broadly. In this context, the Pacific salmon case points both to the utility and to the limits of transparency in international environmental agreements. It points as well to the potential effects on environmental negotiations of federal politics and of the politicization of environmental management.

Chapter 12

North American Integration and "Green" Electricity

Ian Rowlands

Introduction: Greening the Grid

Electricity systems around the world are experiencing unprecedented rates of change, driven – at least in part – by a combination of three forces: electricity industry restructuring, growing environmental concern, and increasing internationalization. The result is that both opportunities and challenges are arising as efforts grow to ensure that electricity is provided in a sustainable manner.

Canada and the United States are no exceptions. Across these two countries, these three forces are at work. Notwithstanding substantial concerns in the wake of the so-called "California crisis" – that is, power reforms that resulted in high prices, load shedding and numerous claims of market manipulation (for more, see Bushnell, 2004) – electricity systems at the state or/provincial level are continuing to be restructured (EIA, 2003; NRCan, 2003a). And in spite of the United States' withdrawal from the Kyoto Protocol process, air quality concerns (at local, regional and global levels) are high on the list of priorities of many across these two countries (Rosenbaum, 2002:189-205; VanNijnatten and Lambright, 2001). Finally, renewed attention to security issues – in the wake of the 11 September terrorist attacks – has only served to push the state of bilateral relations up the political agenda (Roussel, 2003).

The first two of these forces mean that greater attention is being paid to how renewable electricity – that is, "electricity which may be characterized as environmentally friendly by virtue of the energy resource used" (Holt, 1997:13), which often means electricity generated from solar, wind, small hydro and biomass resources – might be encouraged. Given that it has largely been left to the state or province level to determine not only the appropriate support scheme for renewable electricity, but also the very definition of the term "green power", different approaches have been taken. The result is a patchwork quilt of actions across Canada and the United States.

In light of the third of the aforementioned forces, however, such variations may be inconsistent with aspirations for closer economic, social and/or political relations – or at least, more-harmonious relations – between the two countries. It is within this context that this chapter explores the issues associated with the interaction between

Canada-U.S. relations and the attempted "greening" of power systems through increased use of renewable electricity. More specifically, the chapter focuses upon three areas.

First, after briefly describing electricity supply systems within Canada and the United States, the chapter reviews the different support schemes that exist for renewable electricity across these two countries. It is shown that different jurisdictions have adopted different strategies: among the approaches are various financial incentives, outreach and voluntary programs, and rules, regulations and policies. The aim of this part of the chapter is to identify the extent to which differences exist – between, and within, countries. Second, the chapter identifies the ways in which the "internationalization" of electricity is increasing; it also reveals the growing interest in stronger bilateral relations between Canada and the United States on electricity issues. There are a variety of factors – including both technological advances and policy developments – that are pushing the various parts of these countries' electricity industries closer together.

Finally, given the existing predominance of "local approaches" for promoting renewable electricity, and the pressures for a single "international approach" towards all electricity matters (promotion of renewable electricity included), the chapter investigates ways in which the promotion of renewable electricity might be achieved against a background of closer international ties. A "middle ground" approach – that is, one that does not entirely rely upon local priorities (as is now the case) or a single bilateral vision (as might be the direction in which policy is heading) – is advocated. This option is advanced in light of recent international organizations' activities and recommendations in this area.

Electricity Supply and Support Schemes for Renewable Electricity

In 2001, Canada was the world's fifth largest generator of electricity – the 588 TWhr produced within its territory represented 3.8 percent of all power generated, worldwide (IEA, 2003:27). Moreover, Canada is the world's largest producer of hydropower – 12.6 percent of all electricity in the world produced in this manner (2001 data, taken from IEA, 2003:19). In 2000, 60.1 percent of the electricity generated in Canada was by means of large-scale hydropower facilities (NEB, 2003, Table A4.2.12). Coal-fired power stations (18.3 percent) and nuclear power stations (11.7 percent) made more modest, though still significant, contributions (NEB, 2003, Table A4.2.12). Other renewable resources – including wind, biomass and small-scale hydropower – contributed 2.3 percent (NEB, 2003, Table A4.2.12).

The United States is the single largest producer and consumer of electricity in the world – responsible for 25.0 percent of the worldwide total (2001 data, taken from IEA, 2003:27). In 2002, 3,858.5 TWhr of electricity was generated in the country (EIA, 2004, Table 5). The majority of this (50.1 percent) was by means of coal-fired power stations; nuclear power stations (20.2 percent) and natural gas-fired power stations (17.9 percent) were also significant contributors (EIA, 2004, Table 5). Those resources often called "renewable" – that is, hydropower (6.6 percent) and the entire suite of other renewables (that is, solar, wind, biomass, and so on (2.3 percent)) – made only modest contributions (EIA, 2004, Table 5).

Many argue that these patterns of electricity supply (and use[1]) are unsustainable. Significant use of fossil fuels for power generation (particularly coal) creates air quality problems at a variety of scales – local (smog), regional (acid deposition) and global (climate change). Moreover, the challenges associated with nuclear power not only relate to short-term safety (the possibility of an accidental release of radioactive material), but also long-term environmental issues (the safe disposal of waste) and economic viability over various time-scales. Finally, irrespective of one's position regarding the sustainability of existing large-scale hydropower facilities (see, for example, World Commission on Dams, 2000), it is important to recognize that many of the "best" sites (that is, those that have the smallest environmental and social impact) in North America have already been exploited. Thus, the problems facing present modes of electricity generation are encouraging a reconsideration of how power is supplied.[2]

The potential advantages of renewable sources of energy are also stimulating new thinking about power supply. Goldemberg (2004), for example, enumerates a range of benefits arising from the greater use of renewable energy. These include catalyzing environmental and health improvements (mitigating air pollution, in particular), stimulating innovation and local economic development, diversifying energy supply, advancing energy security, preventing conflicts about natural resources and alleviating poverty. For a variety of reasons, therefore, many are calling for increased use of renewables in energy supply.

Given, however, that the financial cost of renewables (that is, what potential purchasers must spend to secure access to green energy) is usually higher than the conventional means of energy provision, many argue that there is a need for some kind of "support scheme". In other words, actions must be taken in order to "level the playing field", so that the subsidies that large, centralized means of electricity generation have traditionally received (and continue to receive) can be countered. These subsidies are both direct – financial resources provided – and indirect – the ability to "externalize" some of the costs (for example, health care requirements arising from air pollution) onto others.

The Database of State Incentives for Renewable Energy (DSIRE) provides a useful overview of different kinds of "renewable energy incentives" (analogous to the "support schemes" term introduced above). They divide incentives into three different categories (DSIRE, 2004a):

1 The focus in this chapter is upon "supply" – that is, the provision of electricity. Of course, increased energy sustainability also requires that "demand" be examined as well – for example, conservation and efficiency strategies.

2 For more information about the sustainability consequences of conventional means of electricity supply, see CEC (1999), CEC (2002) and Holdren and Smith (2000).

(1) Financial Incentives: tax incentives, grants, loans, rebates, industry recruitment, solar energy equipment leasing and sales by utilities, and production incentives.

(2) Outreach and Voluntary Programs: utility green pricing programs, outreach programs, and voluntary installer certification programs.

(3) Rules, Regulations and Policies: public benefits funds, renewables portfolio standards, net metering, interconnection, extension analysis, generation disclosure, contractor licensing, equipment certification, solar/wind access laws, and construction and design standards, required utility green power options, and green power purchasing/aggregation policies.

Worth noting here is that support schemes for renewable electricity have been, to date, primarily introduced at the state or provincial or substate or subprovincial levels. (More information about specific programs may be found in Dogterom et al.(2002), DSIRE (2004b) and CEC (2004).) What is significant for the investigation in this chapter is that there appears to be a wide degree of differences across state/provincial programs. Not only have organizations in individual jurisdictions selected different broad approaches (as represented by the three categories noted above), but even among those that have taken the same general tack, the details are often quite dissimilar.

Under the heading of "financial incentives", for example, consider the example of wind power tax incentives at the federal level. In Canada, there exists the "Wind Power Production Incentive" (NRCan, 2002), while the United States had the "Federal Renewable Production Tax Credit" (DSIRE, 2004b). While both can be considered to be an example of a "feed in policy" (Rowlands, forthcoming), there are significant differences between them. For one, the former is a payment, while the latter was a tax credit. Additionally, their values are different: the Canadian incentive is set, initially, at a 1.2 (Canadian) cents per kilowatt-hour payment, while the American one provided for a 1.8 USD cents per kilowatt-hour tax credit. Thus, while each has a similar general goal – that is, to expand wind power production in their respective countries – they contain different operational details.

To take but one more example of differences among "financial incentives", consider the rebates for the installation of residential photovoltaic systems that are offered by a number of U.S. states. Bolinger and Wiser (2002) found that six U.S. states have "buy-down programs" – that is, financial payments for those who purchase photovoltaic systems for their homes. Even among this relatively limited number of jurisdictions, however, rules varied widely. The amount of the rebate differed across every state – between $3 and $6USD. Moreover, some states had complementary "production incentives" (that is, additional payments would be made for every unit of electricity generated by the photovoltaic system), while others did not. There were also differences with respect to the size that the solar electric system had to be – some had limits like 5 kW or 10 kW, while others did not (though they might have had lower rebates for larger systems). Thus, a wide range of requirements were in evidence.

Turning to "outreach and voluntary programs", consider utility green pricing programmes that exist in the two largest cities in Alberta (Canada). In Calgary, Enmax offers its "Greenmax programme" (Enmax, 2004), while in Edmonton, Epcor offers its customers the opportunity to purchase "Eco-Packs" (Epcor, 2004). While both assure the customer that a set amount of green power will be added to the provincial grid for a small monthly payment, they differ with respect to the kinds of renewable resources they rely upon. Enmax focuses solely upon wind, while Epcor draws its green power from a range of small hydro, wind, biomass and solar facilities. Given the sheer number of such "green pricing programs" in existence in the United States (126, according to DSIRE (2004b)), it would be easy to find similar differences among U.S. cities and states.

Under the heading of "rules, regulations and policies", meanwhile, different jurisdictions have used different definitions of "renewable" to structure their legislation. While virtually everyone agrees that solar and wind should be called renewable (and that oil and coal should not be called renewable), differences of opinion arise with respect to other resources, particularly hydropower and biomass (Patterson and Rowlands, 2002; Rowlands et al., 2002). This is perhaps most evident in how different states in the United States elaborate their respective "renewable portfolio standards". (A renewable portfolio standard (RPS) is a "law or policy which requires that a certain percentage of a organization's generating capacity, new investments in energy capacity or total energy sales/purchases, must be derived from specific renewable resources" (CEC, 2003a:3).) Under the terms of the RPS for the state of Illinois, for example, hydropower does not qualify as a renewable source of electricity (and thus does not enjoy legislative support). Alternatively, in the state of Maine, any hydropower facility up to 100 MW qualifies under that state's RPS (DSIRE, 2004b).

Where the renewable electricity is generated is also important in the definition used in RPS legislation in some jurisdictions. A number of states require "electricity from these sources to be produced in-state… whereas others… require particular fuel sources to be in-state" (CEC, 2003b:6). Other states, however, place no similar "location of origin" restrictions upon the renewable electricity.

The age of the facilities generating the renewable electricity is also relevant, for a number of jurisdictions require a particular share of the green power to be sourced from "new" facilities. "New", however, is often defined by different cut-off dates. In the RPS in Massachusetts, "new" means after 31 December 1997, while in Texas, it means something 20 months later – namely, after 1 September 1999 (DSIRE, 2004b).[3]

Turning to another "rule, regulation and policy", consider the diversity in rules regarding "net metering" that are in place across Canada. (Net metering refers to the process whereby, for individuals who are generating their own power – with, for example, photovoltaic panels – electricity can flow both to and from the customer through a single, bi-directional meter. See Bell (2003) for a discussion about different

3 For more about the similarities and differences among RPSs, see CEC (2003a) and CEC (2003b).

definitions of the term.) Bell (2003:ix) found that "eight Canadian utilities currently have policies in place which allow small renewable generators to be compensated at the retail rate and another seven utilities provide below retail compensation." Many others, however, have no formal policy in place.

Thus, it is evident that there are differences across both Canada and the United States regarding the "kinds" of renewable electricity that are supported and the "ways" in which they are supported.

Pressures for "Internationalising" Support Schemes for Renewable Electricity

One might immediately wonder why the fact that there exist different approaches to supporting renewable electricity across Canada and the United States is an issue of consequence. After all, electricity, by its very nature – economically unfeasible to store, physical (and economic) losses associated with its long-distance transmission – appears to be a commodity that is largely-contained within a local system. Little is usually made of the global trade in electricity, like it is for many other goods and services. Why then, even in the presence of increasing internationalization, should there be interest in the existing diversity of local support schemes for renewable electricity?[4]

It certainly is the case that electricity has, traditionally in Canada and the United States, been predominantly a "local" concern. Approximately 1.5 percent of the electricity generated in 2000 in either Canada or the United States was exported to the other country (NEB, 2003, Table A.4.2.12).[5] This is, of course, an extremely small share of these two countries' total electricity supply. Nevertheless, given the significant total value of the electricity supply industry in both Canada and the United States, this still represents more than C$2 billion (NRCan, 2003b) – a substantial figure in absolute terms.

Indeed, it is important to recognize the various institutional and physical links – in terms of electricity – that currently exist between Canada and the United States. For one, governance of different parts of these countries' (interconnected) power systems is already international: the presence of organizations like the North American Electricity Reliability Council and its various committees (including the Western Electricity Coordinating Council, the Mid-Continent Area Power Pool and the Northeast Power Coordinating Council) are all evidence of existing institutional links in electricity between the two countries.

The 14 August 2003 blackout also revealed how closely these two countries' electricity systems are linked, physically. Accidents and errors in the state of Ohio "cascaded" out of control, so that eventually both countries – an estimated 50 million

4 For an earlier, exploratory, discussion of some of these issues in a North American context, see Rowlands (2002).

5 The figures for the individual countries are as follows: In 2000, 8.7 percent of the electricity generated in Canada was exported to the United States, while 0.4 percent of the electricity generated in the United States was exported to Canada.

people in eight states and the province of Ontario – were affected. (For more about the blackout, see U.S.-Canada Power System Outage Task Force (2003).) With "51 electricity grid connections that cross the Canada-U.S. border" (NRCan, 2003b), electricity is, every minute of every day, a transnational issue.

Moreover, various organizations on both sides of the border are calling for greater international cooperation on energy issues. The United States, for example, produced its "National Energy Policy" in March 2001. In that report, it was recommended – in a broad and general sense – that "a North American Energy Framework [be supported] to expand and accelerate cross-border energy investment, oil and gas pipelines, and electricity grid connections by streamlining and expediting permitting procedures with Mexico and Canada" (NEPDG, 2001:xv).

Focusing explicitly upon electricity, the report also noted that international interconnections between Canada and the United States "provide important trade and clean air benefits, while allowing both countries to benefit from load sharing and integration. The reliability of the North American electricity grid can be enhanced yet further through closer coordination and compatible regulatory and jurisdictional approaches" (NEPDG, 2001:8-8) Recommendations for closer electricity ties – both institutional and physical – thus followed.

In a similar vein, the Canadian Prime Minister and the U.S. President (along with the Mexican President) agreed at the Summit of the Americas in Quebec City (22 April 2001) that their newly-created North American Energy Working Group "will be a valuable means of fostering communication and coordinating efforts in support of efficient North American energy markets ..." (quoted in CEC, 2002:iv). This group issued its report the following year (NAEWG, 2002). Thus, not only are there substantial connections, in terms of electricity, between Canada and the United States already in place, but some are calling for these links to be strengthened and replicated.

When the focus turns to renewable electricity, in particular, the prospects for increased interconnections between Canada and the United States seem to heighten even further. Consider three additional ways in which renewable electricity could become a larger bilateral issue. First, it should be recognized that goods "made with" renewable electricity could travel much further than the electricity itself could travel. For example, soft drinks contained in "green-powered" aluminium cans produced in one country could be marketed for its environmental attributes in the other country. This could mean that the "embedded" electricity ("green power", in this case) generates international attention. Second, the promising prospects for hydrogen fuel cells in power generation suggest that it might soon be economically practical to store electricity and to move it over long distances. By transporting hydrogen instead of electrons, it is conceivable that Canada's reserves of large-scale hydropower could be used to generate hydrogen for small-scale electricity generators in parts of the United States. Similarly, American coal reserves could be used to generate hydrogen for the same purpose in parts of Canada. Either case would also give electricity heightened international standing. Third, many feel that the existing trade and investment regimes in North America might further direct attention to Canada-U.S. relations and renewable electricity. Here, some possibilities are considered in depth.[6]

Trade disputes could conceivably arise as a result of – for example – differing RPS qualifications. Horlick et al. (2002, 8) argue that electricity as a "good" is basically all "alike" – that is, the electrons generated by a wind-powered turbine are indistinguishable, at the user's electrical outlet, from those generated by a coal-fired power plant. What distinguishes them is the way in which they were produced – that is, in the language of the international lawyers, the "non-product-related processes and production methods" (Appleton, 1999).

Recent precedents in international trade law have led Horlick et al. (2002) to believe that an RPS in jurisdiction A that excludes, for instance, large-scale hydropower, could effectively be challenged as discriminatory by hydropower interests in jurisdiction B. As argued above, the "products" are alike. Moreover, many would argue that there is nothing in the processes and production methods that justifies any restriction upon their importation – that is, they are just as "environmentally-friendly" as those various resources that qualify as part of jurisdiction A's RPS (Klimpt, Guérard and Arsenault, 2002). Indeed, the hydropower producer's case would appear to be strongest in cases in which jurisdiction A's RPS was intended to "reduce local smog"(for example, Texas's RPS, which aims to reduce "air pollution in Texas from fossil fuel electric generation" (noted in DSIRE, 2004b)). If, alternatively, the intention of the RPS was to mitigate climate change,[7] perhaps the hydropower exclusion from the RPS would have a greater chance of successfully meeting a legal challenge.

At this point, of course, it remains largely academic, for there is "no GATT/WTO case law on trade in electricity and ... the only jurisprudence relating to the energy sector deals with petrol or gasoline. ... [And] there is no NAFTA jurisprudence dealing with trade in electricity" (Horlick et al., 2002:8). Indeed, Hempling and Rader (2002) argue otherwise – that disparate RPS requirements are consistent with NAFTA (an agreement which could be key in determining the outcome of international disputes on this issue).[8] The point is simply that if trade tribunals call for – or if it is even simply perceived that trade tribunals could call for – a harmonized approach to supporting renewable electricity, then a uniform, bilateral strategy could effectively be encouraged.[9]

---

6 For a similar discussion, examining relations between North America and the European Union, see Rowlands (2003).

7 For the debate about the global climate change impacts of large-scale dams, see, for example, World Commission on Dams (2000), 75-77.

8 Their argument that these are not "like" products (that is, electricity generated by wind is different than electricity generated by coal, because the former has customer appeal, among other attributes) is their potentially most powerful one (Hempling and Rader, 2002:6-7).

9 Having said that it is largely an "academic" issue is not meant to suggest that disputes like this could not arise soon. Indeed, Canadian officials have been watching – with some degree of anxiety – debates surrounding the development of a federal RPS in the United States. In its 2003 review of international trade priorities, the Canadian government noted that "Canada remains concerned over proposals in recent U.S. federal and state legislation

Investment disputes could also serve to catalyze a common bilateral approach. It is possible that certain provisions of NAFTA's Chapter 11 (the investment chapter) could apply even in the absence of "true deprivations of property" (that is, one's traditional view of corporate expropriation by host governments – "nationalising" foreign companies and taking over their assets). Instead, there might need to be "compensation for any government action which has a significant impact on the profit-making ability of an investment" (Horlick et al., 2002:24). Horlick and colleagues go on to argue that: "If the approach set out there [in the Metalclad case] is maintained, then any post-investment environmental measure applied in the electricity generation and distribution sectors that impact on the profitability of a foreign investor will require compensation to be paid" (Horlick et al., 2002:24-25).[10]

An example of such a challenge, involving renewable electricity in Canada and the United States, can be envisaged. Consider fictional jurisdiction A. Its government had traditionally taken a "laissez-faire" attitude towards renewable electricity. As a result, a company from jurisdiction B sets up a landfill gas recovery-to-electricity unit in jurisdiction A, and markets the resulting power under the national "green power" logo scheme. Further imagine that the leadership in jurisdiction A then has a change of heart, and decides to actively advance renewable electricity by introducing its own support scheme (rather than having the "default" national one – the labelling scheme – be the only one in existence). Legislators there decide to introduce an RPS. Following the results of local polling, these legislators decide that "renewable" consists exclusively of solar and wind. As a result, the company from jurisdiction B can no longer market its biomass-sourced electricity as a premium (environmental) product. That company's officials may then argue that because biomass is just as "renewable" as the privileged sources (solar and wind), the legislation is unfair. They then proceed to argue that the introduction of the RPS amounts to "de facto expropriation of assets" and they demand compensation for lost revenues. Although it is hard to anticipate the outcome of such a case, it is certainly reasonable to state that the case put forward by the company from jurisdiction B could be viewed sympathetically by a NAFTA panel. And, in anticipation of an outcome favourable to the company from jurisdiction B, every conceivable jurisdiction A in Canada and the

---

to exclude Canadian-origin renewable energy resources and hydroelectric power from U.S. renewable energy programs. Canadian advocacy in this sector has raised U.S. awareness of a North American electricity market and the impact that discriminatory measures could have on this market" (Government of Canada, 2003, 40). Moreover, the Canadian ambassador to the United States has written to US legislators, arguing that: "All hydroelectricity, not just incremental hydroelectric generation, is renewable energy. Should an RPS emerge in your legislation, we would request that hydroelectricity not be disadvantaged. We wish to point out that given NAFTA and WTO obligations, any RPS must be non-discriminatory vis-à-vis Canadian and U.S. generated electricity" (Kergin, 2003).

10 In the Metalclad case, a US waste management company challenged "decisions by Mexican local government to refuse it a permit to operate a hazardous waste landfill … and by state government to create an ecological preserve in the area" (CCPA, 2004). A NAFTA tribunal found in favour of the US company, following Chapter 11 of the NAFTA.

United States may want to ensure that its support scheme for renewable electricity is as "compatible" with neighbouring jurisdictions as possible.[11]

Thus, a variety of factors may continue to encourage the increasing internationalization of Canada-U.S. electricity issues. There may be, therefore, growing pressure to have support schemes for renewable electricity to be as "common", bilaterally, as possible. This may manifest itself in the form of any or all of the following (and more):

- common definition for "green power"single loan program for solar energy systems
- centrally-designed and implemented "education campaigns"
- identical legislation regarding generation and pollution disclosure obligations

Indeed, calls for centralising (to a greater degree) the way in which support schemes for renewable energy are developed are already in evidence. The Canadian Electricity Association, for example, has stated that it believes that it is "critical for the Canadian government to develop a clear and consistent stance with respect to the definitional question of ... renewable 'green power'" (quoted in Vaughan et al., 2001:43). Similarly, the Joint Public Advisory Committee (of the Commission for Environmental Cooperation of North America) called upon the CEC to promote "the adoption of similar criteria by the NAFTA parties for defining green power" (JPAC, 2001).

The Way Forward: Finding a Middle Ground Between Local Approaches and Internationalization

Thus, it is evident that support schemes for renewable electricity have their roots – within Canada and the United States – at the local level. It is also clear, however, that there are existing factors that are serving to encourage the harmonization of these same support schemes for renewable electricity. Should support schemes for renewable electricity be allowed to be swept up in increasing internationalization, with the result being that there exists a single way of supporting renewable electricity across Canada and the United States? Or, alternatively, should local authority in such decision-making be somehow preserved, with the result being that individual communities continue to decide how best to support renewable electricity? Or, finally, should some "middle ground" be developed?

As the title of this section suggests, the argument advanced here is that some kind of "middle ground" should be developed. It is acknowledged that neither an entirely local approach (as is now dominant) nor a wholly-international approach (as would appear to be the direction in which policy is heading) is the most desirable. That is

11 What makes the potential Chapter 11 challenge all the more intriguing is that it would not need to be instituted by (or even supported by) the government in jurisdiction B; private companies have standing in such cases under NAFTA.

not, however, to argue that there are not advantages to either – for there certainly are.

A local approach may provide the "flexibility necessary to increase the sustainability of [individual electricity supply systems]. By acknowledging, and responding to, regional differences in the resource content of electricity systems, in resource endowments and in health and environmental challenges, communities could ... identify their own path for sustainability" (Rowlands and Patterson, 2002). Alternatively, a uniform international approach might increase "confidence in the investment climate [which] may lead [renewable electricity] developers to produce large quantities of renewable energy technologies for the [international] market. [An international] standard would also provide consumers with a simple and singular definition for green electricity. This may lead to greater trust and confidence in green electricity on the part of the general public" (Rowlands and Patterson, 2002). But there are also drawbacks to each approach – for the benefits of one approach equally serve as the costs of the other approach.[12] This encourages consideration of how some kind of "middle ground" might serve to capture the respective benefits, without also encompassing the costs.

The fact that renewable electricity is promoted for both local and global reasons would also seem to encourage some kind of "middle ground" approach. Examining the case of environmental policy harmonization more broadly, Jha argues (1997:311) that different approaches should be taken, depending upon whether the environmental goal is a global one or a local one. If it is a global goal, then harmonization should be pursued. In the case of renewable electricity, addressing global climate change is often one of the key motivators (for example, Canada's EcoLogo program for "renewable low-impact electricity"; see Patterson and Rowlands, 2002, for a discussion). Alternatively, if it is a local goal, then mutual recognition is what may be most appropriate. Jha's general comments in this regard would seem to apply quite well to renewable electricity: "For example, pollution thresholds differ, based on such variables as climate, soil characteristics, pollution assimilative capacities, as well as ability and willingness to pay. Even to achieve identical environmental quality between two nations, their individual standards need not be the same" (Jha, 1997:311). Given that local goals often motivate support schemes for renewable electricity (see, for example, the Texas example, above), it is clear that this approach is also relevant.

This issue – that is, the appropriate way in which support schemes for renewable electricity and internationalization should be considered together – has recently been taken up by international organizations. The CEC Secretariat, for example, following the mandate given it by Article 13 of the North American Agreement on Environmental Cooperation (in which it is noted that "The Secretariat may prepare a report for the Council on any matter within the scope of the annual program'), launched a major initiative on "Environmental Challenges and Opportunities of the Evolving Continental Electricity Market".

12 For an elaboration, see Rowlands and Patterson (2002).

The Secretariat – guided by the advice of an international advisory board – prepared a draft report that examined "recent developments in the electricity sectors in Canada, Mexico and the United States, possible environmental quality impacts resulting from restructuring and other developments, and also explores policy issues related to recent developments in the adoption of environmentally preferable electricity, including so-called 'green electricity' labelling and certification systems"(CEC, 2001). This draft report was the subject of a public symposium, held in San Diego, California at the end of November 2001. After a period of public input, the Secretariat produced a final report for the governments of Canada, Mexico and the United States. This report (CEC, 2002) was released to the public in June 2002.

In that report, the Secretariat appears to be calling for greater "cooperation and compatibility" on environment-related electricity issues.[13] Although they do not necessarily advocate "identical ... environmental laws, policies and programs in [the electricity] sector," they do nevertheless argue that there are "compelling reasons for North American cooperation in developing compatible policies and progress related to the electricity sector" (CEC, 2002:22).

The aforementioned international advisory board appears to have endorsed a similar tack: while explicitly ruling out a single, unidimensional international approach, they nevertheless advance calls for greater coordination of effort across North America. Consider, for example, the following two recommendations:

> 5.2 A dialogue should be commenced among industry, government and non-government organizations to explore opportunities for developing a more consistent regional approach to defining "renewable" energy;
>
> 5.3 The Advisory Board encourages the NAFTA Parties, through the CEC, to discuss mutually agreeable clarifications that would indicate whether and to what extent the way that electricity is generated is an integral part of the electricity "good" itself, for purposes of construing the Treaty and related agreements. (CEC, 2002:32)

Indeed, similar sentiments have been voiced elsewhere. The aforementioned National Energy Policy of the United States observed that as "state and federal governments consider energy reforms, there will be a need to ensure compatible regulatory frameworks with our neighbours while recognizing differences in jurisdictions" (NEPDG, 2001:8-8).

Thus, although it is clear that many stakeholders are also calling for some kind of "middle ground" approach to the interaction between internationalization and support schemes for renewable electricity, such calls remain relatively vague. To date, there has been little specific advice offered as to how to proceed.

To work out the details, there is clearly a need for international, multi-stakeholder discussions on the issue. For reasons that are elaborated elsewhere (in the transatlantic context, see Rowlands, 2003), representatives from a range of different

13 The term is taken from the title of one of the main sections of the report – namely, "The Need for Greater Environmental Cooperation and Compatibility" (CEC, 2002, 22).

organizations need to investigate the issue so that benefits from different forms of (and degrees of) coordinated activities in renewable electricity can be maximized, while potential costs can be mitigated or averted altogether. The established Canada-U.S. links that exist on electricity issues may provide an appropriate framework for these discussions.

Turning attention to renewable electricity, however, it is interesting to see that – in perhaps the best "functional'" tradition – players "on the ground" are already beginning to grapple with many of the issues that have been identified in this chapter. They are "learning by doing", through binational linkages on renewable electricity issues.

More specifically, there are already at least two instances of international activity regarding certification of "green power products". And they cross the Canada-U.S. border in both directions. For one, the Western New York Wind Corporation (a U.S. company) has received (Canadian) EcoLogo certification for the "alternative source electricity" produced at its facility in Gainesville, New York (ECP, 2004). And second, Vision Quest Windelectric (a Canadian company) has had its tradable renewable certificates certified by the (U.S.) Green-e program (GreenBiz, 2004). Thus, practitioners are active on this issue. Although this does not replace the need for multi-stakeholder discussions, the experience can inform those same discussions, so that the effective solutions – that is, appropriate approaches occupying the "middle ground" – can be found and followed.

Conclusion

The purpose of this chapter has been to explore the issues associated with Canada-U.S. relations and support schemes for renewable electricity. To do this, the argument was developed in three main sections. First, the wide diversity in support schemes for renewable electricity, across Canada and the United States, was revealed. Given that such schemes have largely emerged from the state or provincial level, it is not particularly surprising that different paths have often been chosen. Second, the pressures concerning increased "internationalization" in Canada-U.S. electricity issues were identified and examined. In light of these two apparently divergent phenomena, it was argued that explicit efforts must be made to make them compatible. Although the ideal "middle ground" approach still has yet to be fully elaborated, its importance was identified and key directions for further action highlighted. Indeed, this provides the impetus to continue to conduct research, and to experiment with different options, in this critical area.

Chapter 13

Uniquely Positioned: Global Economic Integration and Canada-U.S. Environmental Relations

Robert Paehlke

Canada-U.S. environmental relations are usually thought of in terms of bilateral cooperative ventures dating from the century-old Migratory Bird Treaty and following on through the International Joint Commission, the Great Lakes Water Quality Agreement, and the acid precipitation treaty signed by Brian Mulroney and George H. Bush. Alternatively, in Canada, the relationship is sometimes discussed in terms of threats to the Canadian environment that might result from actual, potential or even hypothetical U.S. demand for Canadian resources including lumber, minerals, paper, fish, oil, gas, electricity or water. Or, in a more positive vein, the focus is on what might be done to protect cross-border wildlife corridors from Yellowstone to Yukon or from the Adirondacks to Algonquin or to improve multilateral undertakings such as the Commission for Environmental Cooperation.

I argue that, while all of these things are important, both Canadians and Americans should also consider our environmental relationships in a wider context, a context that revolves around globalization and sustainability. Accordingly, this chapter comments on Canadian-American environmental relations from a global rather than from an exclusively bilateral perspective.

Globalization and Sustainability

Global economic integration poses challenges to both national sovereignty and democratic practice. In the 18th and 19th centuries the expansion of economic activity beyond local political boundaries was instrumental in the rise of the liberal democratic nation-state, but advocacy of a parallel expansion today appropriately provokes wariness. This is because effective democratic governance at a global scale is not easily imagined. At the same time, it is difficult to conceive any other way to resolve the unintended consequences of accelerating globalization that include: 1) increasing inequality within most nations; 2) trade-related environmental problems; 3) downwards pressure on taxation and social policy; and 4) tensions between a dominant secular commercialism and intensifying ethno-religious orthodoxies frighteningly now combined with terrorist opportunities that are also in many cases themselves an unintended consequence of global integration.

It is important to reflect on how each of these concerns relates to sustainability and identify some mechanisms for advancing sustainability despite (or through) global economic integration. Sustainability here is understood as a greater balance among environmental, social and economic objectives to maximize social equity and well-being and to minimize ecological damage through recognition of the need to constrain or ameliorate the effects of extracting raw resources from nature. Renewable resources should not be extracted faster than they are renewed and non-renewable resources should be used judiciously. Such change will require adaptation at every level of governance from the personal through the local and national to the global.

Canada is particularly well positioned to play a role in this adaptation. Should it choose to accept a true leadership role in advocating and in achieving sustainability, Canada would significantly advance its reputation for leadership in international environmental and ethical affairs. This chapter will credit several recent Canadian initiatives in this regard, most notably Canada's ratification of the Kyoto accord, its leadership on the POPs agreement and its pro-equity, anti-subsidy position regarding agricultural subsidies at the trade talks in Cancun and since. The chapter will also discuss ways that these and some new initiatives might be advanced in the future.

The broad conclusion is that Canada is well suited to playing a role in any possible transition to more democratic and balanced global-scale environmental governance. Support for this assertion includes the fact that Canada is a leading trading nation, both resource-rich and broadly prosperous (an unusual combination), culturally diverse, historically inclined to multilateralism, located in North America but with European instincts regarding many aspects of public policy, and thoroughly informed regarding the merits and perils of federalism. Also an important asset in this regard is the sheer reality of Canada's land to population ratio and the stewardship and sustainability obligations and possibilities thereby imposed. All of these factors would serve it well both in taking and in encouraging bold sustainability initiatives.

Before turning to Canada's possible role let me briefly summarize my perspective on the effects of global economic integration on social and environmental policy as set out in a recent book (Paehlke, 2003).

Toward Environmental and Social Policy at the Global Scale

Globalization does not generate an unambiguous race to the bottom in either equity or environmental protection. Some nations, those at the cusp of industrialization, are clearly able to launch an export-driven rise out of desperation. Japan perhaps did it first and has been followed by Taiwan, Korea, Hong Kong, Singapore and Malaysia. China and India are now advancing dramatically. Internal inequality is rising within those nations as entrepreneurialism and a middle class develop. Inequalities are increasing as well within wealthy nations as industrial and mobile service jobs are exported to these nations and others. But, on a global scale inequality has not increased because whole nations such as China are lifting themselves out of poverty as North American and European steelworkers, call center workers and light manufacturing employees are supplanted by growing numbers of lower-paid Wal-Mart greeters and cashiers.

Globalization *has* likely created downward pressure on social programs and on corporate taxation so that domestic industries might compete, in Canada's case, with low tax rates in the United States and lower wages in Mexico (and almost everywhere else save Europe). And, global economic integration combined with recent environmental policy resistance within the United States imposes downward pressure on domestic environmental protections globally only partially offset by technology transfers and the so-called California effect (upward pressure on environmental standards within products exported to wealthy environmentally-oriented jurisdictions).[1] The exception here appears to be Europe where there is a sufficiently large market, sufficient wealth and a broad-based desire to see through environmental policy advances.

Global economic integration likely has positive effects in terms of overall economic growth. Some nations have done very well overall from trade and economic integration including Canada, China, India and the United States (which has invested heavily in all of those economies). But there are a number of unintended consequences, especially social and environmental consequences. Some of these are listed in Table 13.1.

Table 13.1 Some consequences of global economic integration

1. Increasing domestic inequality within many nations, but not necessarily increasing overall global inequality;
2. Some increased fuel use associated with the increased transportation of goods and people;
3. Increasing political separation between extraction, production and consumption resulting in reduced visibility of the environmental damage associated with production and consumption;
4. An increase in exotic flora and fauna as well as new global disease vectors associated with increased trade and transportation;
5. A limited "California effect" race to the top on some environmental concerns;
6. A general, though highly inconsistent, restraint of the political capacity of national governments to tax corporations in the face of mobile investment dollars, to take positive social policy initiatives, or to achieve more stringent environmental regulations;
7. Accordingly, a growing democratic deficit, an overall decline in the effectiveness of democratic governance within many nations.
8. Increased terrorist opportunities through rising international mobility.

---

1 The California effect and its limits are discussed in Paehlke (2003:20-21).

Despite these possible consequences of economic integration in the absence of political integration, for altogether sensible reasons (doubts regarding the possibility of effective democracy at that scale and fears regarding the opportunities for global-scale malfeasance), few advocate global government as a means of coping with these problems. Many, however, advocate multilateral global governance initiatives to cooperatively address these consequences and others.

During the Bush II Administration, however, the United States has moved in the opposite direction at full speed, developing an ever-increasing inclination to and capacity for unilateralism. Along the way it has undermined virtually every small step toward global governance and international law, especially in the realms of environmental protection (rejecting Kyoto and simply neglecting POPs) and human rights (especially regarding the International Criminal Court but including nearly every other established institution as well, most notably the Geneva Conventions).

At the same time, trade agreements seem to most people (including those involved in the process) more than sufficiently complicated and difficult to achieve without any attempt to incorporate social and environmental considerations. This is, in my view, a profound mistake. Cross-national cooperation could significantly limit the extent to which economic competition between nations is based on reducing taxes, shrinking social programs and diminishing environmental standards. This approach is somehow taken to be a barrier to trade, a violation of sovereignty and a road that leads straight to the imposition of a stifling global bureaucracy.

This need not be the case, but there exists a cult of expertise (and an array of exclusionist norms and closed processes) regarding trade that leaves ordinary citizens utterly uninvolved in the process and unwilling to challenge the economistic character of existing trade agreements. The complexity of adding some social and environmental standards or pro-equity and pro-environment pressures to trade treaties would add a degree of complexity, but one that is modest when compared to the massive complexity that is already there.

The claim of governments of impotence in the face of competitive economic pressures is, I think, mostly disingenuous dissembling (and reflects an ethical indifference to environmental and social outcomes protestations to the contrary by Canadian leaders notwithstanding). It is at the least a failure of imagination. There are many possible routes to limited global standards (and thereby governance) that do not establish anything like sovereign global government.

Shifting the pressures on social and environmental policy that global economic integration imposes would require an agreement to measure three-dimensional (economic, environmental and social) outcomes and a collective willingness to experiment with trade rules as if we all lived on a planet where our destinies are increasingly intertwined. Agreements of this sort would diminish the negative social and environmental tendencies of globalization, and could become a part of the existing trade treaty processes.

This possibility should be more widely understood. In a world where global economic integration is now the norm, effective citizenship of any kind requires some opportunity for expression at the global scale, and meaningful expression must reside somewhere within the economic heart of the integration process. World environmental summits and environmental treaty processes are not without merit, but there must ultimately be some links between sustainability objectives and the trade treaty process. What are those objectives?

Sustainability relocates green thought from the environment ("out there" in nature) into the core of what it means to have, and to create, more effective human societies and economies. Sustainability analysis evaluates two things: 1) how much prosperity does an economy generate for and from each extraction of materials and energy from nature? And, 2) how much human well-being do societies produce for each increment of prosperity? The idea is very simple and yet despite the enormous costs and risks even to the global economy itself, poor sustainability performance is the norm most of the time in most places. Sustainability is in effect an alternative measure of societal (and thereby global-scale economic) success. Its advance must be part and parcel of the rules by which the global economy is integrated.

Sustainability focuses first on total material requirement (TMR), the sum total of energy and physical mass extracted from nature. Every extraction carries an environmental price, some are large and some are small, but none is zero. We can reduce that environmental price (per TMR), but it is often easier to reduce the material requirement itself, or at least the extraction of new materials – something that Canada has been doing preeminently for all of its history. Make a paper towel from recycled newspaper and extraction is eliminated (almost). On a personal level, walk or cycle to work even sometimes and your car will last longer and extractions are reduced.

Sustainability and economic efficiency are closely linked. Time lost to long commutes to work could be in part redirected to productive work time. Making a quality sound system lighter reduces extractions but also likely lowers production costs for the manufacturer. However, making it more durable, while it reduces extractions also reduces sales. Reducing the average distance traveled by food from a norm of 1000 miles reduces extractions (and improves freshness), but would likely diversify crops in any particular location and might increase the labour-intensity of the food system. Increasing the price of energy and materials will increase the extent to which most sustainability options are also the more economically efficient options.

Determining the efficiency with which society's and the global economy as a whole creates human well-being at any given level of prosperity is more difficult. There is less agreement on the meaning of well-being. But, most people would agree that longer, healthier lives, less crime, greater social cohesion and improved educational levels are part of it. But, can we have prosperity, social justice and environmental protection at the same time? Does more of one get us more of the other? Under what conditions and circumstances, and in what societies and policy mixes, and (most important within a global economy) what set of trade arrangements can three-dimensional benefits be optimized?

Most sustainability analysts agree that we could get a lot more prosperity for each extraction of materials and energy from nature. Almost everyone (maybe even including those that extract resources if they got more money for each unit of extraction) would agree that the "double efficient" production of well-being from prosperity and prosperity from extraction is a worthwhile objective. The average best guess for what level of improvement is possible over time is about four times more. That would mean that humans could be four times richer with no more damage to the environment, or as rich with one-fourth the damage. Or, probably best, somewhat richer with a reduced environmental cost.

The distinction between well-being and prosperity within sustainability analysis places environmental policy in the heart of the contemporary debate over globalization. It rejects trickle down economics *as an assumption* (and demands proof that richer is better). It also casts doubt on the unchallenged celebration of economic growth achieved through undermining health care and social programs by demonstrating that at least a semblance of social equity is essential to overall societal well-being. Strikingly, this is a view that sounds very Canadian. It recognizes that all humans (and with a simultaneous focus on eco-efficiency and environmental protection all of living nature) are a part of a global community.

Within a sustainability framework, citizenship cannot be confined within any one nation. An environmental sense of citizenship is unlike citizenship of any other sort in that the claiming or granting of citizenship in this form does not imply differentiation in terms of rights and duties from any other persons – there are no outsiders. There are no Athenian slaves and there are no foreigners. Canadian multilateralist, multicultural sensibilities are very much at home with this emerging perspective.

That's the good news. The bad news is the nearest thing global environmental citizens have to a seat of global governance in any form is a growing but unevenly accepted body of only-sometimes-enforced environmental treaties, a widely ignored United Nations Declaration of Human Rights, a United Nations in crisis, and perhaps nearest to being global governance organizations: the WTO, World Bank and IMF. At least the latter has recently noticed on several occasions that post-2000 fiscal policies in the United States are a potential threat to global economic stability. Perhaps that assertiveness will prove to be a beginning of sorts.

National citizenship, in T. H. Marshall's sense, is a kind of basic equality and full membership in a community (Marshall and Bottomore, 1992). As such, it could in principle be experienced at the global level without a global sovereign state – globally focused citizen initiatives could be undertaken at the local, national or multilateral level. Trade treaties, or domestic legal actions, or consumer pressure might hold international corporations to more stringent social and environmental standards wherever they operate. Trade treaties could, for example, specify minimum standards for third world employees producing for export, or establish trade-enforced common rules with regard to environmental protection.

Consumer pressures have already led to certification of sustainable forest cutting practices and, under pressure from citizen activists some retailers have established child labour standards regarding clothing imports (when exporting nations would or could not). In another example of global citizenship U.S. expert opponents of farm subsidies supported Brazil's successful WTO appeal of U.S. cotton subsidies –

subsidies in the billions of dollars that radically undermine cotton farming in Brazil and West Africa where in the latter case cotton is the *only* internationally competitive economic activity. At the same time many noted chefs in both North America and Europe are now consciously selecting local, fresh, organic ingredients.

In each of these cases there are equity and/or sustainability arguments for change and the effort has been carried by citizens rather than governments. Indeed governments (other than the government of Brazil) have been on the wrong side of the issue. It is also clear from these and other examples that there is some potential for progress toward sustainability through green citizen initiatives through both global and local efforts. Arguably such citizen and citizen-driven commercial initiatives are steps toward global governance progress. That progress can continue even in the absence of any prospect of even a semblance of global government, but it would be advanced considerably if there were national governments that were consistently on side with these efforts.We could, however, go much further.

Getting Beyond Economistic Global Governance

In *Democracy's Dilemma* I offered a number of politically plausible global scale initiatives (plausible at least to those not totally blinded to future possibilities by hyperrealism), four of which are noted here. A variant of the second possibility is obvious enough to have been advanced by at least one U. S. Democratic candidate for the nomination for President, but his proposal was controversial enough to alarm a leading *New York Times* columnist (as noted further below). The four proposed initiatives are:

1. Peg energy and materials (commodity) prices to the average price of manufactured goods starting with oil. The price of oil should rise sufficiently fast to at least double the historic rate of dematerialization (GDP per TMR).
2. Develop a global minimum wage system pegging wage levels in export-oriented industries to GDP/capita within each nation or region.
3. Enforce existing and new multilateral environmental and social (labour, human rights) treaties through adjustments to trade access and establish thereby, for example, a global right to unionize, at least within industries that produce for export.
4. Begin on an experimental basis a world pension beginning with the oldest citizens of the poorest nations with a comparable amount also paid to UNESCO agency operations or recognized international NGOs operating within those same nations. Fund the system via the Tobin tax and/or a tax on energy exports.

The first two of these possible initiatives, or something like them, would advance environmental, social and even economic sustainability – and would, in effect, help to humanize global economic integration. The first initiative recognizes the centrality of energy and the importance of the fact that sufficient economic and environmentally benign alternatives to oil and natural gas are not yet known let alone available. Accordingly, any transformation from oil as society's core energy source will take a very long time and will affect every aspect of human existence, especially in wealthy nations. This sort of initiative assumes that to even approach sustainability, we must accelerate technical, economic and social change in order to understand what our post-oil options really are while sufficient fossil fuel reserves exist to see through the transition.

One thing that was learned following the 1979 OPEC-forced oil price increase (and which was largely forgotten by 1985) was that everything – economic, social and environmental – depends on the price (and availability) of oil. The good news was that even after an extreme price shock not only did the global economy recover but gasoline consumption in most advanced economies declined absolutely and economic output per unit of energy accelerated (until energy prices fell in 1985).[2] Pegging energy prices to the average price of manufactured goods (or "just" assuring an agreed slow and steady increase in oil prices unless and until something better actually comes along) is necessary to encourage accelerated long-term investment in alternative energy supplies and increased energy efficiency (including expansion of public transit use, recycling and product and infrastructure redesign).

The second suggested initiative might seem radical. It certainly did when Richard Gephardt advanced a proposal for a global minimum wage in the Democratic presidential primaries. *New York Times'* correspondent Nicholas Kristoff argued in response that the widespread economic desperation in places like Cambodia were sufficient grounds for avoiding minimum wages in third world export industries.[3] However, a global minimum wage would slow but not stop the pace of job transfers and might also restrain the downward pressure on low-end industrial wages in wealthy nations. Pegging the limit to GDP/capita, not a part of Gephardt's proposal, would leave some advantage with the poorest nations relative to less poor nations.

The third initiative could substitute for the second or might serve as a complement, but might also be even more strongly resisted by the economic elites of poorer nations and/or multinational corporations. A pegged global minimum wage (the second possible initiative) could be used to introduce reform in a measured and even-handed way and might have a goal of reducing the gap in industrial wages (between, say, Canada or Germany and Indonesia, Cambodia or China) from something like fifty-fold to something like twenty-or-ten-fold over an extended period of time, much more by change upwards in the latter than downwards in the former.

The effect of such change might lower by a small measure the incentive to relocate and raise the price of imported goods slightly in rich nations. But, even doubling or tripling the wages of those that produce our shoes and clothes and stereos would not affect prices anything like proportionately. It might force some restraint on the value

2 For further discussion on this point see the editorial and articles in Alternatives: Canadian Environmental Ideas and Action 30 (Winter, 2004).

3 New York Times, op ed, 14 January 2004.

of the endorsement contracts for running shoes or bump the price from $70 to $75 per pair, but it might also mean that the person who made those shoes could buy a cell phone designed, if not manufactured, in Finland or afford to go to a Hollywood movie (depressing as that thought might be). Even Henry Ford was more radical than today's "liberal" columnists when he imagined that his assembly line workers might eventually buy his (and their) products.

Finally here, what of what one might call a world pension? Such a proposal will appear to many economists and policy analysts (not to mention the neo-conservative and middle-of-the-road ideologues that dominate the airwaves of North America) to be unadulterated lunacy, especially in the face of widespread pressures on public pension systems in most wealthy nations (mostly a function of slower birthrates and increased longevity).

I suffer no illusion that such a measure is likely to be adopted. Obviously, any such initiative would be fraught with problems not the least of which would be determining individual eligibility and actually delivering payment to those eligible. The elderly within the poorest states are likely to be illiterate and many of the poorest states are failed states or dominated by corrupt bureaucracies. And, it would also be argued, such an initiative would in effect be a tax on those nations that trade the most, redistributed within those nations that trade the least and thereby a trade barrier.

However, that is the point. Comprehensive global economic (and transportation and communications) integration requires that there be some way to lift the weakest nations out of desperation. This is true for many reasons, not the least of which is the fact that failed states are terrorist havens. Moreover, new diseases can more easily gain a foothold among the poorest peoples in the world and now can move around the world in days not months. As well, environmental protection is all but impossible in the face of poverty and so too is restraint on family size in the face of infant mortality. Increasingly, we all live in one environment. Economic destitution all but guarantees overfishing, overgrazing, the spread of desertification, poaching of endangered species, eating bush meat, and indifference to long-term environmental and social concern of all kinds (including the production of opiates for export). Many or all of these perils systematically come back to haunt everyone everywhere.

The amount of money necessary to make a real difference to individuals in the very poorest nations would represent a very small percentage of the value of *any* dimension of global trade and exchange. At the same time an externally-funded pension scheme, however modest, would be a godsend in many African nations where AIDS is decimating the working age population and only the oldest remain available to care for the youngest. Even a modest program – one that involves helping the small number of living elderly in but a small number of nations, a few of the poorest in each poorer region of the world – could make a meaningful difference especially if one realizes that nations like Afghanistan, Burma, Sudan and potentially Palestine might qualify. In brief an initiative of this sort recognizes that we now live in one world and we all bear some responsibility for each other across legal and cultural borders. Idealism can be self-interested without being less idealistic.

The industrial revolution of the 19th century transformed the nations of Europe and North America in a positive way (in the end) in part because they were nations or became nations (Germany, Italy) as the industrial revolution advanced, political entities comparable in scale to the productive capacities of their day. Political entities, especially democratic ones, eventually limit the worst excesses of both trade restraint and social maldistribution. They provide essential education opportunities, environmental protection and resource management. Global governance, matching the scale of today's economy, at present *only* seeks to avoid trade restraint and to provide additional incentives to the already wealthy.

This economistic form of global governance will not (now or ever) maximize the human benefits that *could* flow from global economic integration.[4] Nor does it, or will it, contend with sustaining economic growth over the long run as industrialization moves beyond the fossil fuels. Human population levels, global integration and simple social justice all require that we become both more efficient at converting wealth into well-being and nature into wealth. Environmental citizens know that the one-dimensional pursuit of prosperity on a global scale is an ethical disaster, achieving too little socially at a higher environmental cost than is necessary. This realization imposes an ethical obligation to participate, to behave as citizens even in the absence of a system of global governance that welcomes the participation of individuals or even non-governmental organizations.

This is not entirely fair. There are points of entry for both individual citizens and NGOs at the global scale. They can attend open sessions of Conference of the Parties (COPs) related to various environmental treaties. Individuals can join the United Nations Association or can get involved in NGOs that play an on-going role in various international processes. If one had enough money and time one could do such things almost every day for the rest of one's life. But, it is arguably the case that economic and trade bodies and meetings are more important to environmental and social outcomes than international institutions that focus on environmental and social issues. They are decidedly less welcoming to non-business organizations or points of view either directly or through national delegations.

National run-ups to trade treaty negotiations are about making sure that all of the important economic voices are heard. In the treaty process some industries may be hurt and some may benefit. The goal is to maximize national economic benefits and minimize national economic hurts. Social and environmental outcomes within one's nation or in the world as a whole are rarely considered within that process. Trade and economic growth are presumed to be the primary objective and always an unqualified benefit. Within negotiations protecting against over-exploitation of resources or negative environmental outcomes is presumed to be the concern of each nation and there is no one there concerned that some nations are in no position to worry about such things. A declining average global industrial wage (through the

4 For a further discussion of how such benefits might be understood and measures see the discussion in *Democracy's Dilemma*, chapters 4 and 5.

replacement of high earners in rich nations with low earners in poor nations) is even presumed to be a positive outcome (since profits rise and price of goods falls).

The process is clearly flawed and one-dimensional. Social and environmental considerations need to find a way to the table within national run-up debates, within multilateral trade talks and within trade policy administrative procedures and hearings. At present, only nations have a real voice within this process. Some nations will need to be consistent advocates of change, must speak on behalf of environmental protection and social justice within international trade processes, even sometimes at their own economic expense. This would require in turn strong domestic citizen initiatives within those wealthy democratic nations that might take the side of what progressive forces exist within poorer nations at the trade talk level.

For this to succeed, citizens from many nations must learn to interact directly and then seek to influence the international stance of their nations through domestic politics. One such initiative is the World Social Forum; others are human rights and environmental NGOs.[5] Influencing foreign policy through citizen action is a daunting task because foreign policy, more than any other aspect of public policy, is widely seen to be an elite prerogative. It is the realm of the foreign office, the trade office, international lawyers, concerned corporations and select academics of a discrete and tempered demeanour. Foreign policy is only rarely fought in electoral campaigns unless a nation has involved itself in an unpopular war or someone is advocating a popular one.

International politics is alleged to be the realm of realism and national interest, not idealism and citizen participation. Citizens, it is assumed, can always be convinced to orient to global governance through a nationalist lens. While this view remains valid, it also misses what has changed in the past 30 years. The professional employment market is now a global market. The economy is increasingly organized on a global basis, what happens throughout the world affects everyone's life dramatically and quickly, and everyone understands this. Climate change, the global movement of toxic substances in nature, terrorism and the increasingly rapid movement of global disease are readily apparent to educated people everywhere. Moreover, the internet makes substantial information about all of these things much easier to come by and international contacts through this means (as well as increased travel and international educational experiences and immigration) have burgeoned. It is in fact hard to imagine that a cosmopolitan sense of citizenship will not continue to increase.

Very large nations, however, are frequently inward looking and prone to being somewhat self-absorbed. If there is going to be leadership from any nation in moving towards cosmopolitanism, towards thinking in terms of sustainability on a global basis, it will likely come from smaller nations. Poorer nations large or small have special challenges when thinking beyond economic growth at any cost. Canada is as well placed as any nation to take a leadership role, to set an example in terms of sustainability and social justice advocacy and action.

---

5 Probably the best book on the subject is still Keck and Sikkink, 1998.

Canada's Potential Role

Canada is uniquely positioned to play an influential role in helping to establish a more sustainable global economy and thereby a more politically and economically stable world. Canada is pre-eminently a trading nation; few other nations export and import as high a proportion of their GDP. More than that, the Canadian economy is dominated by foreign direct investment, while at the same time Canadians have heavily invested in the economies of other nations. Canadians, accordingly, cannot help but understand that policy autonomy and economic autarky are no longer an option. It does not require a belief in the existence of a cult of impotence to suggest that global economic integration alters a government's range of domestic policy flexibility (McQuaig, 1998).

Canada is also, as noted above, pre-eminently multilateralist. Our governments and most Canadians have understood for a very long time that Canada's best chance for influence, or even for policy autonomy, is to be one among many, not locked away within a bilateral quasi-union with the United States. Most Canadians instinctively welcome attempts at global governance and instinctively distrust unilateralist tendencies, especially when they arise in the United States. These instincts are essential to any Canadian role in moving the world toward a path that incorporates environmental and social balancing. As noted, the best prospect for such an outcome is within a system of global governance that rather than being almost exclusively on global economic integration, seeks at least to ameliorate the negative effects of such change.[6]

Equally important to a leadership role in such an undertaking is the fact that Canada is one the most culturally diverse nations in the world. Canada indeed is one of the few nations that are truly comfortable with that reality, one that celebrates diversity rather than taking a melting pot approach to immigration. Canada, bilingual at its core, thereby also has natural ties of language and culture to almost every nation on the planet. Combined with a preference for multilateralism and the fact of being one of the most trade-oriented nations in the world, Canada is uniquely placed to punch above its weight in international affairs, including international environmental affairs.

It is even also arguable that Canada's habit of modest expenditures on military capacity is not necessarily a disadvantage in terms of the diplomacy that surrounds international economic, social and environmental governance. While limited military expenditures do not gain respect with U.S. governments or most NATO officials, Canadians might gain in influence with the emerging globally-oriented citizens of every nation were Canadian governments more forthright and comfortable with their lack of enthusiasm for conventional military assertiveness.

Canada's role in the world does not lie in the realm of nation-to-nation combat. There is no need to be embarrassed about this. Given the scale of the challenge that sustainability poses, heavy military expenditures might be better seen as a potentially fatal distraction and thereby actually a threat to human security. To put it

---

6 Note environmental treaties, but note also failure to get to effective regime on climate change or on biodiversity or on the switch from fossil fuels.

another way, military expenditure beyond that needed for counter-terrorism activities (including the collective stabilization of failed states) and territorial self-defence carries an opportunity cost in terms of the enormous task of advancing sustainability. More than that, the unilateral use of military power is at least as likely to exacerbate the problem of terrorism as to quell it and excessive North American dependence on imported oil does not ease that prospect. Indeed, heavy dependence on oil imports from the Middle East renders *any* involvement in the Middle East suspect.

Such things need to be said even though it is not easy to say them diplomatically in the present context. One way to do so is the way in which comments were made about Iraq during former Prime Minister Martin's first trip to Washington, D.C. – the toughest comments about the rightness and usefulness of Canada's refusal to participate in the Iraq invasion came from an American (Democratic Senator Joseph Biden) who spoke on that occasion. Many Americans will always be onside with progressive initiatives undertaken by Canada. There is no more important issue regarding which Canada might seize the North American initiative than the looming and spectacularly challenging transition from fossil fuels.

Canada needs to be clear that anything less than an equitable sharing of what remains of global fossil fuel supplies is a recipe for catastrophe. More than that, those nations, including Canada, that have the capacity to develop alternative energy sources have a profound moral obligation to exert every imaginable national effort. Doing so is also the basis of an excellent national economic strategy. It is even better as a means of helping to prevent the destruction of the planet within a long series of resource wars.[7] In this effort Canada should also remain steadfast in its historic reluctance to participate in military incursions not sanctioned by the United Nations and should continue to frankly state why it follows this course.[8]

Canada, because it is both a leading energy producer and a leading energy consumer, could also play a much more significant role in moving the world toward sustainability. Canada is singularly well placed to be self-sustaining in terms of energy supplies, *even with very limited domestic use of fossil fuels*, given our very low population density and abundant potential for hydropower, wind energy and biomass. Canadians have not fully appreciated how unique this makes us: not only do we have stores of fossil energy, but we have the option of extracting them judiciously. Moreover, given its social policy traditions and wealth, Canada could champion and in fact achieve a consistent drive toward greater domestic social equity and social well-being. Given its technological capabilities it could also be as innovative as any nation in advancing sustainable production (Toner, forthcoming).

---

7 See Klare, 2001 and Heinberg, 2003.

8 Cases like Kosovo complicate this generalization. All that one can say is that strategic affairs inevitably involve difficult judgments and there can be no iron clad rules. A predisposition to avoid armed conflict except as a last resort would certainly avoid blatantly illegal interventions such as in Iraq where multilateral agencies clearly had the purported concern (the possible possession of weapons of mass destruction) well in hand and this was well known before the war began. See, for example, Blix, 2004.

Needless to say, following such a path would not be easy in terms of Canada-U.S. bilateral relations or in terms of Canadian domestic politics. Canadian use of fossil fuels has already risen to something approaching 30 percent above our Kyoto target of reductions of greenhouse gases to 6 percent below 1990 levels. Some significant efforts are now finally underway, but it would still be optimistic to predict that we will soon stabilize at *present* levels. One problem is that there are heavy new investments in the tar sands and extracting oil from that source is enormously more energy intensive than drilling for conventional oil.

If Canada is ever to achieve actual *reductions* (as opposed to slower growth) in greenhouse gas emissions, we may well need to establish some ceiling on total annual production of fuel from the tar sands, a ceiling that would almost certainly be rejected by the government of Alberta which has constitutional jurisdiction over natural resources and the government of the United States that is eager to import more energy from Canada. The question is clearly one of Canadians' commitment to environmental protection and global treaty obligations versus provincial powers, the political clout of multinational and domestic energy companies, and bilateral (U.S.-Canada) relations.

Until the 1990s, Canada had a singular reputation in international affairs on environmental issues and in recent years has begun the task of restoring that reputation. Part of the original reputation was based on our natural heritage of vast lands, waters, forests and wildlife, but it was also based on effective policy actions. Environment Canada was established in 1971 and in its early years was reasonably well funded. As a nation, we campaigned for action against acid precipitation on a North American basis though the United States likely acted when it eventually did primarily for domestic political reasons. Canada also championed the Biodiversity Convention at Rio in 1992 and earlier individual Canadians took leading roles in the Stockholm conference, in submissions to and the writing of the Brundtland report *Our Common Future*, and later in the United Nations Environment Program and other international environmental bodies.

In the 1990s, however, Canada's reputation in international environmental initiative was diminished. Both federally and in Ontario environmental protection expenditures were cut disproportionately in the urgent drive toward balanced budgets in the face of extensive and prolonged deficits. The Harris government of Ontario was openly hostile to environmental protection and went out of its way to avoid the enforcement of existing environmental legislation. It ultimately perished politicallly in large part on the ensuing pollution events at Walkerton.[9] At the same time the federal government pursued the defence of asbestos exports at the World Trade Organization, resisted a precautionary approach to genetically modified organisms in international trade and seemingly opposed for some time the Kyoto accord having originally agreed to it. And, for a decade the federal government was

9 In May 2000, following heavy rains, seven citizens of Walkerton, a small Ontario town, died and more than a thousand were made seriously ill by contaminated public water supplies. This tragedy followed the privatization of water testing and severe cutbacks in the provincial Ministry of the Environment.

unable to secure domestic legislation on the protection of endangered species despite its leading role on the Biodiversity Convention.

Only in its waning days did the Chrétien government reverse its position on Kyoto to join with European and other advocates on this crucial multilateral initiative. At the same time Canada played a leading role in the development of the initiative on Persistent Organic Pollutants (POPs), primarily pesticides that have found their way into food chains throughout the Arctic region from Alaska and Canada to Greenland and Siberia. At the date of this writing the United States is still resisting Kyoto and has not ratified the POPs convention less out of hostility than primarily as a result of distraction by the war in Iraq.[10] The Harris government has given way to a more environmentally oriented provincial government and the Canadian federal government has finally passed legislation on endangered species.

Canada, it might be said, has partially restored its international environmental policy credibility. It is not, however, in a leadership role, a role which clearly now resides in Europe, especially in Germany, the Netherlands and Scandinavia. There is an opportunity to re-assert Canadian leadership in the realm of sustainability. In this Canada could serve as a bridge between Europe and the United States and (with Australia), as the world's wealthiest resource producer, serve as a bridge between the rich industrialized North and the poor resource-oriented South. Instinctively, in the Cancun discussions on agricultural subsidies Canada did just that. Almost alone among the wealthy nations Canada sided with those poorer nations whose agriculture is undermined by heavily subsidized agricultural imports from the United States and Europe while at the same time they are pressured to remove tariffs and subsidies to their domestic manufacturing industries.

Canada, in summary, is uniquely positioned to take sustainability and global governance initiative. The basis for this uniqueness is summarized in Table 13.2.

Table 13.2 Canada: uniquely positioned

1. The world's wealthiest resource-producing nation, able thereby to relate to the economic perspective and resource-economy related insecurities of poorer nations.
2. Historically and in terms of political culture a "mid-Atlantic" nation in terms of social policy, state activism, and orientation to global politics.
3. Historically inclined to peacekeeping, international organizations and multilateralism.
4. Until recently a reputation as a global leader in environmental policy.
5. Wealthy and innovative enough to contribute technical solutions to the extent that they exist, were we to adopt policies that would foster such innovations.
6. Potentially the western hemisphere nation most open to three-dimensional (non-economistic) multilateral global governance at a time when the world

10 See Downie and Fenge, 2003.

desperately needs it and the United States is rushing headlong in the opposite direction.

7. Multi-cultural and federalist, attributes essential to such an undertaking.
8. One of the highest ratios of land per person in the world. This low population density, combined with Canada's technological capabilities makes it a natural for some forms of renewable energy and for land-based solutions to greenhouse gas emissions (enhanced carbon sequestration).

Needless to say, Canada alone cannot lead the world to greener, fairer global economic integration, but it is well positioned to join with others in pointing the way. To do this Canada must not just bask in having signed Kyoto but actually come into conformity with its provisions. It must also be clear that this is not "just" about climate change, but also about the future of industrial society and world peace. It must work toward bringing high growth poorer nations into meaningful participation – perhaps by modifying Kyoto to require rapid improvement in fossil energy use per dollar of GDP until some GDP/capita threshold at which point a freeze on use, or something very near to it, takes effect. This would remove the stated objections of the United States.[11]

Canada should above all think globally and in the long term. In this context it only makes sense – economically, strategically and environmentally to aggressively fund research and effective action on environmentally benign energy options and to learn to accommodate, and assure, a smooth and gradual rise in commodity, especially energy, prices relative to the price of other goods and services. Energy prices in 2006 are thought to be high, but are lower in real terms than they were in the early 1980s. They must be higher to assure movement toward sustainability, but change must be smooth and increases assured in order to facilitate investment in efficiency and alternatives. Finally here, Canada could take an assertive lead on gradually adjusting trade agreements to include some social and environmental minimum standards – such as global minimum wages scaled to GDP/capita.

There is no avoiding the fact that in today's context such a stance would sharply differentiate Canada from the United States on the global stage. The United States, once a clear world leader on environmental matters, has shifted away from this view so sharply in recent years that U.S. environmental activists are left wondering where they went so wrong and how things can be turned around. Opposition to all multilateral environmental initiatives by the United States may, however, be only temporary and, while a greener standby Canada might invite tensions in U.S.-Canadian bilateral relations in the short term, it could lead to stronger bonds in the future.

---

11 The United States might well find other objections, but some other administration might be persuaded to join since neither China nor other high growth poorer nations would ever agree to participate unless the United States were to sign.

Is Environmentalism Dead in the United States?

Much has been made of a recent essay in the United States entitled "The Death of Environmentalism."[12] The essay, by environmental activists Michael Schellenberger and Ted Nordhaus, argues that the central error made by U.S. environmentalists is to have operated for too long as technically-oriented lobbyists seeking narrow and incremental environmental change rather than concentrating on building broad coalitions that seek more fundamental social and political change. The result of this, they believe, is a failure to capture the imagination of Americans, a failure that contributed to today's entrenched neo-conservatism and the current rejection of all environmental initiatives and the rollback of existing protections at the federal (and therefore the international) level.

Schellenberger and Nordhaus are part of a larger coalition called the New Apollo Project, named after the 1961 commitment by President John F. Kennedy to put a man on the moon. The New Apollo Project advocates requiring that a minimum proportion of electricity be produced from renewable sources and providing monetary incentives to individuals and industries to become more energy efficient. The objective is to do nothing less than restore the industrial strength of the United States by limiting greenhouse gas emissions and moving rapidly towards energy independence. Advocates of this approach argue that it can result in simultaneous improvements in the economy (reducing balance of payments problems, for example), social justice (through the restoration of skilled blue collar employment) and, seemingly at time incidentally, the environment.

The undertaking now has the support of many state and local governments, in for example Pennsylvania, unions, community activists and environmental organizations. In related developments more than 175 U.S. mayors (representing 40,000,000 Americans) have signed Kyoto compliance initiatives, even extremely conservative states like Texas have taken renewable energy initiatives, and the governors of the Northeast states have taken a number of related initiatives.[13] The point is that the present posture of the United States government with regard to sustainability and climate change may well only be a temporary posture.

Conclusion: Real Friends Tell the Truth

It has been fashionable for many years in Canadian intellectual circles to be highly critical of the United States and to see it as monolithically insensitive to all things progressive. Some U.S. administrations make this an easy stance to adopt, but Canadians do not have the excuse of distance for missing the more complex reality that is our neighbour to the south. Historically, the United States has been an

12 Michael Schellenbacher and Ted Nordhaus, "The Death of Environmentalism," available as a pdf file from www.thebreakthrough.org.

13 See, for example, the editorial "States to the Rescue," www.nytimes.com (25 August 2005) and www.cityofseattle.net/mayor/climate/, and chapter five.

environmental policy leader, the nation where the first national park was established and where environmental impact assessment, for example, was invented.

As an American might say, though, what have you done for me lately? In terms of environmental policy initiatives, there is no doubt, as noted, that the United States has been eclipsed by many European nations and the European Union as a whole. It is important to remember, however, that the United States once led the way in environmental protection and that it may well do so again.

Indeed environmental innovation still abounds in the United States. Even during the administration of George W. Bush, as openly hostile to environmental protection as any government in American history, land trusts designed to protect in perpetuity both farmland and wildlife habitat in private hands have thrived and were even funded as part of a general aid package to the Republican's rural base under the Farm Act of 2002.[14] As well, without help from the government, the natural and organic food industry is thriving, and wind energy and urban core restoration stimulated by supportive tax arrangements at the state level, and (as in Canada but not so consistently in Europe) smoking has been banned in most indoor public locations. Moreover, green building products (including many made from recycled materials) and green building projects abound, especially in the commercial sector.

Canadians can see these things because U.S. events and every nuance of American opinion are visible to us on a continuous basis. Understanding the United States is almost an industry in itself in Canada.[15] Canadians could use this special knowledge; combine it with being one step removed from an American perspective, and directly remind American citizens of their own potential for moral leadership. One way to do this is by conveying this potential to a wider world at present bewildered by the United States government's current hostility to anything multilateral and its seemingly endless capacity for in your face self-absorption.

Yet regarding the environment Canadians too easily see themselves as champions and Americans as despoilers when this is far from an accurate assessment.[16] We celebrate our signing of Kyoto but quickly forget that we resisted that initiative for many years and are yet to even approach compliance. The United States has flatly refused to sign, but many U.S. states have taken what are in effect compliance initiatives that exceed what has been done in Canada. We also need to remind ourselves that Yellowstone preceded Banff and that the Americans invented environmental assessment in the National Environmental Protection Act (NEPA) of 1969. Canada did not pass comparable legislation until the 1990s, and Canada took decades to pass endangered species legislation.

Indeed in these latter two initiatives, Canadian governments were slow to follow because they actively sought to avoid the challenges that U.S. governments were quite prepared to accept. Canadian bureaucracies observed the U.S. experience

---

14 See www.farmland.org the website of the American Farmland Trust or the websites of the more than one thousand land trusts in the United States for details.

15 Most recent and interesting is Adams, 2003.

16 See Hoberg, 2002 et Hoberg, 1996, pp. 341-385.

and concluded that both NEPA and endangered species protection could irritate entrenched economic interests and accordingly have delayed proceeding for as long as possible. Other Canadian governments have, however, been more than happy to hide behind U.S. governments' reluctance to challenge entrenched interests on behalf of the environment. Canada has also refused to label GMOs and we have been very cautious with mounting any challenge to the auto industry regarding fleet average fuel efficiency standards (or regarding the ludicrous exemption of SUVs and pick-up trucks from automobile fleet average fuel efficiency standards).

In fairness, Canada has recently been somewhat more audacious with regard to environmental protection than it was in the 1990s. Canada did take a leading role on the POPs treaty while the Bush II Administration in United States dragged its heels. Prior to POPs, perhaps Canada's most determined environmental initiative in the face of both intensive corporate lobbying and inaction in the United States was the 1999 ban on the use of recombinant bovine somatropin (rBST), the growth hormone used in dairy cattle.

In combination with changing course on the signing of Kyoto and a refusal to participate in the invasion of Iraq, Canada is as out of step with the environmentally relevant aspects of United States foreign policy as it has ever been.[17] However, finally here, it must be noted that two out of three of these initiatives were taken in the waning days of the Chrétien government and, though strongly supported by public opinion, arguably are quite out of character for Canadian governments.

Overall, one way to characterize the present situation is that Canada is nearer to Europe in spirit and instinct in social and environmental policy matters, even as Europe has systematically sought to distinguish itself from the United States. Yet, Canada's economic linkages run North-South. Were Canada not irretrievably a part of the North American economy, Canadians might feel more at home within the European Union – in a space that is both greener and more socially progressive than the United States and profoundly multilateralist. Could Canada, then, come to be so audacious as to dare to try to bring the two diverging Western giants nearer to each other?

The first thing to realize is that Canada would not be left to undertake such an initiative alone. There are many other nations that might prefer a greener, fairer, "softer" (more multilateralist) United States. Many governments are frequently these days caught between their historic and empathetic links to the United States and the current opinions of their own citizens. More than that, Canadians understand as few other nations do that the United States itself is not a monolith. Canada can perhaps help to draw out America's better self. Arguably, Canada can best influence the United States by actually being even more of a living model of that better self.

---

17 Iraq is environmentally relevant because it is at least in part a resource war not unrelated to a refusal by the United States to take the short term economic risks associated with energy use restraint. Note the claim of 450,000 jobs that would be lost in association with tougher energy efficiency standards within the auto industry.

Ironically, that in turn requires that Canada work to maintain its autonomy in any way that it can.

Canadians can see the wisdom in *New York Times'* columnist Thomas Friedman's words like too few Americans can. In April, 2004 he wrote, following a discussion about the extent to which the U.S. economy is losing science-based competitiveness: "Right now we should have a Manhattan Project to develop a hydrogen-based energy economy – it's within reach and would serve our economy, our environment and our foreign policy by diminishing our dependence on foreign oil. Instead the Bush team says let's go to Mars. Where is Congress? Out to lunch – or, worse, obsesses with trying to keep Susie Smith's job at the local pillow factory that is moving to the Caribbean – without thinking about a national competitiveness strategy" (Friedman, 2004).

While some in Canada are determined to replace the Caribbean and grab that pillow factory, most Canadians can see that the future of the global economy (as well as avoiding an endless series of resource wars) requires a leap into sustainability and that that in turn requires nothing less than a concerted effort by all of the technologically advanced nations of the world. Canada is positioned as well as any nation to help to demonstrate to Americans why it is necessary that they be involved in an important way in a multilateral strategy to see through a transformation of the fossil fuel-based, industrial economy on which we all depend. Given their military and economic might, they can (and do) imagine access to the oil wealth of the world for as long as it lasts. Canada could signal to them: 1) that that is not necessarily the case, and 2) that it is in any case urgent that all nations begin to move decisively out of that past.

Canada could do that by threatening the future curtailment of energy exports in violation of NAFTA provisions, but this is beyond improbable.[18] However, if Canada is serious about climate change it may ultimately have to accept some constraints on oil sands development (because oil sands extraction and processing is far more carbon-intensive than conventional oil production). Given Kyoto obligations, it is arguable that Canada can never radically increase its oil exports to the United States. Only in a context of multilateral commitments to Kyoto and sustainability, and a deeply held public commitment to those goals, could Canada hope to get away with extracting only enough to meet its own, hopefully slowly declining, domestic needs and perhaps only a very small increase in exports.

To be fair to the United States, Canada needs to say this sooner rather than later. It then needs to expend the funds – in energy efficiency improvements, urban redesign and reconstruction, public transit, and sustainable production – necessary to come into compliance with Kyoto domestically. Just as with acid precipitation, one must walk the walk before one can legitimately talk the talk.

---

18 However, in 2005, ex-Prime Minister Martin did suggest, to the great distress of Alberta's Premier, Ralph Klein, that Canada might look to expanding energy sales to China if the soft wood lumber dispute could not be resolved.

In time the United States would have little choice but to believe that Canada was serious. In time, as well, Canada's economy and global reputation would only benefit from adopting such a course. In the end Canada must speak truth to power, through deeds more than words, but loudly enough that the United States and its citizens, our neighbours and long-standing friends, can hear. Real friends may not always be able to tell the truth, at least not loudly and in public, but they can live it. Perhaps the best way to tell the truth, given our proximity and the obvious power imbalances, is just to behave differently.

Bibliography

Abbott, F. (1996), "From Theory to Practice: The Second Phase of the NAFTA Environmental Regime", in Rudiger Wolfrum, ed., *Enforcing Environmental Standards*, Berlin: Springer, pp. 451-478.

Abbott, F. (2000), "NAFTA and the Legalization of World Politics: A Case Study", *International Organization* 54 (Summer), pp. 519-548.

Abbott, K., Keohane, R., Moravcsik, A., Slaughter, A-M, and Snidal, D. (2000), "The Concept of Legalization", *International Organization* 54 (Summer), pp. 401-420.

Aboriginal Pipeline Group (2004), "Funding Agreements Reached and Preliminary Information Package to be Submitted, Mackenzie Delta Producer Group Confirms." *News Room* (18 June 2004) http://www.aborginalpipline.ca/04_News/release08.htm, accessed 18 June 2004.

ABST (1992), *Committee on the Competitiveness of the Resource Industries*, a report presented by the National Advisory Board on Science and Technology to the Prime Minister of Canada, Ottawa.

Adams, M. (2004), *Fire and Ice: The United States, Canada and the Myth of Converging Values*, Toronto: Penguin.

Adler, E., and Barnett, M. (1998), *Security Communities*, Cambridge: Cambridge University Press.

Alanis Ortega, G. (2002), "Public Participation within NAFTA's Environmental Agreement: The Mexican Experience," in Kirton and Maclaren, (2002a), pp. 183-186.

Alaska Department of Fish and Game (2003), *Salmon Ex-vessel Price Time Series by Species*. Juneau: Alaska. Accessed at http://www.cf.adfg.state.ak.us/geninfo/finfish/salmon/catchval/blusheet/84-03exvl.pdf, accessed 12 April 2004.

Alaska Highway (1998), "History of the Alaska Highway." 1998, http://themilepost.com/history.html accessed 25 January 2005.

Albright, M. (1998), Remarks in Press Briefing, Ottawa, Canada, 10 March.

Allison, J. (1995), *International Environmental Cooperation: North American Air Quality Agreements as Bargaining Outcomes*, PhD dissertation, Los Angeles: University of California.

Allison, J. (1999), "A Fortuitous Consequence: the Domestic Politics of the 1991 Canada-United States Agreement on Air Quality", *Policy Studies Journal*, 27 (2) pp. 347-359.

Allum, J. (1995), *Smoke Across the Border: The Environmental Politics of the Trail Smelter Investigation*, PhD dissertation, Kingston: Queen's University.

Alper, D.K. (1997), "Transboundary Environmental Relations in British Columbia and the Pacific Northwest," *The American Review of Canadian Studies – Red, White and Green: Canada-U.S. Environmental Relations*, 27(3).

Alyeska Pipeline (2004), "Pipeline Facts", 23 June http://www.alyeskapipe.come/Piplinefact.html, accessed 23 June 2004.

American Bird Conservancy (2004), "International Programs", www.abcbirds.org/international/ accessed May 2005.

Andrews, E. (2002), "Outside Halls of Power, Many Fear Free Trade", *New York Times,* 3 November p. B4.

Appelton, A.E. (1999), "Shrimp/Turtle: Untangling the Nets", *Journal of International Economic Law* 2(3) pp. 477-96.

Arctic Climate Impact Assessment (2004), *Impacts of a Warming Arctic*, Cambridge: Cambridge University Press, 2004.

Arctic Environment: Second Ministerial Conference (1993), *The Nuuk Declaration on Environment in the Arctic* (Nuuk Greenland, 16 September pp. 3-4.

Arrow, K., et al. (1995), "Economic Growth, Carrying Capacity, and the Environment", *Science* (April 28) 268: 5210, pp. 520-521.

Asia Pacific Economic Cooperation (APEC, 2004), *Report on Initiatives of The North American Commission for Environmental Cooperation* (CEC), Marine Resource Conservation Working Group Puerto Varas, Chile 6-7 May 2004.

Askins, R. (2000), *Restoring North America's Birds: Lessons from Landscape Ecology*, New Haven: Yale University Press.

Attfield, R. (1991), "Attitudes to Wildlife in the History of Ideas", *Environmental History Review* 15:2, pp.71-8.

Audley, J. (1997), *Green Politics and Global Trade: NAFTA and the Future of Environmental Politics*, Washington D.C.: Georgetown University Press.

Audley, J., Polaski, S., Papademetriou, D. and Vaughan. S., (2003), *NAFTA's Promise and Reality: Lessons from Mexico for the Hemisphere*, Washington, D.C.: Carnegie Endowment for International Peace.

Aulisi, A., Layke, J., and Putt del Pino, S. (2004), *A Climate of Innovation: Northeast Business Action to Reduce Greenhouse Gases*, Washington D.C.: World Resources Institute.

Aulisi, A., Farrell, A., Pershing, J., and VanDeveer, S. (2005), *Greenhouse Gas Emissions Trading in U.S. States: Observations and Lessons from OTC* NO_x *Budget Program,* White Paper, Resources for the Future.

Axline, A., et al., (eds) (1974), *Continental Community? Interdependence and Integration in North America*, Toronto: McClelland and Stewart.

Axworthy, L. (1997), "Sustainable Development and Human Security", *Canadian Speeches* (April) 11:1) pp. 43-7.

Axworthy, L. (1998), Remarks in Press Briefing, Ottawa, Canada, 10 March.

Barkin, S. and Mansori, K. (2001), "Backwards Boycotts: Demand Management and Fishery Conservation", *Global Environmental Politics*, 1(2) pp. 30-41.

Barkin, S., and Moseley, C. (2003), "Sustainable Development, Political Institutions, and Scales: The Management of Pacific Salmon", in Bressers, H. and Rosenbaum, W., *Achieving Sustainable Development: The Challenge of Governance Across Social Scales*, New York: Praeger.

Barkin, S. and Shambaugh, G. (1999), *Anarchy and the Environment: The International Relations of Common Pool Resources*, Albany: State University of New York Press.

Barkin, S. and Shambaugh, G. (1999a), "Hypotheses on the International Politics of Common Pool Resources", in Barkin and Shambaugh.

Baskin, Y. (1996),"Curbing Undesirable Invaders", *Bioscience* 46, pp. 732-736.

Bates, D.V. and Sitzo, R. (1983), "Relationship between Air Pollution Levels and Hospital Admissions in Southern Ontario", *Canadian Journal of Public Health* 74, pp. 117-122.

Beamish, R. J. (1976), "Acidification of lakes in Canada by acid precipitation and the resulting effects on fish", *Water, Air, and Soil Pollution*. 6, pp. 501-514.

Beamish, R. J. and Harvey, H. (1972), "Acidification of the La Cloche Mountain Lakes, Ontario, and Resulting Fish Mortalities", *Journal of the Fisheries Research Board of Canada*, 29(8), pp. 1131-1143.

Beier, P. and Noss, R. F. (1998), "Do Habitat Corridors Provide Connectivity", *Conservation Biology*, 12, pp. 1523-1739.

Beissinger, S., et al. (2000), "Report of the AOU Conservation Committee on the Partners in Flight species prioritization plan", *The Auk*, 117(2), pp. 549-561.

Bell, J. (2003), *A Survey of Canadian Policies to Compensate Small Power Producers for Electricity Fed to the Grid: Net Metering and Net Billing*, Dalhousie University, Halifax, December.

Bellona (2003), "Decommissioning of Nuclear Submarines", *Submarine Decommissioning – Bellona.* http://bellona.no/en/international/russia/navy/northern_fleet/decommissioning/index.html accessed 25 January 2005.

Bernstein, S. (2002), *The Compromise of Liberal Environmentalism*, New York: Columbia University Press.

Bernstein, S., and Cashore, B. (2002), "Globalization, Internationalization, and Liberal Environmentalism: Exploring Non-Domestic Sources of Influence on Canadian Environmental Policy", in VanNijnatten and Boardman, pp. 212-230.

Betsill, M. (2001), "Mitigating Climate Change in U.S. Cities: Opportunities and Obstacles," *Local Environment* 4 (4), pp. 393-406.

Bibby, C. (2002), "Why Conserve Bird Diversity?", in *Conserving Bird Biodiversity: General Principles and Their Application*, K. Norris and D. Pain (eds), Cambridge: Cambridge University Press, pp. 20-33.

Bilder, R. (1972), "Controlling Great Lakes Pollution: A Study in U.S.-Canadian Environmental Cooperation", *Michigan Law Review* 70, pp. 469-556.

Blair, D. (2003), "The CEC's Citizen Submission Process: Still a Model for Reconciling Trade and the Environment?" *Journal of Environment and Development* 12 (September), pp. 295-324.

Blix, H. (2004), *Disarming Iraq: The Search for Weapons of Mass Destruction*, New York: Pantheon.

BNA (1982) "Canadian official accuses administration of manipulating acid rain scientific work", *BNA Environment Reporter*, 13(23), pp. 782.

Boardman, R. (1992), "The Multilateral Dimension: Canada in the International System," in Robert Boardman (ed.), *Canadian Environmental Policy: Ecosystems, Politics, and Process*, Toronto: Oxford University Press.

Boardman, R. (2006), *The International Politics of Bird Conservation: Biodiversity, Regionalism and Global Governance*, Cheltenham, UK and Northampton, MA: Edward Elgar.

Boardman, R., and Beazley, K. (eds) (2002), *Politics of the Wild*, London: Oxford University Press.

Bolinger, M. and Wiser, R. (2002), *Customer-Sited PV: A Survey of Clean Energy Fund Support*, Montpelier, VT: Clean Energy Group.

Bowman, J. (2001), "Citizen Submission Process Proves Valuable in BC Hydro Case", *Trio* (Fall), www.cec.org/trio/stories/index.cfm?ed=5&ID=70&varlan=english#top>.

Brennan, R. (1998), "Smog plan toothless, critics say", *The Windsor Star*, Wednesday, 21 January 1998, p.A1.

Brigham, Lawson (1997), "Commentary: An International Polar Navigation Code for the Twenty-First Century", *Polar Record* 187(33), pp. 283.

Bright, C. (1999), "Invasive Species: Pathogens of Globalization", *Foreign Policy*, Fall, pp. 50-58.

Bryden, J. (1998), "Minister Sees Something Fishy Everywhere: David Anderson Has Declared Himself Minister of Fish", *The Ottawa Citizen*, 1 July 1998 (final edition), A6.

Bulkeley, H. and Betsill, M. (2003), *Cities for Climate Change: Urban Sustainability and Global Environmental Governance*, London: Routledge.

Burnett, A. (2003a), *A Passion for Wildlife: The History of the Canadian Wildlife Service*, Vancouver: University of British Columbia Press.

Burnett, A. (2003b), "All bird conservation: First steps", www.nabci-us.org (accessed January, 2005).

Burnett, J. (1999), "A Passion for Wildlife: A History of the Canadian Wildlife Service, 1947-1997", *Canadian Field-Naturalist* 113, pp. 1-183.

Burton, P. J., et al., (2003), "The current state of boreal forestry and the drive for change," in Burton, J., et al. (eds) *Towards Sustainable Management of the Boreal Forest*, NRC Research Press, Ottawa, pp. 1-40.

Bushnell, J. (2004), "California's Electricity Crisis: A Market Apart?", *Energy Policy*, 32(9) (June), pp. 1045-52.

Caldwell, L. and Weiland, P. (1996), *International Environmental Policy: From the Twentieth to the Twenty-First Century*, Durham and London: Duke University Press.

Calgary Herald (2003), "Offshore Alaska oil drilling ardently promoted by U.S.", *Calgary Herald* (14 October 2003) D5.

Cameron, J. (2001), "The Precautionary Principle in International Law", in T.O'Riordan, Cameron, J., and Jordan, A. (eds) *Reinterpreting the Precautionary Principle*, London: Cameron May.

Canada, Acidifying Emissions Task Group (1997) *Towards a National Acid Rain Strategy*. Report submitted to the National Air Issues Coordinating Committee, October

Canada, Government of (1970), *Foreign Policy for Canadians*, Ottawa: Queen's Printers.

Canada, Government of (1985), *Competitiveness and Security*, Ottawa: Queen's Printers.

Canada, Government of (1991), *Canada's Green Plan: The First Year*, Supply and Services, Ottawa: Queen's Printers.

Canada, Government of (1995), *Canada and the World*, Ottawa: Queen's Printers.

Canada, Government of (2002), *Climate Change Plan for Canada*, 21 November Supply and Services, Ottawa.

Canada, Government of (2003), *Opening Doors to the World: Canada's International Market Access Priorities*, Supply and Services, Ottawa.

Canada, Government of (2005), *Project Green – Moving Forwards on Climate Change: A Plan for Honouring our Kyoto Commitment*, Government of Canada, Ottawa.

Canada-United States Research Consultation Group on the Long-Range Transport of Air Pollutants (1979) "The LRTAP Problem in North America: A Preliminary Overview", Ottawa.

Canada-United States Research Consultation Group on the Long-Range Transport of Air Pollutants (1980) "Second Report", Ottawa.

Canada-United States, Air Quality Committee, Progress Reports on Air Quality Agreement, 1992-2006 <http://www.ec.gc.ca/pdb/can_us/qual xx (accessed July 2005).

Canada-United States, Ozone Protocol, 2000 http://www.ec.gc.ca/cleanair-airpur/CAOL/air/can_usa_e.html, accessed November 2005.

Canada-U.S. Air Quality Committee, Subcommittee on Scientific Cooperation (2004) *Canada-U.S. Transboundary PM Science Assessment* <http://www.msc.ec.gc.ca/saib/smog/transboundary/toc_e.html (accessed July 2005).

Canadian Broadcasting Corporation (CBC, 2002), "Chrétien promises 10 new national parks", 3 September 2002. Accessed 12 December 2004.

Canadian Council of Ministers of the Environment (CCME, 2003), *Climate, Nature, People: Indicators of Canada's Changing Climate*, Winnipeg: Manitoba.

Canadian Press/Leger Marketing (2001), "A Study of the Perception of Canadians with Regards to the Environment: Executive Report 13 July", *http://www.legermarketing.com/documents/spclm/010813eng.pdf* (Cited 24 June 2004).

Caporaso, J. (ed.) (1978) "Dependence and Dependency in the Global System", (special issue) *International Organization*, 32(1).

Cardoso, F. H. and Faletto, E. (1979) *Dependency and Development in Latin America*, Berkeley: University of California Press.

Carlton, J. and Cohen, A. (2003), "Episodic global dispersal in shallow water marine organisms: the case history of the European shore crabs *carcinus maenas* and *c. aestuari*", *Journal of Biogeography*, 30, pp. 1809-1820.

Carroll, J. (1980), *Environmental Diplomacy*, Ann Arbor, Michigan: University of Michigan Press.

Carroll, J. (1981), "Patterns Old and New", in R. Spencer, ed., *The International Joint Commission Seventy Years On*, University of Toronto: Centre for International Studies.

Carroll, J. E. (1983), *Environmental Diplomacy: An Examination and Prospective of Canadian-US Transboundary Environmental Relations*, Ann Arbor, Michigan: University of Michigan Press.

Carroll, J. and Mack, E. (1982), "On Living Together: Canada, the United States and International Environmental Relations", *Denver Journal of International Law and Policy.*

Cassesse, A. (2001), *International Law*, Oxford: Oxford University Press.

Cattaneo, C. (2004), "Pipeline behemoths square off", *National Post* (December 23, 2004) FP1.

Chacko, C. J. (1932), *The International Joint Commission Between the United States of America and the Dominion of Canada*, New York: Columbia University Press.

Chatterjee, P. and Finger, M. (1994), *The Earth Brokers: Power, Politics, and World Development*, New York: Routledge.

CIDA (Canadian International Development Agency) (1997), *CIDA and the Environment*, Canadian Development Agency, Ottawa.

CITES (2004), How CITES Works? http://www.cites.org/eng/disc/how.shtml accessed 12 December 2004.

Clark, W. (2000), "Environmental Globalization", in Nye, J. and Donahue, J. (eds) *Governance in a Globalizing World*, Washington:Brookings Institution Press, pp. 86-108.

Clarkson, S. (1973), "Lament for a Non-Subject: Reflections on the Teaching of Canadian-American Relations", *International Journal* 27, pp. 265-75.

Clarkson, S., Davidson Ladly, S., and Thorne, C. (2005), "A North American Community of Law with Minimal Institutions: NAFTA's Committees and Working Groups", in Kirton and Hajnal, forthcoming.

Clarkson, S. (1982), *Canada and the Reagan Challenge*, Toronto: Lorimer and the Canadian Institute for Economic Policy.

Clement, W. (1977), *Continental Corporate Power: Economic Linkages Between Canada and the United States*, Toronto: McClelland and Stewart.

Cohen, A. (2003), *While Canada Slept: How We Lost Our Place in the World*, Toronto: McClelland and Stewart.

Cohen, D. and Murray, T. P. (2002), "State Must Protect Our Climate Now", *Boston Globe*, 1 September 2003.

Cohen, M. (1975), *The Regime of Boundary Waters: The Canada-United States Experience*, Hague Academy, Recueil.

Cole, E. and Ensign, P. (1997), "An Examination of United States Foreign Direct Investment into Mexico and its Relation to the North American Free Trade Agreement: Towards a Balanced Understanding of the Effects of Environmental Regulation and Factor Endowments That Affect Location Decision", paper presented at the annual meeting of the Academy of International Business, Monterey, Mexico, 8-12 October.

Condon, B., and Sinha, T. (2003), *Drawing Lines in Sand and Snow: Border Security and North American Economic Integration*, Armonk, New York: M.E. Sharpe.

Commission for Environmental Cooperation (CEC) (1995a), Second Annual Regular Session of the Council of Ministers, CEC, Oaxaca, Mexico, October 13.

CEC (1995b), *Report on the Death of Migratory Birds at the Silva Reservoir (1994-95)*. Oaxaca, October.

CEC (1996), "North American Environment Ministers accelerate environmental protection efforts", http://www.cec.org/files/PDF/COUNCIL/96-00_EN.pdf, accessed 28 June 2006.

CEC (1997a), *Continental Pollutant Pathways: An Agenda for Cooperation to Address Long-Range Transport of Air Pollution in North America*, Montreal: Commission for Environmental Cooperation.

CEC (1997b*), Long-Range Transport of Ground-Level Ozone and its Precursors: Assessment of Methods to Quantify Transboundary Transport with the Northeastern United States and Eastern Canada*, Montreal: Commission for Environmental Cooperation.

CEC (1999), *Issue Study 3 – Electricity in Canada, Mexico and the United States: Some Environmental Implications of the North American Free Trade Agreement*, in #6 in the Environment and Trade series, Assessing Environmental Effects of the North American Free Trade Agreement (NAFTA): An Analytic Framework (Phase II) and Issue Studies (Montreal: Commission for Environmental Cooperation of North America).

CEC (1999), *Assessing Environmental Effects of the North American Free Trade Agreement (NAFTA) An Analytic Framework (Phase II) and Issue Studies*, Montreal: CEC.

CEC (1999a), *North American Important Bird Areas: A Directory of 150 Key Conservation Sites*, Montreal: CEC.

CEC (2001), *North American Agenda for Action, 2002-2004*, Montreal: CEC.

CEC (2001a), "Electricity and the Environment" (Montreal, QC: Commission for Environmental Cooperation of North America, http://www.cec.org/programs_projects/other_initiatives/electricity/index.cfm?varlan=english. accessed 15 August 2001.

CEC (2002), *Environmental Challenges and Opportunities of the Evolving North American Electricity Market: Secretariat Report to Council Under Article 13 of the North American Agreement on Environmental Cooperation*, Montreal: Commission for Environmental Cooperation of North America, June).

CEC (2003), *Strategic Plan for North American Cooperation in the Conservation of Biodiversity*, Commission for Environmental Cooperation, Montreal.

CEC (2003a), *Renewable Portfolio Standards as a Policy Instrument for Promoting Renewable Electricity: A Survey of Canada and the United States*, (Montreal: Commission for Environmental Cooperation).

CEC (2003b), *What is Renewable? A Summary of Eligibility Criteria Across 27 Renewable Portfolio Standards*, Montreal: Commission for Environmental Cooperation of North America, 15 December.

CEC (2003d), Final Factual Record for Submission SEM-99-002 (Migratory Birds), Prepared in Accordance with Article 15 of the NAAEC. 22 April. Published in CEC, North American Environmental Law and Policy Series, vol. 11.

CEC (2004), "Electricity and Environment Database" (Montreal: Commission for Environmental Cooperation, http://cec.org/databases/certifications/Cecdata/index.cfm?webisteID=3; accessed 10 February 2004).

Convention on Biological Diversity (CBD, 1996), "An Ecosystem Approach to the Management of Northern Coniferous Forests", Subsidiary Body on Scientific, Technical and Technological Advice (SBSTTA) Second Meeting Montreal, 2 September 1996.

CBD (2000), "The Ecosystem Approach under the CBD, from Concept to Action", Report from Southern Africa Regional Pathfinder workshop Victoria Falls, Zimbabwe, 17-19 July.

CBD (2001), *Review of the Efficiency and Efficacy of Existing Legal Instruments Applicable to Invasive Alien Species*, CBD Technical Series No. 1. Montreal: Secretariat of the CBD.

CBD (2003), "Ecosystem Approach: Further elaboration, guidelines for implementation and relationship with sustainable forest management", SBSTTA Ninth Meeting, 10 November 2003.

Cowling, E.B. (1982) "Acid precipitation in historical perspective", *Environmental Science & Technology*, 16(2):110A-123A.

CPA (2004), "NAFTA Chapter 11 Investor-State Disputes" (Ottawa, ON: Canadian Centre for Policy Alternatives; http://www.policyalternatives.ca/publications/chapter11-table.pdf; accessed 11 February 2004).

Crawford, S. (2001), *Salmonine Introductions to the Laurentian Great Lakes: An Historical Review and Evaluation of Ecological Effects*, Ottawa: NRC Press.

Cristancho, S., and Vining, J. (2004), "Culturally Defined Keystone Species", *Human Ecology Review* 11:2:153-164.

Daley, B. (2004), "Wind Farms find unlikely foe in environmentalists", *Boston Globe* August 1, 2004: A1 and B5.

Dansereau, P. (1978), "Canada-U.S. Relations in an Environmental Perspective", in Carroll, J., ed., *Canada-U.S. Natural Resources and Environment Symposium*, University of New Hampshire, Institute of Natural and Environmental Resources, pp. 2-7.

Day, A. M. (1949), *North American Waterfowl*, New York: Stackpole and Heck.

Dearden, P. (2001), "Endangered Species and Terrestrial Protected Areas", in Beazley and Boardman (2001), pp. 75-93.

Deere, C. and Esty, D. (eds) (2002) *Greening the Americas: NAFTA's Lessons for Hemispheric Trade*, Cambridge, Mass.: The MIT Press.

Defenders of Wildlife (2000), *The Public in Action: Using State Citizen Suite Statutes to Protect Biodiversity*, Washington: Defenders of Wildlife.

Defenders of Wildlife (2004), *State of the Wolf, 2004*, Washington: Defenders of Wildlife.

De Lafontaine, Y., et al. (2002), "Testing a new anti-Zebra mussel coating with a multi-plate sampler", *Biofouling* 18:1, 1-12.

Depalma, A. (2005), "Northeast States Welcome U.S. Rule Cutting Pollution", *New York Times*, 11 March.

Depalma, A. (1995), "Bird deaths in Mexico are a test for trade pact", *New York Times*, 8 June A14.

Department of Foreign Affairs and International Trade (DFAIT, 2000), Canada-U.S. Ozone Negotiations: Joint U.S.-Canada Statement. News Release: Ottawa, 16 February 07/24/2000.

Desai, N. (2000), "Implementing Agenda 21: A United Nations Perspective", in Dodds, F., ed., *Earth Summit 2002: A New Deal*, London: Earthscan, pp. 21-30.

DeSombre, E. (1995), "Baptists and Bootleggers for the Environment: The Origins of United States Unilateral Sanctions", *Journal of Environment and Development* 4.

DeSombre, E. (2002), *The Global Environment & World Politics*, London: Continuum.

DeSombre, E. and Barkin, S. (2000), "Unilateralism and Multilateralism in International Fisheries Management", *Global Governance*, 6(3):350-351.

Deutsch, C. H. (2005), "Saving the Environment, One Quarterly Earnings Report at a Time", *The New York Times*, 22 November 2005.

Dewailly, E., et al. (1989), "High Levels of PCVs in Breast Milk of Inuit Women from Arctic Quebec", *Bulletin of Environmental Contamination and Toxicology* 43 (5): 641-6.

Dillon, P. J., Jeffries, D. S. and Schneider, W. A. (1978) "Effects of Acidic Precipitation on Precambrian Freshwaters in Southern Ontario", Ontario Ministry of Environment, April.

Dillon, S. (1995), "Scientists say raw sewage killed 40,000 birds", *New York Times*, 29 September:A9.

Dinwoodie, D. H. (1971) "The Politics of International Pollution Control: Trail Smelter Case", *International Journal*, 27:219-35.

Doering, R. and Runnalls, D. (1993), "Sustainability: The Key to Competitiveness in the 21st Century", *Prosperity and Sustainable Development For Canada: Advice to the Prime Minister*, Ottawa: National Round Table on the Environment and the Economy (NRTEE) March.

Dogterom, J. et al. (2002), *Green Power Marketing in Canada: The State of the Industry*, (Drayton Valley, AB: Pembina Institute for Appropriate Development, December).

Donaghy, G. (2002), *Tolerant Allies: Canada and the United States, 1963-1968*, Montreal and Kingston: McGill-Queen's University Press.

Dorsey, K. (1998), *The Dawn of Conservation Policy*, Seattle: University of Washington Press.

Dosman, Edgar (1976) "The Northern Sovereignty Crisis 1968-70", in Edgar Dosman (ed) *The Arctic in Question*, Toronto: Oxford University Press, pp. 1-206.

Dowie, M. (1995), *Losing Ground: American Environmentalism at the Close of the Twentieth Century*, Cambridge MA: MIT Press,

Downie D. L. and Fenge, T. (eds) (2003), *Northern Lights against POPs: Combating Toxic Threats in the Arctic*, Montreal: McGill-Queen's University Press.

Driscoll, C. T., Lawrence, G. B., Bulger, A. J., Butler, T. J., Cronan, C. S., Edgar, C., Lambert, K. F., Likens, G. E., Stoddard, J. L. and Weathers, K. C. (2001), "Acid rain revisited: Advances in Scientific understanding since the passage of the 1970 and 1990 Clean Air Act Amendments", Hubbard Brook Research Foundation, Science Links TM Publication, Vol. 1, No. 1.

Dryzek, J., and Hunter, S. (1987), "Environmental Mediation for International Problems", *International Studies Quarterly* 31:87-102.

DSIRE (2004a), "Frequently Asked Questions", (Raleigh, NC: Database of State Incentives for Renewable Energy. http://www.dsireusa.org/faq/faq.cfm?&CurrentPageID=9; accessed 10 February 2004).

DSIRE (2004b), "Database of State Incentives for Renewable Energy", (Raleigh, NC: Database of State Incentives for Renewable Energy; http://www.dsireusa.org/index.cfm?&CurrentPageID=3; accessed 10 February 2004).

Duffy, A (2000), "Provinces pledge to cut smog by 2010," *Edmonton Journal*, Wednesday June 7, 2000:A6.

Dwivedi, O. P., Kyba, P., Stoett, P., and Tiessen, R. (2001), *Sustainable Development and Canada: National and International Perspectives*, Broadview Press, Toronto.

Eayrs, J. (1961), *The Art of the Possible*, Toronto: University of Toronto Press.

Eayrs, J. (1972), *In Defence of Canada: Peacemaking and Deterrence* Toronto: University of Toronto Press.

Economic Policy Institute (1997), *The Failed Experiment: NAFTA at Three Years*, Economic Policy Institute, Washington DC, 26 June.

ECP (2004), "Western New York Wind Corp", (Ottawa, ON: Environmental Choice Program; http://www.environmentalchoice.com/dbform0.cfm?companyid=295&group=5; accessed 11 February 2004).

EIA (2003), "Status of State Electric Industry Restructuring Activity – as of February 2003" (Washington, DC: Energy Information Administration; http://www.eia.doe.gov/cneaf/electricity/chg_str/regmap.html; last accessed 10 February 2003).

EIA (2004), *State Electricity Profiles 2002* (Washington, DC: Energy Information Administration, January).

Enmax (2004), "Greenmax", (Calgary, AB: Enmax; http://www.enmax.com/Energy/Residential/Greenmax/How+Greenmax+works.htm; accessed 10 February 2004).

Environment Canada (1997) *1997 Canadian Acid Rain Assessment*, Ottawa (five volumes).

Environment Canada, news release, (2000) "Canada and the US Embark on New Era of Cleaner Air", http://www.ec.gc.ca/press/001207_n_e.htm and http://www.ec.gc.ca/press/001207_b_e.htm (accessed 22 July 2005).

Environment Canada (2000), "Fact Sheet: Ozone Annex under the 1991 Canada-U.S. Air Quality Agreement", accessed 24 July 2000.

Environment Canada (2001) *Precursor Contributions to Ambient Fine Particulate Matter in Canada*, Report by the Meteorological Service of Canada, May.

Environment Canada and the United States Department of the Interior, Fish and Wildlife Service (EC and USFWS) (2001), Conserving *Borderline Species: A Partnership between the United States and Canada*, Washington and Ottawa.

Environment Northeast (2003), Climate Change Roadmap for Connecticut: Economic and Environmental Opportunities, Part II: Strategies.

Epcor (2004), "Green Power Program Overview", (Edmonton, AB: Epcor; http://www.epcor.com/Residential/Products+and+Services/Green+Power/Program+Overview.htm' accessed 10 February 2004).

Esty, D. and Geradin, D. (1997), "Market Access, Competitiveness and Harmonization: Environmental Protection in Regional Trade Agreements", *Harvard Environmental Law Review* 21(2):265-336.

Faucheux, S., O'Connor, M., and Nicolai, I. (1997), "Economic Globalisation, Competitiveness, and Environment", *OECD Proceedings Globalisation and Environment: Preliminary Perspectives,* pp. 101-139.

Financial Times (1997), "Canada-US Fish Row Grows", 29 May 1997 (London edition): 8.

Findlay, J., and Coates, K. (eds) (2002), *Parallel Destinies: Canadian-American Relations West of the Rockies*, Seattle: University of Washington Press.

Fitzmaurice, M. (2003), "Public Participation in the North American Agreement on Environmental Cooperation", *International and Comparative Law Quarterly* 52 (April):333-368.

Fitzpatrick, J. (2002), "The AOU and bird conservation: Recommitment to the revolution", *The Auk*, 119(4):907-913.

Fletcher, T. (1998), *Environmental Justice and Hazardous Waste: A View From the Canada-United States Border*. PhD dissertation, McGill University, Hamilton, Canada.

Florini, A., ed. (2000), *The Third Force: The Rise of Transnational Civil Society*, Carnegie Endowment for International Peace, Washington, D.C.

Foreign Affairs, Canada, Devil's Lake website, http://www.dfait-maeci.gc.ca/can-am/washington/shared_env/devilslake-en.asp (accessed September 2005).

Foster, D. and Motzkin, G. (1998), "Ecology and conservation in the cultural landscape of New England: Lessons from Nature's History", *Northeastern Naturalist* 5(2):111-126.

Fox, A., et al., (eds) (1974), Canada and the United States: Transnational and Transgovernmental Relations, Special Issue, *International Organization* 28.

Friedman, T. (2004), "Losing Our Edge?", *The New York Times*, 22 April.

Gailus, J. (2000), *Bringing Conservation Home: Caring for Land, Economies and Communities in Western Canada*. A Project of the Sonoran Institute and the Yellowstone to Yukon Conservation Initiative.

Gaines, S. (2002), "The Masked Ball of NAFTA Chapter 11: Foreign Investors, Local Environmentalists, Government Officials, and Disguised Motives", in Kirton and Maclaren (2002a), pp. 103-130.

Galloway, J. N. and Whelpdale, D. M. (1980), "An Atmospheric Sulphur Budget for Eastern North America", *Atmospheric Environment* 14: 409-417.

Gal-Or, N. (1998), "Private Party Direct Access: A Comparison of the NAFTA and the EU Disciplines", *Boston College International and Comparative Law Review* 21 (Winter): 1-42.

Gilligan, M. (1997), "Lobbying as a Private Good with Intra-Industry Trade", *International Studies Quarterly* 41(3): 455-474.

Glicksman, R. (2003), "The CEC's biodiversity conservation agenda", in Markell, D., and Knox, J., (eds) *Greening NAFTA: The North American Commission for Environmental Cooperation*, Stanford University Press, pp. 57-79.

Goldemberg, J. (2004), *The Case for Renewable Energies*, Secretariat of the International Conference for Renewable Energies, Bonn, Germany.

Gorham, E. (1955), "On the Acidity and Salinity of Rain", *Geochimica et Cosmochimica Acta* 7: 231-239.

Gorham, E. and Gordon, A. G. (1960), "The influence of smelter fumes upon the chemical composition of lake waters near Sudbury, Ontario, and upon the surrounding vegetation," *Canadian Journal of Botany*, 38: 477-487.

Gorham E. and Gordon, A. G. (1960), "Some effects of smelter pollution northeast of Falconbridge, Ontario", *Canadian Journal of Botany*, 38: 307-312.

Gorham, E. and Gordon, A. G. (1963), "Some effects of smelter pollution upon aquatic vegetation near Sudbury, Ontario", *Canadian Journal of Botany* 41: 371-378.

Graham, B.(2002), "Civil Society and Institutions of Global Governance," Address to the Third Annual EnviReform Conference on "Sustainability, Civil Society and International Governance: Local, North American and Global Perspectives", Toronto, 8 November 2002.

Graves, F. (2003), "Climate Change, the Environment and Continental Policy Convergence", Part of the "Rethinking North American Integration" Study, Ekos, Presentation to the Public Policy Forum conference, Ottawa, 30 October 2003.

GreenBiz (2004), "Green-e Certifies First Canadian Green Tags for U.S. Sale", (http://www.greenbiz.com/news/printer.cfm?NewsID=26400; accessed 11 February 2004).

Greene, S., and Keating, T. (1980), "Domestic Factors and Canada-United States Fisheries Relations", *Canadian Journal of Political Science*, XII: 4, 731-750.

Griffiths, F. (2003), "The Shipping News: Canada's Arctic Sovereignty not on thinning ice", *International Journal*, 58(2).

Griffiths, F. (2004), "Is Canada's arctic sovereignty threatened?" *Arctic Bulletin – WWF* no.1(4).

Grigorovich, I., et al. (2003), "Ballast-mediated animal introductions in the Laurentian Great Lakes: retrospective and prospective analyses", *Canadian Journal of Fisheries and Aquatic Sciences* 60:740-756.

Groetzinger, J. (1997), "NAFTA's Environmental Provisions: Are They Working as Intended? Are They Adequate?" *Canada-United States Law Journal* 23: 401-428.

Grossman, P. (2000), "Globalization and the Linkage of Trade and Environmental Issues: A Comparative Analysis of the Canada-United States and North American Free Trade Agreements", PhD dissertation, New York University.

Groves, C., et al. (2000), "Planning for Biodiversity Conservation: Putting Conservation Science into Practice", *Bioscience* 52(6):499-512.

Haas, P. (1990), *Saving the Mediterranean: The Politics of International Environmental Cooperation*, Columbia University Press, New York.

Haglund, D. (2003), "North American Co-operation in an Era of Homeland Security," *ORBIS* 47 (Fall):675-691.

Hamel, S. (2003), "Climate Change Action Plan: 2003 Update", Presentation given at the 28th Annual Meeting of the New England Governors and Eastern Canadian Premiers, Groton, Connecticut, 9 September.

Harrison, K. (1996), *Passing the Buck: Federalism and Environmental Policy*, Vancouver: University of British Columbia Press.

Hasegawa, Koichi (2004) *Constructing Civil Society in Japan: Voices of Environmental Movements*, Melbourne: Trans Pacific Press.

Hawkins, A. (1984), "The US Response", in A. S. Hawkins, R. C. Hanson, H. K. Nelson, and H. M. Reeves (eds) *Flyways: Pioneering Waterfowl Management in North America*, US Fish and Wildlife Service, Washington, D.C., pp. 2-9.

Hay Opinion Leader Research Program (1989), "What Price Success? Sustainable Development in Canada: Promise or Paradox?" (November).

Hazell, S. (1999), *Canada v. The Environment: Fearer Environmental Assessment 1984-1998*, Canadian Environmental Defence Fund, Toronto.

Head, I. (1991), *On a Hinge of History: The Mutual Vulnerability of South and North*, Toronto: University of Toronto Press.

Head, I. and Trudeau, P. (1995), *The Canadian Way: Shaping Canada's Foreign Policy, 1968-1984*, Toronto: McClelland & Stewart Inc.

Health Canada – Environment Canada (1998), *National Ambient Air Quality Objectives for Particulate Matter: Science Assessment Document* (www.hc-sc.gc.ca/ewh-semt/ pubs/air/naaqoonqaa/particulate_matter_matieres_particulaires/science_evaluation_scientifique/index_e.html (accessed December 2005).

Hebert, J. et al. (1989), "Ecological and genetic studies on *dreissena polymorphia* (Pallas): a new mollusc in the Great Lakes", *Canadian Journal of Fisheries and Aquatic Science* 46:1587-1591.

Hebert, J. et al. (1991), "Demography and ecological impacts of the invading mollusc *dreissena polymorphia*", *Canadian Journal of Zoology* 69:405-409.

Hebert, J. (2003), "US House, Senate agree on energy policy", *Ottawa Citizen* (15 November 2003) D10.

Heinberg, R. (2003), *The Party's Over*, Gabriola Island: New Society Publishers.

Hempling, S. and Rader, N. (2002), *Comments of the Union of Concerned Scientists to the Commission for Environmental Cooperation*, Union of Concerned Scientists. 31 January, Cambridge, Mass.

Henton, D. (1997), "B.C. May Up Ante to Get Salmon Deal: Province Working on Plan to Turn up Heat, Clark Says", *Toronto Star*, 30 May (final edition):A18.

Henton, D. (1997a), "Blockade of Alaska Ferry is Lifted, But Angry B.C. Fishermen Want Ottawa to Resolve Salmon War", *Toronto Star*, 22 July (final edition):A1.

Herman, F A and E Gorham (1957), "Total Mineral Material, Acidity, Sulphur, and Nitrogen in Rain and Snow at Kentville, Nova Scotia", *Tellus* 9, no. 2: 180-183.

Hoberg, G. (1996), "Governing the Environment: Comparing Canada and the United States," in K. Banting, G. Hoberg and R. Simeon, (eds), *Degrees of Freedom*, Montreal: McGill-Queen's University Press, pp. 341-385.

Hoberg, G. (2002), "Canadian-American Environmental Relations: A Strategic Framework", in VanNijnatten and Boardman (2002), pp. 171-189.

Hocking, B. (1996), "The Woods and the Trees: Catalytic Diplomacy and Canada's Trials as a 'Forestry Superpower'", *Environmental Politics* 5:3, 448-75.

Holdren, J. and Smith, K. (2000), "Energy, the Environment, and Health", in *World Energy Assessment: Energy and the Challenge of Sustainability*, United Nations Development Programme, New York, pp. 61-110.

Holmes, J. (1971), *The Better Part of Valour: Essays in Canadian Diplomacy*, Toronto: McClelland and Stewart.

Holsti, K. J. (1971) "Canada and the United States", in S. Spiegel and Kenneth N. Waltz, (eds) *Conflict in World Politics*, Cambridge: Winthrop, pp. 375-96.

Holt, E. (1997), *Disclosure and Certification: Truth and Labeling for Electric Power*, Renewable Energy Policy Project, Issue Brief No. 5, Washington D.C.

Horlick, G., Schuchhardt, C. and Mann, H. (2002), *NAFTA Provisions and the Electricity Sector*, Background Paper 4, Environmental Challenges and Opportunities of the Evolving North American Electricity Market (Montreal, QC: North American Commission for Environmental Cooperation. June).

Housman, R. (1994), "The North American Free Trade Agreement's Lessons for Reconciling Trade and Environment", *Stanford Journal of International Law* 30: 379-422.

Howard, Ross (1977), "Industrial Pollutants 'Time Bomb' LeBlanc Warns", *Toronto Star*, 21 June 1977, p. B2.

Howatt, T. (2003), "Gas Piped by 2010: After 30 years it looks like a Mackenzie Valley Pipeline will be built. But there's lots of work ahead", *Opportunities North* (December 2003) http:www.nnsl.com/ops/jan2_04piped.html, accessed 20 June 2006.

Huebert, R. (1998), "New Directions in Circumpolar Cooperation: Canada, the Arctic Environmental Protection Strategy and the Arctic Council", *Canadian Foreign Policy* 5(2): 37-58.

Huebert, R. (2001), "Article 234 and Marine Pollution Jurisdiction in the Arctic", in Alex Oude Elfernik and Donald Bothwell (eds) *The Law of the Sea and Polar*

Maritime Delimitation and Jurisdiction, The Hague: Maritinus Nijhoff, pp. 249-267.

Huebert, R. (2003), "The Shipping News Part II: How Canada's Arctic sovereignty is on thinning ice", *International Journal* 58(3).

Huebert, R. (2004), "The coming arctic maritime sovereignty crisis", *Arctic Bulletin – WWF* No. 2 .04.

Hufbauer, G., et al. (2000), *NAFTA and the Environment: Seven Years Later*, Institute for International Economics, Washington DC.

Hughes, L. (2000), "Biological Consequences of Global Warming: Is the Signal Already Apparent?", *Trends in Ecology and Evolution* 15:56-61.

Hunter, D., Salzman, J., and Zaelke, D. (2001) *International Environmental Law and Policy*, 2nd ed., Foundation Press.

Huntington, Henry and Michelle Spark (2003), "Pops in Alaska: Engaging the United States," David Downie and Terry Fenge (eds) *Northern Lights against POPs: Combating Toxic Threats in the Arctic* (Montreal and Kingston: McGill-Queen's University Press.

Hutcheson, John (1978) *Dominance and Dependency*, Toronto: McClelland and Stewart.

IEA (2003), *Key World Energy Statistics*, International Energy Agency, Paris.

IISD (International Institute for Sustainable Development) (1996), *The World Trade Organization and Sustainable Development: An Independent Assessment Summary*. Winnipeg, Ontario: IISD.

IISD (2001), *Private Rights, Public Problems: A Guide to NAFTA's Controversial Chapter on Investor Rights*, International Institute for Sustainable Development, Winnipeg.

Imbeau, L., Monkkonnen, M., and Desrochers, A. (2001), "Long-term effects of forestry on birds of the eastern Canadian boreal forests: A comparison with Fennoscandia," *Conservation Biology*, 15: 1151-62.

IMD International and the World Economic Forum (1992), *World Competitiveness Report* Lausanne; Geneva: IMD International and the World Economic Forum.

International Air Quality Advisory Board (1998), *Special Report on Transboundary Air Quality Issues*. Accessible at: http://www.ijc.org/boards/iaqab/spectrans/exec.html.

International Joint Commission (1997), *The IJC and the 21st Century*.

International Joint Commission (2000), *Transboundary Watersheds*, December 2000.

International Joint Commission (2002), *Eleventh Biennial Report on Great Lakes Water Quality*.

Jackson, I. (1992), "Mixed Signals From the International Joint Commission" *J. Great Lakes Res.* 18(3): 355-356.

Jahn, L., and Kabat, C. (1984), "Origin and Role", in A. S. Hawkins, R. C. Hanson, H. K. Nelson, and H. M. Reeves (eds) *Flyways: Pioneering Waterfowl Management in North America*, US Fish and Wildlife Service, Washington, pp. 374-86.

Janofsky, Michael (2005) "E.P.A. Sets Rules to Cut Power Plant Pollution," *New York Times*, 11 March.

Jansen, H. (2001), "Induced Institutional Change in the Trade and Environment Debate: A Computable General Equilibrium Application to NAFTA with Endogenous Regulation Setting", *Environmental and Resource Economics*, 18: 149-172.

Jewell, S. (2000), "One continent for all", *Endangered Species Update*, 17(2), March/April: 26-27.

Jha, V. (1997), "Harmonization and Mutual Recognition: Are They Feasible?", in S. Zarrilli, V. Jha and R. Vossenaar (eds), *Eco-Labelling and International Trade*, Houndmills UK: Macmillan Press Ltd, pp. 310-17.

Johnson, P. (1999), "Five windows for the future of NAFTA's environment commission," *Policy Options*, 20(5): 27-32.

Johnson, P. and Beaulieu, A. (1996), *The Environment and NAFTA: Understanding and Implementing the New Continental Law.* Washington DC: Island Press.

Jockel, J. and Schwartz, A. (1984), "The Changing Role of the Canada-United States International Joint Commission", *Environmental Review* 8(3).

Jones, L., Griggs, L. and Fredricksen, L. (2000), "Environmental Indicators," 4th ed. *Critical Issues Bulletin* (April), Fraser Institute, Vancouver.

JPAC (2001), "Letter to the three NAFTA Environment Ministers", dated 13 December 2001, http://www.cec.org/files/PDF//Coun29-en1_EN.pdf. accessed 10 January 2002.

Judd, N. (2000), "Smog Control Tops the Agenda at Canada-U.S. Talks," *Environment News Service*, wysiwyg://74/http://ens.lycos.com/ens/jun2000/2000L-06-15-01.html, accessed 6 June 2001.

Juillet, L. (2000a), "Aboriginal Rights and the Migratory Birds Convention: Domestic Institutions, Non-State Actors and International Environmental Governance", Ph.D. dissertation, Carleton University.

Juillet, L. (2000b), "Domestic institutions and non-state actors in international governance: Lessons from the US-Canada Migratory Birds Convention", in Cohn, T., McBride, S., and Wiseman, J. (eds) *Power in the Global Era: Grounding Globalization*, London: Palgrave, pp. 125-38.

Keck, M. and Sikkink, K. (1998), *Activists Beyond Borders*, Cornell University Press, Ithaca.

Keohane, R. (1982), "The Demand for International Regimes", *International Organization*, 36(2):141-171.

Keohane, R., Haas, P., and Levy, M. (1993), "The Effectiveness of International Environmental Institutions", in Haas, Keohane, and Levy, (eds), *Institutions for the Earth: Sources of Effective International Environmental Protection,* Cambridge, MA: MIT Press.

Keohane, R. and Nye, J. (1977), *Power and Interdependence: World Politics in Transition*, Boston: Little, Brown.

Keohane, Robert and Joseph Nye (1989), *Power and Interdependence*, Boston: Little Brown.

Keohane, R., and Joseph Nye (2001), *Power and Interdependence*, 3rd ed., New York: Longman.

Kergin, M. (2003), "Ambassador Kergin's Letter to Rep. W.J. Tauzin and Sen. P. Domenici", (Washington, DC: Canadian Department of Foreign Affairs and International Trade, 12 September).

Kibel, P. S. (2001), "The Paper Tiger Awakens: North American Environmental Law After the Cozumel Reef Case", *Columbia Journal of Transnational Law* 39: 4-3-82.

Kincaid, J. (1990), "Constituent Diplomacy in Federal Politics and the Nation State: Conflict and Cooperation", *in* Michelmann, H. and Soldatos, P. (eds), *Federalism and International Relations: The Role of Subnational Units*, New York: University of Oxford University Press,

Kirkby, C. (1997), "Moving Alaskan Oil to Market: Canadian National Interest and the Trans-Alaska Pipeline, 1968-1973", *The American Review of Canadian Studies* 27(4): 495-511.

Kirton, J. (1997), "NAFTA's Commission for Environmental Cooperation and Canada-U.S. Environmental Relations", *American Review of Canadian Studies* 27(4) (Winter): 459-486.

Kirton, J. (1997), "The Commission for Environmental Cooperation and Canada-U.S. Environmental Governance", *The American Review of Canadian Studies* – Red, White and Green: Canada-U.S. Environmental Relations 27(3).

Kirton, J. (1998a), "The Impact of Environmental Regulation on the North American Auto Industry Since NAFTA", in S. Weintraub and C. Sands, (eds), *The North American Auto Industry under NAFTA*, Washington DC: CSIS Press, pp. 184-220.

Kirton, J. (1998b), "NAFTA's Trade-Environment Regime: Implications for the Hemisphere", Center for International Relations, University of Southern California, Columbia International Affairs Online www.ciaonet.org.

Kirton, J. (1998c), "NAFTA, Foreign Direct Investment and Economic Integration: A Canadian Approach", in Organisation for Economic Co-operation and Development, Migration, Free Trade and Regional Integration in North America, *OECD Proceedings*, Organisation for Economic Co-operation and Development, Paris, pp. 181-194.

Kirton, J. (1999), "Successful Strategies for Environmental Regulation in the North American Automotive Industry under NAFTA", Paper prepared for the project on *The North American Automotive Industry Under NAFTA*, Centre for Strategic and International Studies, Washington DC.

Kirton, J. (2002), "Winning Together: The NAFTA Trade-Environment Record", in J. Kirton and V. Maclaren (2002a), pp. 73-99.

Kirton, J. and Fernandez de Castro, R. (1997), *NAFTA's Institutions: The Environmental Potential and Performance of the NAFTA Free Trade Commission and Related Bodies.* Commission for Environmental Co-operation, Montreal.

Kirton, J. and Maclaren, V. (2002a), *Linking Trade, Environment and Social Cohesion: NAFTA Experiences, Global Challenges*, Aldershot: Ashgate.

Kirton, J. and Maclaren V. (2002b), "Forging the Trade-Environment-Social Cohesion Link: Global Challenges, North American experiences", in Kirton, J. and Maclaren, V. (2002a), pp. 1-23.

Kirton, J. and Rugman, A. (1999), "Regional Environmental Impacts of NAFTA on the Automotive Sector", *Canadian Journal of Regional Science* 21 (Summer): pp. 227-254.

Kirton, J. et al. (1999), *Assessing the Environmental Effects of the North American Free Trade Agreement (NAFTA): Final Analytic Framework and Methodological Issues and Empirical Background.* Commission for Environmental Co-operation, Montreal.

Kitchen, V. (2004), "Smarter Co-operation in Canada-U.S. Relations?" *International Journal*, LIX:3, 693-710.

Klare, M. T. (2001), *Resource Wars*, New York: Henry Holt /Owl Books.

Klimpt, J., Guérard, Y. and Arsenault, E. (2002), "Comments on the CEC's Working Paper (and Related Papers)", http://www.cec.org/files/PDF//JEKlimpt-Hydro-Quebec-comments.pdf. 10 January 2002; accessed 10 July 2002.

Kochan, J., and Schenker E. (1970), *Overseas Shipping at Great Lakes Ports: Projections for the Future*, Centre for Great Lakes Studies, University of Wisconsin-Milwaukee.

Laursen, F., ed. (2003), *Comparative Regional Integration: Theoretical Perspectives*, Aldershot: Ashgate.

Legault, L.H. (2000), "The Roles of Law and Diplomacy in Dispute Resolution: The IJC as a Possible Model", *Canada-United States Law Journal* 26.

Levesque, H., McCullough, G., and Mohr, P. (1984), *A Review of Migratory Bird Sanctuaries in Ontario*, Canadian Wildlife Service, Ontario Region.

Levitt, Kari (1970), *Silent Surrender*, Toronto: Macmillan.

Leyshon, A. (1992), "The Transformation of Regulatory Order: Regulating the Global Economy and Environment", *Geoforum* 23: 249-267.

Leyton-Brown, D. (1976), "The Multinational Enterprise and Conflict in Canadian-American Relations", in Baker Fox, A., Hero, A. and Nye, J. (eds), *Canada and the United States: Transnational and Transgovernmental Relations*, New York: Columbia University Press, pp. 140-161.

Leyton-Brown, D. and C. Sands (1997), "Introduction", *The American Review of Canadian Studies* – The Thomas O. Enders Issue on the State of the Canada-United States Relationship, 27(2).

Likens, G. E. and F. H. Bormann (1974), "Acid Rain: A Serious Regional Environmental Problem", *Science*, 84: 1176-79.

Likens, G.E., Bormann and N.M. Johnson (1972), "Acid Rain", *Environment*, 14(1): 33-39.

Litfin, K. (1994), *Ozone Discourses*, New York: Columbia University Press, Lipschutz, R. (2000), *After Authority: War, Peace and Global Politics in the 21st Century*, New York: SUNY Press, Albany.

Lowry, A. (1992), "North American free trade and the environment", *Business America*, 113(21): 22-24.

Ludwig, D. (1994), "Missed opportunities in natural resource management", *Natural Resources Modelling*, 8: 111-17.

Lumsden, Ian (1970) *Close the 49th Parallel*, Toronto: University of Toronto Press.

Macdonald, D. and Smith, H. A. (1999-2000), "Promises Made, Promises Broken: Questioning Canada's Commitment to Climate Change", *International Journal* 55 (1):107-124.

Mack, C. M. and Holyan, J. (2004), "Idaho Wolf Recovery Program: Restoration and management of gray wolves in central Idaho", *Progress Report 2003*, Nez Perce Tribe, Department of Wildlife Management, Lapwai, ID.

MacKinnon, M. (2000), "Smog-fighting strategy to be unveiled", *The Globe and Mail*, 19 2000:A1.

MacNamara, K. (2004), "TransCanada Optimistic on Mackenzie Line: First Nations' dDispute", *National Post*, 15 October 2004, FP5.

MacNeill, J. (1992), "Trade-Environment Links: The Global Dimension," in Kirton, J., and Richardson, S. (eds) *Trade, Environment and Competitiveness: Sustaining Canada's Prosperity*, National Round Table on Environment and Economy, Ottawa, pp. 7-20.

Magrath, C. (1924), *Magrath Papers*, M30 E87, vol. 6, File 20, Archives Canada, Ottawa.

Magraw, D. and Charnovitz, S. (1994), "NAFTA's repercussions: is green trade possible?" *Environment*, 36(2):14-27.

Mahant, E. (2001), "An Assessment of Citizen Submissions to the NAFTA Commission for Environmental Co-operation", paper presented at the International Studies Association Conference, Hong Kong, 26-28 July.

Mann, H. (2001), *Private Rights, Public Problems: A Guide to NAFTA's Controversial Chapter on Investment Rights,* International Institute for Sustainable Development: Winnipeg.

Mann, H. and Araya, M. (2002), "An Investment Regime for the Americas: Challenges and Opportunities for Environmental Sustainability," in Deere, C. and Esty, D. (eds) *Greening the Americas: NAFTA's Lessons for Hemispheric Trade,* Cambridge, Mass.:The MIT Press, pp. 163-182.

Mann, H., and von Moltke, K. (1999), *NAFTA's Chapter 11 and the Environment: Addressing the Impacts of the Investor State Process on the Environment,* International Institute for Sustainable Development, Winnipeg.

Mansour, M. (2001), "Excessive 'Precaution' Threatens Food Consumers and Foreign Trade", WLF *Legal Backgrounder*, vol 16 (44) 19 October.

Markell, D. (2000), "The Commission for Environmental Co-operation's Citizen Submission Process", *Georgetown International Environmental Law Review* 7 (3) (Spring).

Markell, D. and Knox, J. (eds) (2003), *Greening NAFTA: The North American Commission for Environmental Cooperation*, Palo Alto, California: Stanford University Press.

Marshall, T. H. and Bottomore, T. B. (1992), *Citizenship and Social Class*, London: Pluto Press,

MASSPIRG Education Fund (2003), "Cars and Global Warming: Policy Options to Reduce Greenhouse Gas Emissions from Massachusetts Cars and Light Trucks", MASSPIRG Education Fund, Boston, MA.

Mayer, F. (1998), *Interpreting NAFTA: The Science and Art of Political Analysis*, New York: Columbia University Press.

Mazur, A. and Welch, E.W. (1998), "State Policies to Improve Air Quality", Unpublished Manuscript, Syracuse University.

McGucken, W. (2000), *Lake Erie Rehabilitated: Controlling Cultural Eutrophication, 1960s-1990s*, Akron: University of Akron Press.

McNamee, T. (1997), *The Return of the Wolf to Yellowstone*, New York: Henry Holt.

McNeely, J., et al., (eds) (2001), *Global Strategy on Invasive Species*, IUCN, Gland, Switzerland.

McQuaig, L. (1998), *The Cult of Impotence*, Toronto: Penguin Books.

McRae, Don (1987), "The Negotiation of Article 234", in Franklyn Griffiths (ed.) *Politics of the Northwest Passage*, Kingston and Montreal: McGill-Queen's University Press: pp. 98-114.

Michele, R. (2004-5), "The State of US Shipbuilding: US Outlook: As order books shrink, shipyards scan the horizon for signs of hope", *American Ship Review 2004-2005* Issue 84:2-8.

Miles, P. and Wright, J. (1978), "An Outline of Mineral Extraction in the Arctic", *Polar Record* 19:11-38.

Miller, B. et al. (2001), "The Importance of Large Predators to Healthy Ecosystems", *Endangered Species Update* 18(5):202-210.

Miller, P. et al. (1997), "The Long-Range Transport of Ozone and Its Precursors in the Eastern United States", Northeastern States for Coordinated Air Use Management, Boston.

Miller, P. and Grumet, J. (1998), "Binational and regional issues in air quality science and policy", *Environmental Science & Policy*, 1:223-230.

Minister of the Environment (2000), "U.S.-Canada Ozone Annex Negotiations, Negotiators Joint Statement", News Release: Washington, 13 October 2000.

Mirovitskaya, N. and Ascher, W., (eds) (2001), *Guide to Sustainable Development and Environmental Policy*, Durham: Duke University Press.

Mitchell, R. (1994), *Intentional Oil Pollution at Sea: Environmental Policies and Treaty Compliance*, Cambridge, MA:MIT Press.

Mitchell, R. (1998), "Sources of Transparency: Information Systems in International Regimes", *International Studies Quarterly*, 42(1):109-130.

Mittelman, J. (2000), *The Globalization Syndrome: Transformation and Resistance*, Princeton, NJ: Princeton University Press.

Mittelstaedt, M. (2000), "Ontario moves to cut smog, acid rain", *The Globe and Mail*, 25 January 2000:A8.

Moffett, Samuel E. (1972), *The Americanization of Canada*, Toronto: University of Toronto Press (original edition, 1907).

Montpetit, E. (2003), *Policy Networks and the Environment in France, the United States, and Canada*, Vancouver. University of British Columbia Press.

Moomaw, W. (1992), "Regional Boundaries and Global Climate Change: Northeast North America", *in* Schmandt, J. and Clarkson, J. (eds) *The Regions and Global*

Warming: Impacts & Response Strategies, Oxford: Oxford University Press, pp. 275-289.

Morrison, S. (1997), "US, Canada Restart Talks over Salmon", *Financial Times*, May 28 (London edition):4.

Mumme, S. and Duncan, P. (1996), "The Commission on Environmental Co-operation and the US-Mexico Border Environment", *Journal of Environment and Development* 5 (June): 197-215.

Munton, D. (1981), "Paradoxes and Prospects," in Spencer, R., (ed.), *The International Joint Commission Seventy Years On*, Centre for International Studies, University of Toronto.

Munton, D. (1980-81), "Dependence and Interdependence in Transboundary Environmental Relations", *International Journal*, 36 (1): 139-184.

Munton, D. (1981), "Acid Rain and Basic Politics", *Alternatives*, 10 (Spring-Summer):21-28.

Munton, D. (1983) "Life, Liberty and the American Pursuit of Acid Rain", *Alternatives*, 11(2):13-20.

Munton, D. (1997), "Acid Rain and Transboundary Air Quality in Canadian-American Relations", *American Review of Canadian Studies*, 27(3).

Munton, D. (1998), "Dispelling the Myths of the Acid Rain Story" *Environment*, 40(6) (July-August):5-7, 27-34.

Munton, D. (2002), "Forests, Fumes and Further Studies: Environmental Science and Policy Inaction in Ontario", *Journal of Canadian Studies* 37(2) (Summer):130-163.

Munton, D. (2004), "Using Science, Ignoring Science: Lake Acidification in Ontario", in N. Harrison and G Bryner (eds) *Science and Politics in the International Environment*, Lanham, MD: Rowman and Littlefield.

Munton, D. (2005), "Acid Rain Politics in North America: Conflict to Cooperation to Collusion", Paper presented to a conference on acid rain, Connecticut College, April.

Munton, D. and Castle, G. (1992), "The Continental Dimension: Canada and the United States" in Boardman, R. (ed.) *Canadian Environmental Policy: Ecosystems, Politics, and Process*, Oxford University Press, Toronto.

Munton, D. and Kirton, J., (eds) (1992), *Canadian Foreign Policy: Selected Cases*, Scarborough: Prentice Hall.

Munton, D. and Kirton, J. (1994), "North American Environmental Co-operation: Bilateral, Trilateral, Multilateral", *North American Outlook* 4 (March): 59-86.

Munton, D. and Kirton, J. (1996), "Beyond and Beneath the Nation-State: Province-State Interactions and NAFTA", paper presented to the International Studies Association Annual Conference, San Diego, CA, April 17.

Munton, D., Soroos, M. , Nikitina, E. and Levy, M. (1999), "Acid Rain in Europe and North America", in O. R Young (ed.), *The Effectiveness of International Regimes*, Cambridge: MIT Press, pp. 155-247.

Myers, H. and Munton, D. (2000), "Cold War, Frozen Wastes: Cleaning up the DEW Line", *Environment and Security* 4:122-124.

NAEWG (2002), *North America – The Energy Picture* (North American Energy Working Group, June).

National Assessment Synthesis Team (NAST, 2000), *Climate Change Impacts on the United States: The Potential Consequences of Climate Variability and Change*, National Assessment Synthesis Team, US Global Change Research Program. Available at http://www.gcrio.org/NationalAssessment/.

National Science and Technology Council (NSTC, 2000), "Fact Sheet: North American Research Strategy for Ground-level Ozone Research Initiative", National Science and Technology Council, Committee on Environment and Natural Resources http://www.whitehouse.gov/WH/EOP/OSTP/Environment/htm/fac_trop_oc.html accessed 10 October 2000.

Nature Conservancy (2001), *Conservation by Design: A Framework for Mission Success*, Nature Conservancy, Washington.

Nature Conservancy (2003), *The Five-S Framework for Site Conservation. A Practitioner's Handbook for Site Conservation Planning and Measuring Conservation Success*. Volume 1, 3rd Ed., Nature Conservancy, Washington.

NEB (2003), *Canada's Energy Future: Scenarios for Supply and Demand to 2025*, Calgary, AB: National Energy Board.

NEPDG (2001), *Reliable, Affordable, and Environmentally Sound Energy for America's Future: Report of the National Energy Policy Development Group*, Washington, DC: U.S. Government Printing Office, May.

New England Climate Coalition (NECC, 2003). *Global Warming and New England: Progress, Opportunities and Challenges After Two Years of the Regional Climate Change Action Plan*, www.newenglandclimate.org, accessed 29 June 2005.

New England Climate Coalition (NECC, 2004), *Report Card on Climate Change Action*, www.newenglandclimate.org, accessed 29 June 2005.

New England Climate Coalition (2005), *2005 Report Card on Climate Change Action: Second Annual Assessment of the Region's Progress Towards Meeting the Golas of the New England Governors/Eastern Canadian Premiers Climate Change Action Plan of 2001*. August, 2005, www.newenglandclimate.org, accessed 29 June 2005.

New England Governors and the Eastern Canadian Premiers (NEGECP, 2001), *Climate Change Action Plan*, The Committee on the Environment and the Northeast International Committee on Energy of the Conference of the New England Governors and the Eastern Canadian Premiers.

New England Governors and the Eastern Canadian Premiers (NEGECP, 2001a). *Climate Change New Directions for the Northeast: Background Paper*. A Workshop of the Conference of the New England Governors and the Eastern Canadian Premiers, March 29-30, 2001, Fredericton, New Brunswick, Canada.

New England Governors and the Eastern Canadian Premiers (NEGECP, 2003), *Report to the New England Governors and the Eastern Canadian Premiers on Climate Change Project.*

New England Governors and the Eastern Canadian Premiers (NEGECP, 2004), "College and University Climate Change Symposium", University of New Hampshire, 18 June 2004.

New York Times, (1968), "Big Oil Reported on Alaska's Article Slope", (19 July) 47.

Newell, P. (2000), *Climate for Change: Non-State Actors and the Global Politics of the Greenhouse*, Cambridge: Cambridge University Press.

Nicol, H., and Townsend-Gault, I., (eds) (2004), *Holding the Line: Borders in a Global World*, Vancouver: University of British Columbia Press.

Nilsen, Thomas (2000), "Sunken nuclear powered submarines", *Northern Fleets incidents Bellona* http://www.bellona.no/en/international/russia/navy/northern_fleet/incidents/index.html accessed 25 January, 2005.

Nordstrom, H. and Vaughan, S. (1999), *Trade and Environment*, WTO Special Studies, Geneva, WTO.

Norris, R. S. and W. Arkin (2005), "Known Nuclear Tests Worldwide, 1945-1994", *Bulletin of the Atomic Scientists* 2005 http://www.thebulletin.org, accessed 29 June 2005.

North American Bird Conservation Initiative (1998), "Puebla Minutes – Conservation Objectives."

North American Bird Conservation Initiative (1999), NABCI: Strategy and Action Plan.

North American Bird Conservation Initiative (2001), NABCI, Second Trinational Meeting, February 14-16, 2001, Queretaro, Mexico.

North American Bird Conservation Initiative (2002), Review of Progress on the North American Bird Conservation Initiative. May. (Art Martell, Humberto Berlanga, David Pashley, and Jurgen Hoth)

North American Waterbird Conservation Plan (2002), Waterbird Conservation for the Americas.

North American Waterfowl Management Plan (1998), Expanding the Vision: 1998 Update.

North American Waterfowl Management Plan (2002), Canadian Habitat Matters.

Northeast States for Coordinated Air Use Management (NESCAUM, 2004), *Greenhouse Gas Emissions in the New England and Eastern Canadian Region, 1990-2000*, Boston, Massachusetts, April 2004.

Norton, B. (1991), *Toward Unity Among Environmentalists*, New York: Oxford University Press.

Norton, R. (1998), "Posture and Policymaking in Canada-U.S. Relations: The First Two Mulroney and Chrétien Years," *Canadian Foreign Policy* 5 (Winter): 15-36.

Norwegian-Russian Expert Group for Investigation of Radioactive Contamination in the Northern Areas (1994), *Dumping of Radioactive Waste and Investigation of Radioactive CFontamination in the Kara Sea: Extended Summary*, Standing Committee on Foreign Affairs.

Noss, R. (2003), "A Checklist for Wildlands Network Designs", *Conservation Biology*, 17(5):1270-1275.

Nossal, K. R. (1978), *The Unmaking of Garrison: United States Politics and the Management of Canadian-American Boundary Waters*, Behind the Headlines 37, CIIA, Toronto.

NRCan (2002), "Wind Power Production Incentive (WPPI)," (Ottawa, ON: Natural Resources Canada, 17 May; http://www.canren.gc.ca/programs/index.asp?CaId=107&PgId=622; 10 February 2004).

NRCan (2003a), "Background: Cross-Canada Electricity Snapshot", Ottawa, ON: Natural Resources Canada, 27 November; http://www.nrcan-rncan.gc.ca/media/newsreleases/2003/2003106a_e.htm; accessed 10 February 2004.

NRCan (2003b), "Backgrounder: Canada-U.S. Electricity Facts – 2003", Ottawa, ON: Natural Resources Canada, 27 November, http://www.nrcan-rncan.gc.ca/newsreleases/2003/2003106b_e.htm; accessed 10 February 2004.

NTI, Monterey Institute of International Studies (1999), "The Nunn-Lugar Cooperative Threat Reduction (CTR) Program", http://www.nti.org/db/nisprofs/shared/ctr/orverview.htm, accessed 22 March 1999.

Nye, J. (1976), "Transnational Relations and Interstate Conflicts: An Empirical Analysis," in Baker Fox, A., Hero, A., Nye, J., (eds), *Canada and the United States: Transnational and Transgovernmental Relations*, New York: Columbia University Press, pp. 367-404.

Odén, S. (1968). "Acidification of Air Precipitation and its Consequences on the Natural Environment" (title translated from Swedish) *Bulletin No. 1*, Ekologikommitten Statens Naturvetenskapliga Forskeningsrad, Stockholm.

O'Malley, M. (2004), "The Mackenzie Valley Pipeline", *CBC News – Indepth: Aboriginal Canadians* 2 July 2004 http://www.cbc.ca/news/background/aborginals/mackenzie_pipeline.html, accessed 2 July 2004.

Omernik, J. M. (1995), "Ecoregions: A framework for environmental management", in Davis, W., and Simon, T. (eds) *Biological Assessment and Criteria*, Boca Raton: Lewis.

Orbuch, P. and Singer, T. (1995), "International Trade, the Environment and the States: An Evolving State-Federal Relationship", *Journal of Environment and Development* 4 (Summer): 121-144.

Ottawa Citizen (1997), "Canada to Get Tough on U.S. Fish Boats: B.C. Premier Vows More Pressure in Salmon War", 22 May 1997 (final edition):A3.

Oye, K. (1986), "Explaining Cooperation Under Anarchy: Hypotheses and Strategies", in Oye, ed., *Cooperation Under Anarchy*, Princeton: Princeton University Press.

Paehlke, R. (2000), "Environmentalism in One Country: Canadian Environmental Policy in an Era of Globalization", *Policy Studies Journal.* 28(1):160-176.

Paehlke, R. (2003), *Democracy's Dilemma: Environment, Social Equity and the Global Economy*, Cambridge: MIT Press.

Park, C.C. (1987), *Acid Rain: Rhetoric and Reality*, New York : Methuen.

Parker, L. and Blodgett, J. (1999), "98-236: Air Quality: EPA's Ozone Transport Rule, OTAG, and Section 126 Petitions – A Hazy Situation?" Congressional Research Service: Updated 15 June 1999.

Parker, L. and Blodgett, J. (1998), "Air Quality and the New Ozone NAAQS: the OTAG Process", Congressional Research Service, Report to Congress, Washington, DC: Committee for National Institute for the Environment.

Parks Canada (2004), Nahanni National Park Reserve of Canada. Parks Canada. http://www.pc.gc.ca/pn-np/nt/nahanni/index_e.asp accessed 12 December 2004.

Patterson, M. J. and Rowlands, I. (2002), "Beauty in the Eye of the Beholder: A Comparison of 'Green Power' Certification Programs in Australia, Canada, the United Kingdom and the United States", *Energy & Environment* 13(1):1-27.

Pedynowski, D. (2003), "Prospects for Ecosystem Management in the Crown of the Continent Ecosystem, Canada-United States: Survey and Recommendations," *Conservation Biology*, 17(5):1261-1269.

Pentland, C. (2003), "Odd Man In: Canada and the Transatlantic Crisis", *International Journal LVIII* 2:145-166.

Peterson, M.J. (1993), "International Fisheries Management", in Haas, Keohane, and Levy (eds) *Institutions for the Earth: Sources of Effective International Environmental Protection*, Cambridge, MA: MIT Press.

Pew Center on Global Climate Change (2004), "Learning from State Action on Climate Change," in Brief #8, http://www.pewclimate.org/policy_reports_and_analysis/state/index.cfm accessed 29 June.

Poinani, K., and Richter, B. (1999), "Functional Landscapes and the Conservation of Biodiversity", *Working Papers in Conservation Science, No. 1*. Washington: Conservation Science Division, The Nature Conservancy.

Price, D. (2000), "Chapter 11 – Private Party vs. Government Investor-State Dispute Settlement: Frankenstein or Safety Valve?" *Canada-US Law Journal* 26.

Public Citizen (1995), *NAFTA's Broken Promises,* Public Citizen, Washington DC.

Purver, Ron (1955), "The Arctic in Canadian Security Policy, 1945 to the Present," in David Hewitt and David Leyton-Brown (eds) *Canada's International Security Policy* Scarborough: Prentice Hall Inc.

Putnam, R. (1988), "Diplomacy and Domestic Politics: The Logic of Two-Level Games", in *International Organization*, 42(3):427-460.

Rabe, B. (1997), "The Politics of Ecosystem Management in the Great Lakes Basin", *The American Review of Canadian Studies – Red, White and Green: Canada-U.S. Environmental Relations* 27 (3):411-431.

Rabe, B. (1999), "Federalism and entrepreneurship: Explaining American and Canadian innovation in pollution prevention and regulatory integration", *Policy Studies Journal*, 27(2): 288-306.

Rabe, B. (2004), *Statehouse and Greenhouse: The Emerging Politics of American Climate Change Policy*, Washington, DC: Brookings Institution Press.

Rabe, B. (2004a), "Beyond Kyoto: Designing Policies to Reduce Greenhouse Gases in Multi-level Governance Systems". Unpublished manuscript.

Rabe, B. (2005), "Moral Super-Power or Policy Laggard? Translating Kyoto Protocol Ratification into Federal and Provincial Climate Policy in Canada", Paper Presented at the Annual Meeting of Canadian Political Science Association, London, Ontario, June 2005.

Rajakoski, E. (1989), "Multilateral Cooperation to Protect the Arctic Environment: The Finnish Initiative", in *The Arctic: Choices for Peace and Security*, Vancouver: Gordon Soules Book Publisher.

Rausch, U. (1997), "The Potential of Transborder Cooperation: Still Worth a Try", Halifax, NS: Centre for Foreign Policy Studies.

Raustiala, K. (1995), "The Political Implications of the Enforcement Provisions of the NAFTA Environmental Side Agreement: The CEC as a Model for Future Accords", *Environmental Law* 25 (Winter): 31-56.

Ray, J. (2000), "Mesocarnivores of Northeastern North America: status and conservation issues", WCS Working Papers 15:1-84. Wildlife Conservation Society, New York.

Redekop, J. (1976), "Reinterpretation of Canadian-American Relations", *Canadian Journal of Political Science* 9.

Reiser, A., Spiller, J. and VanderZwaag, D. (1986), *Environmental Decision-Making in a Transboundary Region*, New York: Springer-Verlag.

Reisman, J. (2003), "Governors and Greens," Au Groton, Tech Central Station, 5 September, 2003. Available at http://www.techcentralstation.com . See also http://www.maineinstitute.com.

Roberts, John (1980) "The Urgency of Controlling Acid Rain", speech by the Minister of the Environment, Canada, to the Air Pollution Control Association, Montreal, 12 June , *Statements and Speeches*, No. 80/8, Department of External Affairs, Ottawa.

Roberts, J. and Jones, C. (2003-2004), "From Talking the Talk to Walking the Walk – The Challenge of Improving Canadian Air Quality", *Policy Options* (December 2003-January 2004): 1962-67.

Robinson, R. M. (1982), "The Rule of Law Between Nations – An Acid Test", Address to National Academy of Sciences, Seventh Symposium on Statistics and the Environment, Washington, DC, 4-5 October.

Robinson, S. K., et al. (1995), "Regional forest fragmentation and the nesting success of migratory birds", *Science*, 267:1987-1990.

Rosenbaum, W. (2002), *Environmental Politics and Policy*, Fifth Edition, Washington, D.C: CQ Press.

Roussel, S. (2003), "The US", *International Journal* 58(4) (Autumn):571-90.

Rowlands, I. (2002), "North American Integration and Support Schemes for Renewable Energy: Exploring the Issues", in United States Association for Energy Economics and International Association for Energy Economics, *22nd North American Conference Proceedings*, United States Association for Energy Economics, October, Vancouver, B.C.

Rowlands, I. (2003), *Renewable Electricity and Transatlantic Relations: Exploring the Issues,* San Domenico, IT: Robert Schuman Centre for Advanced Studies, Working Paper No. 2003/17.

Rowlands, I. (2005), "Envisaging Feed-in Tariffs for Solar Photovoltaic Electricity: European Lessons for Canada", *Renewable & Sustainable Energy Reviews* 9(1) (February):51-68.

Rowlands, I, Parker, P. and Scott, D. (2002), "Consumer Perceptions of 'Green Power'", *Journal of Consumer Marketing* 19(2):112-129.

Rowlands, I. and Patterson, M. (2002), "A North American Definition for 'Green Electricity': Implications for Sustainability", *International Journal of Environment and Sustainable Development*, 1(3).

Rugman, A. and Kirton, J. (1998), "Multinational Enterprise Strategy and the NAFTA Trade and Environment Regime", *Journal of World Business* 33 (4) (Spring): 438-454.

Rugman, A. and Kirton, J. (1998), "MNE's and Environmental Regulation: The NAFTA Experience," *Business and the Contemporary World* (Summer).

Rugman, A. and Kirton, J. (1999), "NAFTA, Environmental Regulations and International Business Strategies", *Global Focus* 11(4).

Rugman, A., Kirton, J. and Soloway, J. (1997), "A Canadian Corporate Strategy in a North American Region", *American Review of Canadian Studies* 27 (Summer): 199-219.

Rugman, A., Kirton, J. and Soloway, J. (1999), *Environmental Regulations and Corporate Strategy: A NAFTA Perspective,* Oxford: Oxford University Press.

Ruiz, G., and Carleton, J. (eds) (2003), *Invasive Species and Management Strategies*, Washington: Island Press,

Runnalls (1991), "Toward a Canadian Strategy," in *On The Road to Brazil: The Earth Summit,* UN Association in Canada, Ottawa.

Runnalls D. (1995), "The Road from Rio", in Osler Hampson, F., and. Maule, C., (eds) *Canada Among Nations 1993-94: Global Jeopardy,* J. Lorimer and Co., Toronto, pp. 133-153.

Sampson, G. (2002), "Environmentalist Paradox: the World Trade Organization's Challenges", *Harvard International Review*, (December 2001 - February 2002) 23:4, 56-61.

Sanderson, I. (2002), "Evaluation, Policy Learning and Evidence-Based Policy Making", *Public Administration*, 80(1):1-22.

Schelling, T. (1960), *The Strategy of Conflict*, Cambridge, MA: Harvard University Press.

Schloesser, D.W., and Nalepa, T. (1994), "Dramatic decline of native unionid bivalves in offshore waters of western Lake Erie after infestation by the Zebral Mussel, *Dreissena polymorpha*," *Canadian Journal of Fisheries and Aquatic Science* 51: 2234-2242.

Schmandt, J. and Roderick H., (eds) (1985), *Acid Rain and Friendly Neighbours: The Policy Dispute between Canada and the United States*, Durham: Duke University Press.

Schmidheiny S. (1996), "Financial Markets and the Development Process", *Financing Change: The Financial Community, Eco-Efficiency, and Sustainable Development*, Cambridge: MIT Press.

Schwartz, A.M. (2000), "The Canada-U.S. Relationship at the Turn of the Century", *The American Review of Canadian Studies* – The Thomas O. Enders Issue on the State of the Canada-United States Relationship, Summer.

Schwartz, A. and Jockel, J. (1983), "Increasing the Power of the IJC", *International Perspectives,* Nov/Dec.

Scott, A. (1976), "Transfrontier Pollution and Institutional Choice", *Studies in International Environmental Economics*, Ingo Walter (editor), New York: Wiley, pp. 303-317.

Scrivener, David (1989), *Gorbachev's Murmansk Speech: The Soviet Initiative and Western Responses*, Norwegian Atlantic Committee, Oslo: 1-75.

Scrivener, David, (1996), *Environmental Cooperation in the Arctic: From Strategy to Council*, Security Policy Library 1, The Norwegian Atlantic Committee: Oslo: 1-35.

Seattle Times (1997), "Yet Another Collapse in U.S.-Canada Fish Talks", *Seattle Times*, 25 May 1997 (final edition):B6.

Seguin, R. (2000), "Ministers agree to air-quality target", *The Globe and Mail*, Wednesday 7 June 2000: p.A7.

Selin, H. and VanDeveer, S. D. (2005), "Canadian-US Environmental Cooperation: Climate Change Networks and Regional Action", *American Review of Canadian Studies* 35 (2):353-378.

Shabecoff, P. (2000), "Chapter 6: The Environmental Revolution", in *A Fierce Green Fire: The American Environmental Movement.* (New York: Hill and Wang, 1993) 142-148, (reprinted in L. Benton and J. Short *Environmental Discourse and Practice: A Reader.* Oxford: Blackwell Publishers, pp. 139-142.

Shared Species Table [Trilateral Committee] (2002), "Shared Species Table: Summary Report", VII Meeting of the Canada/Mexico/United States Trilateral Committee for Wildlife and Ecosystem Conservation and Management, Nuevo Vallarta, Nayarit, Mexico, 23-26 April.

Shelby, A. (2004), "Whatever it takes", *Nation* 278 (13) 5 April:16-21.

Shrybman, S. (2000), "Trade now, pay later: that's the credo of the World Trade Organization ... environmentalists have much to learn from such a powerful opponent", *New Internationalist* (January-February) 320:29-30.

Smith, D., Stahler, D., and Guernsey, D. (2004), *Yellowstone Wolf Project Annual Report 2003*, National Park Service, Yellowstone Center for Resources, Wyoming.

Smith, P. J. (2002), "Cascading Concepts of Cascadia: A Territory or a Nation?", *International Journal of Canadian Studies*, 25: 130.

Smythe, E. (1980), "International Relations Theory and the Study of Canadian-American Relations", *Canadian Journal of Political Science*, XIII:1, 121-147.

Soloway, J. (1999), "Environmental Trade Barriers in NAFTA: The MMT Fuel Additives Controversy", *Minnesota Journal of Global Trade* 8(1).

Soloway, J. (2002), "Environmental Expropriation Under NAFTA Chapter 11: The Phantom Menace," in Kirton, J. and Maclaren, V. (2002a), *Linking Trade, Environment and Social Cohesion: NAFTA Experiences, Global Challenges,* Aldershot: Ashgate, pp. 131-144.

Soloway, J. (forthcoming), "NAFTA's Chapter 11: Investor Protection, Integration and the Public Interest", in Kirton, J. and Hajnal, P. (eds), *Sustainability, Civil*

Society and International Governance: Local, North American and Global Contribution, Aldershot: Ashgate.

Sossin, L. M. (1999), *Boundaries of Judicial Review: The Law of Justiciability in Canada*, Toronto: Carswell Thomson Profession Publishing,

Soulé, M. and Noss, R. (1998), "Complementary Goals for Continental Conservation", *Wild Earth,* Fall:19-28.

Soulé, M. and Terborgh, J. (1999), "Conserving nature at regional and continental scales: a scientific program for North America", *Recovery: An Endangered Species Newsletter*, published by the Canadian Wildlife Service #17.

Spencer, R., Kirton, J. and Nossal, K. (1981), *The International Joint Commission Seventy Years On*, University of Toronto, Centre for International Studies, Toronto.

Sproule-Jones, M. (2002), *Restoration of the Great Lakes: Promises, Practises, Performances*, Vancouver: University of British Columbia Press.

Stairs, D. (2003), "Myths, Morals, and Reality in Canadian Foreign Policy", *International Journal* LVIII: 2, 239-256.

Standing Committee on Foreign Affairs and International Trade (1997), *Canada and the Circumpolar World: Meeting the Challenges of Cooperation in the Twenty-First Century*, House of Commons.

Stattersfield, A., Crosby, M., Long, A. and Wege, D. (1998), *Endemic Bird Areas of the World: Priorities for Biodiversity Conservation*, BirdLife International, BirdLife Conservation Series No. 7, Cambridge, UK.

Steele, S. (1997), "A Haul of Hard Cash", *Maclean's*, 4 August 1997:19.

Stein. R. E. and Grenville-Wood, G. (1984), *Between Neighbours: How U.S. States and Canadian Provinces Settle their Shared Environmental Problems,* Environmental Mediation International, Ottawa and Washington.

Steinberg, R. (1997), "Trade-Environment Negotiations in the EU, NAFTA and WTO: Regional Trajectories of Rule Development", *American Journal of International Law* 91(2): 231-267.

Stevis, D. and Assetto, V., (eds) (2001), *The International Political Economy of the Environment: Critical Perspectives, International Political Economy Yearbook Vol. 12,* Boulder, Colorado: Lynne Rienner Press.

Stoddard, J. L., Kahl, J. S., Deviney, F. A., DeWalle, D. R., Driscoll, C. T., Herlihy, A. T., Kellogg, J. H., Murdoch, P. S., Webb, J. R., and Webster, K. E. (2003), "Response of surface water chemistry to the Clean Air Act Amendments of 1990", EPA620-R-03-001, U.S. Environmental Protection Agency, Washington.

Stoett, P. (2000), "Mission Diplomacy Or Arctic Haze? Canada and Circumpolar Cooperation", in Cooper, A. and Hayes, G. (eds) *Worthwhile Initiatives? Canadian Mission-Oriented Diplomacy*, Toronto: Irwin, pp. 90-102.

Stoett, P. (2001), "Fishing for Norms: Foreign Policy and the Turbot Dispute of 1995", in. Irwin, R., (ed.), *Ethics and Security in Canadian Foreign Policy,* Vancouver: University of British Columbia Press, pp. 249-268.

Stoett, P. (2004), "Wildlife Conservation: Institutional and Normative Considerations", in Schrijver, N. and Weiss, F. (eds), *International Law and*

Sustainable Development: Principles and Practice, Leiden, Netherlands: Martinus Nijhoff, pp. 501-518.

Stupples, P. (2001), "Green globalization: from emissions reduction to Third World debt, green parties unite on a charter to create a sustainable future", *Alternatives* (Fall) 27:4, 12-13.

Sturino, I (2000), "Ontario smog may hinder cleanup talks", *The Globe and Mail*, Friday, 11 February 2000:A23.

Suckling, K., Slack, R., and Nowicki, B. (2004), *Extinction and the Endangered Species Act*, Center for Biological Diversity, Washington.

Summers, P. and Whelpdale, D.M. (1976), "Acid Precipitation in Canada", *Water, Air and Soil Pollution* 6:447-455.

Susskind, L. (1994), *Environmental Diplomacy: Negotiating More Effective Global Agreements*, Oxford: Oxford University Press.

Sutherst, R. (2000), "Climate Change and Invasive Species: A Conceptual Framework", in Mooney, A. and Hobbs, R. (eds), *Invasive Species in a Changing World*, Washington: Island Press, pp. 211-240.

Tollefson, C. (2002), "Stormy Weather: The Recent History of the Citizen Submission Process of the North American Agreement on Environmental Cooperation", in Kirton and Maclaren (eds) (2002a), pp. 153-182.

Tollefson, C. (forthcoming), "NAFTA's Chapter 11: The Case for Reform", in Kirton, J. and Hajnal, P., (eds), *Sustainability, Civil Society and International Governance: Local, North American and Global Contribution*, Aldershot: Ashgate.

Tomblin, S. G. and Colgan, C. S. (2004), *Regionalism in Global Society: Persistence and Change in Atlantic Canada and New England*, Toronto: Broadview Press.

Toner, G. (ed.) (forthcoming), *Sustainable Production*, Vancouver: University of British Columbia Press.

TRAFFIC (2004), Traffic North America http://www.traffic.org/about/in_field_tna.html accessed 25 January 2005.

Trebilcock, M. (forthcoming), "Trade Liberalization, Regulatory Diversity, and Political Sovereignty", in John Kirton and Peter Hajnal, (eds), *Sustainability, Civil Society and International Governance: Local, North American and Global Contribution*, Aldershot: Ashgate.

Trilateral Committee (1996), *Memorandum of Understanding establishing the Canada/Mexico/United States Trilateral Committee for Wildlife and Ecosystem Conservation and Management.*

Trilateral Committee (2002), "Shared Species Table: Summary Report. VII Meeting of the Canada/Mexico/United States Trilateral Committee for Wildlife and Ecosystem Conservation and Management", Nuevo Vallarta, Nayarit, Mexico, 23-26 April.

Trio (2004), "Three species get trinational protection", *Trio*, Summer 2004 http://cec.org/trio/stories/index.cfm?varlan=english&ed=13&ID=155, 29 June 2006.

Tsebelis, G. (2002), *Veto Players: How Political Institutions Work*, Princeton: Princeton University Press.

United Nations Economic Commission for Europe (1979), Convention on Long-Range Transboundary Air Pollution, www.unece.org/env/lrtap/full%20text/1979.CLRTAP.e.pdf, accessed June 2005.

United Nations Environment Programme. (2002) *Global Environment Outlook 3 (GEO-3): Past, Present and Future Perspectives*. Nairobi: UNEP.

United Nations Environment Programme. (2005), *GEO Year Book 2004/5.* UNEP, Nairobi.

United States-Canada Air Quality Committee (USCAQC, 1998), *Canada-United States Air Quality Agreement: 1998 Progress Report.*

United States-Canada Air Quality Committee (USCAQC, 1999), *Ground-Level Ozone: Occurrence and Transport in Eastern North America.* A Report by the United States-Canada Air Quality Committee, Subcommittee 1: Program Monitoring and Reporting.

U.S.-Canada Framework for Cooperation (2003), in "Conserving Borderline Species: A Partnership between the US and Canada", www.speciesatrisk.gc.ca/publications/cbs/index_e.cfm, accessed January 2005.

U.S.-Canada Power System Outage Task Force (2003), *Interim Report: Causes of the August 14th Blackout in the United States and Canada* (Ottawa, ON: Natural Resources Canada, November).

United States-Canada, Memorandum of Intent on Transboundary Air Pollution (1983) "Executive Summaries, Work Group Reports", February 1983.

U.S. Department of the Interior (USDOI, 2004), Minerals Management Service, Alaska OCS Region, "Proposed Notice of Sale Beaufort Sea Oil and Gas Lease Sale 195", *Leasing Activities* October 8, 2004 http://www.mms.gov/alaska, accessed 8 October 2004.

United States, Environmental Protection Agency (1995), *Human Health Benefits from Sulphate Reductions under Title IV of the 1990 Clean Air Act Amendments*, EPA Publication No. EPA-430/R-95-010.

U.S. Fish and Wildlife Service (1986), *North American Waterfowl Management Plan.*

U.S. Fish and Wildlife Service (2002), *Birds of Conservation Concern 2002*, Division of Migratory Bird Management, Arlington, Virginia.

U.S. Fish and Wildlife Service (2004), *A Blueprint for the Future of Migratory Birds: Migratory Bird Program Strategic Plan 2004-2014*, Division of Migratory Bird Management, Arlington, Virginia.

United States, House Committee on Interior and Insular Affairs (1990), Subcommittee on water, Power and Offshore Energy Resources, *Investigation of the Exxon Valdez Oil Spill, Prince William Sound Alaska: Oversight Hearings*, pts 1-5, 29 March -5 May. United States, National Acid Precipitation Assessment Program (1987), *Interim Assessment: The Causes and Effects of Acidic Deposition*, 4 Volumes. Washington, D.C., U.S. Government Printing Office.

United States Trade Representative (1997), *Study on the Operation and Effect of the North American Free Trade Agreement*, United States Trade Representative, 1 July.

VanDeveer, S. (2004), "Ordering Environments: Regions in European International Environmental Cooperation", in Jasanoff, S., and Long Martello, M. (eds) *Earthly Politics: Local and Global In Environmental Governance*, Cambridge: MIT Press.

Van Driesche, J., and van Driesche, R. (2000), *Nature Out of Place: Biological Invasions in the Global Age*, Washington, DC: Island Press.

Van Dyke, J. (1996), "Applying the Precautionary Principle to Ocean Shipments of Radioactive Materials", *Ocean Development and International Law* vol. 27(44):379-397.

VanNijnatten, D. (2003), "Analyzing the Canada-US Environmental Relationship: A Multi-faceted Approach", *American Review of Canadian Studies* 33(1):93-120.

VanNijnatten and Boardman, R., (eds) (2002), *Canadian Environmental Policy: Context and Cases*, Second Edition, Oxford: Oxford University Press.

VanNijnatten, D., and Lambright, H. (2002), "Canadian Smog Policy in a Continental Context: Looking South for Stringency", In VanNijnatten and Boardman, (2002) pp. 253-273.

Vaughan, S. (2002), "Sustainability, Civil Society and International Governance: Local, North American and Global perspectives", presentation given at Third Annual Envireform Conference, Munk Centre for International Studies, University of Toronto, 8 November.

Vaughan, S., Patterson, Z., Miller, P. and Block, G. (2001), *Environmental Challenges and Opportunities of the Evolving North American Electricity Market*, Working Paper 2 in the 'Electricity and the Environment' series, North American Commission for Environmental Cooperation. 22 October, Montreal.

Vayrynen, R. (2003), "Regionalism, Old and New", *International Studies Review* 5(1):25-52.

Veitch, C., and Clout, M., (eds) (2002), *Turning the Tide: The Eradication of Invasive Species*, IUCN, Gland, Switzerland.

Vermont, State of (2003), *Climate Action Plan for State Government Buildings and Operations.*

Von Moltke, K. (2002), "Investment and the Environment: Multilateral and North American Perspectives", in Kirton and Maclaren (2002a), pp. 145-151.

Wagner, M. (1999), "International Investment, Expropriation and Environmental Protection", *Golden Gate University Law Review* 29: 465-527.

Wapner, Paul (1995), *Environmental Activism and World Civic Politics*, SUNY Press, Albany, New York.

WBCSD, (World Business Council for Sustainable Development), (1998) *Trade, Environment and Sustainable Development: A Briefing Manual*. Geneva: WBCSD, 1998.

WCED (World Commission on Environment and Development) (1987), *Our Common Future*, Oxford: Oxford University Press.

Webber, Bob (2005), "Environmentalists fear Mackenzie Valley Pipeline", *Canadian Press* (January 4, 2005).

Weibust, I. (2000), *Federalism and the Environment: Regulatory Competition and Cooperation in Federal Systems*. PhD dissertation, Massachusetts Institute of Technology, United States.

Weinberg, M. S. (1999), "Technical Barriers to Trade (Non-tariff Measures)", *Metro. Corp. Couns.*, October: 48.

Weintraub, B. A. (1992), "Science, International Environmental Regulation, and the Precautionary Principle: Setting Standards and Defining Terms", *NYU Environmental Law Journal*, vol 1: 173-181.

Weintraub, S. (1994), "Current State of U.S.-Canada Economic Relations", *American Review of Canadian Studies* 24 (Winter):473-488.

Weintraub, S. (1997), *NAFTA at Three: A Progress Report*, Center for Strategic and International Studies, Washington DC.

White, D., et al. (1993), *Invasive Plants of Natural Habitats in Canada*, Canadian Wildlife Service, Ottawa.

Whitehorse Star (2004). "US Lawmakers set aside measure to drill in refuge", *Whitehorse Star*, June 21:7.

Whitehorse Star (2004a), "Canada won't block pipeline: Governor", *Whitehorse Star*, December 29:7.

Wiken, E. (1986), *Terrestrial Ecozones of Canada*, Environment Canada, Ecological Land Classification Series, no. 19, Ottawa.

Wiken, E. Marshall, I., Lawton, K. and Hirvonen, H. (1996), *A Perspective on Canada's Ecosystems: An Overview of the Terrestrial and Marine Ecozones*, Canadian Council on Ecological Areas, Occasional Papers, no. 14, Ottawa.

Wilkinson, T. (1997), "Nagging Border Problems Boil Over in British Columbia", *Christian Science Monitor*, 21 July:3.

Willems, S. and Baumert, K. (2003), "Institutional Capacity and Climate Actions", Paris: OECD. COM/ENV/EPOC/IEA/SLT(2003)5.

Williams, Glen, (1983), *Not for Export: Toward a Political Economy of Canada's Arrested Industrialization*, Toronto: McClelland and Stewart.

Williams, M. (2001), "In Search of Global Standards: The Political Economy of Trade and the Environment", in Stevis D. and Assetto, V. (eds) *The International Political Economy of the Environment: Critical Perspectives, International Political Economy Yearbook Vol. 12*, Boulder: Lynne Rienner, pp. 39-61.

Williams, M. and Gilmore, S. (1997), "Salmon War – Sockeye Catch off Alaska is Key in U.S.-Canada Salmon Dispute", *Seattle Times*, 22 July.

Wilson, J. (2003a), "The Commission for Environmental Cooperation and North American Migratory Bird Conservation: The Potential of the NAAEC Citizen Submission Procedure," paper presented to the Annual Meetings of the Canadian Political Science Association, Halifax, Nova Scotia, 30 May-6 June.

Wilson, J. (2000b). "'Internationalization' and the Conservation of Canada's Boreal Ecosystems", *Canadian-American Public Policy*, Number 56, December.

Wilson, S. (2002), "Article 14-15 of the North American Agreement on Environmental Cooperation: Intent of the Founders", in Kirton and Maclaren (2002), pp. 187-193.

Winfield, M. (2002), "The North American Commission for Environmental Cooperation: A Case Study in International Environmental Governance", Paper presented to conference on Globalization, Multi-Level Governance and Democracy, Institute for Intergovernmental Relations, Queen's University, May 2002. Available at http://qsilver.queensu.ca/iigr/conferences/globalization/pdfs/winfield.pdf.

Winham, G. (1994), "Enforcement of Environmental Measures: Negotiating the NAFTA Environmental Side Agreement", *Journal of Environment and Development* 3 (Winter): 29-41.

Wise, C. (2004), "Property rights and regulatory takings", in R. F. Durant, D. J. Fiorino, and R. O'Leary (eds) *Environmental Governance Reconsidered: Challenges, Choices, and Opportunities*, MIT Press: Cambridge, pp. 289-322.

Wittenberg, R., and Cock, M. (2001), *Invasive Alien Species: A Toolkit of Best Prevention and Management Practices*, GISP, Oxon, UK.

Woolcock, S. (2002), "The Precautionary Principle in the EU and its Impact on International Trade Relations", CEPS Working Document No. 186, October.

World Bank, UNDP, UNEP (1992), *Global Environmental Facility – The Pilot Phase and Beyond*. Working Paper Series Number 1, Washington, DC, (May).

World Commission on Dams (2000), *Dams and Development: A New Framework for Decision-Making,* Earthscan, London, UK.

World Economic Forum and CID (2001), *Global Competitiveness Report 2001* Geneva: World Economic Forum. Excerpts available at: *http://www.cidharvard.edu/cr/index.html* (Cited June 24, 2004).

Y2Y (1998), *A Sense of Place: Issues, Attitudes And Resources In The Yellowstone To Yukon Ecoregion*, Yellowstone to Yukon Conservation Initiative, Canmore, Alberta.

Y2Y (2000), *Y2Y Framework Dataset Demonstration Project*. www.Y2Y.net, accessed 29 June 2006.

Y2Y (2004), Yellowstone to Yukon Conservation Initiative. www.Y2Y.net, accessed 29 June 2006.

Young, O. (1989), "Science and Social Institutions: Lessons for International Resource Regimes", in Andresen, S., and Ostreng, W. (eds) *International Resource Management: The Role of Science and Politics*, Belhaven Press, London.

Young, Oran (1989), *International Cooperation: Building Regimes for Natural Resources and the Environment*, Ithaca, Cornell University Press.

Young, Oran (1999), *The Effectiveness of International Environmental Regimes*, Cambridge, Massachusetts Institute of Technology Press.

Youth, H. (2003), *Winged Messengers: The Decline of Birds*, Worldwatch Institute, Worldwatch Paper 165, Washington.

Index

Global Environmental Governance

Also published in the series

The Politics of Irrigation Reform
Contested Policy Formulation and Implementation in Asia, Africa and Latin America
Edited by
Peter P. Mollinga and Alex Bolding
ISBN 0 7546 3515 5

Governing Global Biodiversity
The Evolution and Implementation of the Convention on Biological Diversity
Edited by
Philippe Le Prestre
ISBN 0 7546 1744 0

Agricultural Policy Reform
Politics and Process in the EU and US in the 1990s
Wayne Moyer and Tim Josling
ISBN 0 7546 3050 1

Linking Trade, Environment, and Social Cohesion
NAFTA Experiences, Global Challenges
Edited by
John J. Kirton and Virginia W. Maclaren
ISBN 0 7546 1934 6

International Equity and Global Environmental Politics
Power and Principles in US Foreign Policy
Paul G. Harris
ISBN 0 7546 1735 1